confessions of an
INNOCENT MAN

TORTURE AND SURVIVAL IN A SAUDI PRISON

WILLIAM SAMPSON

M&S

Library and Archives Canada Cataloguing in Publication

Sampson, William, 1959 –
    Confessions of an innocent man : torture and survival in a Saudi prison / William Sampson.

ISBN 0-7710-7903-6

    1. Sampson, William, 1959-.   2. Torture victims – Saudi Arabia – Riyadh – Biography.   3. Prisoners – Saudi Arabia – Riyadh – Biography. 4. Prisoners – Canada – Biography.   5. Judicial error – Saudi Arabia.   6. Western countries – Foreign relations – Saudi Arabia.   7. Saudi Arabia – Foreign relations – Western countries.   I. Title.

HV9780.S24 2005   365'.6'092   C2005-900989-6

We acknowledge the financial support of the Government of Canada through the Book Publishing Industry Development Program and that of the Government of Ontario through the Ontario Media Development Corporation's Ontario Book Initiative. We further acknowledge the support of the Canada Council for the Arts and the Ontario Arts Council for our publishing program.

Typeset in Sabon by M&S, Toronto
Printed and bound in Canada

This book is printed on acid-free paper that is 100% recycled, ancient-forest friendly (100% post-consumer recycled).

McClelland & Stewart Ltd.
The Canadian Publishers
75 Sherbourne Street
Toronto, Ontario
M5A 2P9
www.mcclelland.com

1 2 3 4 5   09 08 07 06 05

To my father and step-mother, James and Nelia, for being just that.

To Geoffrey Bindman for his patience and for fifty years
of dedication to the cause of human rights and the
protection of civil liberties.

Stone walls do not a prison make,
Nor iron bars a cage;
Minds innocent and quiet take
That for an hermitage;
If I have freedom in my love
And in my soul am free,
Angels alone, that soar above,
Enjoy such liberty.

"To Althea from Prison"
by Richard Lovelace (1618–1658)

CONTENTS

INTRODUCTION

In starting this book, I began another journey, one of many that I have undertaken in my life. This one has been conducted not so much in physical time and space, but mainly within the recesses of my mind. Where to begin and how to proceed should have been easy enough to determine, but proved otherwise. The more I thought of what happened during the three years of my imprisonment and the time since, the more intricate the patchwork of events surrounding my imprisonment and release became. Many questions remained to which I needed answers.

In my pursuit for redress, what came to the fore were the questions "How?" and "Why?" The questions were simple, the answers were not. The explanations my investigations eventually revealed produced a picture less clear and more strange than I had envisaged. So much was new to me when I was first released because of the isolation that I had endured; so much happened after my release that what had seemed clear in prison became less so. I found myself unable to impose order on my thoughts while still unsettled by my unexpected freedom. With time, my ability to make sense of things has coalesced, though much detail remains hazy and nebulous.

The other important questions, posed both by myself and by those who have discussed with me the time I spent caged and alone, delved into the very essence of my being. What was it that I did to survive? Where did those ideas come from? Where did I find the resolve to enact them? Immediately after my release, I had no specific answers. Without reflection, it seemed to me that I did what was natural and necessary at the time. In looking back, I have come to realize that the peculiarities of my personality helped me to easily adopt strategies that allowed for the reclamation of my identity and my integrity while in the hands of barbarians. Yet what I did is neither remarkable nor courageous nor beyond the capabilities of any person that finds themselves in similar circumstances.

What I have come to believe is that there exists in all of us the potential to stand and fight and to reclaim. All that is necessary is an understanding of the process of brutalization and the personal realizations that such knowledge can bring. I have met and talked with a number of survivors of torture who behaved much as I did even though we are a disparate range of personalities from different backgrounds. For each of us, there were points of realization, personal epiphanies that, once reached, liberated the sufferer. This mental freedom actualized our ability to resist in a manner that was subtle or unsubtle but was appropriate. This in turn has allowed us to endure, to heal, and to bear witness more effectively than might otherwise have been the case.

It is not my place to tell the stories of others; I can only bear witness to what I experienced and learned, hoping that in so doing light is shed on both the barbarity of torture and on the resilience of our individual humanity. This then is my story. Horrendous though it might seem, it is the story of a journey that enlightened me in spite of the efforts taken by the security apparatus of a sovereign state to destroy me, and the efforts of other states to deny me justice.

William James Sampson
July 30, 2005

GLOSSARY

Bhisht – Traditional Arabian cloak or robe. It is also called a mishlah.

Ghutra – Arabian cloth headdress, usually white

Hajj – Annual pilgrimage to Mecca

Iqal – Corded black rope circlet worn atop the shemagh or ghutra, originally from the cords of the camel's halter. The Bedouin still use old halter ropes cut for this purpose.

Iqama – Identity card

Jellaba (also spelled djellaba) – Loose, long-sleeved hooded woollen cloak

Khawaja – Literally, foreigner but often used in a pejorative sense – "dirty foreigner"

Mabaheth – Intelligence Division of the Ministry of Interior

Mutawa – Council for the Promotion of Virtue and the Prevention of Vice

Sharia – Islamic law

Shemagh – Traditional white and red checkered Saudi headdress

Shukran – Thank you

Sid – Homemade alcoholic beverage

Sidiqi – Friend

Thobe – Long shirt-like garment worn by Arabian men

Wadi – Rocky watercourse, dry except in the rainy season

Wasta – Influence

one

THE FALL

/

At 7:00 a.m. my alarm clocks began ringing at their allotted intervals, dragging me to consciousness. I felt tired and unrefreshed. The previous weeks had been tense and stressful, leaving little time for relaxation and making what rest I had fitful and inadequate. When I finally roused myself, I was running late. It was Sunday, December 17, 2000.

I showered, shaved, and dressed, proceeding downstairs to the kitchen. Preparing my extra-strength espresso, a concoction I referred to as rocket fuel, I began trying to order my thoughts. I was in the midst of preparing a report on water treatment and purification in Saudi Arabia, which was due for submission at the end of the week. I was finding it difficult to concentrate on it. A wave of car bombs had begun in November 2000. I was certain that my friend Raf Schyvens, almost the victim of one such bomb, was being framed for these events. He had been arrested seven days earlier. I still did not know where he was being detained, and my mind constantly returned to thoughts of his fate. I mapped out in my mind my contact list for the day: the first counsel of the Belgian Embassy, a couple of Saudi friends, and a couple of our mutual associates. Some were sources of information; others were friends I had promised to keep informed as I searched for our friend.

As I walked from the kitchen to the living room, I began drinking my coffee and lit a cigarette. Thus, my breakfast was complete – an infusion of legal stimulants necessary to jump-start my higher functions into operation. I turned on the television to catch Sky News on satellite. The time was 8:00 a.m. I wondered if the latest bombing in Saudi Arabia would be reported. The most recent

7

bombing had occurred the previous Friday in Al Khobar on the east coast of the country. A friend had called and told me about it, but had provided few details as the local news service had not been informative. It was the third in a recent series of attacks on western expatriate workers.

The other bombings had occurred in Riyadh. The first bomb exploded on November 17. It had killed Christopher Rodway and injured his wife, Jean. The second exploded on November 22. It severely injured Mark Payne. Three of his friends in the same car suffered less severe injuries. Each of these attacks had targeted British nationals. Raf had witnessed the second bombing and had provided emergency medical assistance – for which he had been arrested.

To say I was worried was an understatement. In Saudi Arabia, whenever a major crime occurred, the authorities immediately looked to the expatriate communities for a scapegoat. There exists a culture of denial in which all malfeasance was blamed on foreigners or external influences. It was the most culturally and politically xenophobic country in which I had lived. I was certain that the local police and intelligence services would be looking for a *khawaja* (foreigner) to blame. The arrest and disappearance of Raf had all the hallmarks of such a conspiracy. Because we were close friends and because we saw each other frequently, I realized that I might be implicated through nothing more damning than my association with him. I believed that my time of freedom was probably limited. I worried about my fate, and also about the fate of other friends who might be implicated in a fabricated conspiracy simply because they were my friends. I hoped that they had listened to my warnings, but feared they would not heed my advice.

With these thoughts worrying me, the news program reported on the most recent bombing. Another Briton, David Brown, had been injured in the blast. Would the authorities be forced to admit the true nature of the problem, now that there was a trio of incidents across the Kingdom? As the news round finished, I called my father to tell him of the new event. We chatted about my plans for Christmas, and my desire for a break from life in the Kingdom. I did not tell him of my fears.

I collected my briefcase and headed out the door into the morning air. It was 8:15 a.m.; the weather was clear and cool, but still warm enough for just a long-sleeved shirt and tie, no jacket. I walked past the swimming pool to the front gate, resigned to another day of frustration and stress. As I stepped through the front gate, I caught sight of my Nissan Patrol 4 by 4. It looked odd and it was a second or so before I saw that it had a flat tire. This hardly improved my mood. Swearing under my breath, I headed off to one of the main streets nearby to hire a taxi. I had no intention of changing a tire while dressed for work. I was late. I should have been in the office by eight, but true to form, I had timed my departure to arrive there at eight-thirty or so.

As I turned away from my car, something caught my eye at the T-junction fifty metres away. It was a grey beige American four-door sedan. For some reason the model name Intrepid has stuck in my mind. Why I should remember such a detail, I have no idea. What my eye had noticed was movement. As the sedan pulled out of its parking space and rapidly turned onto my street, I caught the look on the driver's face. I knew. I knew at that instant that it was coming for me. I had nowhere to turn, nowhere to hide, and little time to react. The car pulled up within a couple of inches of me, causing me to jump back. Much later I realized that a corpse at this stage would have ruined their tortuously planned scenario. At that moment it appeared I was going to be run over. Two Saudis dressed in thobes and ghutras burst from the passenger doors. The first to reach me was a man in his twenties, stockily built and about my height. He had a broad sallow face and thin slit-like eyes. His pencil-line moustache brought to mind pictures of Frank Sinatra from the 1940s.

He grabbed my briefcase with one hand and my wrist with the other. The driver, a slender man slightly taller than I with a dark pockmarked face and a wispy attempt at facial hair, had sprinted around the car, grabbed my other arm, and began stripping me of the rest of my possessions. The third individual, short and squat, with a neatly trimmed beard and moustache, waved a warrant card in his left hand and a revolver in his right. These three I would come to know intimately, more intimately than ever I would have wanted.

In as level a voice as I could muster, I asked what they were doing and why they were being so aggressive. I was told to shut up. The two men who had grabbed me began slapping and punching me as they checked my pockets. I did not resist, thinking that it would only make matters worse. In hindsight, I was both right and wrong. It would have resulted in my being shot and possibly killed, but as I was later to be sentenced to death, that would not have mattered. My death might have caused the diplomatic hiatus that could have spared my friends their ordeal. That is hindsight, and in such a situation as I was in, the textbook says that resistance is both dangerous and inappropriate. Nothing should be done to make one's captors angry, insecure, or nervous. I tried to stay calm, to give them no reason to mistreat me, and to appear cooperative. After all, it was possible my arrest was a mistake.

So I stood there, let them force my hands behind my back and cinch on handcuffs too tightly. The punching and slapping continued as I was pushed into the back of the car. I tried to speak, but before a sensible word was uttered, I was slapped on the neck and hit on the hinge of the jaw with a revolver. I felt something crack in my mouth. My wrist and hands were already burning from the pressure of the metal, and now I wondered if my jaw was broken (it was not, my teeth were). I sat with my legs awkwardly balanced on the well of the drivetrain. Fear consumed me, but I worked to maintain an outward appearance of calm. It was difficult, the most difficult performance of my life. I watched as the thug with the thin moustache climbed in beside me, while the others returned to their original positions. The doors slammed shut.

As the car pulled away, the thug to my right pulled my legs apart, and the officer in the front passenger seat turned around to face me. With a smile on his face, he struck between my legs with the revolver. The pain was electrifying. Instinctively, I closed my legs, tears welling in my eyes. Exclamations in rapidly spoken Arabic were followed by my captors' howls of laughter. The car came to a halt outside an office building eight hundred metres from my home. A fourth be-thobed individual climbed in on my left side. After a brief agitated conversation, not a word of which I understood, he placed a ghutra over my head, covering my eyes. Something, I know not what, was used to tie it in place, putting pressure on my eyes, giving a red glow to the light permeating my impromptu blindfold. Again the car pulled away, again my legs were held apart, but more effectively as my new companion assisted in the fun. The thug in the front began again to work over my scrotum and testicles with the barrel of his gun. I assume it was the gun, for what slammed into my flesh was hard, cylindrical, and metal. Bloody painful it was.

We drove for what seemed an eternity, but was probably no more than forty minutes. Even that was an excessive time, given our final destination. The car twisted and turned, the punches rained down, questions poured forth. What was my name? What was my religion? Did I speak Arabic? Where did I work? All asked, all performed to keep me from establishing where, in more than one sense, I was being taken. The journey to our ultimate destination should have taken less than twenty minutes, as I was to establish later.

Eventually the car came to a halt. I heard the electric window roll down, and incomprehensible words shouted. The clanking sounds of a metal security gate opening confirmed to me that we had arrived. The car rolled slowly forward for a few metres and the gate clanked shut. The car doors opened and I was pulled out by my tie to the giggled glee of my captors. Dragged like a recalcitrant dog on a leash, I stumbled forward. As we entered a doorway, my blindfold was removed and I saw the entrance to my new residence.

The control room was to my left, filled with banks of CCTV screens watched by a slovenly uniformed individual drinking tea and looking bored. Slightly to my front and left was a corridor and set of stairs. To my right was another doorway through which I was led. This opened into a hallway in the centre of which was a desk. Pushed to the desk, I was asked my name and assigned a number: 23. My tie was removed, as was my belt, but not my shoelaces. Then I was led forward to another doorway on the left behind the desk. Through this, I could see another corridor lined with metal doors. Painted a sickly yellow, illuminated by fluorescent light, it exuded fear and degradation.

My guards, now a coterie of pimply uniformed hirelings, pushed me into the cell, the number 23 marked in chalk on the lintel. The handcuffs were released, and then clasped again onto my right wrist, the other end being affixed to the grill in the door, located about five feet from the floor. The door was pushed shut and with it I was pushed into the cell. Standing there, I surveyed my new accommodation.

The cell was the same colour as the corridor, sickly yellow and in need of repainting. It measured two by three metres, with a height of three metres. In the upper left corner of the far wall was a CCTV camera. Mounted through the centre of that wall was an air conditioner. Ill-fitted in its position, daylight penetrated around its edges. The floor was bare grey concrete, dusty and cold. On it was a cheap, thin mattress with a garish floral pattern. At the end of the mattress nearest the door was a thin grey blanket. As I finished my survey, I shivered with cold and fear. Stretching out my leg, I reached the blanket, dragging it toward me. I stretched down with my left hand collecting it, then wrapped myself in it. It smelled of sweat and urine, a crude pheromonal stench that belonged to countless others.

I am not sure how long it was that I stood there in a state of near shock, chained upright. Just as I was getting to grips with my fear and trying to calm the turmoil of my mind, I heard the guards approach. The door was unlocked. As it opened outward I was pulled forward. Harshly they stated a single English word: "Number!" In an instant, I had been reduced to a nonentity. The handcuffs were released and then re-clasped behind my back. Shackles were fixed around my ankles and a rectangular black blindfold was tied over my eyes. Then I was roughly pulled from the cell along the corridor.

From my measured pace and the short distances involved, I knew that I was being led back to the control room and the stairs opposite. I was led up them, stumbling, trying to keep my footing. At the top, after two flights of ten steps, we turned right and walked maybe eight or ten metres down a corridor. Again, I assume that it was a corridor. Initially, every time I was in this part of the building, I was blindfolded and had to depend on other senses to provide the necessary details. In this case, from our footfall it sounded like a corridor.

I was pushed through a door to my right and brought to a halt by a desk barring further progress. I both felt and heard the presence of at least three or four others. Someone moved beside me and I felt his fist slamming into the back of my neck, causing me to sprawl across the desk. Commanded to stand up, I struggled upright. The blindfold was pulled off, and I saw before me the three thugs who had arrested me. Behind me was a uniformed guard who had acted as my guide in this underworld.

The room was a small office with a desk and four metal chairs. Its walls were off-white, and the floor was carpeted with a cheap synthetic fabric that had once been brown (probably) but was now just dark and dirty. In the far wall was a window through which I could see another building and the white metal gate I had passed through only an hour or so earlier.

At this point, I was told to sit down. As I tried to do so, the officer to my right laced his fingers through my hair, pulling me violently down as he himself sat. This was the one with the pencil-thin moustache. Already I had given him a name, my own point of reference. In my mind, I named him The Spiv. He never said a word to me in all the time we spent together. He spoke no English, as I spoke no Arabic, but even so, he never directed a word in any language to me. He sat beside me, stroking and playing with my hair, occasionally caressing my right thigh. He kept sniffing me like a carrion feeder inspecting the flesh of a potential, rotting meal. It was unsettling, as I knew it was meant to be.

The others sat on the other side of the desk. To my left was the short one, who preened himself and ceaselessly adjusted his ghutra. I named him The Midget. He had a dull stupid aspect to his eyes, and his intelligence was limited but not his dedication to the power of his employment. He called to mind the cartoon characterization of Dopey the dwarf with his habit of continually nodding his head while his eyes remained glazed over. His name, I later worked out, was Ibrahim. Since my release, I have come to know his full name: Ibrahim Al Dali. He was then a captain but through his dedication later gained promotion to the rank of major and is now lieutenant-colonel. To my right was the dark-skinned one with the acne-ravaged face. I named him Mr. Acne, though his real name is Khaled Al Saleh. He had hard aggressive eyes, burning with the hatred of a true fanatic. While at times he was the least brutal, he seemed to gain the most personal enjoyment from the pain, humiliation, and grief of his victims. Of the three, he seemed the most intelligent and as such the most dangerous. These then were members of the dreaded Mabaheth, the Saudi Arabian secret police, a law unto themselves, feared by everyone but their masters – though I recommend that their masters never slip the lead.

Mr. Acne asked if I knew why I had been arrested. I was hardly going to reply that I knew that they wanted to frame me for the bombings, so I said no. This prompted The Spiv to forcefully dig his fingers into my thigh, clucking as he did so. Again, Acne asked, again I said no. The Midget glanced at The Spiv, who then stood up, slapped me across the face, and dragged me to my feet by my hair.

I was pushed into the centre of the room and surrounded by the three of them. Rapid-fire questions were directed at me by Acne, and I realized that he was the English speaker among them. Their response to my dumb answers was a flurry of slaps and punches directed at my stomach, lower back, crotch, and the side of my face. They seemed then, as they did at all times in the future, to exert inordinate caution not to hit me in the face, given the level of violence directed elsewhere. I was curious about this at first, but soon realized they were well practised at not leaving obvious signs of their handiwork.

The Midget, in a fit of rage, pushed me off my feet and kicked me in the back as I floundered about on the floor. Screamed at to stand up, I awkwardly struggled to my feet, encumbered by the restraint of the handcuffs and shackles. I was dragged back to my chair and was pushed into it by The Spiv, who resumed his affectionate attentions, as Acne began to recite a litany of my crimes. He told me that they knew everything, that I had planted and detonated all three of the bombs that had recently disturbed the Kingdom and the expatriate community. He told me I would confess because everyone did, it was only a matter of time. I was told they would make me beg to confess, for they had the power to do anything they wanted. The pain they would inflict on me was beyond my imagination. I do not know why I replied flippantly.

I said that I had a pretty good imagination so that must truly be something.

The Midget exploded across the desk. His fists slammed into me, knocking me and my chair onto the floor. Kicks were directed at my stomach and crotch. I screamed as he directed his foot into my testicles. My interrogators giggled and laughed; they were enjoying playing with me.

For a moment, the brutality subsided as they suppressed their amusement. As I lay there, it flitted through my mind that this was getting just a bit repetitive and tedious. I fought not to smile through my pain. My mouth had already caused me enough trouble. As this passed over, I was roughly pulled upright and pushed into the chair. The three resumed their appointed positions. I was told to detail my movements on the days of the three bombings: Friday, November 17; Saturday, November 22; and Friday, December 15. Slowly and carefully with as much detail as was possible, I described my activities on those days. With the exception of Friday, December 15, my whereabouts were verifiable only by one or two close friends, Raf being one of them. It would be easy for my interrogators to break my alibi by arresting the few people I had been with. I knew it was not beyond them to arrest others to destroy the proof of my innocence and that their arrest and abuse were now likely if not guaranteed (and I believe this was the reason for the later arrests of my friends Les Walker and Carlos Duran). It was a terrifying prospect.

Again and again, I went over the same statements. Each time I declared my innocence. Each time I was accused of lying and threatened with the prospect of more violence to be delivered with more force, but the violence did not come. Hope reared its naïve head. Maybe this was as far as it would go? Maybe they would realize that whatever they had planned was mistaken? Just then, I heard the plaintive call to prayer of the muezzin. To my relief, I was blindfolded and taken to another room down the corridor some distance past the stairwell.

Once I was in this new office, the blindfold and handcuffs were removed but not the shackles. I saw the office was much like the other, but without a window. I also saw an older man with a greying beard. He sat in a chair and politely invited me to sit in another. We sat looking at each other for a few moments, each trying to size up the other. I restrained the impulse to break the silence and explain myself. This was a struggle. The desire to talk and make oneself understood at moments like these is quite strong. I guess it is driven by fear and an impulse toward self-preservation, but it is inappropriate.

Finally he spoke. "What is your name?" His English was very good, with a hint of a British accent.

I answered tersely.

"Why are you here?" he asked.

"Because a mistake has been made," I said.

He smiled. "But our officers never make mistakes."

Yeah, and bears never shit in the woods – the words formed on my tongue. Instead I said, "There is always a first time."

His response was a sphinx-like smile. "Tell me why you think you are innocent."

Tell me why you think you are innocent, I repeated silently. What a thought. I did not think, I knew. To him, though, my presence there was proof of my guilt, or at least my guilt as he needed to see it. It was like a scenario by Kafka, only badly written. I began my story again, relating how I could have had nothing to do with the events, nor did I have any involvement in the crimes with which I was accused. Surely, he would see this. He continued to smile seraphically before finally replying.

"Allah in his infinite wisdom protects the innocent. They alone will feel no pain. You say that you are innocent, then Allah will protect you."

This was a statement borne of the fanaticism that accompanies trials by fire and water and other such acts of pious control and conformity. It chilled me to the very marrow of my bones. If ever there was a statement designed to terrify me, this was it. My body was in the hands of perverted zealots; my soul was their next target for possession. I had entered a very real temporal hell and I was scared. The memory of that fear is enough to send a chill down my spine and raise goose pimples. Even now, it can on occasion cause tears to well up in my eyes.

After this pronouncement, we sat in silence; me with my jumbled confused thoughts and fears, he in his smug sense of power and self-righteousness. Eventually, the door opened and my inter-rogators returned to collect me. Blindfolded, handcuffed, and shackled, I was led back to the original office. The blindfold alone was removed and I was kept standing.

The Spiv leaned against the wall while Khaled and Ibrahim set about enjoying themselves. I was punched, kicked, and thrown around. I was a thing, an object in a violent game of pass the parcel as I was thrown from one to the other. This continued for a couple of hours without a word being spoken by my tormentors until they were interrupted by the next call to prayer. As uniformed guards came into the room, I was blindfolded and then led back to my cell.

In the cell, the shackles were removed along with the blindfold, and the handcuffs were rearranged to chain me to the door. As I stood, fear gripped me. My stomach tightened into a ball. My legs were shaking, my heart was pounding in my ears. I tried to calm myself. I had been arrested at 8:15 a.m. and it was now between three and four in the afternoon, estimated by the passing of two prayer calls. I told myself again and again that this was all a mistake that could easily be cleared up. Yet the cold reason of my analytical mind told me that this was no mistake, that this must be where Raf was being held. As my captors had already embarked on this course, there was little chance of easy resolution. I told myself that I must endure and hold out against the coming brutal-ity for as long as possible, though the outcome was inevitable, as I knew. Thus, naïve hope and cold realism fought a battle for my mind and my heart.

Realism won.

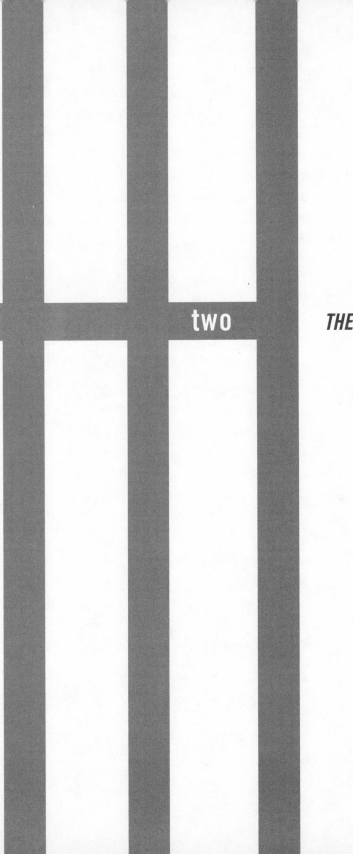

two

THE KINGDOM AND I

//

I had no sense of foreboding or concern when I caught my first sight of the desert Kingdom through the oval window of the Emirates Airbus. I was curious to see exactly what Riyadh was like, for I had travelled extensively throughout the Middle East, but had never had the opportunity to travel in Saudi Arabia.

The land below was a light brown, dusty and crenulated with wadis, like a crumpled pair of chinos. A few long straight roads cut through the landscape like flat seams. Little else was visible, no vegetation, and only a few scattered areas of settlement or habitation. This was the central province of Saudi Arabia as seen from the air. As the aircraft began its descent, I was able to see Riyadh, the capital, rising out of the surrounding desert plains. The buildings making up this cityscape and the scope of its layout were in stark contrast to its desolate surroundings. There seemed no gradual buildup of development before the city itself started, almost as if it had been parachuted into the middle of nowhere.

Saudi Arabia was a place I wished to visit. Its remoteness, its barrenness, and its closed nature were all things that intrigued me, and the only way I could see it was by going there on business. I had been travelling since the previous day from Vancouver via London and Dubai, and I felt my usual surge of interest and anticipation as I approached another new horizon. I wondered if all the rumours I had heard were true.

I had heard that the Kingdom presented two faces. The public face was that of a country controlled by a royal family governing to a strict interpretation of the Koran and Sharia law where all activities taken for granted in more liberal or western societies are proscribed. The private face was one of corrupt governance where behind closed doors everything and anything was indulged in. I had met expatriate workers who loved their time in Saudi Arabia, and I had met those who hated it. I had never met anyone whose opinion was neutral, and all passed comment on the inconsistency and corruption of those who ruled Saudi Arabia.

I was on my way to take up a post as a marketing consultant with the Saudi Industrial Development Fund. The Fund is a development bank responsible for providing soft loans to start-up manufacturing projects, in order to help diversify the industrial base of the country. My responsibilities were to review the marketing and business plans of applicant companies and comment on the potential viability of the project under review. I was assigned to the medical, veterinary, and pharmaceutical sectors and some of the specialty chemicals sectors because of my background in biomedical research and pharmaceutical marketing (I have a Ph.D. in biochemistry and an M.B.A.).

As I walked through the vaulted chamber of the arrivals hall, I noted the airiness and attempted grandeur of my surroundings, and also the obvious lack of attention to essential maintenance. I proceeded without incident through passport and immigration control into the baggage hall, where I discovered that my luggage had not arrived. Fortunately, I had purchased some short-sleeved shirts and underwear in London during my stopover.

I registered my complaint at the lost luggage counter and proceeded through to customs clearance, where I explained my lack of baggage to a bored-looking official. In the main airport concourse, it appeared that no one had been sent to meet me. While I was searching for an information desk, I was approached by a limousine driver. He had correctly assumed that I must be the individual he was to collect because I was the only westerner wandering around in this part of the airport. When we stepped from the air-conditioned airport into the covered parking area, I felt the searing heat and the dryness of the air. I had arrived in Saudi Arabia in the middle of July 1998, well into the heat of the summer season. I knew that the temperatures would easily be above 45°C, or even 50°C.

The drive from the airport revealed the flatness and brownness of the landscape on either side of the highway into Riyadh. The highway was lined with palm trees and acacia bushes, though little shrubbery was apparent anywhere else, which made me wonder why such efforts would be made in a country that lacks water resources.

When I arrived at the Hyatt hotel, a letter was waiting for me from the Fund, welcoming me to the Kingdom and inviting me to present myself. As it turned out, the office block was next door to the hotel. I showered and made myself somewhat more presentable, before I ventured out into the heat and walked the fifty or so metres to my new office.

Within an hour I had been assigned my apartment, and a temporary company vehicle was allocated to me. I surrendered my passport, applied for my *iqama* (identity document), and submitted a claim for my travel expenses. I was then taken to the department where I was to work and was introduced to the department head, a Saudi Arabian whom I had met at the interview for this job, who in turn introduced me to the other consultants in the Marketing Department. Then I was assigned a cubicle and given my first project for review.

There was a general lack of activity and a dearth of personnel in my department. A fellow consultant, an expatriate from the Netherlands, pointed out what I should have realized. A lot of people were taking their annual summer leave. He gave me the usual advice one would expect from an expatriate who had more experience dealing with the Fund and with life in Saudi Arabia, as well as his dictum on the only true advantages of life in Saudi

Arabia: "The sun always shines, there are no taxes, and women cannot drive."

Later that afternoon, a Saudi from the general services section of the Fund took me to the company recreation centre and then on to my apartment, a very large, sparsely furnished, two-bedroom flat. Because I was on what was termed a bachelor contract, the bare minimum of furnishings had been provided. The effect was the denotation of second-class status. The logic of my employers was that to completely furnish the accommodation was not necessary because I did not have a spouse or children. It was my first introduction to the suspicion with which bachelors were regarded in the Kingdom. For someone of my age and background to be unmarried was unthinkable in the local culture.

Thus at the end of my first day, I found myself alone in a flat that was part of the company's bachelor accommodation, without a telephone, television, or any other distractions, wondering what to do for entertainment. So why was I here?

This is a question that must be asked by hundreds of thousands of expatriate workers who make this journey. Saudi Arabia has one of the largest populations of migrant workers relative to the local population, where estimates vary from between one million and four million migrants in a total population of twenty-one million. For most who find themselves in the Kingdom the principal answer to the question is "Money." I had been unemployed after a failed business venture for which I had left behind a good job in management in the pharmaceutical industry. The work at the Fund sounded interesting if not necessarily challenging, and was reasonably well paid, with accommodation, car, holiday allowances, and comprehensive medical coverage.

I had organized my travel so as to arrive in the Kingdom on Monday at the beginning of the working week. I discovered that the working week runs from Saturday to Wednesday with Friday being the Sabbath, something I should have realized. So I had only a couple of working days before the weekend arrived and was able to take up the offer of one of my expatriate co-workers to show me around Riyadh; I could also begin to explore on my own the surrounding countryside.

Thus it was that I found myself on my first Thursday evening eating pizza and drinking home-brewed beer while being regaled with stories of the problems and difficulties that living in the Kingdom can produce for expatriates. The strict social control that the government enforces alongside the imposition of a very strict interpretation of Sharia law meant that almost everything one would take for granted in the West was absent.

There were no cinemas or theatres, concert halls or music clubs. Restaurants, of which there were a wide variety, were internally seg-regated by sex and marital status; men would be in one section while women and families were in another. Men and women were allowed to be together only if they were married or were members of the same family. The practice of all religions other than Islam was prohibited. Raids on clandestine religious ceremonies organized by groups of Indians or Filipinos were triumphantly reported in the local press. And then there was the ban on alcohol, which I was breaking as this information was imparted to me.

At the time I arrived, the authorities had been turning a blind eye to a lot of the activities of the western expatriate community, and an active social scene had developed around the major housing compounds where many expatriates lived. There was a theatre group running in one compound, various amateur music groups, and the ubiquitous pubs and bars. The most famous were those on the Izdihar compound housing British Aerospace employees where there was a weekly disco. Most of these bars were open only to residents and their friends. Because I was working for a Saudi employer and because I was living in company bachelor accom-modation, I was not immediately part of the life that existed on the major expatriate housing compounds.

At the time I arrived in the Kingdom, a number of off-compound bars were run more or less discreetly from smaller, less secure compounds or from villas or houses in the better neighbourhoods.

Among the off-compound bars that were operating while I was a free man in the Kingdom were the Dewdrop Inn (run by Americans working for the Vinnell Corporation), the Tudor Rose (run by a British design engineer, open since the late 1980s, and unofficially the officer's mess for various RAF and USF groups during the Gulf War in 1991), the White Elephant (run by employees of Cable & Wireless), Melrose Place (run by employees from Lucent), and the Dog's Bollocks (run by an Irish expatriate who worked for the Saudi Industrial Development Fund). Other bars and clubs were the Leg's Arms, the Celtic Corner, the Consulate, and Shenanigans.

These bars primarily served homemade beer and home-distilled alcohol (known by the name of *sid* or *sidiqi,* from the Arabic word for friend). The beer was usually made by the curious expedient of using yeast (often bakers' yeast), sugar, and alcohol-free beer that had passed its expiry date and that was available at a discount from shops and supermarkets. The quality of the liquor varied. Some people were able to adapt the process to produce reasonable facsimiles of gin or bourbon, though most produced something just the right side of drinkable. Some commercially produced liquor was available, but that was particularly expensive (500 Saudi riyals for a one-litre bottle – about $100 U.S.) and the choice was usually limited to Johnnie Walker Black Label. Furthermore its supply was not very regular, being dependent on the chaotic delivery schedules of a number of underground networks.

It amused me that I encountered more alcoholics in Saudi Arabia, among both the local population and the expatriates, than anywhere else I have lived. It was a fact of life. On more than one occasion at work, usually after the lunch hour, I found myself in an elevator surrounded by a miasma of alcohol emanating from one or other of the senior members of the Saudi management. As for the expatriates, the country seemed to be a magnet for people with this problem. Maybe they arrived in Saudi hoping that the supposed absence of alcohol would cure them of their problem or possibly it was that their problem had made employment in the West untenable and Saudi Arabia was their last chance at remunerative employment. Whatever the reason, I have never before or since found myself in a social milieu where alcoholism appeared to be so ubiquitous.

Probably the most sought-after invitations, primarily due to the availability of free alcohol, were to the parties and receptions held by the various western embassies. (Interestingly, in a country that was supposed to be free of alcohol, the embassies seemed to have more than adequate supplies. No doubt there was an agreement that accommodated the needs of the embassies and the Saudis.) Developing the contacts to ascend the pecking order necessary to gain access was something indulged in as a matter of course by many in the expatriate community. For those in the British and American communities in Riyadh, this could take some time, given the large number of their fellow citizens in the Kingdom (in 1998, this was approximately thirty thousand for the British and fifty thousand for the Americans). For others, such as those from Finland, Italy, or Belgium, the size of whose communities numbered in the hundreds at most, access to embassy social life was almost a given.

One common belief among my Saudi colleagues, provoked by the common knowledge that the embassies were not "dry," was that the legations supplied their compatriots with a monthly ration of a bottle of whisky (along with other items such as GPS locators and pornographic videos). Funnily enough, my interrogators held this conviction. My efforts to disabuse them and other Saudis of this fantasy failed even though such generosity would have cost the British Embassy in the region of £1 million per annum in whisky alone. I cannot imagine that any embassy would maintain such an expensive and foolish policy. Nevertheless, it was a persistent rumour believed even by many of my western-educated Saudi Arabian work colleagues.

The rumours that circulated among the local Saudis and the expats concerning the access that westerners had to imported alcohol were just that, rumours. The ultimate control of the smuggling was in the hands of Saudi Arabians, with expatriates (both westerners and non-westerners) acting as the middlemen arranging shipping and distribution. Not surprisingly, Saudi-based companies were involved in logistics. One bootlegger I would become acquainted with worked as the transport manager of Zahid tractors, a dealership for heavy trucks and mobile plant that was also a haulage contractor.

Apart from the bars, organizations like the Paradise Group threw ticketed parties on the larger compounds that were also open to non-residents. For a short time there was a cinema on one of the Al Ramazan compounds opened by an enterprising American bootlegger, in an attempt to diversify his source of income. Schedules of films were sent by e-mail around the expatriate community. The cinema was shut down after one expatriate posted the schedule on a bulletin board where he worked, and the Saudi owner of the compound was contacted by the authorities.

All these facilities were open only to western passport holders, with a few exceptions made for special friends of the regulars of these establishments or social clubs. This was due primarily to the nature of the segregation that existed throughout Saudi Arabia. This exclusivity was not because of racism on the part of the western expatriate community, though such attitudes were common enough.

Everyone who arrives in Saudi Arabia is identified, paid, and housed according to the country of nationality. The broad designations used in employment terms were Saudi Nationals, western expatriate workers (Americans, Britons, Australians, Canadians, etc.), other Arab nationals, and third-country nationals (Filipinos, Bangladeshis, Sri Lankans, Indonesians, Africans, etc.). Salaries were paid according to these designations with westerners at the top of the heap, and the third-country nationals down at the bottom. Housing and other benefits followed the same pattern, with each national group being housed separately with a descending scale of quality. Where skills were nominally identical between individuals across these groups, as was the case for, say, electricians or nurses, a western expatriate worker would be paid more than a third-country national. Even within the groups there was differentiation of pay for equivalent jobs, with the Filipinos being the highest paid among the third-country nationals and Americans being the highest paid among the western expatriates.

The system was almost identical to the apartheid regime imposed in South Africa and was just as rigid. Thus one lived and operated within what were effectively state-imposed ghettos, which in turn created an air of mistrust among the various national groups, each suspecting the other of happily working as informants for the Saudi authorities. Whether or not this was the desired intention of the government is a matter for conjecture, but this is the effect that it had, further reinforcing the segregation at all levels, particularly the social.

Just after receiving my iqama, less than a month after my arrival, I experienced the treatment the Mutawa accorded third-party national groups. The Mutawa, whose full title is "the Council for the Promotion of Virtue and the Prevention of Vice," are the religious police controlled by the Ministry of the Interior, the department responsible for policing the Kingdom. Trained only as religious fanatics, their role is to enforce the strict interpretation of the religious laws applied in the Kingdom.

I was standing in one of the larger modern shopping complexes just off Oleya Road when evening prayer was called, and the shops began to shut for the duration of the prayer as required. Just as the shops finished closing, a group of Mutawa appeared, distinguished from the other Saudis present by short thobes that reached only to the mid-calf, sandals, plain white ghutras without iqals, and by their full, bushy beards. They took to their task of ensuring the attendance at prayer of all the Muslims in the mall with alacrity, and then began to round up all the Indians and Filipinos present, pushing and shoving them, delivering the occasional slap to those who protested, while demanding their iqamas as proof of their religion.

The few westerners present assiduously ignored what was going on and were just as assiduously left alone. I observed the actions of these thugs too closely, and my interest was noted by two of the younger Mutaween, who immediately bore down on me demanding my papers. After examining my iqama, they began to demand in a mixture of Arabic and English if I was Indian. I was frankly nonplussed. I hold dual British and Canadian citizenship. I explained as best I could that I was Canadian, for that was the nationality under which I was registered in the Kingdom. The shouts and exclamations of my two interviewers attracted the attention of others of the Mutawa, and a few more of them began to cluster around me. Things seemed to be getting not a little dodgy, and I realized something must be wrong with my identity documents. What was most noticeable was the change in the demeanour of the Mutawa once they thought that I was Indian. Their behaviour had been surly and arrogant, now it became aggressive and threatening. I learned this was usual. The Mutawa meted out quite brutal treatment to Asian and African nationals as a matter of course. Westerners rarely experienced this treatment.

Fortunately for me, an English-speaking Saudi Arabian stepped into the fray and retrieved my iqama. He did not have the same appearance as the Mutawa, for he was clean-shaven, wearing a thobe of normal length along with a red checkered shemagh and iqal. At the time, I thought he was just a concerned citizen. I realized much later that he was a regular police officer accompanying them on their rounds. Within a couple of minutes, after I handed him a business card from the Fund, he managed to establish that I was not in fact Indian but Canadian, and that my iqama had been issued with the wrong designation for my nationality. Thankfully that was the end of it, except for the admonition that I must get my employers to resubmit my iqama for correction.

Oddly enough when I raised this issue at the Personnel Department the following day, I was met only with a shrug of the shoulders, and the assurance that it would be rectified when my new iqama would be issued two years hence. (At the time of my arrest two years later, my recently reissued iqama still recorded my nationality as Indian.) My iqama was not the only government-issued identity document with errors.

A few weeks later when driving home, I was caught up in one of the irregular roadblocks performed to check identities and catch illegal immigrants. As required, I handed my driving licence over to a young uniformed policeman, who looked at it and then walked away to one of the patrol cars that formed the roadblock. He returned with a sergeant, who indicated that I had to pull my car to the side of the road. I did this and stepped out of the vehicle into a strange discussion concerning the invalidity of the licence that became more confused when I handed over my iqama. The sergeant and his young assistant now had an invalid driving licence that stated my nationality as Canadian, and an iqama that stated my nationality as Indian.

At the point when our limited dialogue was exhausted, and I was probably about to be arrested, a plainclothes officer appeared to sort out the mess. The problem with my licence was that it was technically out of date by five years, having an expiry date set at a time long before my arrival in the Kingdom. Thankfully, the plainclothes officer discovered that the issue date, which I knew to be correct, was in advance of the expiry date, making the licence paradoxical. He also established that I had not lived in the Kingdom previously, so it was obvious that the licence had been issued with this fault. I was also fortunate that he was more amused than perturbed by the error in my iqama. Thus, I once again found myself making a complaint in the Personnel Department, but this time I was able to get my driving licence reissued.

I explored all the various souks and markets within the Riyadh area, even those not frequented by westerners. During these urban peregrinations I soon learned that while the presence of expatriates in the Kingdom was tolerated (at least on the surface) by the educated and affluent of Saudi society, it was actively resented in other quarters. On a Thursday morning, a couple of weeks after arriving in the Kingdom, I was wandering alone in one of the markets in the Baatha area of Riyadh, when a couple of men, whom I thought might be Mutawa from their appearance, approached me. As they drew close to me, I was spat upon and subjected to a few angry imprecations, not a word of which I understood. I balled my fists expecting a fight, but they just hurried off, casting nervous glances over their shoulders lest I follow them. Angry though I was, I let this pass, wiping the saliva from my face. This was not the last such demonstration I experienced. But at that time in 1998, such incidents were infrequent, if not rare.

While I was developing my personal assessment of the political stability of the regime, mistakenly confident of my ability to duck, I gained my introduction to the bar scene in Riyadh. It occurred on Remembrance Day 1998, when I met Sandy Mitchell and Gerry McGeoch at a service held at the British Embassy. I discovered from them that they had set up a bar known as the Celtic Corner on the Al Fallah compound, located by Coffee Pot roundabout (so known because a statue of a coffee pot had once graced the traffic island), just opposite the old Riyadh airport (which had become a base for the Saudi Air Force). I soon became a regular at this bar, and from there came to know and be invited to the other bars on the circuit.

During my time as an habitué of the scene it became clear to me that the expatriate community held the view that while all this was illegal, it was tolerated, and that one had to be quite unlucky to be arrested for these activities. I came to realize that the risks of any given bar or club being raided were not a matter of luck, but simply a matter of *wasta* (influence) of the owner of the bar or compound. Whenever a raid was conducted on a bar, it was conducted by the Mutawa under the supervision of the uniformed police, who stayed in the background. It was almost as if the raids served to uphold the religious purpose of the Mutawa, allowing them to focus their ire on the expatriates, who after all were the source of all corruption in the Kingdom.

When I first arrived, it was always the bars located on the smaller compounds or in individual villas that were hit. That was where the wasta of the compound owners came into play. All the large compounds had been instructed to serve the needs of the western expatriate community whose members were working on large infrastructure or defence-related projects for the Saudi government. In such cases, the compound ownership was either through a company or individuals connected to Princes of the House of Saud, effectively making the compound immune from the prying eyes of the Mutawa, even though it was guaranteed that the intelligence services of the Ministry of the Interior were well aware of the activities taking place. Effectively, the larger the company that you worked for and the more important the contract in which it was involved, the safer one was from harassment or arrest.

Compounds such as Eid villas, Jedawal, Al Nikhail, Najj, Seder, or Izdihar housed large numbers of personnel involved in defence contracts from companies such as Raytheon and British Aerospace, and the authorities avoided doing anything to disturb expatriate life for these workers. These compounds also provided through their exorbitant rents a means of channelling government funds to the retainers of the various government ministries. Part of the contracts signed by the western companies required them to house their employees at approved locations, which usually meant on a compound owned directly or indirectly by the family or retainers of the minister concerned. It is one of the hidden costs of doing business in Saudi Arabia; however, it seems not to present an obstacle if the contracts concerned are lucrative enough.

It was with this growing awareness that I became a regular patron of the Celtic Corner, and my association and friendship with Sandy Mitchell grew and developed. At the time we met, his wife, Noy, was expecting their first child, and Sandy, who worked as a senior anaesthetic technician at the Security Forces Hospital (run by the Ministry of the Interior for the benefit of its personnel) was wondering whether to continue running the bar. When their son, Matthew, arrived, Sandy stepped back from running the Celtic Corner, hiring Les Walker to act as a manager in his stead. Les had been searching for a new job because his then Saudi employer had not paid him for eight months (a not uncommon occurrence in the Kingdom). He took this unofficial (and illegal) position temporarily until he was hired as the manager for the Izdihar compounds at which British Aerospace employees are housed.

Les had been resident in Saudi Arabia for more than twenty years and had witnessed all the changes that oil wealth had brought to the country, as well as the changes to the expatriate community. He also understood the intricacies of Saudi life. If there was a story or rumour, he had heard it and had both the experience and knowledge to judge its accuracy. I often found myself at his house on the weekend.

Gradually over the first few weeks and months of my residence in the Kingdom, I began to adjust, muddling through the odd hiccough in the bureaucracy and settling in to a work routine that included a daily excursion to the Desert Inn for lunch. The establishment was located on a facility run by the USAF and other American defence contractors (though it was in the process of being handed over to the Saudi Air Force). It was a place where one could be served bacon and other pork products, which were illegal in the Kingdom. The weekend buffet brunches served each Thursday and Friday were always packed.

As for the mechanics of my job, I did not find it unduly difficult, though I did have to learn a substantial amount about the politics of the game. I soon developed the view, not uncommon among other of my expatriate work colleagues, that while some of the projects that passed through the Fund were reasonable enough, quite a few amounted to little more than an elaborate means of providing welfare for the well-heeled and well-connected. Many of the projects were based on the manufacture of overpriced products for sale to Saudi Arabian government agencies as part of the drive for import substitution.

The basic remit of the Fund, providing soft loans for Saudi-based manufacturing projects, was and is in itself perfectly sensible. However, application of this *raison d'être* proved otherwise. Too many of the projects that I reviewed were attempts to access financing by classifying repackaging operations as manufacturing to gain exemption from import duties. Duties were imposed on finished goods coming into the Kingdom, but not on items classified as raw materials. Naturally, there was an incentive to find the means to get around these fees. One project that springs to mind involved the production of an anti-scaling chemical used in water desalination plants. At the time I looked over that particular application, this chemical was shipped in bulk into the Kingdom through a Saudi Arabian agent. The end stage of producing the active chemical agent entailed the mixing of two precursor chemicals, so a project was hatched that involved the importation of the two precursors with the final mixing taking place in the Kingdom.

The project required minimal capital investment, and most of the increase in profits that came from the sale of the final product was derived from the savings from the exemption of duty that the importing of the two precursor molecules (classed as raw materials) produced. In my report I remember stating that the project would be viable given that the Saudi company involved would be supplying the same final product to the same few clients whose demand was well established and easy to forecast, but I questioned whether this was what was meant by development. The project could barely be described as a screwdriver operation, yet I know it was approved, probably in part because of the connections or wasta of the Saudi Arabian sponsors of the project.

As for the value of wasta, I was delivered of another lesson in the importance of this commodity through a project that involved the production of veterinary pharmaceuticals. While this was ostensibly another repackaging operation, it did involve investment in manufacturing plant beyond a couple of mixing and storage tanks, as was the case in the former project. Where this project ran into trouble was in the relationship between the Saudi sponsor and the Ministry of Agriculture, which was responsible for control of veterinary pharmaceuticals. The sponsor had fallen foul of the authorities through the importation of certain banned anti-parasitic compounds used in the poultry industry. The viability of the project was dependent on this conflict being resolved. Furthermore, my review of the industry sector indicated that the project's sales projections were too high. However, even at more conservative estimates of sales, the project was probably viable, should the other problem be rectified.

I myself fell foul of the politics surrounding this project when I assessed the project on lower sales figures and mentioned the political problems. On the day the final report was submitted to the senior lending officer, I received an unexpected visit from the rather irate Saudi sponsor. As I later discovered, this project was of interest to a couple of senior members of the management of the Fund, who tried to keep their involvement hidden. Over the next year I was subjected to varying degrees of pressure to revise my appraisal to one more favourable to the project, and to remove any reference to the problems arising at the Ministry of Agriculture. Eventually, this project disappeared from view, and I was spared any further impromptu visits, for the Saudi sponsor ended up in prison as a result of charges laid by the Ministry of Agriculture. Not that the sponsor was necessarily guilty of any crime – he just didn't have the appropriate influence in the ministry even though he did have the appropriate influence at the Fund, for it seemed that there were those at the ministry with a more vested interest in some of the sponsor's competitors.

As for my social life, it was hardly raucous. Most social activities, but not all, were associated with alcohol at least in part, and thus illegal because of that if nothing else. Activities such as those that were part of the natural history society or the various off-road trekking clubs, which one would have thought innocuous, were monitored to such a degree as to confirm the institutional paranoia of the authorities. I can remember the cloak-and-dagger arrangements that were made to set up a rendezvous to head off on a weekend desert trip. Should a collection of westerners in 4 × 4 vehicles have been spotted by the police, the group would have been broken up and arrests would probably have been made. The authorities looked with suspicion on any large group wandering the hinterlands exploring the Kingdom. The concept that anyone would do such exploration as a hobby was alien to them, and thus it was viewed as a potential threat to the security of the Kingdom.

I found the means to keep myself supplied with books and magazines; those that were not readily available in the Kingdom, I was able to have shipped to me. Some did not make it past the censors, but that was due to the obtuseness of the censors and not the subject matter of the books. I developed a few good friendships, but kept my own company for the most part, as I always have done.

I spent weekends away in the desert, an activity I indulged in more and more as my competence and confidence in my off-road driving abilities developed. I saw the Hijaz, the Empty Quarter, the Red Sands, and the mountains of Asir. This represented my most dangerous activity, for most of these excursions were conducted alone. I look back in fondness to my times spent wrapped up in a sleeping bag or a *bhisht*, head torch in place, book in hand, out in the middle of nowhere under a starlit sky. Occasionally, on my more far-flung trips I would come across Bedouins with their goats and camels, and find myself at the mercy of their sincere and generous hospitality. All in all, life was good then.

Like most expatriates, I was not unduly worried when the first of the small compound or off-compound bars were raided and closed down. The first to go was Tricky Dicky's in December 1998; it had been run by an Irish chef. It was assumed that it had been raided because the owner had the misfortune to choose a location only a few doors away from a villa used as a dormitory by the local Mutawa. In 1999 a bar called K2 was raided, followed in the late summer of that year by a raid on the Dewdrop Inn.

Every once in a while, warnings would be sent out by the embassies concerning security, but they would not provide information about the incidents that provoked their issuance. As the local media were tightly controlled by the Ministry of the Interior, little was reported about any attacks on expatriates. In such a situation, where accurate information is unavailable, inaccurate information fills the vacuum. The rumour mill of the expatriate community worked overtime in this capacity.

One heard of buses full of nurses attacked at shopping centres, of Americans beaten up in coffee shops in Jeddah, of Brits being attacked at petrol stations, most of which were third-hand accounts that I was not able to substantiate. Still, even discounting for the exaggeration that a rumour mill imposes on such information, and relying primarily on first-hand accounts, the hostility toward foreigners in general and western expatriates in particular that I had encountered while exploring Riyadh when I first arrived seemed to be increasing.

None of this particularly worried me, for no one was being killed, and it all seemed fairly random. Most expatriates seemed to accept the picture painted of a country free of crime, except that caused by the immorality of the various expatriate communities. The local papers had occasional items heralding raids on bars, clubs, or distilleries run by Indians or Filipinos, government crackdowns on those who overstayed their visas, or campaigns to clamp down on speeding or other traffic offences. There were few if any reports on major crime as one would see in the western media, and no crime figures were published by the Ministry of the Interior. As most westerners lived on compounds or in the more affluent areas of the cities where there was a heavier police presence, we had as a collective group a somewhat distorted perspective. I had fewer illusions than most. My suspicions were confirmed by a couple of friends who worked in the Shamasi hospital, a rather dilapidated facility run by the Ministry of Health with a prison wing operated by the Ministry of the Interior. They described to me a steady flow of casualties resulting from violence or violent crimes that would not be uncommon in any northern European city, though probably fewer than seen in North America.

All in all, life in the Kingdom was reasonably safe. Not as safe as most expatriates believed, but certainly no worse than any major western city. In 2000, at the end of my second year in the Kingdom, two incidents brought me to the attention of the Ministry of the Interior. The first came about because of the raids in April of that year on two bars run by Gary O'Nions, Shenanigans and the Consulate. At the time I was not unduly worried; probably, I should have been. However, that is hindsight.

I was at work when, just before lunch, I answered a call from Sandy Mitchell, who informed me that Shenanigans and the Consulate had been raided and a number of people, including the proprietor, Gary O'Nions, had been arrested.

Sandy had long acted as an unofficial prison visitor helping expats who fell foul of the law on anything from traffic violations through to alcohol offences. On a number of occasions Sandy had managed to affect the release of those arrested without charge and without their employers or their embassy becoming involved, usually to the relief of all concerned. He used contacts that he had developed where he worked at the Security Forces Hospital, run by the Ministry of the Interior for its employees, to prevent the typical complications that occur when officialdom enters the fray. To be successful he usually needed to intervene within a few hours of the arrest, and the offence needed to be relatively minor.

As O'Nions had been arrested the previous night in a raid on his bar, success was unlikely. However, Sandy hoped to locate the other individuals who had been arrested. We could at least speed up the process of informing embassies and employers in hopes of decreasing their time spent in jail. In these situations, individuals would be paroled into the care of their employers, to await disposition of their cases. If the offence was a minor one, such as a traffic offence, or if the offence was related to identity document problems or being in the company of a member of the opposite sex to which the offender was not a related, nothing further would happen, though one consequence might be that an employment contract was not renewed.

Running a bar was a serious offence. It was punished by a period of imprisonment followed by deportation. Typical official sentences would be two years in prison, a fine, and two hundred to four hundred lashes, which would be rigorously applied to offenders who were third-country nationals. Westerners were granted some leniency. They could expect to be imprisoned until the following Ramadan, when a pardon would be granted, and the offender would be deported without paying the fine or experiencing the public flogging.

Sandy called me because I had recently begun to help him in these matters. During our lunch hours, we located the police jail at which everyone was being held. We were able to persuade the senior officer in charge to allow us to speak to Gary, who told us the details of what happened and the names of those arrested with him. Everyone, including Gary O'Nions, was eventually released within a few days, under guarantees from their employers. Officially, Gary was employed by Eurocatering, a small company owned by a member of the Al Aidan family who full well knew the nature of his activities. It is curious that someone whose sole occupation in Saudi Arabia was the management of illegal bars, as Gary's was, would have a Saudi Arabian employer, but that is how things work. It must have been the wasta of his employer that expedited Gary's release.

This was not the first time that an illegal bar run by Gary had been uncovered. In the late 1980s Gary set up the Empire Club, which had become a focal point of social life within Riyadh. In early 1998, while Gary was briefly out of the Kingdom, the Empire Club was raided. His wife was arrested and held for three months before being deported. For reasons best known to Gary, he decided to return to the Kingdom in 1999, under a new name, Gary Dixon, to once again run illegal bars. Through his lucky escape, and his initial luck in returning to the Kingdom, "The Saga of Gary O'Nions" became part of the folklore of expatriate life there.

Gary fostered an image of himself as the Scarlet Pimpernel. Unfortunately, the Pimpernel had now been plucked. It would not be too long before the authorities realized who Gary Dixon was, and I expect they would not have appreciated having their noses tweaked in such a manner. Gary was not happy with what he faced. He knew his arrest and detention would prove embarrassing for the British Embassy, the Ministry of the Interior, and his Saudi sponsor. The prospect of a harsh sentence, in conjunction with the sobering sight of the damage wreaked upon his establishments by the Mutawa, made Gary eager to flee while he still had his liberty.

Gary informed Sandy that Frank Murray, the former transport manager at Zahid tractors, whom Gary knew through the boot-legging network, had offered a means of escape to Dubai. Sandy, when informed of this, spoke to Ian Wilson, then consul at the British Embassy, to find out if this was a sensible option, and to find out if Gary would receive assistance from the British Embassy if he fled to Dubai. Sandy believed that Wilson gave this plan tacit approval when he agreed that it would be best if Gary just disappeared. This message was passed on to Gary who, through Frank, made his arrangements to leave Riyadh for Dammam, on the east coast, within a few days.

On the Friday that Gary was due to depart, Sandy Mitchell came around to see me at my home. He had planned to drive Gary to Dammam, but his car was acting up. Given that he had also just worked through the night at his hospital, I offered to collect Gary and undertake the journey of three and a half hours to take him to his rendezvous in Dammam. So began an unfortunate comedy of errors.

About sixty kilometres from Dammam my car suffered a flat tire. If that was not bad enough, I discovered that my spare tire was also flat. This meant that all we could do was wait for a passing good Samaritan or for the highway patrol, a prospect that made Gary distinctly nervous. When a police car eventually arrived, the officer flagged down a passing juggernaut and had the driver use his air line to reflate my tire, in the hope that the puncture was a minor one. With this done, the police officer departed and we drove tensely toward Dammam. About five minutes later the tire went flat again, and we were forced to await the arrival of another police car.

When this occurred, the police officers put one of my wheels into the trunk of their patrol car and took me to a motorway service station where an emergency repair was done. I was then taken back to my car. Before the police officers left, they took my details (fortunately they did not take Gary's) and reported the incident. It was the first time I had an encounter with the authorities in which I was not perfectly in the right. What should have been a simple drive could easily have resulted in arrest.

We were late and missed our rendezvous. Gary and I spent the afternoon reading the papers and drinking coffee in the reception area of the Meridien hotel, while we waited for Gary to be collected by an American named John Koukawski, who worked for Saudi Aramco (the state oil company that is an American-Saudi joint venture). About six in the evening, Koukawski arrived, collected Gary, and helped me purchase a new tire and have the other repaired. Both Gary and I were relieved that there were no further incidents. I headed back to Riyadh, and Gary went into hiding on the Saudi Aramco housing compound.

That, I hoped, was the end of it, but unfortunately it was not. Gary ended up stuck in Dammam for a couple of months while arrangements were made for his clandestine trip to Dubai. Sandy and I visited him at his hideaway on the Aramco housing compound on the night before his departure, Sandy bringing with him a small rucksack containing spare clothing and sundries for his trip. The following morning we returned to Riyadh, while John Koukawski, Gary's host, departed with Gary for the desert. From my understanding, Gary was taken to an unguarded spot on the

Saudi-Emirates border, and that night he walked a couple of kilometres due east into Dubai and was collected by Koukawski's contacts there. Apparently that occurred without a hitch, and so Gary successfully left Saudi Arabia. That was the last thing to go right, and a few weeks later I heard that Gary was arrested while trying to leave Dubai.

For whatever reason, I was not concerned from a personal point of view, I just considered it damned unfortunate, inconvenient, and embarrassing, all the things that I had tried to prevent. I wondered how long it would take before Gary would be returned to Saudi from Dubai and if I would be implicated in the mess.

Toward the end of the summer in August, the Tudor Rose was raided and another group of expats were arrested, finding themselves stuck in Malaz police station in Riyadh. The Tudor Rose was one of the oldest and smallest of the bars, run by its owner more for his personal entertainment than for profit. He was content if he covered the cost of rent from his takings (which he did not always manage). Again, most of his guests were released the next day. Unfortunately, the owner and a compound resident who had been running a still were not so fortunate and spent more than a year in prison before being deported, by which time I was in prison myself, facing a more serious penalty.

In quick succession, the Consulate, Shenanigans, and the Tudor Rose had all been shut. Interspersed with these closures had been the arrests of a few bootleggers and the closure of a couple of stills. No raids or interventions had occurred against the clubs located on the major compounds; still, it appeared to me that the authorities were finally clamping down on the bar and club scene.

No one else seemed to find this too worrying. Everyone seemed to think that the bars located on the Al Fallah compound (the Celtic Corner and the Leg's Arms) were in no danger, because of their proximity to a Saudi Air Force base. I believed that the authorities knew full well about most of these clubs, along with all

44

the others, and could close them down at will, meaning that none of them were safe.

I was also aware of a growing expression of anti-western sentiments. The intifada had begun, and condemnations of America's, and thus the West's, policies toward Palestine had become rife. Incidents of confrontation between westerners and the local population, both rumoured and real, were on the increase, and one had to take care if one travelled alone in certain districts. I began to feel that it was only a matter of time before a lethal confrontation occurred, and I became increasingly wary, as did many in the expatriate community. I knew that there was trouble brewing in Saudi Arabia. Nevertheless, I could not have predicted that innocent people, including myself and my friend Les Walker, would be framed for a series of lethal attacks on westerners in order to help maintain the culture of denial cultivated by the Saudi government.

On October 12, the second incident occurred. At the close of the working day on Wednesday, the start of the weekend, I drove over to visit some friends, Peter and Annie Goldsmith, and arrived in the middle of a raid by the Mutawa. The Mutawa had stormed the villa next to the Goldsmiths', looking for a bootlegger who was running a still in their neighbour's house. When they did not find him, they turned their attention next door. Unfortunately, Peter had a large quantity of wine brewing in his house, making Peter and Annie a satisfactory catch. I was arrested with them.

Both of the Goldsmiths had been in the Kingdom for a number of years. Peter was an electrical engineer, and he was employed at the King Khaled Military Hospital. I first met them almost twelve months earlier, after they had taken in the girlfriend of the owner of the Dewdrop Inn. She had been arrested with the owner, an American employed by Vinnell, when the Dewdrop Inn was shut down. Her name was Marie, and Sandy had visited her when she was in prison. She was being allowed to stay with Peter and Annie until her enforced departure. Her boyfriend had been released into the parole of his employer and was living under house arrest until his deportation.

I became a regular visitor of Peter and Annie's, sitting at the poolside or in the garden, enjoying the occasional sundowner and their company. I was on my way to their house for exactly that purpose on that Wednesday evening.

As I turned onto their street and approached the Goldsmiths' villa, the Mutawa poured forth from the garden, surrounding my vehicle and pulling me from it. Once I had been pulled free from the vehicle, I was handcuffed while the Mutawa danced around, gleefully raining punches and kicks on me. Luckily for me they were either inexpert or not trying too hard. Eventually they tired of this game, and I was taken to join Peter and Annie, who were sitting in a police vehicle.

All of us were hustled into the covered driveway of the original target villa where we were placed in the back of a large GMC Suburban. The Mutawa pulled another western couple off the street, an American employee of Raytheon and his Filipino wife, arresting them for the same offences. At one point we were taken into the villa and seated around a coffee table in the living room, upon which glasses were then placed. A plainclothes police officer joined us, and photographs were taken. From there our group, which now numbered six in total, was taken to the Mutawa station in the southern part of my neighbourhood, before being driven to the Sulimaneh/Oleya police station.

When we arrived at the police station, our identity documents were handed over by the Mutawa and we were put into a communal cell with about twelve others, whose nationalities ran the gamut from Saudi, Yemeni, Egyptian, and Pakistani through to those of the newly arrived westerners. It was crowded and cramped, filled with cheap bunk beds, and there was little room to move. Fortunately there was a separate toilet and shower room that was in passable condition, so we were able to maintain a minimum level of cleanliness. The Ritz it was not.

One of my new cellmates, a Saudi arrested on alcohol charges, lent me his mobile telephone. I knew I would be able to reach Raf, who worked as the trauma coordinator for the King Fahd National Guard Hospital, the major medical facility for the Saudi Arabian National Guard. I let him know where we were, and I asked him to pass the message along to Sandy.

Raf and Sandy then spent the evening of my arrest trying to find the police station in which we were being held. This was to no avail, for the station had not long been open and had had few if any western occupants, keeping it off our radar. Eventually, they managed to contact the duty officers at the British, American, and Canadian embassies, passing along the details of all those arrested, as well as contacting someone at Raytheon on behalf of our American co-detainee.

I was not a little perturbed and I wondered if the false claims put forward by the Mutawa would be accepted. Because I was working for a Saudi government organization, I expected that they would not be pleased, even if they accepted that my arrest was wrong. Peter, who also worked for the Saudi government, was in a worse position because alcohol had been found in his house, so I expected that he and Annie would face more difficulties than I. As for our new-found American friend, his situation was the least problematic. He worked for an American defence contractor operating within the Ministry of Defence and Aviation. This incident had few if any ramifications for him. Nevertheless, he alternated wildly between despair and near hysteria throughout the weekend till his release.

The following morning, I received a visit from Raf and Sandy, who were more amused than worried about my situation, but they were concerned about the predicament that Peter and Annie faced.

An official of the Canadian Embassy, Omar El Soury, an Egyptian working for the embassy as the property management officer, visited me. He was polite and helpful, inquiring about my treatment, and promising to contact my employers. I had hoped this would not be necessary, but understood the complexity of the situation might require their intervention. The American was visited by his embassy and people from his company: his immediate superior arrived with their company's government affairs officer, a Saudi national whose job was to deal with problems such as this. Later that morning, we were all dutifully trooped out to complete statements, which we obediently did. I am grateful to the Raytheon government affairs officer, for he stayed behind not only to assist his co-worker with the required statement, but also to help Peter and me. Then it was back to the cell, and a jolly weekend cursing our misfortune.

One particular worry that I expressed to Sandy, Raf, and Omar El Soury concerned the security of my house. The Mutawa had taken my keys at the time of my arrest and had not handed them over to the police. My worry was not only about damage or theft. I knew the Mutawa was not above planting evidence at my now empty villa. This general lack of security had earlier been driven home to me with a jolt.

I had moved into the villa about fifteen months previously, when I tired of living in the company's bachelor accommodation. I elected to take the company rent allowance and find my own accommodation. I ended up renting a small, three-bedroom villa with its own pool. It was more than spacious enough for me. It was conveniently located in the northern part of the Sulimaneh district of Riyadh, an area that was once the embassy district, before the diplomatic quarter was set up on the outskirts of Riyadh. I was better able to entertain friends there, holding the occasional barbecue and dinner party, which were technically illegal. The villa had made a pleasant change from the bachelor quarters and made me even more settled and comfortable in Saudi Arabia, though now my situation looked like it might have to change once again.

That evening another western expat joined us in the cell. His arrest showed that the aggressiveness of the Mutawa was intensifying. He was a Canadian of Lebanese origin who was working for Nortel. He had been arrested as he was leaving a restaurant where he had dined with a married couple, friends he had not seen for a number of years. When taking leave of his friends, he had made the simple mistake of kissing the woman on the cheek, whereupon he was descended on by the Mutawa and now found himself kicking his heels beside me. To say he was angry was an understatement, though fortunately his company obtained his release the next afternoon without further problems. An arrest such as that would not have occurred when I first arrived in Riyadh, but the atmosphere was changing to one that was less tolerant. Expats were now encountering the roughness of the Mutawa I had seen two years earlier, when I was mistaken for an Indian. What this meant was that the western expat community had to learn to do what the locals and the communities of third-country nationals had been doing for years: fading from sight whenever the Mutawa appeared on the street.

On Friday both the American and the other Canadian were released sometime in the late afternoon, leaving Peter and me as the only westerners. Our cellmates were a mixed bunch, most held on minor charges, trying to amuse themselves as they took it in their stride that time in prison was not at all unusual in the Kingdom. Despite the overcrowding, their attitudes made the time spent in confinement amusing if not pleasant.

When I was arrested, the Mutawa had tried to say that the target villa belonged to me. Once they failed to establish this, they then said that I had been arrested while having a drinks party with my friends and that a case of alcohol had been found in the back of my car. The young uniformed police officer who had the pleasure of accompanying them filed a more accurate report, which stated that I was arrested on the street and that in my car were two boxes, one containing a television and the other a video recorder. His statement confirmed the information I gave to the police during my interview the next day.

I was released on Saturday, just after midday, through the auspices of the Fund. The charges against me were dropped, though I suspected that I was not completely in the clear. Certainly, there would be a black mark against my name at the Ministry of the Interior, as well as at my employer's. I settled back into the routine of my life, with most of those whom I knew treating this hiatus as just one of those things. Peter was not as fortunate. The charges against him were more serious, and his employer, the military hospital, was not understanding and would not recommend his release.

Raf and I began to visit Peter every second day. On alternate days, other friends would go in to see him. We all took him spare clothes, cash, and the odd book to try to make his stay more comfortable. Seeing Annie was more difficult. She was being held at the Malaz women's prison, and she received few visits.

We managed to get in touch with Annie's daughters who lived in the U.K., apprising them of the situation, and tried to coordinate whatever activities were deemed necessary to affect a resolution, keeping the situation out of the press for the time being. Raf and I even managed to get permission for Peter to speak to the family back in the U.K. The hope was that, while it was unlikely that the charges would be dropped, with Ramadan only a few weeks away, the couple would be granted clemency and expelled without a lengthy stay in prison.

During my visits to Peter at the jail, I came across a number of the Mutaween who had arrested us. Their expressions showed their displeasure that I was wandering around free, but I was not subjected to any harassment. When I think back on it, it was probably not the best of ideas to parade myself in front of them. The police officers were not concerned that I was visiting Peter, accepting my concern for a friend as natural and not taking my arrest seriously. That, however, was not the case for the Mutawa.

On Friday, November 17, as arranged, Raf collected me at my villa, and we went to visit Peter. There was nothing new to tell him, so we just chatted for a few minutes and agreed to pass a message along to another of his friends whom we had intended to visit anyway. After the visit, Raf and I went to Rosa compound to check in with Peter's friends. It was while we were there that we first heard rumours of the bombing. Our host was phoned by a friend from British Aerospace who informed him that a car bomb had gone off on Ouraba Road at about midday. I was a bit perplexed by this information for I lived not far from one end of that street and mistakenly assumed that I would have heard something. When Raf and I left, we returned to my villa by a circuitous route that took us the length of Ouraba Road. Just past the junction with Oleya Road, we both noticed a sizeable crowd and a couple of police vehicles, but saw nothing to indicate that a car bomb had gone off; we assumed that a car bomb would have left a noticeable impression.

Later that evening, while in Jareer bookstore, we received confirmation of the event. Raf answered a call on his mobile from a fellow nurse who was listening to the details being broadcast on the BBC news and who in turn relayed them to us. It was not until a couple of days later that we learned the identities of the victims, Christopher Rodway, who was killed, and Jean Rodway, who was injured. We also learned that Christopher Rodway was a coworker of Peter Goldsmith, which meant we had to give Peter this unhappy news.

In the expatriate community, the news of Christopher Rodway's death was met with both shock and nervousness. With little accurate information being available, other than the brief announcements broadcast on BBC and Sky News, the rumour mill worked overtime. The fact was that most people were nervous and wondered what this heralded.

On Wednesday, November 22, I had arranged to meet Raf after work in order to visit Peter. Unfortunately, I left work later than anticipated and then got stuck in traffic. I was going to be too late to visit Peter, so I phoned Raf to cancel our appointment. We both decided to visit Peter the following day and arranged instead to meet at Sandy's house. When we arrived there, we sat at the poolside of his small compound, relaxing into the start of another weekend. About six o'clock, I bid Sandy and Raf goodnight, telling them that I had to drop in on Les Walker, and that I might see Raf at the Celtic Corner later on.

I didn't get to the Celtic Corner that night. Having gone home, I showered and changed before dropping in on Les as I said I would. Once there, I simply spent the evening in Les's company, not leaving for home until well into the early hours of the morning. I was completely unaware that a bomb had gone off earlier that night and that Raf had witnessed the explosion. I learned of these events when Sandy woke me the next morning by banging on the front gate of my villa. Sandy told me of the incident and wanted me to go with him to see Raf. On our way there, Sandy told me what he had learned from his calls from Raf.

When Sandy and I arrived at Raf's shared villa, located on the housing area of the National Guard Hospital complex on the eastern outskirts of the city, Raf was already awake and looking somewhat shocked. Witnessing an explosion as closely as he had is bound to make one feel vulnerable and exposed; Raf was no exception. He decided to spend the weekend at my place, so we returned to central Riyadh, watched a lot of television, and talked. I got from him a more complete version of events, which I would mull over in my mind repeatedly during the coming weeks.

He had arrived at the Celtic Corner on the Al Fallah compound around seven o'clock, where he spent his time in the company of a friend who was recovering from cancer. During the evening, Raf was joined at various times by other friends; among them were two nurses who invited him to a party on the Al Salaam compound, a place that housed people who worked for an aircraft maintenance company. At 11:15 p.m., just after the bar closed, Raf left with those attending the party. They travelled in three cars, with Raf's vehicle in the middle of the impromptu convoy. The lead vehicle was a GMC Blazer that had been parked beside Raf's car, up against the wall of the compound, only twenty or thirty metres away from the security checkpoint at the entrance to the Saudi Air Force offices nearby.

About a kilometre from the pub, less than five minutes after the journey had begun, a bomb exploded in the right front wheel arch of the lead vehicle as they passed the first set of traffic lights on old Airport Road. The car came to a halt at the side of the road, and the other vehicles also pulled over. The driver, Steve Coghlan, was slightly injured and suffered perforated eardrums. Unfortunately, Mark Payne, the passenger in the front of the car, suffered critical injuries to his right leg and was bleeding profusely. The two other passengers in the rear of the vehicle were only slightly injured, suffering mainly from shock and having their eardrums perforated by the blast.

Raf got out of his car and approached the damaged vehicle and, with the help of the others in his party, removed the two passengers from the rear of the vehicle. Raf remained on the scene, along with the driver of the damaged vehicle, the injured and immobile Mark Payne, and one of the other passengers. Everyone else got into the third vehicle and left the area, going directly to the Al Salaam compound. In retrospect, this was a mistake for their car could also have had a bomb planted on it, and by leaving the scene like that they suffered the ire of the authorities.

At the accident scene, Raf quickly assessed the injuries to Mark Payne before turning away to phone the emergency services. As he redialled the number, having done so incorrectly initially, he was confronted by two Saudi Arabians in thobes and ghutras. These were members of the secret police, the Mabaheth, and with them was a uniformed officer of the rank of major. As it turned out, one of them was none other than Ibrahim Al Dali, who would figure so prominently in our lives over the next couple of years. They had arrived on the scene within five to ten minutes of the explosion. Within another couple of minutes, the scene was swarming with police and ambulance men, whom Raf assisted in their ministrations to the injured, leaving Raf covered in blood.

Raf was tersely interviewed by the plainclothes officers, before being taken by them back to the Al Fallah compound to show them where the cars had been parked. There followed a thorough investigation by the police of the only vehicle remaining on the open ground outside the compound. Raf was then left there, while the police returned to the original scene, where his car still remained. He had to wait for three hours before the police returned, at which point they took him back to his car and allowed him to leave.

Raf had tried to call me that night sometime after the explosion but had been unable to reach me because I had turned off my phone while recharging the battery. Given the time of the explosion, I would have still been with Les, and the route from his house to mine meant that I had passed by the scene of the explosion. Interestingly, when I had driven home in the early hours of the morning, I had not noticed anything untoward for the scene had been thoroughly cleaned up by that time.

The more I went over Raf's version of events, the more something did not seem quite right about the events of that night. It was highly unusual to see a senior officer in uniform on the streets late in the evening, and it was even more unusual for one to arrive at the scene of a crime with the secret police after so short a time had elapsed. While their early arrival could have been a coincidence, it seems to me more probable they had anticipated the explosion or had some intelligence about it. Alongside this was the worrying fact that the bomb was most probably planted just outside the Al Fallah compound.

As I have said, the Al Fallah compound was located next to a Saudi Arabian Air Force compound, and in front of it was a large open space of wasteland used as a car park. It was overlooked by a three-storey office building, from the top of which one could see into both compounds. Given the presence of air force guards so close to the entrance of Al Fallah, and the openness of the surrounding area, it has always struck me as a poor choice of venue to do anything without being observed, such as planting bombs. These were unsettling thoughts.

If the first explosion had worried the expatriate community, this second one ramped up the level of paranoia. Security warnings circulated from the embassies, including advice on how to inspect one's vehicle. Every conversation seemed to be about the bombings, with everyone trying to reassure themselves that it could not happen to them because their housing compounds or workplaces were secure.

Over the next couple of weeks, all the witnesses and victims of the second bombing were hauled in for questioning. The problem for everyone was not that they had been nearly killed by a bomb, for no one suspected that the police would try to frame one of their number for the crime. The problem was the nature of their activity in the early evening, involving alcohol and attendance at an illegal drinking den. Everyone was concerned about the possibility of arrest.

Raf was the last to be interviewed. His interview was scheduled on the evening of Wednesday, December 6. This preliminary interrogation lasted through the night. Raf was not released until the early hours of the next day, having been through his first interview with Ibrahim and Khaled. He came around to see me immediately. He was distressed by the accusations that had been levelled at him.

His interrogators had been verbally abusive, and they had accused him of planting and detonating the bomb. They had set up an appointment to interview him again in the afternoon of that day, only a few hours after Raf was released from the first interview. I tried to allay his fears; I said they were trying to confuse and disturb him. If this was their sole aim, they were already successful. I worried that it was not. I worried that they might be considering hanging a scapegoat. I began to fear that Raf, and others, were in some danger from the accusations of the secret police.

It seemed sensible for him to contact his embassy to describe what had just happened, but there was not time before his second interrogation. I phoned the Belgian ambassador, Franz Michiels, whom I had met at an embassy reception a week or so earlier, to inform him of my fears concerning Raf. I paid a visit to the Belgian Embassy early in the afternoon on that Thursday, while Raf headed off for his next interview.

I met with the Belgian ambassador and the first consul, Olivier Quineaux. The three of us discussed Raf's predicament and also the deteriorating security situation. I learned from them that all the embassies had been noticing an increase in attacks on and arrests of westerners. The first consul provided me with a list of lawyers to help in Raf's defence should that prove necessary, for all three of us operated under the mistaken assumption that the Saudi Arabian government would grant westerners a little more of the due process of law than was usually accorded in their country.

It was late in the afternoon of the next day when Raf's second interview ended. He swung by the Belgian Embassy to give his own report of what had happened. He was in such a state of nervous tension that the ambassador sat him down and gave him a cognac before he allowed Raf to tell his story. Raf told him the second interview had gone much as the first had, with similar threats and accusations. Raf calmed down a little after delivering his account to his ambassador, but remained worried. He came to see Les, Sandy, and me before heading home.

On December 9, Saturday, Ibrahim and Khaled, along with numerous uniformed police officers, arrived unexpectedly at Raf's shared villa. There they performed a search of the premises. They found no alcohol in Raf's quarters; unfortunately, they did find some beer in a room belonging to another member of the house-hold, an Australian nurse. For this crime, both he and Raf were arrested. I found out about this event in a somewhat serendipitous telephone call, for I chose to phone Raf just before I left work. When he answered his mobile phone, he had just enough time to tell me that the police were at his house and that they had found alcohol in the part of the villa belonging to his housemate. I knew then that Raf was in trouble, but was still unsure as to how serious it was.

While the disturbing events of the past couple of days were unfolding, a story had appeared in the local papers claiming that an American named Mike Sedlak had been arrested as the one responsible for the bombings. I had met Sedlak, a former American army officer who worked for Vinnell, on the bar scene. Though I considered him to be a highly dubious character, he was more often than not too drunk to stand, so it was my opinion that he was being framed. As it turned out, he had been at the Celtic Corner on the night of the second bombing and was in such an inebriated state that had he involved himself with anything explosive he would have been the victim. He had lived for a brief time on the same small residential compound as the Rodways, making him the perfect fall guy. So here his name was in the papers, being accused of serious crimes, the nature of which was more indicative of the growing boldness among the homegrown dissidents in Saudi Arabia than it was of any Byzantine conspiracy theory that the security services were trying to concoct.

My contact with Raf was broken. I phoned James and Moira, a married couple who worked as nurses at the National Guard hospital and lived near him. Within a few minutes they were able to confirm that Raf and his housemate had been arrested on alcohol charges, but they had no idea where he had been taken. I then called the first consul of the Belgian Embassy, informing him of what had just transpired. Up until the time of my arrest, we talked on a daily basis and passed on what little information we had gleaned. None of my inquiries turned up information about Raf's whereabouts, nor did any of the inquiries made by his embassy. Raf had disappeared as one can do only in a police state.

He was, however, not the only one to disappear at that time. In the weeks prior to Raf's arrest, Kelvin Hawkins and David Mornin, proprietors of the Celtic Corner, had been arrested. No one knew their whereabouts. Along with their arrests were the arrests of three bootleggers, whose whereabouts were also unknown. It appeared that the bombings had unleashed a whirlwind cleanup operation on the bar scene. A disturbing rumour began to circulate that made Raf's arrest seem all the more sinister.

The gist of it was that the bombing campaign had been started by two people, a Belgian and an Irishman, who were believed to be spies. While Raf was still free, he and I had managed to trace this rumour to its source, an Irish nurse and her Saudi/Sudani/American husband. To this day I have no idea why this woman or her husband had begun spreading that rumour. There had long been suspicion concerning this couple among a number of people in the expatriate community, and I will admit that I was among those who thought they might be informers. What end did they think they would achieve? Were they were acting under someone's instruction? However, such thoughts lead into the realm of arcane conspiracies – but then given what subsequently happened to my friends and me, such thoughts may not be groundless.

I had two conversations in the few weeks prior to my arrest that further contributed to my suspicions. A couple of months after I arrived in the Kingdom, I had made an acquaintance within the police force. This happened by accident at a small but pleasant café near the Specialist Hospital. I would sometimes go there to have coffee and strudel while reading the paper. It was there that I met Moussa. We struck up a conversational friendship that revolved for the most part around his interest in rugby and football. I learned from him that he worked in the Ministry of the Interior and found him to be a useful occasional source of information. There did not seem to be a bar that he had not heard about. I learned of their existence and their names from him, long before I gained my own introduction to those places. I discovered from him the procedures for arrest and the jails to which people would usually be taken. I also learned that there were prisons to which one would not wish to be introduced.

Moussa had first warned me that a number of raids were going to take place, using the security risk posed by the bombings as an excuse. With the Celtic Corner having been raided just prior to his warning, I wondered what was left to be shut down, other than the bars on the large compounds, which were not raided then nor have they been. However, given the number of arrests among various bootleggers that happened subsequently, his warning was not inaccurate. He also informed me that some people had been arrested in connection with the bombings, most of whom were Saudis and had some connection with the Mutawa. I was told this was not going to be admitted to, at least publicly. As far as I was concerned, this was something to be worried about for it meant that the government must be looking for a scapegoat.

Just after Raf's arrest, Moussa and I spoke again for the last time – he declared it would be the last time. I asked him for help in locating my friend and he told me it was not something he could do. He told me quite simply that if I had the means to get out of the Kingdom, I should do so at once. He confirmed by his simple statement what Raf's arrest had made me realize. None of us on the bar scene were safe, and those close to any of the witnesses or victims were even more at risk. I was certain that I was going to be arrested. I was also certain that I would not try to abscond before they came for me. It was just not something I could have done, for I believed that by leaving the Kingdom in such a manner, I would only make things worse for my friends. In truth, I was wrong about this, for no such action could have made things any worse for any of those they arrested.

Time was now running out for me. I had come to realize that it was short, but did not know exactly when I too would disappear. On Thursday night, December 14, I went around to see James and Moira at their flat at the National Guard Hospital. I did not have much to tell them. Raf was not in any police station that I knew of, otherwise I would have been able to locate him. It was clear to me that the secret police were holding him at one of their centres, wherever they were. I was told by a Belgian nurse present in the flat that the embassy had not told his family, and I suggested that it was time they did. I explained to them my fears that the Ministry of the Interior was going to try to frame him and would cast the net wider to implicate his friends in a concocted conspiracy. I also told them that should I disappear, they should not attempt to look for me. For their own safety I recommended that they should not bring attention to themselves on my behalf, certainly not while they remained in the Kingdom. Specifically addressing James and Moira, I pointed out that given their close relationship with Raf, it might be an idea to consider leaving the Kingdom.

As chance would have it, some weeks later while James was out of the Kingdom on leave, the Mabaheth came looking for him. It appeared that his name had featured in a large number of e-mails on Raf's computer, confiscated during the search of Raf's villa. He was warned not to return to the Kingdom. Fortunately, Moira was able to leave without any difficulties, so they were clear of any involvement in the ensuing drama.

On Friday, December 15, I was by chance delivered of an alibi for at least one of the claims against me. About noon, Sandy brought an Egyptian doctor around to my villa to arrange for him to view Peter Goldsmith's car. Much to my relief, Peter and Annie had been released and sent back to the U.K. not long after the first two bombings. I had taken responsibility to sell Peter's car.

We all arranged to meet at eight o'clock that evening at the car souk, where I brought the car for inspection. This meeting occurred as planned, though the sale of the car did not go through. What this meant to me in the future was that it proved my presence in Riyadh at times that made it impossible for me to have driven to Dammam, planted and detonated a bomb, and returned to Riyadh. It did not help with two of the accusations levelled at me but it at least removed the third. There are small mercies after all, though this one was small indeed.

three THE INQUISITION

///|

So I stood there, arm hanging in its shackles, body sore from the work-over. I was unsure of the time and completely at a loss as to my location. Jumbled disconnected thoughts raced through my mind, chased by my fear. One part desperately clutched at the hope that this was all a mistake that would resolve itself. The other acknowledged that, mistake or not, my interrogators had chosen a particular path. In the inexorable logic of its direction, events would follow this path of their choosing. All the landmarks were there. I was to be forced to confess to crimes that I had not committed in order that they, in conforming to the needs of their government and culture, could maintain the façade of the social order prevalent in their country.

I was terrified. Waves of blind panic and fear threatened to overwhelm my attempts at coherent thought. Straining not to succumb, I forced myself to think as clearly as circumstance allowed. I assessed my situation, depressing as it was. I tried to locate myself in time and place. I worked out in my mind different scenarios, focusing on the worst possible. I had to find some way to prepare myself for what lay ahead. In reality no preparation is adequate, but the process helps give one some semblance of control, which is exactly what my captors intended to destroy.

I estimated that I had been in their care for eight hours at the most. The sequence of prayer calls told me this. Their erratic driving told me that their objective was to confuse me. The time it should have taken to deliver me to the interrogation centre was twenty minutes or thirty minutes at the most. The journey seemed to take twice that amount of time. In my mind, I projected a map of Riyadh, trying to establish a likely location. I was in one of the detention and interrogation centres of the Ministry of the Interior's Intelligence division (the Mabaheth). This one was the Al Ulaysha centre located toward the outskirts of Riyadh, which fell well at the outer edge of my estimates. Weeks later, through one of their errors, I was able to firm up this estimate. The correctness of my estimate provided some small affirmation and comfort to me. Even in my distress, my mind had been working.

I scanned my memory for any words or names that I had heard that might give me a clue as to the identities of my tormentors. I thought of ways to keep track of time, to encapsulate and reinforce my memories. It was important for me to do this to counteract the mounting fear and desperation that my treatment instilled in me and the disorientation that my circumstances caused. This, the first stage in the process through which I would be passed, can best be described as the disorientation phase.

During this period, your captors break the connection with normal reality. You are blindfolded or hooded to deprive you of your ability to determine your location. You are denied access to information as to time and place in order to imbue a sense of disembodiment. Initial physical brutality is not as severe as it could be for two reasons: to instil a sense of immediate fear that adds to the disorientation and to instil a sense of anticipation of worse to come. In stepping over the fine and invisible line that marks the difference between legitimate questioning and coercive interrogation, your captors indicate that they are prepared to be even more brutal. They show that they are not governed by any of the rules you might expect in a legitimate interview.

This initial disorientation and the method of processing you into your cell, the assignment of a number, and the effective eradication of your name are there to strip you of your assumed place in the world. Thus the victim now has lost time, place, and identity, existing without any ability to communicate with the outside world or to make reference to the cues of everyday life. As the victim, it is important to replace what has been taken, to find some inconsistency in the process that will allow you to anchor yourself in time and place, to analyze your surroundings and make a mental record of everything that is happening. The effect of your initial disorientation is to produce fear and loss of control. You cannot eradicate the fear or regain control as you knew it, but you can go some way toward ameliorating the fear and gaining other means of control within the process. It is essential to keep your eyes and ears open to every stimulus, however insignificant it might seem, because these act as anchors around which your mind builds some semblance of understanding amid the deliberate confusion.

I hung there, listening to every sound, reviewing my surroundings: the cold concrete floor, the CCTV cameras staring down at me, the dirty foam mattress with the garish floral pattern, and the equally filthy blanket. It lay crumpled at the foot of the mattress where I had left it when taken for my first interrogation. I reached out with my foot, dragged the blanket to me, and wrapped myself in it again. The atmosphere in the cell was so cold and dank that I welcomed the little warmth this disgusting item provided. I looked at the CCTV camera and wondered about its efficacy. I pulled the blanket over my head. Would this action be noticed? I heard footsteps approaching my cell down the corridor. The small panel in the door was opened and a guard peered in at me, his face close enough for me to smell his breath. Without a word, his duty done, he closed and locked the panel, finally walking away. I had my answer – the camera worked. My every action was to be observed. Even in my misery I was to be denied privacy, another unsettling element to assist in keeping me off balance and vulnerable.

I kept the blanket wrapped around my head and speculated about what was to come. The next prayer call passed, the minutes ticking by like hours, followed shortly after by the sounds of activity outside my cell. Doors opened and closed in rapid succession, interspersed with brief snatches of Arabic. I heard a voice I recognized, that of David Mornin, the owner of the Celtic Corner, speaking English and the odd word of Arabic, demanding more bread. The panel of my door opened, followed by the door itself. I was released from the handcuffs and given a plastic food tray with chicken, rice, pita bread, a small bottle of water, and a paper cup full of tea. This being Ramadan, I knew that sunset had occurred and I was being served my main meal. I was allowed to sit at the end of the mattress to enjoy my feast.

I tried the chicken, but its greasy, rubbery texture killed any remnants of an appetite already suppressed by adrenaline. So I drank the water and tea and left the food alone. The guards had instructed me in broken but adequate English "No sleep." At this time sleep was impossible, given the tension and stress that I felt. I leaned against the wall and thought, pulling the blanket over my knees and sipping slowly on the water to make this respite last. I explored my environment from this position, looking for anything I could turn to my advantage. I felt a small tear in the seam of my mattress that I enlarged a little, considering it a possible hiding place. A hiding place for what I did not know. As I listlessly pawed at the rice in a pretence of eating, I realized it could act as the only time-counter I would likely have or be able to fashion. Cautiously, I extracted a single long grain of rice and slid it into the hole in the mattress. These were my first actions that had not been properly observed since my arrest, and they formed a small but important victory.

Too soon the tray was collected and I was returned to my enchained position, left to contemplate my stark future. The last prayer call of the day was intoned, and I could see, through the gaps in the brickwork around the air conditioner, that the day was now most definitely night. I was going to be able to track time – I could determine daylight, and with the assistance of the prayer calls, I could at least estimate the time to within an hour or so during the day. Night was another matter, as the time between the last prayer call of the day and dawn prayer on the next was then about nine hours, during which it would be difficult to estimate time with any accuracy. However, as I was beginning to learn, estimating time during the night was not going to be a prime concern.

Not long after I was chained again to the door, I heard other cell doors open and the sounds of other people, including the shuffled gate of prisoners as their ankle shackles rattled accompaniment to their restrained movement. Then the door panel opened and the guard asked me for my number. When I answered, the door opened and I was released briefly, only to have my hands cuffed behind my back, a blindfold placed across my eyes, and shackles clasped on my ankles. This was to be the normal procedure for removing me from my cell for interrogation while I was held at this place of torture and denigration.

Again, I was led upstairs to the "offices," better described as torture suites, and made to sit in a metal folding chair. I sat and waited, leaning slightly forward in the seat due to the restrained position of my hands and arms. Time dragged slowly, as my mind raced through different levels of fear. This was a new element added to that mix, this being held in suspense, awaiting the arrival of my torturers. It was a calculated part of the interrogation/torture process. As a hostage, I knew to some extent what was to come and rather than allowing one to build up one's resistance to the inevitable, this enforced delay caused mounting apprehension and fear. Such a heightened emotional state makes one more suggestible, more amenable to conforming to the requirements of the torturers, more willing to do anything to end the process, and I believe it makes the subsequent pain of the beatings worse. It is not that the actual blows are fiercer or the damage done worse than might be the case, just that the effect of the subsequent physical brutality is more damaging to your emotional state than would have been an immediate assault, and due to its greater emotional impact the pain is felt more acutely. I learned there was a discernible pattern to their methods of destruction.

The door opened behind me, the blindfold was forcefully pulled off, and the short barked command "Stand up" was directed at me. As I stood and turned in the direction of the voice, I saw again my interrogators: Dopey (whom I also called The Midget), Acne, and The Spiv. While I came to know the names of the first two, the name of the other is still unknown to me. The Spiv grabbed me by the arm and pushed me into the wall. Ibrahim, nicknamed Dopey, stepped forward and slapped me across the side of the head a few times, once again being careful not to strike me in the face. The blows were delivered with sufficient force to be very painful, and at first they caused little damage. This changed over the next few days and weeks as the repeated violent contact took its toll.

During this part of the session, not a word was spoken nor any intelligent sound uttered. All that could be heard were my occasional expressions of pain followed by Khaled's barking of the words "Shut up." The dominant sounds were sharp cracks as Ibrahim's hands and fists made contact with my head and body, accompanied by the childish giggling of all three as they enjoyed the pain and humiliation that they inflicted on me. Once again, this was to form part of the pattern of the interrogation process and their behaviour during these sessions. These all but mute assaults were characteristic of the second phase of each period of questioning.

At this point, I should indicate that the use of words such as interrogation or questioning to describe these interviews is somewhat inaccurate. The words "demanding," "controlling," and "implanting" form a much more appropriate description. Except for the questions pertaining to my activities on the days of the first three bombings, few of the interrogation and torture sessions ever required me to reveal information. Everything related to the bombings was put to me as a series of statements, frequently contradictory, as to what they said I had done. The "confessions" I was eventually to provide were simply restatements of the scenarios that they repeated to me ad nauseam.

Having become bored with simply hitting me, Ibrahim violently grabbed me by the arm, pulling me toward the centre of the room. Due to the shackles, I stumbled and fell to the floor, to be met by kicks to my legs, abdomen, and lower back. I was commanded, "Stand up." With difficulty, I struggled awkwardly to my feet. The seemingly simple act of standing is no mean feat when one's arms are pinned behind one's back and one's legs are restrained by shackles with only fifteen centimetres of chain links separating them. As I began to regain my feet by rolling against the wall for support in my efforts, Ibrahim and Khaled slapped me in the back of the head, adding to my difficulties and their amusement. When I finally managed to stand, Khaled pushed me from behind into The Spiv, who slapped me, then pushed me away into the path of Ibrahim. Once more, I was subjected to a violent game of pass the parcel, occasionally being let to fall to the floor, where I would be met by vicious kicks to my lower body.

Eventually, I was led back to the chair and made to sit down. The Spiv sat to my left. Ibrahim and Khaled sat on the opposite side of the desk between us. The lecture began. Ibrahim spoke in Arabic. Khaled translated. I was told in no uncertain terms what they could do to me. I was threatened with numerous descriptions of the beatings they could inflict. I was even threatened with the possibility that should they so choose electric shocks would be applied. At the same time The Spiv stroked and caressed my left leg from the knee to the crotch, every once in a while delivering a forceful squeeze to my testicles, and giggling at the sharp intake of breath that the pain extracted.

Acne had begun to use two euphemisms for the process of torture, which in their minds was a legitimate tool on the path to the goals they had been ordered to achieve. The phrases "putting you in the right way" and "getting your mind right" were repeated again and again in the session and over the next few months. These euphemisms were more for their own benefit than they were for mine. If I said that their brutality constituted torture, I would be met with the angry refutation that "putting me in the right way" was not torture. Whenever, in my few moments of defiance, I asked them how their claims of piety and religious observance meshed with the brutality in which they engaged, I was given convoluted arguments.

What they were doing was correcting me and "getting my mind right." It could not be torture. In other words, any act that they could justify as purging their victims of the corruption in which said victims were steeped could not be considered wrong. Their definition of corruption would best be explained as being anything that constituted difference from their accepted frame of reference. Guilt or innocence was not a consideration – only their orders mattered and if those required that someone be "put in the right way" then whatever means necessary were justified.

Perhaps unwisely, when first I heard the phrase "getting your mind right," I laughed.

The phrase triggered a specific memory. It brought to mind the film *Cool Hand Luke*, which deals with life on a Georgia prison farm. In one particular scene the brutal and sadistic governor describes to the prisoners the punishment being meted out to one of their number. I heard the echo of the actor's squeaky high-pitched drawl delivering the same line as Khaled finished his delivery of this phrase.

When I laughed Khaled rose to his feet and reached across the desk, punching my left cheek, one of the very few times that such a strike was directed to the front of my face.

The Spiv now hauled me to my feet, and once more I was thrown around the room, knocked to the floor, kicked and punched over most of my body (except the face). By now though, the shock of the initial brutality was wearing off, even though I was shaking from fear and excess adrenaline. Sore and bruised as I was, I had come to feel that if they limited themselves to this simple level of thuggery, then I might be able to endure and not give them what they wanted. A small inappropriate glimmer of hope formed in my mind. Was this what they wanted? By threatening me with incredible brutality and not delivering it, they lulled (if lulled is the right word) me into a false sense of security. Being wrenched from it was all the more devastating when the beating became more brutal.

I was taken back to my chair and seated. I expected another round of questions and demands. Instead, my three interrogators left the room, ushering in a uniformed guard to stand over me. I tried to analyze what had just gone on, for I had been with my interrogators for at least an hour and yet no specific demands had been made or questions asked, just simple statements that I could stop this by complying with their wishes. In fact, this was pretty much the usual pattern of each interrogation session to which I would be subjected. The period of awaiting my interrogators, their arrival and deliberate mute brutality, a lecture on what they could do to me and how only my compliance was needed to prevent it, followed by more vicious brutality, then their departure, leaving me to contemplate and wait, these were all part of the formula. This was in fact the second phase, which can be best described as the debilitation phase. In itself, it consisted of the five distinct subphases just described, the latter couple of which would be repeated during the sessions. Admittedly, my Saudi Arabian tormentors should not have proceeded in such a predictable or definable pattern, but this in itself was indicative of their laxity and their failure to absorb all the lessons with which they had surely been provided. It also conforms to my wider experience within Saudi Arabia, where regardless of the quality of the training or education provided, nothing there is ever applied properly or very effectively. The fact that my tormentors had been trained by professionals was obvious (British, American, and Israeli intelligence services have all provided assistance and training to operatives of the Saudi Arabian government at various times). However, as I have now investigated various discussions of professional torture and coercive interrogation methodology, I have realized that there were flaws in the way they were applied in my situation for they established too formal a routine. There were departures from the routine, but these were rare and only for specific reasons or purposes. This predictability, even though what was being applied was terrifying, was something upon which my mind could anchor itself, alleviating some of the disorientation and debilitation.

Where my captors had gone during this intermission, I did not know, assuming at the time that they were having a tea break. Doubtless to say, this was one of their potential activities, but I soon knew, via the screams that percolated through the door of the office, that they were demonstrating some efficiency by repeating the process on one or other of my fellow captives. At that moment, I understood that Raf was one of their probable victims, but I did not know who else was held there and being tortured, though I had my suspicions. I knew a number of expats who had been arrested or who had disappeared in the weeks prior to my kidnapping, and I wondered which of them were being coerced to confess to crimes. Over time the identities of some of my fellow detainees would become clearer, as I would piece together small snippets of information that allowed me to work out who some of the people were who resided in this prison with me. I did not come to know the full scope of the arrests until after I was finally released. Even now, as I write this in the two years since my release, I have only just put together a list of all those arrested, accused of the bombings, and subjected to detention and coercion or torture. The list is amazing in its size and scope, indicative of the lengths to which the Ministry of the Interior was willing to go to cover up the existence of home-grown terrorist cells in their midst.

After what seemed like an hour or so, the door opened and my three tormentors returned. Another round of mute assault took place, with the frequency and the weight of the blows seeming heavier than before. Eventually, they sat me down and began going over what I had told them, telling me that this would not do. The statements made by Ibrahim and translated by Khaled only dealt with the car bomb on November 17, in which Christopher Rodway was killed. No mention of the other two incidents was made by them, which I found curious.

It occurred to me that my alibis for those other two occasions were sufficient to deflect their attempts to frame me for that. However, my alibi for the morning of November 17 was thin, as I had no recollection of anything specific that I had done on that morning. I knew that it had been a Friday morning, part of the weekend in Saudi Arabia, that I had slept late, and that between three-thirty and four-thirty in the afternoon I had, with Raf, visited Peter Goldsmith at the Sulimaneh/Oleya police station near Junction five on the northern ring road. It would therefore be easy for them to make up something interesting to fill in the time during which I would have been alone. This they did with arcane plots, some involving Sandy Mitchell and me conspiring together to plant and detonate a bomb, and others that had me acting alone. No reason was given, no motive suggested. The simple mechanics of the operation were stated to me, followed by the simple assertion that I would confess, that they had the time and the means to ensure I would do so.

This conversation went backward and forward between us. They described what I had done in various permutations, and I refuted it, protesting my innocence. I put to them that if I were guilty, why had the *Arab News* been allowed to report only a week or so previously that Michael Sedlak, an American, had been arrested for and found guilty of the bombings?

I was met by the amused comment that this was just their little joke, and did I not find it funny?

Funny? It was hilarious, for it indicated that they had been forced to change the direction of their plans and find another scapegoat. When I had read the article, I expected that the American government (or at least the ambassador) would not stand for the Ministry of the Interior framing one of its citizens, and that the United States would use its considerable influence to prevent it. I was now faced with the correctness of my assumptions. Was I now Sedlak's understudy in the drama that these goons had constructed to cover up the existence of an internal terrorist threat? This would not be the first time the American government would intervene successfully on behalf of one of its citizens, though its interventions probably resulted in another hapless individual of different nationality being used instead.

My protestations were punctuated by the occasional gasp, as The Spiv had kept up his constant attention to my thigh and groin, squeezing my testicles and occasionally stroking my cheeks and hair. This physical attention and his physical closeness as he leaned into me inspired another distinct feeling of fear. He seemed to enjoy his role in the process, for his caresses and the look on his face seemed imbued with strange feelings of hunger and longing. It was obvious that this was a form of sexual intimidation, designed to be unsettling in a manner different from simple brutality. It certainly worked, for my obvious discomfort and unease only encouraged him and provided the others with amusement.

It was at this point Ibrahim and Khaled changed their questions to those of a more personal nature. They asked about my family and relatives, details that seemed innocuous in themselves but the questions were asked to probe areas of emotional vulnerability: things that could be used against me. They asked detailed questions about my parents, my family, my girlfriends, my education, my interests and hobbies, the reasons for my bachelor status, and other such personal information. They spent a long time questioning me on the details of my qualifications and of my more intimate relationships, particularly the most recent. I was guarded, telling them only that there was no one special in my life at the time and that my last affair was with a woman who had left the Kingdom. This was true up to a point, for the simple act of having an affair in the Kingdom was illegal. I knew that by mentioning any woman currently in the Kingdom, I would be putting her at risk of the charge of adultery or fornication, as any relationship, even platonic, between unmarried men and women is illegal in Saudi Arabia, and this could be used against her as well as myself.

They pored over my reasons for coming to Saudi Arabia in the first place, the basis of which was simple enough. I told them simply that I needed a job and the money was good. This they did not seem to accept and their resentment toward a khawaja such as myself poured forth. Ibrahim and Khaled cursed our presence in their Kingdom, as in their opinion all we did was steal from the pockets of their fellow countrymen, leaving nothing in our wake but our western corruption and filth. This outburst, as with similar others made over the course of my interrogations, was a departure from the script, for it was delivered with such vitriol that it gave me a better understanding of whom I was dealing with, something that should have been denied me.

They hated me and everything that I represented. They were envious of the salaries paid to westerners and resented our very existence and presence. Needless to say, my presence in their country, as was the case for many westerners, was at the behest of the same government employing them, but such facts were ignored in the cognitive dissonance of their hatred and jealousy. Regardless of their attempts to be professional in the conduct of the interrogations, their personal, cultural, and social insecurities showed through. This was of little immediate use to me, but it helped me form an understanding of my tormentors.

They brought this discussion to a close with a series of statements designed to show me once again the power that they had over me. The obvious comments were the threats of greater violence and the reiteration that the British government (for at this point they were referring to me as British) could and would do nothing to help me. What came as a shock was their statement that I was homosexual. Their logic was that as a forty-one-year-old male who had never been married, I must be a homosexual. I was informed that the punishment under Saudi law for such acts or even the potential of someone exhibiting this sexual orientation was death. As this was the case, it would make little difference should I agree to confess to other crimes. I was well aware of the draconian attitudes and laws that attempted to control sexual behaviour in the Kingdom, and I was well aware of the punishment for this supposed crime without having to be given a lecture on their version of sexual morality. In spite of their government's and society's attempts to both deny the existence of and legislate against homosexuality, it was quite common, hidden behind closed doors as is so much in the Kingdom.

In some respects, while they had no evidence for my having such a sexual orientation, their social and cultural prejudices would have pushed them in the direction of this conclusion. Certainly, they seemed convinced of the veracity of their claim given the evidence of my bachelorhood. It provided a convenient lever to use against me, particularly as they said they would locate all my "boyfriends," who would be happy to testify to this fact. I had visions of a collection of Indian, Bangladeshi, or Sri Lankan men being paraded before me at Ibrahim's behest, having been persuaded into their confessions much as I was now being persuaded. It was one more nightmarish image to add to all the rest that they had instilled in my mind. If they were going to manufacture evidence and a confession for something they knew to be untrue (my involvement in the bombings), they would certainly be happy to manufacture evidence and confessions for something they instinctively, though erroneously, believed to be true.

Although initially the accusation shocked me, it also provided some amusement. I pictured the Saudi police or their courts placing such a charge against me with the ensuing farcical publicity that would occur. This wouldn't be the first time in my life that such a claim was made, but it would be the first public announcement. Various and often contradictory rumours about me arose in different work and social circles. At one corporation in which I worked, it was whispered that I was collecting notches on my bedpost by working my way through the stable of the corporation's female personal assistants. Yet, while I worked in that hermetically sealed community I never indulged in a single affair there.

Among a group of climbers I knew, it was assumed I was gay for I never seemed to try scoring with any of the women in the club. I have always protected my privacy. I have gone to great lengths to separate my work life from my personal. What people have never understood about me is my single-mindedness – the workplace was for work and mountains were for climbing. The disparate nature of my interests and ability to adapt to different social environments have made for a wide circle of acquaintances, and from among each distinct group I have found good friends, but this made it difficult for some people to hang a label on me. Thus, anything that could be used to justify my reserved and oft-times solitary nature would be applied. Admittedly, I have tended not to discourage or contradict any of the labels, partly because such refutation is futile unless one makes one's behaviour conform to that accepted by the group and partly because having applied such labels people would then stop prying, granting me the privacy I desired.

My amusement increased as I contemplated the incredulity with which these accusations would be met, once made public, by my former lovers and those of my friends that had got past my reserve to know me well. Needless to say, these accusations were never made public nor made the subject of any of the confessions I subsequently would be forced to write. However, for the next few weeks, I was regularly confronted with them. Eventually they stopped using them as the scenarios they were constructing changed.

When I did not agree to confess, they stopped this round of statements, and I was again hauled to my feet by The Spiv and another round of brutality began. Khaled continued his litany of my crimes as I bounced off walls, fell to the floor, and struggled to my feet, all the while being kicked and punched.

If as you read this it all sounds a little repetitive, it was. This repetitiveness is one of the keys to torture's eventual efficacy. Your body and your mind are cycled through levels of pain and emotional torment that will eventually break down your strength and your will, handing you gift-wrapped and compliant to your captors. It is not a matter of if, only when.

Though darkness still prevailed outside the office window, we heard the sound of dawn prayer. Not that the early arrival of the muezzin's call bothered me, for the session stopped abruptly. Saved by the bell, I thought, a sentiment I did not give voice to, for I did not want to delay their religious observance. The Spiv pushed me into a chair, while Khaled opened the door and called for a guard. When the guard arrived, I was blindfolded and led back to my cell.

I was entering the third day of my captivity, and I had had two sleepless nights. I was now back in my cell, chained to the door in an upright position and deprived of the sleep I craved. Shortly after arriving back in my cell and covering myself with the blanket, I felt another sensation that added to my stress. I developed a massive craving for a cigarette. If ever there was a time that I wished not to be a smoker, it was then. The feelings evoked by nicotine withdrawal did not help my emotional state. At this point, breakfast was served, allowing me to sit down and relieve some of the soreness in my legs. This respite was short-lived, for the guard soon collected my tray, from which I had only drunk the water and the tea.

I kept the orange and was pleasantly surprised to discover that I was allowed to do so. I also realized that the last time I had been to the toilet was just before my arrest, nearly forty-eight hours previously. I spoke a single word to the guard – "Toilet" – and pointed to my crotch, hoping he understood. Thankfully he did, nodding his head. He handcuffed me, leading me from the cell toward the exit from the cellblock.

It turned out that the door just before the exit on the same side of the corridor as my cell was the door to the toilet for the cellblock. The handcuffs were removed and I entered the facility, closing the door behind me and noticing that it could be latched on the inside. I noted the absence of a CCTV camera, providing me with my first bit of privacy since my arrest. Draped around the shower area on my right were a number of thobes and jellabas, indicating that the room was also used as a makeshift laundry. These items probably belonged to other inmates of Arabic origin who had been here a while. On my left was a sink above which was a mirror missing a large section of one corner. In front of me was another door that led into the sole toilet cubicle. I glanced at my reflection and realized how terrible I looked. There was unnatural pallor to my skin and my eyes were puffy and dark. I certainly was not going to win any beauty contests.

As I now had a respite from continuous observation, I took the opportunity to remove my clothes and perform a basic strip wash. It refreshed me more than I expected. Standing there naked, I examined my body as best I could. I noted the reddening weals on my legs, arms, chest, and buttocks. I was going to be covered in a tapestry of bruises. I now availed myself of the toilet, but was surprised by the small volume of urine that I produced and by my inability to defecate. Given the length of time it had been since last I had relieved myself, I wondered what was happening to me internally. The beatings so far had not been severe enough to cause internal organ damage, but the emotional stress of the last couple of days was taking its toll, resulting in significant changes to my physiology.

It did occur to me then that upon entering the toilet, I had closed the internal bolt on the toilet door, locking myself in. As the door was metal, probably mild steel, had I decided to remain where I was it would have taken a considerable effort for my captors to gain entrance. The idea was tempting, for in the time it would take them to realize my intentions, I would have snatched some much-needed sleep. However, I knew that such an action might invite the guards or my interrogators to increase the level of brutality. So I stood and cleaned and dressed myself before finally opening the door.

As I began to open it, I heard the guard get up from the desk at the cellblock entrance. Once in the corridor, I closed the door and he slipped on the handcuffs, this time hesitantly placing a blindfold over my eyes. As he had not done this when he led me to the toilet, it made me realize that, for all his official status, he probably was not well trained in his role as our warder. This suspicion was confirmed over the next few days. Each time I was allowed to go to the toilet, the level of security and the procedures involved varied depending on the level of annoyance my request caused my warder. Yet each time I was taken for interrogation the routine did not vary, being led there blindfolded, shackled, and handcuffed. What was different between these two situations was that my collection for interrogation usually involved two or three officials, one of whom would be dressed in a thobe (and thus probably of officer or senior NCO rank). The guards in the cellblock area were of lower rank, so my forays to the toilet were only ever under the supervision of a solitary private or corporal. This small and seemingly insignificant detail was of interest as it hinted that for all the apparent professional nature of the interrogation, the organization and training of my captors was typical of any Saudi government organization: piss poor.

At some point later that morning, another element was added to the routine. I had no idea of the time except that the event occurred well before the noon prayer. I was collected from my cell in the usual fashion, being led away by a slender talkative individual dressed in a thobe and ghutra who kept up a running commentary in Arabic as he guided me along. My anxious assumption was that an interrogation session was on the immediate horizon. As I hobbled on my way from the cell, I realized that we had passed by the stairwell that led to the area of my initial interrogations. My fevered imagination started to work overtime, conjuring up visions of a Boschian nightmare. We followed this ground-floor corridor, and I felt that we passed through a doorway just as my guide brought me to a halt. As the blindfold and my restraints were removed, I saw I was in what constituted the interrogation centre's medical facility. In front of me was a green examination table; to my right were a desk and a set of cabinets. To my left was a set of scales, and beyond that another doorway led into a room lined with cartons of medications shelved chaotically along its walls.

Half-sitting on the desk was a man dressed in a white shirt, brown trousers, and sandals. From his physical features and his accented English, I assumed he was Pakistani. Poking out of his shirt pocket was the green fascia of his iqama telling me that he was a Muslim and that my first assumption was probably correct. He was what passed for the centre's doctor. He ran through a series of questions concerning my health and any medical complaints from which I suffered. There was little for me to report, for my only chronic medical condition at that time was seasonal hay fever, although I had a list of minor and major sports injuries. He then proceeded to examine me, seeing the bruising and other damage, but not making any record of it.

It was all conducted in a cursory fashion, much as I expected. I was sleep-deprived, suffering the after-effects of numerous beatings and in an emotionally stressed condition; however, my blood pressure and pulse rate were absurdly normal (125/80 blood pressure – 78 bpm pulse – if memory serves me correctly). Unfortunately, these results gave an indication of a robustness that I did not feel at the time, and were to be common to all my medical examinations right up to the point when I had my heart attack.

I was thus passed medically fit. Fit for what, one might ask?

Fit for interrogation and torture. The whole purpose of all my medical examinations was simply to pass me as capable of enduring more brutality. My health was of no real concern, except in the context of whether I would die as a result of the dedication of my interrogators. Unfortunately, I was then in all too robust health, even though at the time of my arrest I was smoking heavily and was badly overweight.

After the examination, I was blindfolded, handcuffed, shackled, and led back to my cell, to spend another day chained upright to the cell door. By this time, the lack of sleep was getting to me and it was a struggle to maintain a coherent or logical line of thought. Even as I tried to daydream to distract myself, it was an effort to engage my imagination. My physical discomfort and the nagging desire for sleep pressed me toward hysteria. Obviously, this confused and emotionally vulnerable condition was exactly what my captors desired and what their methods were designed to induce. The fight against this condition can only go on for so long before either compliance or total emotional and psychological collapse occurs. I was not yet near that point, but I wondered how long I could hold out against their demands.

Prayer calls came and went, the light around the fringes of the air conditioner faded into nighttime darkness, and I continued to wait for the next instalment. Footsteps sounded in the corridor soon after night fell, probably not long after my guards and interrogators broke their daytime fast. At a guess, the time then had been near to six-thirty, but that is a very rough estimate. Anyway, the hatch opened, my number was asked for, the door opened, and the usual restraints were placed upon me. This time, as I was led from the cellblock into the building entrance hall, my guards turned left and we stepped out into the early evening air.

I could hear the noise of vehicles with their engines running and the opening and closing of vehicle doors. There was a tin-like quality to the noise the doors made that made me think of small cargo vans rather than of passenger cars. Mixed in with this were the urgent sounds of Arabic voices, from within which emerged Khaled's voice speaking English. He began by telling me that we were going for a journey. It crossed my mind that I was about to disappear. Maybe their plans to frame me and any of the others they had arrested had begun to unravel, and they needed to dispose of the evidence – me. In this paranoid state, I wondered if I would survive the trip.

My shackles were removed, and Khaled told me to step up into the truck that I had been placed in before. Hesitantly I raised my leg, searching for the step with my foot. As I stood on it, I felt a hand touch my forehead, gently pressing my head downwards. Another hand clutched my shoulder and I was guided into a seat in the back of a police van. The shackles were replaced, and from outside the van, as the doors were closed and bolted, Khaled's voice reiterated that I was to keep quiet. I heard the compound gate rumble open and the van began to move forward. Within another minute or so, we were on the open road as indicated by the increase in speed and the erratic steering of the driver. I was sure I had a companion of sorts with me in my confinement, but there was no way for me to tell. I was having a difficult enough time remaining seated, let alone attempting to explore the vehicle or make other discoveries. My suspicion of companionship was confirmed when the vehicle lurched to a halt and I flew from my seat. A pair of hands gently steered me back to my original position. For the rest of the journey a hand remained on my shoulder, steadying me in my seat.

The van finally came to a stop, and I could hear muffled shouts and the opening and closing of vehicle doors. My companion undid my shackles while the doors were opened. Led from the van and reshackled, I was held by my arms on both sides. As I wondered where I was, for the area was full of sounds that did not fit with those I expected from a prison, my blindfold was removed. Instantly I saw that I was standing in the street outside my house. Just in front of me was my car and to my right was the half-open gate to the yard. In the street along with the police van were three white Nissan patrols with Ministry of the Interior insignia and the grey Intrepid in which I had travelled at the time of my arrest. I found it curious that I could see no other vehicles parked on my street, as usually there would be a large number of them. In addition, I could see no lights on in any of the houses nearby. It was all quite strange, but given the power and authority with which the Mabaheth operates, it would not have been untoward that the area had been in some way cleared on their order. Khaled and Ibrahim were standing to one side of the entrance talking to various uniformed officials, one of whom had the rank of major indicated on the epaulettes of his shirt.

Khaled waved, and the guards either side of me directed me through the entrance to my property. As I entered, I noticed that by the water pump housing was the bicycle belonging to Sultan, my house cleaner. My heart sank as I realized that he had come around to my house as usual, only to be caught up in this nightmare. The place was crawling with police, both uniformed and plainclothes (somewhat of a misnomer as "plainclothes" effectively meant another uniform of thobe, ghutra, and iqal). We entered through the poolside door, and I was taken into the first room on my right, the one I used as a home office and computer room. Khaled joined me and instructed me to keep quiet. Through the doorway, I saw and heard his comrades tearing my house apart.

At one point a young plainclothes officer came into the computer room carrying a glass beer stein, in which a Pepsi can was wedged, aggressively proclaiming, "See! We have found alcohol!"

I said, "Since when has Pepsi been illegal?"

"You must have smuggled this glass into the country as it is illegal" was Khaled's response.

Trying not to laugh, I pointed out that, along with five others, it was bought at the Greenhouse Garden Centre on 747 Rd., and could have been bought in any number of other locations in Riyadh.

The young officer's reaction to my statements was to hit me on the side of the face with the stein.

"It is illegal! You say that I lie?" he screamed.

Khaled barked something in Arabic, and the young fool departed in a fit of pique. As he left the room, I saw another plainclothes officer carrying a scruffy cardboard box into the living room. This was curious, and I wondered about the box's contents. Khaled began asking questions about why I had set up an office in my house, telling me that it was evidence I was involved in illegal activities. Why else would I have a room equipped with a computer, bookshelves, and a desk? By such logic, most of the western expatriate community must have been involved in illegal activities. In Khaled's twisted mind anything could be used, no matter how tenuous, to construct his ludicrous scenarios.

When he had finished his rant, he took me through to the main room that served as both living room and dining room. I noted that sitting on the sofa watching the television were a number of uniformed officers and a solitary be-thobed individual whom I recognized. The be-thobed one stood, turning toward me. I knew I had seen him before. Back in October, only a couple of months previously, I had met him at the local Mutawa office where I had been briefly detained. Apparently, he was the head of the local group of thugs responsible for religious enforcement (or, more accurately, intolerance). For some reason, the fact that I had a television, video, and DVD seemed to excite him into a paroxysm of rage.

He demanded to know how I deserved to have these items. How could I afford them, when his fellow countrymen could not? People like me were robbing him and his kind of what was rightfully theirs. It did not enter his tiny mind that I had been *invited* to work in his country by a Saudi Arabian government organization.

I suggested he direct his questions to the Ministry of Finance, the body responsible for oversight of the Fund. Before he could respond, Ibrahim, who was standing immediately in front of me, slapped me across my neck.

"Shut up." This was the first time Ibrahim spoke to me in English.

In future, though his utterances remained limited to small two- or three-word phrases, I came to realize that he understood English reasonably well, and that only a lack of confidence stopped him from using the language. Odd that this would be the case, given the air of smug arrogance he usually radiated.

Khaled directed my attention toward the dining-room table, informing me that my ownership of this piece of furniture was also evidence of my miscreance, for round it I would chair the meetings of my fellow terrorists. I tried not to laugh, but I could not prevent a smile creeping across my face. This angered Ibrahim, who again hit me on the side of my neck. With the smile wiped off my face, I looked again at the table. On it, beside a stack of my papers dealing with a water purification report, were a dirty plastic bottle with the label Al Ansar and a thin ovoid-shaped object about one centimetre thick, twenty centimetres long, and about ten centimetres at its widest point. This object was wrapped in foil and plastic wrap. The young officer who had hit me with the beer stein grabbed the bottle and opened it. Wafting it under my nose, he informed me that it had been found in my house. As the bottle moved in front of my face, the pungent scent of sid assailed my nostrils.

I knew there was no alcohol in my house, so it had to have been planted there. I glanced back at the table and noticed that on the floor at the right was the scruffy cardboard box I had seen earlier. Obviously, it had been used to bring in whatever evidence they needed to justify my arrest and detention. Then Khaled picked up the other item on the table. As it was held in front of my face, I was told that it contained hashish and that it too had been found in my house. This was nonsense, for I had never had anything to do with hashish in Saudi Arabia, regardless of the fact that it was easier to obtain than alcohol.

At this point another young be-thobed officer entered the room carrying two electrically operated timers that I used with my household lights and on my coffee machine.

"Timing devices for the manufacture of a bomb," Khaled informed me.

As these devices had to be plugged in to an electrical outlet to operate, they would hardly be appropriate for making a portable explosive device, unless of course one had an extremely long extension cord. The absurdity of this was manifest, but I let it pass without comment.

Their game was obvious, to ensure that whatever the outcome, they could justify my arrest by producing this phony evidence. What did surprise me was that no actual material for making bombs, such as timers, fuses, or explosives, had been planted. As I think back on it, planting such real evidence might have complicated things for them. The claim concerning the timers that they found was purely for the purpose of unsettling me. However, by planting evidence of alcohol and drug possession, they had the means to hold me indefinitely according to their laws. With that evidence alone, I could be convicted and, with drugs being part of the case, sentenced to death. This could be, and was, used as a lever against me during ensuing interrogations. However, should they have needed to abandon their claim that I was a terrorist, then a convenient switch could have been made, claiming solely my involvement with alcohol and drugs. This would be a more acceptable way for them to obtain their ends, providing them with a degree of flexibility that direct evidence of bomb-making might not.

At this point, Khaled guided me out of the room and led me upstairs to the bedrooms. Standing inside the door of the main bedroom, I watched as various officers ransacked my property. Trunks, drawers, and wardrobes were rifled through, some of their contents being strewn about the floor, trampled underfoot by the rampaging minions. The process seemed entirely random and deliberately destructive. On reflection, they knew there was nothing remotely incriminating to be found, so the search was being conducted in my presence to show me the planted evidence and to further unsettle me by forcing me to witness their callous disregard for my property. The phony evidence did worry me, but their goonish rampage did not.

From one of the other bedrooms, someone had collected a large cardboard box that had housed my television. It had been put on the landing and into it had been deposited items of my clothing. As I looked at its contents, Khaled left me for a moment in the care of the uniformed officer who had been my companion in the police van. He reached over to my bed and collected a black fleece sweater that had been deposited there, offering it to me. He must have noticed me shivering, as the combination of my fear and the cool night air caused me to shudder intermittently. I nodded to him and shrugged my shoulders, as it was impossible for me to accept his offering with my hands clasped behind my back. His response was to release my handcuffs, allowing me to don the garment. This done, he replaced the handcuffs, taking extreme care to ensure that they were not too tight. His act of kindness was the first humane act that I had experienced since my arrest. In my tired and emotional state, I felt tears well up in my eyes as a result of his gentle concern. Obviously embarrassed by my show of emotion, he looked away from me. Quietly I muttered, "*Shukran,*" the Arabic for thank you.

When Khaled returned, he noticed the change in my appearance and angrily rebuked my guard. I was surprised to see the guard respond even more angrily to Khaled's rebuke. What was said I have no idea, but the fact that this humane individual stood his ground against his supposed superior gave me a fleeting moment of pleasure. I hoped then, as I still do, that this guard did not suffer for his kindness.

When the argument between them ended, I was taken downstairs by Khaled, followed by a be-thobed officer carrying the TV box. Directed back into my office, I watched as my computer equipment was disassembled and dumped roughly into the box. Then books were selected rapidly and seemingly at random from my bookcases, to be dropped on top of my computer. The drawers of my desk were opened and the contents thrown into the box. Then my filing cabinet was opened and all my personal papers, bills, and financial records were also thrown in. Everything that could have contained personal information was confiscated.

From among the remaining books, Khaled casually thumbed a few volumes. Selecting one or two, he opened them and then cast them aside, until he collected a black cloth-covered volume. Holding this in his hands, he asked me what it was. I told him that it was my Ph.D. thesis, which caused him to grin inanely. He pretended to study it seriously and smacked his lips, issuing a few tut-tuts.

Looking me straight in the eye, he said, "This is proof of your training in making bombs."

I remained silent, but wondered how a work titled "The Intracellular Control of Cholesterol Metabolism in Rat Hepatocyte Monolayers" qualified me as an explosives expert. One could say that it did prove a basic level of intelligence, thoroughness, and attention to detail that would be useful in developing the expertise of which I was accused. It could also be said that my background in biochemistry gave me the requisite knowledge of chemistry to manufacture explosives. However, it should be pointed out that anyone with high school matriculation in chemistry also has such knowledge. Moreover, there have been enough explosions set off by individuals without such education to indicate that the manufacture of basic explosive devices is hardly the domain of only the formally educated. This was just another of the straws at which they clutched to support the ludicrous accusations and scenarios that they had formulated.

Khaled put the thesis in the box and reached behind me, collecting what had been offered to him out of my line of sight. What now appeared in his hands was a multi-pocketed sports vest that I usually wore when out in the desert. From the pockets he removed two of the items normally kept there. The first was a Zeiss x 10 monocular, an item that I had found on Cheakamus glacier fifteen years previously. It had accompanied me in all my forays into the wilderness since that time. The other item was a Silva compass, a necessary item if one spends time off the beaten track. Khaled examined these carefully before declaring, "These are what you use for spying."

This was a new twist in the accusations, and in my shock at hearing this I could not contain myself. "Spying? I have had those items on every climbing and trekking trip for the past few years. I am not a spy."

"Only people who are spies do such things," he replied.

In one brief statement, he reduced the activities of everyone who enjoys the challenges offered by remote and difficult environments to something sinister. He probably does believe this is true, making it easier for him to construct his absurd theories.

However, I was speaking the truth. If there is a person less capable of acting in such a capacity, it is me. While I am an intensely private individual, I am too open, direct, and opinionated with those I know to be able to maintain the opacity necessary to operate in clandestine intelligence gathering. I thought it must be just another ruse to unsettle me. I was wrong.

Khaled perused the other items in the box, extracting some photographs my father had taken on our desert trip during his visit in 1999. He showed them to me and said, "These also prove you are a spy."

I remained mute, thinking how absurd it was that they were trying to turn the mundane into the evil, but then it would be necessary for them to do so both as a means of unsettling me and justifying their power over me.

He dropped the photographs and picked up the compass, again stating, "These things are illegal in Saudi Arabia, and only people who are spies know how to use them. Where is your GPS? Where is your camera?"

I told him truthfully that I did not own either item. He reiterated his demand. He asked where all my other photographs were, and I told him truthfully that I had none other than those my father had given me. Again he demanded to know where my camera was and again I told him that I have never owned one. To this day I doubt that he believed me, for in subsequent interrogations and other less violent conversations, he would refer to my lack of ownership of a camera as being strange.

The fact is I have never owned one because I can't be bothered taking photographs. I have always been irritated by having to stop and pose, particularly when in the midst of my outdoor pursuits. More than once have my friends been subjected to obscenities when such requests were made. Even my father has suffered my invective on this point when, during a climbing trip, he decided to play with his camera while we crossed a difficult section of rock face from which there was a thousand-metre drop to the glacier below. It was an absurd and dangerous place for him to stop, a fact I informed him of in no uncertain terms.

It is not that I am camera shy. I just dislike the interruption that stopping for photographs causes. I am unable to see any point in recording the minutiae of one's life on celluloid or in pixels. Why should one stop and pose for a photo album in the midst of something interesting or exciting?

Khaled asked again for my GPS. I assumed that he had not believed me when I had told him that I did not own one. My compass has been all that I have used during my wanderings. Then as now, a compass may be considered redundant in the face of the wide availability of hand-held GPS systems, but not to me. My low-tech means of navigating had served me well enough, and such means did not depend upon batteries. Khaled was never satisfied on this point.

Both the compass that I owned and, for that matter, hand-held GPS systems were readily available in Riyadh for anyone who wished to purchase them. GPS systems had only recently come onto the market in Saudi Arabia, as the government there always restricted any technology that it viewed as having an information-gathering potential. The fact is that even though such items were available does not mean their possession was legal. Technically, satellite dishes were also readily available, but were deemed illegal. These are just a few, among the many, of the inconsistencies of the law in Saudi Arabia. Such inconsistencies are not without their benefits to the police and security forces, as they provided a ready-made justification for the harassment and arrest of nearly anyone. The shops where these items could be purchased were able to ply their trade with impunity as a result of the owners of the businesses having the appropriate wasta or connections, while their customers effectively became criminals through their purchases. In a police state, such a means of control is all too useful, as my arrest and detention demonstrated.

Ibrahim now walked into the room holding an axe handle that had been discovered among my desert trekking equipment that was located in the closet under the stairs. He could barely contain his glee as he waved it in front of my face before placing it in the box with my other personal items.

As he and Khaled spoke to each other, I wondered what they considered significant in this discovery. Would this be used as further evidence of my criminality, demonstrating my possession of advanced weaponry? I learned soon enough that this was not the reason for Ibrahim's pleasure in his find.

Khaled nodded to the guard, and I was taken out into the hallway. Another uniformed guard collected the box containing my property and headed out of my house. A third guard came over to me, fumbling with a blindfold, and yet another entered the house with a Malinoise (a Belgian police dog) on a leash. I whistled softly at the dog, which wagged its tail and strained on its leash to approach me. A sharp jerk on the lead rebuked the poor animal for its friendliness. This was more of their pro forma textbook search procedures.

I looked back into my office where Khaled and Ibrahim stood. They were perusing the remaining objects on my desk. Without any pretence, Khaled picked up my Cross fountain pen and pencil and put them into the chest pocket of his thobe. Ibrahim collected my Tag Heuer watch that I had recently purchased (it was due to be returned to have the strap adjusted). This disappeared into the side pocket of his thobe. I knew then that my personal belongings were no longer my own, but now constituted spoils from which my captors would pilfer to their hearts' content. I had heard of and seen such wanton acts of theft and corruption indulged in by officials of the Ministry of the Interior before. As the country was ruled by what can be best defined as a kleptocracy, such behaviour among its junior officials was not surprising.

Khaled and Ibrahim saw that I witnessed their thefts and laughed at me as the blindfold was placed over my eyes. I was led back to the waiting police van, where my original travelling companion ushered me gently into the back. As the van pulled away, he took off my blindfold and handcuffs, smiling at me as he did so. The contrast that his behaviour provided was stark. I actually felt sorry for him having to work beside thugs such as Khaled and Ibrahim.

As we entered the compound of the interrogation centre, signalled by our coming to a halt and by the sound of the gates opening, he replaced the handcuffs and blindfold, saying, "Sorry" as he did so. It was probably one of the few English words he knew.

I replied, as I had earlier, "*Shukran*," one of the few Arabic words I knew. In the midst of all this darkness, I had encountered some humanity. It had an odd strengthening effect that was much needed.

I was now back in my home-away-from-home wondering what would come next. From the statements made during my last interrogation session and the planted evidence I had seen, I knew that my list of crimes was growing. Everything was being slotted into place to form an impenetrable web of supposed malfeasance that would justify everything they would throw at me. Apart from being a supposed terrorist, I was now a homosexual purveyor of alcohol and drugs with a clandestine security agenda. On this last point, I still was not sure they would bother to go so far. After all, the planted hashish and alcohol were items in themselves that could be paraded publicly, and in the charade of Saudi Arabian judicial and diplomatic affairs would remain unquestioned. However, a monocular and a compass do not an Ian Fleming make. In that I was definitely wrong. One thing I realize now is that once possessed by such people as I was then, no scenario, no matter how absurd, is beyond the realm of possibility if it fits their agenda.

I could not have been in my cell for more than an hour when I was collected for interrogation. I managed to see the watch on the wrist of my guard before the blindfold was put in place. It was five or ten minutes past eleven in the evening and the process now started again: delivery to the office, awaiting the arrival of my tormentors, their first session of the brutality, etc. This time, though the process remained the same, the pain entered another dimension.

Khaled undid my handcuffs and told me to remove my shoes and lie face down on the floor. I was then told to raise my feet and slide back against the wall. As I did this, Ibrahim opened the door and retrieved something from the corridor, but I was unable to see what. Almost the instant the door closed, I felt what he had retrieved as the most intense bolt of pain seared my feet. Involuntarily my body went into a spasm and I screamed, rolling away from the wall. As I did, I saw the rattan cane held in Ibrahim's hands.

The shock of that initial blow was twofold. First, the level of pain that it caused was intense. I had expected physical assaults, but this went far beyond my expectations. I had experienced pain before, having suffered severe injuries such as a broken back, but nothing prepared me for what I now experienced. Second, it wrenched me from the belief that I could endure what they had so far limited themselves to, for this I knew I could not endure indefinitely. It told me in an instant that their promises of increased brutality were now a reality. I immediately wondered when they would begin applying electric shocks (mercifully they never did). So on top of the pain was the immediate increase in my fear and anxiety; another barrier had been breached. From now on everything seemed possible and this was really only the start.

Forced again into position with my feet raised and my legs braced against the wall, the cane descended. I could not stop the spasms that pulled me out of position. Khaled and Ibrahim shouted, "Don't move!"

At least I had discovered that Ibrahim spoke two more words of English, though the means of discovery I could have done without. My jerks were punished by sharp kicks to my torso delivered by Khaled and The Spiv, Ibrahim being intent on his allotted task. Ibrahim brought focus and intensity to his work. Turning my head to watch his movements, I saw how he stood, cane in hand. It was as if he were lining up a million-dollar putt, examining my feet for the exact placement of the cane, reading the soles of my stockinged feet like the nap of a putting green.

After more than twenty strokes, I began to lose count, submerged as I was in a sea of agony. Not only were my feet burning with pain, so too was my whole body, as the spasmodic contractions caused by the blows were causing cramps in my legs, back, and abdomen. My hands and arms, which had remained free to that point, were now constrained behind my back with handcuffs. Khaled grabbed the ankle shackles, pulling my feet toward my buttocks. Then, using another pair of handcuffs, my wrists were tied to my ankles. In this position, a position that I would describe as being hog-tied, I was dragged to the centre of the room.

Freed from the physical limitation caused by the proximity of my feet to the wall, Ibrahim was able to swing the cane more easily. He now marched the cane across my feet, sometimes striking across the width of both feet, sometimes striking along the length of one foot at a time. It was curious to me then, but it seemed that on the longitudinal strikes, Ibrahim favoured my right foot. It also seemed that each strike never hit the same place twice in a row. With incredible accuracy that could only have come from years of dedicated practice and experience, Ibrahim always struck a spot within what felt like only millimetres from where the cane last landed. This maximized the pain, for immediately after a spot had been hit it would be slightly desensitized. Therefore, to maximize the effect, he marched the cane up, down, and across my feet in a particular sequence. The precision was remarkable and devastating.

Three years later, some time after my release, I visited the Parker Institute in Denmark and was examined by doctors whose grim specialty is in providing medical assessments for the survivors of torture. One of the examinations they undertake is an ultrasound scan of the feet, performed under specific conditions that are not comfortable. The objective of the test is to examine the subcutaneous connective tissue (fascia) in the feet for damage indicative of this type of torture. My test results confirmed this abuse, and the doctor told me that my right foot showed more damage than the left. This confirmed Ibrahim's predilection for savaging that appendage more than the other. In the midst of the brutal beatings, I had retained some of my ability to think and to record despite everything.

The test also provided me with other things: incontrovertible medical evidence of the abuse I had suffered and a sense of relief. As the test finished, the doctor told me that the results were positive. I felt tears well up in my eyes; it was all I could do to choke them back. My chest felt as if a weight had been lifted away, allowing me to breathe again. I had approached this and all the other tests with some trepidation, for till then no medical examination to which I had been subjected had provided any direct confirmation of my claims of abuse. This positive result gave me something that I craved, an independent testimony and proof of the abuse. No longer would it be just my word against that of lying bastards of the Saudi Arabian government and their counterparts in the governments of Britain, Canada, and Belgium. I had my proof. It was and is extremely difficult for me to articulate these feelings adequately. As I tried to explain them to the doctor, I clumsily searched for the words. He took my hand and said simply that he understood.

At that moment, I felt an unalloyed sadness for him and his co-workers. I am only one of the many that he examines. I have my pain to live with. He has the pain he sees in the hundreds or thousands that he has examined. I wondered who cares for those at the Parker Institute who care for such as I. Their work is necessary, unfortunately, and their dedication humbling.

The hog-tied position in which I now found myself not only constrained my movements and kept me in the necessary position; it also added new sources of pain. With each strike of the rattan, my legs would forcefully jerk away and downward. This movement would pull on my wrists, threatening to dislocate the joints. In turn, it also would pull on my elbow and shoulder joints, and I could feel the ligaments stretching and tearing. Finally my back would bow, straining the flexure in the centre of my spine. Furthermore, the metal of the handcuffs and shackles would dig into my flesh, pressing into the joints and leaving deep impressions of their position, resulting in further injury. Each strike caused a more pronounced reflex spasm, causing ever-increasing pain in my joints. I was just waiting for something to give. I thought that my vertebrae would be the first to separate, for with the exception of my feet, the pain there was the most intense. In some respects, it might have been a blessing had my back broken, for had that resulted in paralysis of my lower limbs then at least I would have been spared the pain in my feet.

Once a certain level of pain is reached, anything that can provide relief becomes welcome, even if the consequences of such a wish would have been otherwise unthinkable.

Finally the beating stopped. I was partially unencumbered and placed in a chair. I could not stop my body from shaking nor my breath coming in short ragged gasps. Remarkably, I did not cry. I seemed to be beyond tears as a mechanism for relief from pain. I sat and listened as the lecture started. Ibrahim pontificated. Khaled translated.

I heard a litany of my fictitious crimes: homosexuality, alcohol, drugs, murder, and terrorism. The lecture focused on only one of the incidents with which I was originally accused, but this was to be expected. If they could break me to confess to one crime, then the confessions necessary to implicate me in the other crimes would follow. I was well aware of this, and of the possible penalties associated with a murder conviction, but I was also terrified of the pain.

My mind was bombarded by their false promises of relief from pain, by the horrendous physical sensations emanating from all parts of my body, and by the aching desire for sleep. Arrayed against this was my assumption (correct as it turns out) that confession would not end the pain, that confession would put me firmly in the executioner's path, and that confession would require that I implicate others. This certain knowledge that they intended to use me to convict others was uppermost in my mind. Allied with this was my growing hatred of my captors that fostered in me the need not to give the bastards the satisfaction. The simple fact that I was innocent was no longer a factor in my thoughts, much as it never was in theirs. It was an irrelevancy in the game before us. How long would I endure? What would they need to do to "get my mind right"? What would be necessary to deliver me to their complete control?

As usual in these interrogation sessions, Khaled, Ibrahim, and The Spiv left me with a sullen and bored guard. With my hands still free, I reached down to my feet. I gently probed them to assess the damage. The soles felt pulpy and soft, slightly swollen to the touch. There were numerous exceedingly sore pressure points on the bony sections of the balls and heels of both feet, and this after only one session. Next, I massaged my wrists, trying to eradicate the tingling sensation that had spread from there to my thumbs. I suspected that, given the nature of the sensations, I had suffered some damage to the distal ends of the ulnar nerves.

Finished with my limited examination, I stared out of the office window into the night. It occurred to me that should I ever be left unshackled, I could try to crash through the window. I dismissed this thought as foolish for I had no knowledge of the compound's layout should I land successfully after jumping through the window. Most likely, I would break my damn fool neck. Certainly, it would give the Saudi Arabian government something to explain, though experience now tells me that the Canadian and British governments would accept any explanation put forward in order to allow the Saudis to save face. I resolved that any attempt to escape would be possible only if I could get more information on my immediate environment, and so I put it from my mind.

The Three Stooges returned and hauled me to my feet, telling me to pick up my shoes before placing the blindfold and handcuffs on me. My hands were now cuffed in front of me, a slightly more comfortable position than behind my back. I wondered if the session was over, only to be disabused of such hope. I was led across the corridor into another office, the door of which was only a couple of metres down on the opposite side of the corridor. When the door closed behind me, the blindfold was removed.

The office I was now in was of similar size to the previous one. The window was covered by a curtain of a dark material. The room was furnished with two office chairs that had ragged black seat coverings, a desk of rather low stature due to the legs having been truncated for some reason, and the same dark nondescript carpeting. Light was provided by a single fluorescent strip light that seemed to be operating on a rather low setting given the faint illumination it cast.

Khaled told me to sit down on the floor and drop my shoes. As I did this, I noticed the only other item in the room, a hollow metal pipe about two metres long and five to six centimetres in diameter. Khaled kneeled and grabbed my wrists, instructing me to put my hands over my knees and pull them into my chest. While I did this, Ibrahim picked up the pipe. He and Khaled then inserted the pipe behind my knees and over my forearms. Now effectively having locked me in this folded position, Khaled and Ibrahim picked up either end of the pipe, carrying me over to the chairs across which the pipe was then placed. The result of this procedure had me suspended upside down, with the soles of my feet and my buttocks presented in an exposed and vulnerable position.

The weight of my upper body pulled against the handcuffs, placing strain on my wrists and on my shoulders. This, as I learned upon my release, is called falanga, or the chicken position. It is an apt appellation, for that was what I resembled: a live chicken trussed up and on display at market. It was horribly uncomfortable and very convenient for my torturers.

At this point, Khaled and Ibrahim walked around in front of me. From my upside down perspective, the grins on their faces seemed to be both more absurd and sinister. It was then that I saw what was giving them such amusement, other than the spectacle that I now presented. I had not noticed it when I entered the room, so from where it materialized I do not know. There, grasped in Ibrahim's eager hand, was the axe handle that had been taken from my house. It was blindingly obvious that the axe handle had not been taken as evidence, but as an addition to their collection of implements of persuasion. That was the reason for his amusement then and now; Ibrahim had a brand-new toy, one that would last for years, given its solidity.

Khaled remained in front of me as Ibrahim moved away. Knowing what was coming, my body visibly tensed, expanding the smirk on Khaled's face. Then I felt the first blow directed across my buttocks. The pain was intense. The accumulated punishment was having an effect. This part of my anatomy had not previously been targeted – it should not have felt so tender. I did not expect it to be as sensitive as my feet, yet it hurt more than what I had experienced only a few moments ago. After about ten strokes, Ibrahim switched his attention to my feet. Again the blows fell, again the pain coursed through me in waves; again the intensity of both the blows and the pain seemed to have increased. With each strike and subsequent wave of pain that spread from either my feet or my buttocks, my pulse increased, raising my blood pressure. As a result, in my suspended position, the pressure inside my head increased dramatically, producing migraine-like jolts of pain even though no blows were directed there. I could feel my eyes bulge and my eardrums roar with each contact.

With every blow my body jerked and convulsed reflexively. I could do nothing to control it, nothing at all. These spasms only increased my pain, for as they occurred my arms pulled down, grinding my wrists into the cuffs, pressing the metal into the joint space. In turn my shoulder joints strained and felt as if they would rip open. I know that the joint capsules in each was loosened during this time for I could feel the degree of stretch increase, and I now suffer from a concomitant thickening of the joint capsules, which restricts my movements. In pulling down on my arms in that fashion, I also flexed my knee joints around the pipe. As would be expected, the strain on the tendons and ligaments surrounding these joints was intense. On more than one occasion I felt something pop inside one or other of them. Thus each stroke was a symphony of pain from each of my major joints. I wondered which would be the first to fail, and pondered what would be next.

Suddenly, the idea of red hot pokers and branding irons crossed my mind along with images of the *auto-da-fè*. If it seems strange or unbelievable that in the midst of what I was enduring, my mind was trying to anticipate what would be forthcoming, it seems strange to me also. Not only did weird expectations of the *auto-da-fè* come into my mind, so did memories of Monty Python's sketches on the Spanish Inquisition with the possibility of being tortured with a comfy chair. It is strange, I grant you. The only way of explaining it is that when it came to my personal survival, I was driven back on my underlying personality traits and sceptical nature. My cynicism, my humour, and my contrariness have caused me no end of problems at other times in my life, but they were to be part of the key to my survival.

After five or so cycles of buttocks, feet, and scrotum, the beating stopped. Throughout this, my screams had been accompanied by the sounds of Khaled and The Spiv chuckling at my pain, while Ibrahim hummed musically. I can only surmise that the humming was a mark of the intense enjoyment and pleasure that he derived from torturing me. Now though, the only sounds were the gasps of my ragged breathing, as Khaled and Ibrahim lifted the bar from the chair and deposited me on the floor. With the bar still between my knees and forearms, I was unable to stretch out or move, remaining in a folded position, as the three of them departed. No guard was ushered into the room to stand over me nor was one necessary, for I was unable to do anything other than shiver.

I sat there like a discarded carcass, one end of the bar wedged into the carpeting. There was nothing on my mind at all other than the pain that radiated through my body. Eventually they returned, and Khaled immediately began his mantra. He reiterated that it was easy for me to stop the pain; all I had to do was to confess. I was told that I had driven to the Rodways' villa, planted the bomb on the car, followed their car when they had left their villa, and then detonated the bomb by remote control. I was told that they had witnesses who had seen me. I was sure that they did have witnesses, though I was also sure that they would be ones instructed in their testimony. So it went on, though this lecture session was terminated after only a few minutes.

As I expected, I was left alone, trying to steel myself for the next session, which I anticipated would be another beating. In this I was not disappointed. When the Three Stooges returned, I was immediately suspended upside down. Ibrahim began reacquainting my body with the axe handle. All I could do was scream and hope the session would not last too long, though under the circumstances my definition of long meant any length of time greater than a second. The humming and giggling resumed, accompanied by my vocal contributions.

I prayed to lose consciousness, though such luck never did seem to come my way. Eventually, the beating stopped and I was lowered to the floor. Khaled and The Spiv removed the bar, releasing me from at least some of the discomfort. I was told to put on my shoes, an indication that this beating was over. I struggled to put on my shoes, even though my feet had become too swollen for this to be possible. Khaled kept insisting that I complete this task, getting angrier with each failed attempt. In an exhausted and pathetic voice, I insisted that my feet were too swollen. In disgust, Khaled told me to stand and collect my shoes. When I had done so, I was blindfolded and led back to my cell.

As I limped into the cellblock, dawn prayer sounded. Another day had passed. Once in my cell, I noticed that two food trays were awaiting me, one was the evening meal and one was the morning meal. I had not been fed the night before. Released from my restraints, I sat on my mattress, putting my shoes aside and covering my legs with a blanket. I undid my trousers, drawing some little comfort from this act, leaned against the wall, and pawed at some of the food. I extracted a few rice grains to mark the passing of another day. I had decided at that point on the restricted format of what I now termed my rice diary. A single unblemished grain was to mark the passing of each day of my incarceration. A grain bitten in two was to mark each day without sleep. Finally, I decided that a grain stained in some manner would indicate each day of torture. Working out the means of staining the rice grains, I selected one and reached inside my trousers under the cover of a blanket, rolling the grain of rice around between the cheeks of my buttocks. Withdrawing it, I saw on surreptitious inspection that it was adequately stained, and so repeated the process with two further grains. I now had, secreted within the hole in the mattress, nine grains of rice acting as a simplistic record of my first three days of imprisonment. It was the only means available to me for constructing an *aide-mémoire*; it would have to do.

This done, I stood up and banged on the cell door. When the guard arrived I requested to go to the toilet. The guard led me there in only handcuffs. Once in the toilet, I stripped off my clothes and performed very basic ablutions. As I gingerly washed my feet, I noted that they were most definitely swollen; the soles were glowing red, feeling as if they had been burned and were radiating heat. The upper surface was discoloured and swollen. I found that massaging them was too painful, so I finished washing them and continued with the other parts of my body. My contorted investigation revealed kaleidoscopic bruises. A single patch of discolouration spread from just above my hips to the back of my knees. My ankles and lower calves were extremely swollen. I knew that the swellings would have no chance to subside, as I would be spending the time between beatings standing. I wondered what the effects of the increasing fluid pressure would be. With these thoughts in my mind, I called the guard, was walked back to my cell, and was chained to the door. At least the coldness of the concrete floor slightly ameliorated the burning pain in my feet as I stood there with only my socks covering them.

Thus began the daylight hours of my fourth day of captivity.

The routine was now established. The trip to the doctor's office resulted in a cursory examination of my swollen legs. When I re-entered my cell, I was presented with a tube of cream, an anti-inflammatory ointment in all probability. It was indicated to me that I apply it to my legs and feet, which I did liberally before returning the remnants of the tube. Later, the interrogation proceeded as usual though there was one change. The first of the lectures was now delivered by Khaled alone, whose demeanour had changed markedly. No longer aggressive, he tried to appear conciliatory and contrite, apologizing for what had been done to me.

"It is beyond my control," he said, "but I will try to help you but you have to help me."

To help him I had to confess, but as I said to him that I was innocent, I saw the brittle façade of his compassion crack momentarily. His eyes flared with hatred as he struggled to maintain his new demeanour while saying, "But you have always been guilty."

Curious statement that, one upon which I have frequently pondered. I was innocent. Did his religious zealotry make him consider me guilty due to the concept of original sin in the book of our shared religious heritage? After all, Christianity and Islam have in common the Old Testament, making us children of the Book. Was it simply that as someone not of his faith I was by nature evil? Therefore, blame could be justly ascribed to me? Or was it the expressions of the cultural and racial hatred that he had exhibited so far toward me and other ethnic groups? Given the nature of the beast, I believe it was derived from the latter, a deeply rooted hatred and resentment toward anyone or anything that would be considered western. Ultimately, whatever the reason, I was to be found guilty and therefore had to confess. His life's work was simple and obviously satisfying for him: arrest someone you despise and make them confess. The niceties of guilt and innocence were alien concepts, for arrest guaranteed guilt as surely as day follows night.

I had been and was being subjected to disorientation and debilitation via brutality, humiliation, and sleep deprivation. Now an attempt to build an emotional connection was being made to induce dependence. I was already dependent on my captors in certain physical ways. I was dependent on them for food, for toilet privileges, for an end to the beatings, among other things. Beyond the physical, however, is another level of dependence: emotional. Though someone robustly capable of spending long periods alone, I am still a social animal, as are we all. Even after only three days of solitary confinement, I had begun to need human contact of a more pleasant nature. As one reaches this stage in the process, one can all too easily reach out to anyone, even someone such as Khaled or Ibrahim, and thus be manipulated into forming an emotional bond with one's captors. The fear, the pain, and the concomitant distress cloud one's judgement.

In common parlance, this could be called a form of Stockholm syndrome, which arises in situations where hostages realign themselves emotionally with their captors. It is probable that the disorientation and debilitation that follow from being stripped of all normal reference points, subjected to total authoritarian control, and subjected to the fear and pain of physical assault and humiliation, result in the regression of one's personality to a pre-developed state of infantile dependency. When as a small child your personality is still developing from its nascent characteristics, it is dependent on the authority, the affection, and the attention of adults for emotional sustenance and development. Captivity such as I experienced recreates in a very short space of time a grotesque simulacrum of that period of dependency and forces an emotional regression. As this occurs, your captors or even your own mind will trick you into perceiving them as your mentors, and that it is your own behaviour or the behaviour of others (your government, the other prisoners, etc.) that is now seen as the cause of your predicament. Reasonably skilled interrogators can induce this frame of mind in their subjects, though aware subjects can also find a way to resist these overtures and their own emotional impulses. If the subject fails to resist the formation of a bond between themselves and the captor, and the bond is established, the subject becomes more vulnerable. The threatened withdrawal of friendship will be devastating. Thus, the interrogator will gain emotional control as well as physical control over his captive. To say that one, at this stage, is owned body and soul by the interrogators is almost an understatement in such a situation.

The discussion, for that was what it now was, passed back and forth between us. My end was taken up with pointing out my innocence, that I had neither reason nor need to be involved in bombings or any other terrorist activity. Khaled's responses constantly reiterated his desire to help me but that my refusal to cooperate was preventing him from doing so. He assured me there was nothing he could do to keep Ibrahim at bay unless I changed my attitude. His comments were often couched in simplistic analogies. In his twisted syntax, he compared our situation to one where we were on an ocean paddling a raft toward a ship, and without rowing together we would not make it. He compared our situation to one of our trying to board and fly an aircraft: flight depended on both of us at the controls for success. These figurative devices were his crude attempt to link our fates and show that he and I were tied together for a common purpose. Possibly these analogies had worked for him in the past, but with me they did not. I found them insultingly moronic. They helped me reject his attempts at creating an emotional bond. Khaled used this rhetoric in his attempts at brainwashing throughout my incarceration, and I wonder if he ever knew how pathetic I found it.

I wonder also if he ever realized what thoughts I was having during each of the solo and team lecture sessions. Over the early days of my incarceration, my fear and emotional vulnerability grew exponentially. I was aware this was happening and that my captors meant to use it. I tried during the interrogations not to engage my captors and tried not to provoke them, answering only direct questions, though my natural sarcasm and flippancy undermined me at times. To prevent myself from seeing my captors in a benign light or one in which any emotional bond would form, I tried to project certain images in my head as I talked to them. The most effective of them was that as I spoke to Khaled and Ibrahim, I would visualize scenes of sliding thin metal blades into their eyes, savouring in my imagination the pain they would suffer for having caused me so much. While these images danced before me, I tried as best I could to keep any of the hatred or anger that inspired these images from colouring my voice. I am not sure that I was successful in maintaining this pretence, but I think I was, for when some months later I broke from my compliant state and tried to kill Khaled and Ibrahim, their shock and fear were palpable. That event was in my future, and for now I resisted Khaled's entreaties to help him in ending my suffering. Eventually, having made no headway, he called the interview to a close and departed.

I spent the next while contemplating the beating I anticipated. After what seemed an eternity, I was collected and led to the office across the hall where Ibrahim and The Spiv arranged me for suspension. While they were doing this, Khaled said that he had tried to prevent this but I had not helped him. I replied with a simple statement: "Fuck you."

I should not have said it, but I could not restrain myself. On reflection, I knew that all I should have done was to endure.

Defiance should come later and for a specific purpose, not just as an instinctive reaction. I understood this at the time but it was hard for me restrain myself. It would have required that I adopt the traits of a saint, something not remotely possible for me. I know that were I in the same situation again, I would be just as offensive, and I would suffer the same consequences.

The Spiv attempted to kick me in the testicles. As I was sitting on the floor folded around a metal bar, access to that part of my anatomy was somewhat restricted. The result was that The Spiv managed only to crack his shin on the bar, causing me to laugh as he yelped in pain. Ibrahim screamed something in Arabic, bending over to slap me across the side of the head for my insolence. I have no idea what Ibrahim said, but the volume of his outburst told me he was not pleased. Whether this increased his brutality I cannot say, but it is hard to believe it could have been increased without recourse to other methods of torture, for with the falanga position and the subsequent beating it is hard to increase the pain beyond that which is inherent to the method.

So the cycle began again. Feet, buttocks, feet, buttocks, were struck forcefully by the axe handle in the prescribed rhythm. At the tenth cycle, the axe handle crashed into my scrotum. The pain of that single strike was so great as to make those to my feet and buttocks seem mild in comparison. Again, during all of this, I wondered at the precision of each strike, particularly those affecting my scrotum. As a result of my position and the pain of the strikes to the other areas, my scrotal sack had already contracted protectively. The contraction was so strong it induced a feeling of cramp even before the first blow fell there. It felt as if my testicles would disappear into the perineal cavity, yet unfortunately they did not. What was both curious and interesting in a perverse manner was that they were never hit directly. Each blow that connected with my scrotum hit the area immediately behind the testicles, within what felt like only millimetres. It seemed as if the underlying bony structure of the pubic symphysis would break, and my testicles and scrotum would ruptured. This did not happen. Over time, my scrotum, testicles, and penis became swollen and bruised, turning black and purple, coming to resemble rotten oranges in both appearance and size. However, nothing beyond that resulted, and once the beatings stopped they did gradually return to normal, in appearance at least.

I know that I have already mentioned the expertise of Ibrahim, but it cannot be stressed enough. The precision with which these and subsequent beatings were delivered was almost a work of art. Certainly it showed incredible skill. The soft tissue areas of my body were bombarded constantly, yet no visible surface scars are apparent. Only the ultrasound scanning procedure I underwent at the Parker Institute has been able to demonstrate the damage caused to my feet by torture. Muscle trigger points and areas of deep sensitivity indicative of trauma show up in other parts of my body, but they do not necessarily prove torture – that could be their cause, but so too could other events. When I'm exposed to cold I can experience cramps, particularly in my scrotum, and my flexibility is sorely circumscribed but is improving. Only the positive proof from the diagnoses of my feet corroborates my claim of abuse. All that happened to me is bad enough, but the fact remains that nothing was actually ruptured or broken. Never did I lose consciousness during the sessions, though I came close, considering that the brutality was extreme. I was taken to a level of pain and sustained there over hours, days, and weeks with little apparent damage beyond a few broken teeth. To inflict such pain with no record of it on your body requires a particular knowledge, and my captors knew the amounts of force necessary to maximize pain while leaving little if any physical evidence. How does one gain such expertise? What academies teach the requisite skills? On what does one practise? I now have partial answers to these questions, particularly with the information coming from Guantanamo. I also expect that my captors were less restrained with those of other nationalities, as twenty-four hours later I would experience graphic evidence of this, allowing them to develop an understanding of what excessive force did and thus tailor their brutality to the circumstances. What is indisputable is the inhumanity of the practitioners of this art. They and their political masters who encourage and maintain such inhumanity deserve both contempt and imprisonment.

From Ibrahim's perspective at least, all good things must come to an end, so the beating stopped and I was lowered to the floor. Released from the bar, I was walked across the hall back to the other office and deposited with a uniformed guard as my companion. The fact that I had been released from the bar gave me the impression that another round of falanga would not occur that night. With that small glimmer of hope and expecting another lecture, I awaited the return of Ibrahim and Khaled.

In this at least I was not disappointed. Some time later they appeared with smiles resplendent on their faces. They seemed inordinately pleased, though their pleasure was apparently short-lived, given that their persuasive powers were still proving futile, for I was still resisting. The desperation of my earlier screams and cries might have been more dire than previously, giving them hope of an early result. One possibility was that another concomitant interrogation had given them just that. I don't know which it was, but I certainly ruined their mood, and I felt both fear and a fleeting sense of pleasure from being the cause of their displeasure. After a few minutes of Ibrahim sitting and listening impatiently to Khaled's overture of bonding, Ibrahim finally cracked when my protestations of innocence were translated for him. Angrily, he shouted at me, while Khaled translated. I was asked quite simply if I truly wanted my feet to be beaten again. Once again my sarcasm and warped sense of humour came to the fore, as I replied, "Well, at least it keeps my feet warm."

This was in part the truth. My feet were too swollen for me to put on my shoes, so I had spent the preceding hours standing in my stockinged feet on the concrete floor of my cell. My feet, however, did not register the coldness of that unheated surface due to the sensation of heat that emanated from them.

I could not keep a wry smile from appearing on my face, nor did I try to prevent muted laughter from escaping. This sent both Ibrahim and Khaled into a paroxysm of rage, demonstrating at least the hypocrisy of Khaled's attempts at conciliation, if not also demonstrating the poor quality of his acting and self-control. I was knocked to the floor from my chair as they erupted from the other side of their desk to get their hands on me. One of them, I am not sure which, kicked me on the right side of my face, and for the second time I felt something crack in my mouth, though not with as much pain as on the first day. Lifted to my feet, I was taken back for more falanga after probably one of the shortest lecture sessions so far. For some reason the beating that I then received, although horrendous, did not seemed quite as bad as earlier ones had been. Possibly my body was becoming inured to the punishment, but I do not think so. Perversely, I feel that my ability to find humour at such a black moment and to express it helped lessen the pain. Yes, had I kept my mouth shut the beating might not have come so soon, and I would have had a few more moments to recover. That is all I would have had though, minutes, for the beating was inevitable.

Soon this beating was over, followed by a solo lecture by Khaled, who could not but express his sincere disappointment and sorrow, then another round of beating, another solo lecture, and a final session of physical punishment, before dawn prayer was called and I was returned to my cell. Life was predictable, at least, if not pleasant. Was I beginning to get inside the heads of Khaled and Ibrahim, to see through their thinly drawn façades?

I sat in my cell, chewing on pita bread and sipping some water, trying to shift my focus from the pain my body was in. Reviewing the events so far, I could see the pattern. I knew there was no way that I would not confess if things continued in this vein. My body was accumulating damage that made me more and more sensitive, which increased my emotional vulnerability and was sapping my will to resist. I had only one hope: the cessation of these activities due to either the British or Canadian governments becoming aware of my fate and demanding visitation rights. I knew that if this did not happen soon, I would be in serious trouble when eventually I confessed. I knew confession was only a matter of time, and time was something that favoured my captors. I was in part correct in my assumptions; I was also glaringly wrong, as I discovered later.

While I ruminated over these points, I slowly consumed more of the meagre breakfast and modified the grains of rice I had collected from the meal of the previous evening. As I chewed on the leathery bread, I felt a tooth in my upper left jaw disintegrate. This was what I had felt crack when I was pistol-whipped on first being arrested. I spat out the larger fragments and the filling amalgam, washing the small fragments down with a gulp of water. My tongue probed the stub that remained, expecting sensitivity due to the root being exposed, but for once I had some luck, little though it was. The amalgam that had fallen out with the other fragments was in fact only part of the filling, it having split in a horizontal plane, leaving a rough cap that afforded some protection to the root pulp.

I finished my tea, now chewing the last of my pita bread on the right side of my mouth, aware that there was damage there as well. I put the lump of amalgam and some of the larger fragments of the tooth into my pocket in anticipation of a visit to the doctor, before calling for the guard. Once in the toilet, I stripped off and inspected myself. Parts of my body were exceedingly discoloured, with my feet, ankles, scrotal sack, and penis becoming increasingly swollen as well. I wondered just how big they could get before the skin split. I examined my mouth in front of the mirror, noting the damage so far, probing all my teeth with my fingers for any looseness. I discovered that another tooth, one in the back of my mouth on the lower right side, was split and loose, though as yet not too tender beyond the bruising that resulted from being kicked.

When I sat down on the toilet to relieve myself, I discovered difficulties that had not occurred to me. Both urination and defecation were painful. I was able to pass a single small, hard stool with excruciating pain. It felt as if I were passing a bowling ball, splitting myself apart in the process. The subsequent urination provided a burning sensation. Far from giving physical relief, going to the toilet was now an exercise in pain and stress, reminding me all too vividly of the damage I had endured, bringing back to the forefront of my mind anticipation of further brutality. My captors had turned the simplest and most necessary of bodily functions into something to be feared. I was a complete physical mess and I had been their property for barely a hundred hours. It did occur to me again, and with a colder, harder clarity, what a relief death would be.

With that thought in my mind, I finished my ablutions and returned to my cell, resuming my solitary upright vigil. Desperate for some relief, I tried to direct my thoughts to memories of more pleasant times and events. It was hard to maintain the necessary focus, but I knew it was essential that I do so. If all that my mind could render were thoughts of pain received and pain to come, I would slowly drive myself insane. Thus I forced myself to remember the hills and rivers of western Scotland. Gradually I lost myself in images of the Cuillins, of the Morar Peninsula, of Glen Orchy and of Glen Etive, savouring each memory of climbs and long walks. It helped immensely, for I could feel their calming influence as my body relaxed somewhat and my heart rate slowed.

At some point, I was collected for my morning visit with the doctor. Once again in his presence, I complained to him about the developing swellings on my limbs and on my torso, only for him to ignore me. Casually, he examined my right leg by raising my trouser leg by about six inches. While he did this, I retrieved from my pocket the fragments of my tooth for his perusal. He simply threw them into a waste bin with hardly a glance. He took my pulse and blood pressure and informed me there was nothing wrong with me. There was I thinking that I might be in need of medical attention. Obviously, the parameters for defining health and fitness, as laid down by his employers, the Ministry of the Interior, made his diagnosis simple: if it has anything resembling a pulse, then it is fit. I had thought of trying to exaggerate my condition to see if it would secure a temporary medical reprieve, though I rapidly realized that it would be a waste of effort. The reality was that my condition could not be exaggerated. Only a dramatic and permanent collapse might gain such a reprieve, and even then I would have not put money on that providing any relief other than momentary unconsciousness. I returned again to my cell to endure a sleepless vigil of anticipation.

It was during the afternoon, not long after the medical visit, that, with extreme suddenness, I experienced my first period of hallucination. While debate still rages in scientific circles about the reason for or purpose of sleep, one thing that is known is the necessity, if not the purpose, of the dream states that occur during sleep. Deprive someone of sleep for any length of time and their cognitive abilities degrade significantly. Continue to deprive them of sleep and they will be unable to think or control their thought processes. At some point the subconscious or reflex part of one's higher functions cut loose, inducing the dreams or hallucinations that would normally occur during sleep. This uncontrolled manifestation of what is not usually experienced consciously is both strange and probably dangerous. Coherent thought has all but disappeared, except for brief periods during which you experience the paranoid feelings of encroaching insanity, into which I was certainly convinced that I was descending. It is profoundly terrifying and damaging, with little that can be done to ameliorate the experience. As you enter this state, your vulnerability is once again increased, making you even more suggestible and desperate. The extended dimensions of my emotions outpaced my ability for conscious amelioration, starting a swingeing mania beyond control of my feeble attempts to rein it in. To put it simply, I was lost in the surreal landscape that my terrified subconscious created for me.

In my experience, once the hallucinations of sleep deprivation begin the only thing other than sleep that can bring about the return of any reasonably long period of coherent thought is pain. The psychological effect of the physical brutality of torture pushes you through to a level of conscious thought in which reality, albeit an extremely painful one, dominates. Certainly, the structure of my interrogation sessions, in which brutality was always delivered before questioning, woke me from the hallucinatory state with a forceful jolt. I cannot but imagine that this was an inherent flaw in the methodology applied by my captors. The rigidity of their program led to these contradictory effects. Not that I wish to teach my interrogators how to improve their skills, but had they, instead of removing me from my cell for a near immediate beating, arrived at my cell during the first or second day of these hallucinations, they might have achieved the breakthrough they were after earlier than they did.

When the first hallucinations came, driving me from my enforced and artificial reverie, they confronted me with one of my worst fears. As George Orwell posited in his work *1984*, there is at least one overriding fear buried deep in one's psyche that can be exploited to break your will, if not destroy your sense of self also. The picture he painted was of a specific place known as Room 101, where his immobilized protagonist, Winston Smith, was placed by the arresting authorities to face a starving rat. I am now convinced that such a Room 101 exists for all of us, but not quite in the manner that Orwell predicted. Certainly, such a Room 101 does, with limitations, exist for me; however, my captors did not have to design or construct such a place specifically to suit me, I did it for myself. The experience taught me that while one's will can be sapped and even broken by this part of the process alone, it does not go as far as Orwell believed in destroying one's sense of self. That, which I can only describe as the core or essence of one's being, if carefully concealed in one's compliant behaviour, can be maintained and nurtured, though with difficulty.

The effect that the sleep deprivation had on me made me see my cell as full of spiders – large, hairy ones of Amazonian proportions. These are the only things that produce in me feelings of discomfort bordering on fear. Although my dislike of them is not a full-blown phobia, they give me the creeps, sending a shudder of loathing down my spine as I contemplate them even now.

So there I stood, in my own worst nightmare (as if I was not in it already). Struggle as I might with what little strength of reason remained to me, I could not drive these images from before my eyes. The walls and floor were alive with the bastards, and before long I was experiencing phantom sensations of their crawling across my body. I spent hours in spasms of frenetic movement, brushing at my legs and arms to rid me of the imaginary beasts. Hell had only got worse, and it was my own mind that made it so.

It is strange to say that the next interrogation, when it came, was almost a relief. When I was taken for the next session not long after the delivery of the evening meal, the anticipation of brutality was welcome, beginning my awakening; the first strike across my feet brought me to complete, agonizing awareness. The spiders were gone for the time being.

What was worse, the pain of physical torture, or the descent to the edge of sanity that the hallucinations caused? That is a hard, if not impossible, question for me to answer. What I can say is that in conjunction they were bringing about a rapid deconstruction of my personality and the destruction of my will. In the few moments of painful lucidity that remained to me, I knew I was running on empty. My reserves had disappeared, and all that I had left were fear and blind hope: too much of the former and too little of the latter. Probably my only defence left was a permanent and uncontrolled descent into insanity, and thus oblivion. Why this did not occur leaves me asking more questions, for which I have no adequate answers. With time, I came to recognize that alongside my fear and pain simmered an incandescent melange of hatred, rage, and aggression. Maybe that was my last refuge during the time remaining to me before I was broken. Upon reflection now, I cannot think of anything else.

I know that in my life I have oft-times been too aggressive or combative and have exhibited profound dislikes for some of the people with whom I have dealt, but never have I felt the urge or desire to give vent to rage by killing out of pure hatred. For all of my incarceration that desire or need, for that was what it almost became, remained, sometimes seemingly extinct, only to surface, giving me a focus and a perverted source of strength.

Thus it was that having descended into this state of complete disorientation, I was taken for another interrogation. With the first blows that fell across my feet and buttocks, the pain dispelled any lingering hallucinations, and I returned to a conscious appreciation of my situation. I went through all the motions of resistance to the demands of Ibrahim and Khaled, though that part of me no longer cared what happened and another desperately craved an end, any end, to all the torment. In myself, I felt broken and destroyed, no longer really willing myself to resist, but somehow I continued. The night went through its motions also, and for the first time I felt silent tears pouring from my eyes. No sobs or gasps accompanied them, only the screams that each strike elicited, while the water flowed around my temples, moistening my hair. The tears did not stop during the intervals between the beatings, just slowed in their rate of production, falling down my cheeks and dripping on to my clothes now that I was in a more upright position. My captors laughed and cast aspersions on my masculinity for both my tears and my screams.

That night was the fifth I spent in captivity. During the periods of waiting and of being questioned, I was aware of the screams and cries of other prisoners as they received the unwelcome application of correction. I strained to recognize their voices. It is hard to be accurate or precise in determining the identity of someone from the sounds that I heard. I was trying to compare from memory the normal speech patterns of someone I knew with those of someone under extreme duress. At one point, in the latter part of that evening's third period of lecturing, while alone with Khaled, I thought I had finally identified the voice of someone I knew.

On the night my house was searched, I had noted that the bicycle belonging to Sultan, my house cleaner, was inside the walls of my garden, leading me to believe that he had been ensnared in this nightmare. Though I did not see him then, I was correct in believing that he had been arrested. This glimmer of recognition filled me with both shame and remorse. If I had not been arrested he would still be free. As my mind churned with the weight of these emotions, there came a scream so loud and piercing that Khaled halted in mid-sentence to stare at the door. The sheer power of the agony it contained made the hair stand up on the back of my neck, even as accustomed as I had then become to the horrors of that place. How long that scream lasted I do not know, probably no more than four or five seconds, but it seemed to make time stand still. The silence that followed in its wake was eerie, as Khaled and I stared toward its location in anticipation.

Our state of near mesmerization was broken by a be-thobed officer bursting into our room, speaking agitatedly in Arabic. Khaled sprang from behind the desk and scurried out of the room with the messenger. Unusually, no guard was ushered in to sit with me, so I sat there alone, encumbered by both handcuffs and shackles but with my hands in front of me, wondering what had gone wrong. Eventually I became aware of the fact that I *was* alone, and I began to examine the desk, looking for anything that looked like the keys to my restraints. What I would have done had I found the means to remove them I did not know. The objective of becoming unencumbered was all that mattered; my desperation would have directed my actions from that point.

From beyond the office I could hear the opening and closing of doors and terse shouted words in Arabic. Whatever was happening, it was obviously of grave import. After a few minutes of futile perusal, I gave up on my task and stared out of the window into the night. Soon, when the furore outside subsided, the door opened and Khaled entered, accompanied by another officer and two uniformed guards. They stood me up, placed a blindfold over my eyes, then guided me back to my cell.

The blindfold had been applied in haste, providing me with a limited view of the floor for a few feet in front of me. By inclining my head just a little, I could get a reasonable view of the people moving in the hallway. I am certain this was unintentional, and to be frank, I would not have minded being spared what I next saw. As we arrived at the stairwell, I noticed the floor and the descending steps were smeared with a red fluid. As I walked downstairs, my feet could not avoid smearing it further. I could feel the liquid seep through the thin cloth of my socks, leaving a sensation of both stickiness and slipperiness, a somewhat contradictory impression, but that was the sense of it.

I knew that it was blood, quite a copious amount of it. It dawned on me that it had previously been an integral part of the poor bastard whose screams I had heard. Whatever had been done to him, it was severe enough to cause a major haemorrhage, probably resulting in his death.

When finally I was attached to the door of my cell, I went over in my mind the events I had witnessed moments before. I concluded that the blood that now stained my feet belonged to Sultan, and that he was probably dead. So it was that I came to believe I had inadvertently played a part in the demise of a poor Indian man, whose passing left behind a widow and two young daughters who had been dependent on the small remittances he sent from his various jobs. The sense of guilt that I now felt was overwhelming. I believed myself responsible for what had just happened, that his blood was on my hands. These thoughts did not, at that time, help my fragile emotional state. Feeling responsible for the death of another, no matter how indirectly, is not an easy burden to bear, and certainly not under the circumstances I then found myself in. In time, I would learn to use this sense of responsibility to motivate me in my actions, but originally all it did was add to my sense of futility and hopelessness.

I have often wondered whether the events I witnessed that night had been staged to frighten me. The whole thing could have been a performance, but I am sure it was not, particularly with the information I obtained after my release. At that time, though, primary among my reasons for believing that it was not staged and that some ill-fated individual had died that night, was the behaviour of my captors. Khaled and his squalid coterie were, and probably still are, unsubtle in everything they do. Their acting abilities were risible and transparent to me, even in the state they had reduced me to. The sense of panic and urgency that this incident caused was too real, and the expressions on the faces of my captors unguardedly reflected this.

More than two years later, some months after my release, I managed to determine better what happened that night. Having been in prison for as long as I had, and released as hurriedly as I was, I lost contact with several of my friends in Saudi Arabia and had not re-established these links. As a result of my writing a series of newspaper articles, some former colleagues got in touch via the newspaper. One evening in October 2003 I was able to phone a friend with whom I had worked. As I explained what I thought had happened to Sultan, my friend interrupted me, informing me that I was mistaken. He explained that Sultan, whose usual job was as a tea boy at the Fund, had been arrested, but was released within two days and had not been tortured. He also told me that upon his release, Sultan informed some of my colleagues about my fate. Sultan was at least partly aware of what had happened to me, for on the night that my house was searched, he had been arrested entering the property. Thus, while I was shepherded around my house by my captors, so too was he, in order that neither he nor I would catch sight of each other. Although I did not see him, he had managed to catch a glimpse of me and comprehended the difficulties that I would probably face. Sultan informed my colleagues, and they in turn informed both the British and Canadian embassies of my arrest, who would thus have known of my disappearance within five days of my arrest.

As this information was related to me, I felt the burden lift from my shoulders. Sultan had been spared and had not been caught up in my nightmare. The sense of relief, of joy, and of elation that this brought stayed with me for only a brief time. Whose blood was it that I walked through that night in the interrogation centre? In the joy of discovering that Sultan was alive, I had forgotten that someone else must have died instead. Who were they? Did anyone know? Did any government care? To the last question I know the answer to be no. As for my own feelings, I instinctively believed that having gained my own freedom, I now had a duty to speak out not just about the treatment that I received, but also about the treatment that even then was being meted out to those whom I must have left behind. As I watch now the unfolding of current events, I feel this duty more acutely, as hundreds if not thousands are still subject to the inhumane brutality of corrupt dictatorships, and oft-times our own governments collude or assist in this barbarity.

On that night in late December 2000, I had been spared prolonged interrogation through the death of another, and I had my own misery to wallow in, and wallow I did as I stood wrapped in my blanket. Soon the morning meal arrived, and I went through the motions of eating, giving myself as much time as possible to sit on the mattress and stretch out my legs. I attended to my rice diary, for what it was worth, and then called for the guard. Once in the toilet, I stripped off and washed as best I could. I took my socks and began to scrub them under the tap, watching streaks of rose-tinted water drain away. I replaced my clothes, slipping the wet socks onto my feet; their coolness gave some little momentary relief from the burning pain. In the company of a guard, I returned to my cell, to sleepless anticipation, and whatever new depredations lay before me.

The rest of the day passed in something of a haze. I think I was taken to the doctor twice, but am unsure if that was the case. I was little more than a shell of my former self, my nerves stretched taut, and my mind flitting in and out of a semblance of conscious thought. Enforced daydreams of pleasant events were interspersed with hallucinations that grew ever more bizarre. Spiders danced their merry tarantellas across my body; oversized loaves of bread, tomatoes, and joints of meat, bloody and dripping, appeared just out of reach. Through all this I kept repeating the simple mantra "Hold on." But what was I holding on for – rescue? That I knew would not come. I understood that my captors could not and would not release me in my current condition. That being the case, they would need to succeed in their aims before negotiation, if any, concerning my release could occur. Thus, even in my tormented and near demented state, I was certain that I would remain locked in this situation quite possibly permanently. If I was right in that assumption, as time has proven me to be, my holding on was only continuing my suffering to no ultimate purpose, for I was already damned. Still I repeated the mantra ad nauseam, for I had to hold on for my own sense of self, if for nothing else. I knew I would break soon enough, but each hour I resisted was an hour that I was not owned. In my few moments of lucidity, I knew that this was not as bad as it could get, that all I could do was endure and suffer, for nothing would spare me. In this I was right.

When finally the evening meal arrived, I knew another session would soon begin. I could not imagine it being otherwise. Like a zombie, I was led up to the interrogation room, and it began. Waiting, beatings, and lectures and questions followed one after the other. At one point during the first lecture session, which was jointly held by Khaled and Ibrahim, I was shown an A4-sized exercise book with a light green cover. It was the type of thing I remembered from my early schooldays, though here its use was less innocent. Ibrahim opened it, showing me the handwritten text it contained, but holding it far enough away that I could not quite make out the words. As he flicked through the pages, I was sure that I recognized the handwriting it contained and the signature affixed at the end, even though I was unable to read the words. It belonged to one of my fellow detainees, confirming his presence in this place.

When this silent demonstration was over Khaled simply intoned, "You will confess – your friend did."

No names were mentioned, but I took this as another attempt to show me that any resistance was futile, as others, whose arrest I suspected, had already been broken. Oddly, this fact and the manner in which it was presented had no effect on me. I knew others had been arrested, I knew they were being tortured, and I knew that they had their breaking points, as did I. If this was to make me more pliable, it did not, but I was becoming more pliable.

Brought to my feet, The Spiv held my arms, while Ibrahim and Khaled approached me. In Ibrahim's hands was the axe handle, collected from the floor behind the desk. Standing before me, he spoke, Khaled translating, telling me what was about to happen (as if I would not comprehend without his graphic hints). He punctuated his statements by tapping the left side of my head with his toy to the rhythm of his speech. As his fervour and anger intensified, so too did the force with which I was hit, until once again I felt something crack in my lower jaw. All I did, and in reality could do, was stand there mutely. When he was finally bored with this part of the game, I was led away to the inevitable.

Sometime after midnight but before dawn prayer, during the third or fourth round of falanga, as the tears flowed, I could take no more and something broke inside me. The feeling was palpably real, a phantom physical sensation reinforcing the crumbling of my emotional will. My spine seemed to crack and become malleable, as my mind caved in to the pain I was enduring. It seemed as if the physical form of my whole body had been nothing more than the manifestation of my spirit. Now with that destroyed, my body felt limp and formless, like that of a jellyfish.

I screamed and begged to confess, to tell them what they wanted to hear, but my entreaties seemed to fall upon deaf ears. The beating continued, blows fell across my feet, buttocks, and scrotum, no matter how loudly I screamed my willingness to comply. Had my voice become so incoherent? Did they not understand what I was saying? Did they not realize that they had broken me? I suspect that they knew, but such was the pleasure they derived from my destruction, they were loath for it to end. Moreover, they could have thought that I was trying to trick them, though surely the desperation of my cries would have told them I was not. When finally they lowered me down and led me back across the hall for questioning, I do not know how many times I had offered to confess, but it seemed like hundreds and it seemed like an hour before the end of the beating.

Khaled, Ibrahim, and The Spiv sat me down on the chair. I was asked if I would confess to killing Christopher Rodway. That was all they asked, the other accusations were left out, and though some would be revisited at a later stage, they seemed for now to be forgotten. I said I would and was asked what I had done. I simply repeated back to them everything they had told me I had done, implicating only myself and leaving out details of their stated involvement of Sandy Mitchell or Raf Schvyens. This seemed to satisfy them, for I was given an empty exercise book and required to write down what I had said.

As I began to write, I knew there were details I could not give them beyond the general description they had provided so far. I wondered if such extra detail would be important or necessary. I had no idea about any of the timings of the event or even the exact nature of the device that was planted on Christopher Rodway's car. Still I had enough information that this, my initial confession, filled five pages. All the while I was writing, they remained silent, affording me at least a little relief from the sound of their voices. What is strange is that I felt emotionally numb at the moment I was writing out this confession and those immediately following. I knew that I was innocent, but also that I was confessing to a crime that carries the death penalty. I felt no fear of that specific consequence of providing my confession. Nor did I feel any guilt for the use to which my confession would be put in intimidating other prisoners. I just hoped, forlornly, that I would have to endure no more.

When I was finished writing, I was required to initial each page, putting my signature and the date at the end. This last detail took a while for they had to decide if I was to use the Gregorian or Heijira date. When eventually it was decided, I entered "23rd December 2000." An ink pad was produced and I put my thumbprint below my signature. With that they left, taking the book with them, leaving me in the company of another uniformed supernumerary.

They had been gone for what seemed a considerable period of time, for I heard dawn prayer being called and saw the first glimmering of daylight through the window. When eventually they returned, I could tell by the look on their faces that they were not happy with what I had written. My heart sank, as I instantly contemplated a return to being beaten. I was right to assume that they were not pleased, but all they required was that I put the time of my movements in the confession.

So, using the same exercise book I began again writing out the details of my actions. Supposedly I had collected the bomb from my kitchen where I had stored it, driven over to the Rodways' house, and planted it on their vehicle. Now I learned that the device was detonated by remote control. Thus, I had waited until the Rodways had left their house, followed their vehicle onto Ouraba Road, pressed the remote-control detonator, and then driven away. From Khaled I had gathered enough information on the time and events that my suggestions apparently satisfied them. This whole business of writing my confession by gathering information from my captors was surreal. So too was the scenario that they had constructed. That at least gave me some pleasure, for I was sure that if this confession ever saw the light of day, no one in their right mind would believe it, other than the twisted minds of my captors and their mentors. Once again, upon completion of my magnum opus, I initialled, signed, dated, and thumb-printed it. The book was collected and I was left with the uniformed guard. As I sat, I was able to look out of the window and experience the full emergence of daylight for the first time in over six days.

The process of writing and rewriting my confession occurred twice more before they seemed finally satisfied. Nearly all the information each version contained had been provided by my interrogators, Khaled and Ibrahim. With each change required, they would push me to give further details, only to provide them when, through my obtuse lack of comprehension and knowledge, I was unable to guess the details they wanted. It was curiously easy to give them what they wanted, considering the fact that I knew nothing of the events that I was describing and effectively was counter-interrogating them for the information. It was obvious to me that their attempts to get me to guess accurately about the crimes of which I was accused were their means of justifiably claiming that the information had come directly from me. There is too little that I guessed properly for them to be able to make that claim, so frequently their frustration and anger showed at my apparent lack of cooperation. This obtuseness was not lack of cooperation, but was brought on by not knowing the details of the crime beyond what had been reported in the press, by a sluggish mind deprived of sleep, and by my occasionally ineffective attempts to fathom what they needed to be satisfied. I had no desire to be beaten again, and the easiest way to avoid that was to give them what they wanted. To do that, I had first to get the information from them. Thus every misstep I made would be followed by a correction on their part, such was their zeal to get my story right.

With the last of my written confessions over, Khaled and Ibrahim pronounced themselves satisfied, and I was led back to my cell. Even before being chained to the door, I was collected and taken to see the doctor. As I limped away after the cursory examination, I heard the prayer call and realized that it was midday. Collecting my wits as best I could, I tried to calculate the number of hours that I had been in prison, given that I was now well into my seventh day in their hands. I wondered how much longer I would remain alive in this place. I hoped it would not be much longer. I had accepted death as inevitable and hoped only for a respite from pain until then.

Back in my cell, I stood again wrapped in my blanket, waiting. No food had been left for me, nor had any water. For some reason the guards did not let me go the toilet, and as I became desperate to urinate, I simply opened my trousers with my free hand and relieved myself on the wall by the cell door, directing the stream as far from my feet and the mattress as I could. This action provoked an immediate reaction, one I was to remember and to exploit. My actions had been observed through the CCTV cameras, to the obvious consternation and disgust of the watchers. They sent the guards to my cell.

Just as I finished relieving myself for the first time in more than twenty-four hours, the door flap opened. As I awkwardly rearranged myself, I looked into the angry eyes of two guards, who poured forth a hostile stream of invective, ending it with a single English word: donkey. Within their own culture, this word is quite an insult, but it loses something in translation, sounding little more than absurd under the circumstances. I giggled inanely at their anger. They spat on me through the bars. The cell door was unlocked and opened, pulling me forward, as the guards peered into the cell to observe the puddle that was now draining toward the only exit.

I became the recipient of more of their anger, as they pushed me against the door and punched me repeatedly in the back. Whether they were pulling their punches I cannot say, however the blows felt light and ineffectual. It seemed to be a hallmark of my captors that most of their attempts at physical assault had effect only when implements were used.

Having been spat on and punched, I was left alone to stand in the puddle of my own urine that had now reached the doorway. I was still sleepless, and the hours passed with only a few minutes of lucidity breaking the realm of confusion that my mind had descended into. The prayer calls came and went, food was delivered, and I was allowed to sit on my now damp mattress. Again I attended to my rice diary and waited for the tray to be collected. For whatever reason, it was not, and the final prayer of the day was intoned. I huddled under my blanket, wondering at the change.

During this time, I heard another voice that I recognized, emanating from the cell immediately to my left. It was Sandy Mitchell stating his number in answer to a guard's question. I wanted to call out to him, but my fear overrode my impulse to make my presence known and pass on any message of support or apology. I heard the door of his cell open and close, accompanied by the shuffling movements of his departure. His presence confirmed what I had suspected.

Maybe my captors were satisfied. Hoped raised its foolish and futile head. I should have known better, but fear and despair often lead to unreasonable delusions such as that. At some point the door of my cell opened, and I was told to stand. As I did so handcuffs and shackles were immediately placed upon me. Just as the blindfold was being put on, I was able to catch sight of a wristwatch. The time on its analogue face was sometime near half-past eleven. I had been left to sit, almost comfortably, for about four hours. I had wasted the time in near lucid anticipation, when I could have snatched a few hours' sleep. I would not make that mistake again. Quite possibly the worst was over.

Khaled, Ibrahim, and The Spiv were waiting for me, for as I entered the room and the blindfold was removed, there they were in their appointed positions, exercise books placed on the desk. I also recognized my briefcase lying on the far right of the desk. They acted out their pleasure in seeing me, welcoming me to their company in our new spirit of cooperation. The transformation was as remarkable as it was transparent. I was told that there were problems with my confessions and I would need to go over them and make corrections. So it all began again – they talked over things that were wrong, I responded with questions that elucidated what I thought was required. Then I would start to write my confessions in light of the new information gleaned. The confessions would be taken away, brought back, and I would start again with a new composition.

During this time my captors behaved in a manner that could almost be called civilized. Khaled opened my briefcase to retrieve my cigarettes, allowing me to smoke. I noted that my case contained my wallet, mobile phone, cigarettes, and lighter, but was devoid of any of the documents it had held. I was served the occasional cup of tea. Everything was done to make me relax, to encourage my cooperation, and to establish an emotional link. I trusted none of it, motivated only by my need to avoid a return to the brutality of torture. I was encouraged in my suspicions of their behaviour, for after each time I completed writing a new version, I was left alone with The Spiv, whose affectionate attentions took on a greater urgency now that we were alone together. The cycle continued well past dawn prayer before Khaled and Ibrahim announced that they were satisfied.

I was returned to my cell where I found a food tray waiting. Rather than indulge myself immediately, I asked to go to the toilet, for which permission was granted. I enjoyed this respite, taking as much time as possible over relieving and cleaning myself, before returning to my cell. I ate slowly, wondering if I would be allowed to sleep. When I finished, I pushed the tray away, leaned back against the wall, willing sleep to come, seeing if I could get away with it. I received my answer almost immediately as the door was opened and the tray collected. Told to stand up, I complied, and found myself again chained to the door.

Thus the eighth day passed much as the previous ones, though my body did not seem to be in as much pain as on the others. I was still in considerable distress, but the absence of any physical torture the night before allowed my body some small chance to recover. Though still desperate for sleep, I was thankful for this small comfort. As I stood there alone, my thoughts kept returning to my confessions. I felt it was cowardice that made me confess. It is said that confession is good for the soul. If that is the case, then providing false confession is its exact antithesis, even when it is a necessary thing to do. A deep sense of shame and guilt now replaced the numbness.

XXX //

These runaway thoughts and emotions were a cancer eating at my soul, corroding my sense of self-worth, contributing to the emotional destruction wrought by my captors. I kept trying to calculate what would come next, what the next stage would require of me. I had confessed to a crime that carries the death penalty. Given the political and social climate in Saudi Arabia, I could see no way out of my predicament or any alternative to such a sentence being carried out. Even though I had not heard of any westerner being executed in the Kingdom, there would have to be a first time and the judicial system was (and still is) perfectly capable of carrying out this sentence on hundreds of people of other nationalities. I could not see how the Saudi Arabian government would not avail itself of this opportunity to show its resolve and thus satisfy the bloodlust of its more fundamentalist anti-western social elements. Oddly, the prospect of meeting my death at the hands of an executioner did not actually bother me at all, even now that it was no longer something theoretical; with my confession, it was my future. It provided only one concern. I hoped that the event itself would be over quickly, causing not much pain. I hoped that the executioner's blade would be sharp, his arm strong, and his aim sure. Beyond that, the prospect of death offered not fear but relief. If it was the price to pay for the end to the pain, it was a price I would pay, though it was not a fate that I deserved.

With these odd lucid thoughts, mixed with periods of emotional despondency and hallucination, the day went by. When the evening meal arrived, I was allowed to sit once again. As I had resolved to make use of the time attempting to sleep, I pushed the food away, leaned back against the wall, and closed my eyes. I know I slept but it was only briefly, for the meal had been delivered after the fourth prayer call of the day and was collected before the last. At most I had an hour of sitting braced against the wall, allowing myself to drift into unconsciousness. I doubt I even had that long, but it was interestingly refreshing given how brief the time was and how deprived of sleep I was.

Not long after the last prayer, I was removed from the door and taken upstairs. Whatever illusions I had about the brutality being over were shattered when the Three Stooges arrived and I was forcibly hauled to my feet and pushed back against the wall. Ibrahim began by punching and slapping me repeatedly, focusing most of his attention on my testicles, all the while shouting at me in Arabic. Khaled's translations told me that I was a spy for the British government, intent on hurting the Saudi Arabian government. So the rants continued, until I was hauled across the corridor and subjected to falanga. I had no idea what they wanted exactly, for what they had said to me did not make sense.

There is no government any more supportive of the Al Saud regime than the British government. The government of the United States has provided the Al Sauds with assurance of their security, but so too does Whitehall. The degree to which British politicians, ambassadors, and civil servants supplicate before the Al Sauds, literally prostrating themselves at their feet, is quite astonishing if not actually nauseating. So to hear that I was a spy acting to destabilize their regime, in the pay of a government that actually does all in its power to aid and succour the Al Sauds, was bizarre at the least. I could not understand what they wanted from me nor could I comprehend the reasons behind such statements. Where in hell was this going, I kept asking myself?

The cycle had returned to its previous pattern of waiting, brutality, and lecturing, with the lectures listing all the things that

demonstrated I was a spy: dual nationality, work and travel conducted in other parts of the Middle East, compass, monocular,
desert trekking, education, and qualifications. Each of these was
paraded before me as proof that would be used to confirm my supposed operational capacity. Even the nature of my employment in
the Kingdom would be used as proof. I foolishly protested my
innocence in response to their accusations of espionage. I told them
repeatedly that not only were such statements false, they were also
totally ludicrous considering the security assistance provided by the
British government to their country.

I should have simply stuck to a plain denial without adding
such an obvious explanation of the insanity of their charges, for
my discursiveness impinged directly on the cultural ego of these
three. My statements were met by their arrogant denials that Saudi
Arabia needed any assistance in its defence, that its glorious security forces would defend it against all invaders. The reality is
significantly different, for during the first Gulf war, when Saddam's
forces occupied Khafji, a town just inside the Saudi-Kuwait border,
the defending battalions of the same security forces were almost in
Riyadh before the Iraqi battalions were within sight of the border.
Theirs is an army that needs retraining every time it is given a tea
break. Yet before me were three individuals who demanded that I
buy into their propaganda on the expertise, determination, and
bravery of their fellows responsible for the defence of the Kingdom.
However the only thing I knew of in which the Saudi security
forces demonstrated expertise was the brutal subjugation of a
cowed and compliant population. Fortunately as I thought this, my
fear restrained my anger, keeping my tongue still.

The night ended as could be expected, not long after the dawn
prayer call, and I returned again to my less than comfortable
accommodation. I now had no idea where this was going or what
they had in mind. It was one thing confessing to having blown up
the Rodways' car, which was strange enough. It was another thing

entirely to confess to something that made even less sense. It was also one thing for me to betray myself, but somehow more difficult for me to betray my country. For some reason, this made me resist again, even though I had been broken so very recently.

I have tried to analyze the reasons for my emotional reaction and my attempt at that moment to engage in renewed resistance. I have not been able to come up with anything that explains things to my satisfaction. Try to imagine one's nerves stretched taut with fear, your mind fighting at the edge of sanity, your body dirty, bruised, and swollen, with the prospect of death seemingly a relief. In tandem my emotions ran from guilt through hopelessness: guilt because of my weakness in confessing and because of my belief that indirectly I caused the death of my house cleaner; hopelessness, for my horizon had become one bounded only by my destruction. Yet, somehow, for a time, my will to resist had returned. It would, however, be short-lived.

Throughout my interrogations another anomaly had been in my thoughts, and this filled my mind then. During the initial interrogation sessions, threats had been made against me, against my friends, and against their spouses. The supposed crimes of which I was accused were stated to have taken place as part of a conspiracy involving Sandy and Raf. That at least was the story during the first day; however, since that time I had been questioned and lectured as if I were Riyadh's answer to the Unabomber. Few mentions of my personal life beyond accusations of homosexuality were ever made.

This change of direction, the lack of a more personal aspect in the interrogations, came as a surprise. One thing is certain, whenever interrogators wish to soften you up, they probe for areas of emotional weakness, while at the same time engendering it via the interrogation process itself. Khaled had asked extensive questions during the first couple of days concerning the nature of all my friendships in Saudi Arabia. I happily named a number of departed expatriates and Saudi Arabian colleagues who in truth were little more than acquaintances. On questions relating to my family, I answered in apparent honesty, stating that there was little connection with my relatives, parents included. This is at least true in part, for at my own choice I have been estranged from my mother for over twenty-five years. My relationship with my father is, on the other hand, very good, though it has its moments when we lock horns.

Therefore, for my interrogators I must have presented something of an enigma. I could not be threatened with never again seeing my wife or children, nor could they be threatened. Under the circumstances, being a bachelor had certain advantages. Regarding other relationships, particularly familial ones, there appeared to be no levers for them to pull, although in this they were mistaken. When they did discover my close relationship with my father, it did not actually work to their advantage as it might have in this early phase. Instead it worked against them, providing me with a focal point for the release of my rage. Initially then, all they did was make a few vague threats toward friends and their families. Not that this made much apparent difference to me. On the surface all their threats elicited was a shrug of the shoulders, although at a deeper level I felt a more profound sense of concern for my friends' safety.

During my time in prison, and even since then, I have wondered if their cursory probing of my personal life led in fact to a more rapid and severe physical coercion. As I came gradually to comprehend their lack of efficiency in the psychological aspects of their trade, it began to make sense to me that their initial inquiries led them up an apparent blind alley, giving them nothing personal about me that could be manipulated. Certainly, since my release, my conversations with fellow detainees have shown me that in some cases the interrogators spent more time during the initial phases on the manipulation of their personal information, and thus on psychological coercion, delaying the onset of brutality or at least prolonging the periods between beatings.

My singularity, independence, and lack of formal or understandable personal relationships threw them back on pure brutality to break my will. Had they actually bothered to peruse the personal material they had confiscated from me, they might have been more assiduous in profiling me psychologically. In the months and weeks ahead, as I mused over this information, I saw that their expertise was pronounced and demonstrable only in the simpler areas of physical brutality. They were simply lazy.

As I turned my mind again to my immediate predicament, I was once again shocked by the events of the previous night. The hope that had been nurtured by the initial easing of the brutality died a death. My confession had been in vain, it achieved only a day's respite. All I could do now was to hold on through each stage, resisting the torture for as long as possible, buying brief respites by giving them what they wanted to hear at propitious moments. It was not the greatest of strategies, but it was the only one I could construe. It was obvious that the brutality had not ended and would occur every time something was required of me. Therefore, I had no other option.

Almost immediately upon my return to the cell, I was taken to the doctor. It must have been earlier than he was used to, as his demeanour was somewhat sleepy and confused. This time, though, he spent considerable time examining my feet and legs. I expect that he had been instructed to do so, given his prior cursory examinations. The swelling and creeping discolouration must have been causing concern to my interrogators, though doubtless not as much as it was to me. Not that the examination resulted in anything, but he did his duty and then sent me back to my cell.

When I entered the cellblock, I asked to go to the toilet, and was granted permission. As I disrobed and examined myself, I noticed bloodstains in my underwear, and I saw that even though there were no apparent breaks in the skin, sticky plasma had extruded through the skin, more evidence of my rapidly deteriorating condition. I cleaned myself as best I could, before returning to the cell for another long day. Later, on this the ninth day, I was collected just after the fourth prayer before any food was delivered, taken again to the office for interrogation. For all my exhaustion and pain, I was somehow absurdly aware of my surroundings and circumstances, trying to fathom what would come next without letting fear run off with my imagination.

Even with this attempt to curb my paranoia, I sensed that something was wrong when, after waiting for my interrogators, only The Spiv arrived, taking a seat beside me. There was no sign of the other two, and The Spiv indulged himself in his affectionate attentions once again, stroking my hair and cheeks, caressing my legs, and roughly squeezing my testicles. Affection might well be a misnomer for his attention, as it was nothing but sexual intimidation as far as I was concerned. I doubt also that he bore me an ounce of affectionate regard, but I had long since realized that there was something more personal in his touch than would be required to create the impression of a sexual threat. There was an edge of real longing that permeated his actions, making them all the more terrifying and unsettling.

Khaled and Ibrahim did not arrive, and I had begun to wonder how long I would have to spend alone with The Spiv. Suddenly he stood, replacing the blindfold that had been removed when I entered the office. As I was grabbed by the arm, I stood also and was guided across the corridor. The thought of falanga was foremost on my mind, but another nagging fear kept surfacing. Things seemed different, and I was not wrong. My progress was halted by my legs bumping into the foreshortened desk, and I felt The Spiv pushing close to me, the cloying stench of his sickly sweet cologne almost making me retch. I felt his arm snake around my waist, his hand fumbling with the buttons on the waistband of my trousers.

My cuffed hands reflexively pushed his away while I screamed no, as I understood his intentions.

The Spiv shouted back, slapping me hard across the head and pushing me down onto the desk. This made his task of undoing my trousers more difficult, though unfortunately not impossible. With a struggle he managed to undo them, forcefully pulling my trousers and underwear down, leaving me exposed and even more vulnerable. For all my writhing attempts to stand, I had been unable to prevent him from getting my trousers and underwear down. My little resistance only succeeded in inflaming his ire or his desire, though I am not sure there was a difference. Maybe the struggle was part of the foreplay necessary for his arousal – that I cannot say for sure but I suspect it was.

As he continued to push me down across the table, I could feel the cloth of his thobe against my skin, the hardness of his erection pressing through it. Slowly, I could feel the material being shifted until I felt the heat of his skin against mine, and the pulsing movement of his penis hard against my buttocks. By now my screams of no had subsided to a desperate pathetic whisper. I was powerless to do anything to prevent this, ultimately the last possible violation. All I could hope for was that he would lose interest at the last minute.

Then he penetrated me and that hope evaporated. As he separated the cheeks of my buttocks, I felt him thrust his erection against my anus. Fiercer thrusts came as my reflexes contracted my sphincter. This little resistance was futile and with a sharp piercing pain, and the sensation of tearing, I felt him enter me. Waves of pain, nausea, and humiliation passed over me, as he urgently thrust against me. My whole body was tensed against this violation, but it did nothing beyond inducing cramps and the tearing of muscles in my legs and lower torso. As I think back on this now, I feel my body grow rigid and the gorge rise in my throat. It was painful physically, but more painful was the emotional shock that it provided.

What was happening was the violation of my last vestige of physical and thus psychological integrity. I felt so violated and degraded in a way the other brutality could not achieve. I now understand in the most intimate way why rape or pseudo-sexual violation with blunt instruments is so much part of the torturers' array of techniques. It is an effective means in the immediate term of denigrating the subject and destroying their sense of self and personal integrity. In the long term, the emotional scars of such an act last longer than the physical and can be more devastating. With regard to its effects on me, it certainly worked against me as I lay across the desk, silent tears streaming down my face.

While The Spiv took his pleasure from my semi-prone form, the door opened and closed, and I heard a voice that I recognized. It was that of Khaled, who cackled excitedly, before stating that my enjoyment of this event was proof of my homosexuality. How being raped proves such a thing, I am at a loss to understand. I would have thought it proved something else, something more demeaning about the nature of my captors. As Khaled laughed, I felt the force of The Spiv's motions intensify with the increased throbbing I felt inside me. I heard a long gasp, I felt his final spasms, and his body relaxed against mine.

As he separated from me, I prayed that this was the end of it, but it was not to be. I tried to stand, but felt hands push me back down, heard the rustle of cloth, and felt again the warmth of someone's skin against mine, and the hardness of an erection pressing between my buttocks. From the fetid stench of his breath, I knew that Khaled was going to have his turn. I wondered if being second in line discomfited his fastidious sensibilities. Obviously not, as the urgency of his thrusts increased and my nostrils were filled with his stinking exhalations as he panted away excitedly. Finally he too finished, pulling away from contact with me, leaving me totally violated, totally ashamed, and weeping. As the pressure holding me to the desk was relieved, my legs buckled and I slid to the floor. Lying there crying, I felt waves of peristaltic contractions in my lower abdomen and further pain from the pressure in my colon and anal sphincter as a reflex evacuation of my bowels occurred. I tried to contain myself, to stop it from happening, for I was sure that I would be punished if I lost control. I was not successful; I felt myself, in a manner almost disjointed and separate from reality, defecate rapidly and violently onto the dirty carpeting upon which I lay.

The stench from my faeces was overpowering in that small room. Khaled and The Spiv were extremely annoyed. I wonder what they expected, something fragrant, or maybe even a thank you? My response, though involuntary, was appropriate if not a little problematic. In his fury, The Spiv grabbed me by the hair, dragging me up onto my knees, away from the mess that I had just created. Then, as quickly as I had gained my knees, I was pushed forward, off balance again. The smell of my faeces drew closer, and I knew that I was being pushed into it. When finally my face came level with the floor, I felt its wet, sludge-like texture as my face was pushed into its reeking semen-filled mass.

All I could hear now were the angry barks of Khaled.

"Eat it. Eat it," he said repeatedly.

I kept my mouth tightly shut, begging myself not to vomit and add to the mess, as I felt my stomach heave, and my mouth tried to open in response. In this small thing I was successful, and I managed to control myself. When they finally tired of this game, together they pulled to my feet and told me to pull up my trousers. This I found inordinately difficult, for as I bent over, dizziness engulfed me and I could feel a sort of tingling in my head. Eventually I succeeded and, gagging, was led from the room across the corridor to another. From its sound and smell, I thought it was a toilet.

In response to a command, I raised my arms and was released from my handcuffs. Told to remove my now dirty blindfold, I did so. I found myself in a toilet standing next to Khaled and another plainclothes officer. Neither could hide their disgust at the odour I exuded, as they tried to breathe through their mouths alone, holding the tails of their gutras across their faces as impromptu gas masks. Without asking permission, I immediately started to run some water in one of the sinks that was in front of me and began the process of cleaning my shit-smeared face. Gratefully I discovered a dispenser of liquid soap on one of the sinks and liberally made use of it to wash my face, hands, and blindfold reasonably thoroughly, replacing my stench with that of the cheap soap. At least I felt a little cleaner, but it would be some time before I felt truly clean inside.

I asked permission to enter one of the cubicles, disappearing for a brief moment of privacy. Free of handcuffs and shackles, I was able to remove my trousers and underwear. Making use of both toilet paper and the shower-like accoutrement with a flexible hose common to toilets in Saudi Arabia, I continued to clean myself, removing the residue of faeces and semen from my anal and scrotal regions. I noted that I was bleeding, but not profusely. This observation changed when, as a spasm of cramp passed through my abdomen, I sat on the toilet and again involuntarily evacuated my bowels. I passed little solid matter, but seemed to fill the toilet with blood. That worried me little, but it made me wonder what my corpse would present if ever it was subjected to an autopsy. I didn't expect that my body could take much more, and death by rectal haemorrhage would be apt for I was well and truly fucked. I could not help but smile at the perverse logic of my humour.

Robotically, I dressed and rejoined Khaled. I was blindfolded, shackled, and handcuffed with my hands behind my back. We headed down the corridor away from the original interrogation office. Initially this gave me the impression that I was to be returned to my cell. However, just as I realized that the distance covered was too long, a door was opened and I was pushed through it, to hear the familiar voice of Ibrahim.

When I entered this room, hands grabbed me, pushing me down. Forced violently off my feet, I fell forward, face hitting the floor, breath leaving me with a gasp. As I again struggled to regain some semblance of composure, my feet were pulled up by the shackles and attached to my wrists and by another pair of handcuffs. While this was being done, I felt something else being passed between my feet and attached to the handcuffs on my wrists. I was not sure of exactly what this new item was, nor what was happening; it soon became apparent, though, for I felt my hands being pulled backward and my body lifting from the floor. Suspended upside down, the entire weight of my body was being transmitted through my wrists and shoulders. What had been passed between my feet was some sort of cable, and now I found myself hanging in midair, ankles attached to wrists.

Given this awkward position, gravity tried to rotate my body downward, but was prevented from doing so by the cable that suspended me. As Khaled would explain to me later, this position was gleefully referred to as "the swing." In this folded, inverted position, I felt myself rotating slowly on the axis of the cable until hands steadied me in position. How far off the floor I hung, I do not know, but it cannot have been more than twenty to fifty centimetres, otherwise Ibrahim would have needed a ladder to gain the height necessary to perform his task. As it was, his access was at least a little restricted, for when the blows inevitably fell upon my feet, they did so in a longitudinal plane, each foot struck separately. Gone were the strikes that hit both feet simultaneously. Gone also was the axe handle, during this session at least, for the breadth of each strike was narrower and somewhat more intense though the force was transmitted on a smaller area.

As the first blows fell, my body went into a spasm and jerked with the pain, only to be steadied from its involuntary gyrations by hands gripping me on the upper thighs. Not content with my feet as targets, Ibrahim must silently have directed his assistants to turn me toward him, as I felt the hands now rotate my body while my spasms died down. Having had ten or so blows to my feet, I now received the same across my lower abdomen just above the pubic area. When this was finished, a single somewhat lighter blow fell upon my genital area. As was his trademark, Ibrahim struck there with remarkable precision, avoiding my testicles, directing the force of the blow on the swollen stump of my penis. Once this, the last blow of the cycle, was completed, there seemed to be a pause of a few moments before the hands rotated me again to present my feet to Ibrahim. I am unable to say with any accuracy how long this lasted or how many cycles of feet-abdomen-scrotum occurred, though at least seven or eight did before I lost count.

With each blow, my body danced and strained like a crazed marionette and tears flowed from my eyes, soaking my hair. The joints of my wrists and shoulders felt particular pain in this position, feeling even more as if dislocation was only an instant away. I screamed like a banshee, leaving my speaking voice hoarse and ragged. I begged to know what more they wanted, what more was needed, but my screams were in vain, for nothing was said to me.

When finally I was lowered to the floor, I was a gibbering tear-sodden wreck, with no resemblance to what had once been a man. Eventually they released part of my restraints, and I was dragged upright, led from the room and back to my cell. No questions had been asked of me, only sodomy and beating were on the schedule that night. Though effectively brief in comparison to other sessions, that night was undeniably brutal and possibly the most psychologically destructive. I didn't bother going to the toilet on my return to the cellblock, a routine I had tried to establish from the start. It didn't cross my mind. When food was delivered just before dawn prayer, I could not even be bothered to eat or drink, I just sat there with my back against the cell wall, drifting in and out of sleep, or unconsciousness, during the brief time allotted for eating. I no longer felt the rage and hatred that had been supporting me.

Emotionally all that was left to me was fear, and even that was not as enervating as it had been. Whatever personal integrity I had was shattered and I was left as a physical husk devoid of personality.

This emotional limbo, a feeling of total nothingness, lasted for some hours before I felt the faintest of stirrings of my own psychological presence. Gradually painful emotions evoked by this latest violation roused themselves, bringing forth silent tears. I did not try to stop them flowing, just stood there allowing the catharsis they brought to give me some relief. Deliberately, as the tears slowed, I forced my mind to retreat to places more pleasant, to dwell upon memories and imaginings that would help alleviate some of my pain. It took every ounce of my returning emotional strength to do so, for the mire of emotional despondency that my treatment had created seemed a grasping presence drawing me downward.

It was during this brief period in which my sense of self returned, before the hallucinations of sleep deprivation intervened, that I had what I can only describe as an intellectual and emotional epiphany. I had realized from the earliest moments of my incarceration that I had to keep my mind active and use my memories to help support me through the psychological and physical turmoil, but that was a purely intellectual consideration borne from the wide variety of literature that I had read. Possibly because my emotions were so abraded by what I was being subjected to, my ability to separate my emotions from my intellect had disappeared. The result was an uncontrolled merger of feeling and thought, for me something strange. Whatever the reason, this very precise point of joint emotional and intellectual clarity occurred. So sharp and strong was the moment that it remains a focal or reference point for my memories of that time, creating a series of psychological snapshots somewhat like the before and after scenarios beloved of third-rate advertising executives.

Thus, as I drove myself to focus on my memories and experiences, a single piece of poetry coalesced in my mind. Emerging from the depths of my memories, but feeling as if I had just read the work minutes earlier, I silently recited the words of Richard Lovelace from his poem "To Althea from Prison."

"Stone walls do not a prison make,
Nor iron bars a cage;
Minds innocent and quiet take
That for an hermitage;
If I have freedom in my love,
And in my soul am free;
Angels alone, that soar above,
Enjoy such liberty."

The words recited were strangely soothing and uplifting. This was the first time, but it would not be the last, that an apposite meeting of intellect and emotions would be given definition by poetry, lyrics, or quotations dredged from the recesses of my mind. Sometimes it would be only a line or two, other times entire works would flow from my subconscious profoundly crystallizing the moment. Many works that I would review I had not recalled for years; they were seemingly forgotten, but now and then they surfaced at the most necessary of times.

It was as if, as my own mind was losing the ability to protect me against the onslaught, it reached out from within the stone walls and iron bars in which I was confined to the ideas and feelings of others, drawing from them the necessary strength with which to keep me alive, finding by blind instinct words that had once had meaning for me, and now had an even deeper resonance.

So, as I recited Lovelace over and over, like a newfound mantra, I began again to feel whole, racked with pain, with dread, with shame, but still alive in myself. With the words came the feeling, a gut emotional reaction, that I had come through what was the worst of the violations; though techniques could have been and still

could be applied that would be more physically painful, psychologically it was as bad as it could get. They did in fact own my
body, and I would submit to whatever violation or indignity that
they chose to apply. I knew that physically I could stand only so
much pain before acquiescing to their demands and to each of the
betrayals they would require of me. This I had already demonstrated in my first false confessions. I would have to accept this as
inevitable and not destroy myself with guilt. However, I also understood, in a way more profound than earlier, that I had a place of
retreat, for they could not see inside my head. I would have time
and place to slip my fetters, leaving behind my prison cell, as I
walked in the only place I had ever been free: my thoughts. If access
to that freedom was to be granted through the words of long-dead
poets or troubadours, the words were there for me to remember
and thus unlock the door.

In writing this, I give the impression that this was a long drawn-
out process of thoughts and feelings dancing round each other. In
fact it was a single moment, an instant, a millisecond, when all
these thoughts ran through me at once. Now I cried again, but this
time they were not tears of pain, but purely tears of relief. I had
descended as far emotionally as is possible and found that the survival instincts that protect one's sense of self preserved one small
corner of myself that was fortified through the pen of others. This
corner belonged solely to me. It was a strange feeling, even surreal,
but very human, providing me with a sense of calm I had not felt
for days.

Even the hallucinations when they came were not as trouble-
some as they had been, though they were hardly a pleasure. The
day passed, and while the tension of anticipation was still there, I
felt partially disconnected from it. In the early evening, when
finally I was collected for interrogation, I had a heightened air of
resignation and acceptance that had not been there before. I had
gone over their accusation of my being a spy, and the absurdity had

made me realize that this charge would be more of an embarrassment to Saudi Arabia than it would be to either me or the British
government. To be executed as a murderer or as an intelligence
agent would be little different, for the outcome was the same. What
would it matter to me if I did confess to being a spy? Such a confession would only highlight the ridiculousness of the Saudi government claims in this matter, exposing their attempts to cover up
their own internal terrorist problem. My rediscovered clarity put
such thoughts at the forefront of my mind. Any confession provided on these lines would have no basis in fact; no information of
a sensitive nature would be divulged, for there was none. Thus, to
provide such a confession was more to my advantage than to my
disadvantage, regardless of the embarrassment it would cause. I
knew also that probably I had to provide some further resistance,
but that in the end I would confess.

It was in this frame of mind that I was delivered to the interrogation office to sit alone in anticipation of the arrival of my tormentors. When finally someone arrived, it was The Spiv, all on his
own again. His demeanour could only be described as evilly
amused. He had raped me the day before, and from the expression
on his face, I expected that he would do so again. Without any of
what for him must constitute foreplay, I was hauled to my feet and
led across the hall, not even blindfolded this time. Everything happened pretty much as it did the last time. I was pushed against the
desk, trousers and underwear pulled down, and my anus forcefully
penetrated. It was painful, but not as painful as the first time, nor
was it as humiliating or soul-destroying. I said nothing, not even a
mild protest. I hoped that my mute acceptance would decrease his
pleasure. As he was finishing and he had begun to withdraw, I lay
across the desk not moving, except to try to defecate with him in
close proximity. Somehow this did not happen, even though my
effort caused waves of contraction to pass through my rectum.
Given that I had not eaten in the previous twenty-four hours, there

was probably little if anything to expel. At least I did not have to suffer the further indignity of having my face rubbed in my own excrement like a recalcitrant puppy, though that would have been a fair exchange for covering The Spiv in faeces.

While these thoughts passed through my mind, the door opened. Half-turning my head, I saw that Khaled had now entered the room, and expected that he too would seek gratification. Instead he exchanged angry words with The Spiv, before telling me to pull up my trousers. When I had finished this task, I was led to the toilet where I was allowed to clean myself. With these perfunctory ablutions finished, we returned to the interrogation office where Ibrahim was sitting smugly in his appointed place. I long pondered the exchange that had just occurred between Khaled and The Spiv and can only conclude that unlike the previous day, The Spiv had not had permission to conduct his particular game.

A lecture and questioning session began. Each of us repeated the drill that had been defined over the past ten days. I was told repeatedly that I was a spy for the British government, and I was acting under their orders. I quietly protested that this was not the case, knowing full well that eventually I would confess falsely to it being true. With varying degrees of animation, Ibrahim met my denials with further accusations or reiterations. I was told repeatedly that others had confessed to my being an operative of British intelligence and that they also had witnesses to the meetings that I had had with my controllers. I just kept repeating my denials.

When they finally tired of this, they stood, pulled me to my feet, and blindfolded me. I knew what was coming even before we crossed the hallway. Seated on the dirty carpet, I was arranged for suspension from the metal bar, ready for my session of falanga. The blows fell, I screamed and writhed in agony, trying to hold out, trying to endure. This went on for quite a few cycles of feet-buttocks-scrotum, before I was lowered to the ground and returned to the office to endure another session of their wheedling questions and pontificating, before finally I was left alone to contemplate my future and nurse my abused body.

When eventually Khaled and Ibrahim returned, I was again taken for another session of falanga, which I endured in much the same way as all the others. At some point during the beating, in the midst of my screams, I finally relented and told them that I was a spy. This did not end the beating outright for it continued for some time, while they asked what amounted to rhetorical questions and I screamed my replies. Finally they were finished with the punishment; I was released and placed in one of the chairs that had a moment ago acted as a support for holding me upside down.

Now one of the strangest incidents of my incarceration occurred. As I sat in the chair, Khaled went over with me my new confession, filling in details here and there, and then having me reiterate each new and more complete version. During this time, I heard the door open and someone leave the room. I assumed that I was alone with Khaled while I performed most of my reiterations. Then the door opened again and something was said in almost a whisper to Khaled. He told me not to talk before he left my side and went over to the whisperer. When he came back, he told me that in a moment I would be asked to repeat everything that we had just gone over. He told me that I was not to speak until he told me to and that when I was finished my statement I was to shut up and not ask questions. He departed again, and I heard the door open.

A number of people now entered the room, arranging themselves in front of the chair in which I sat. I leaned back slightly and was able to gain a restricted view through the bottom of the blindfold. There were now five pairs of feet standing in front of me. Three of them belonged to Ibrahim, Khaled, and The Spiv, or at least I assumed so. The fourth pair belonged to someone dressed in sandals and thobe, and I assumed them to belong to another Saudi intelligence officer. It was the fifth pair that provoked a sense of surprise, which I fought hard not to show.

I leaned back a little more and was able to see those before me to just a little above what would be waist height. The owner of the fifth pair of feet was wearing lace-up shoes, unlike the others, who wore slip-on shoes or sandals. This for me was significant, for rarely had I seen any Saudi Arabian wearing shoes that required laces even when wearing western business dress. While some of the younger generation who wore western dress might favour running shoes, the form of footwear that I now saw was unusual for even them. Furthermore, he was wearing long dark grey trousers held up by a simple belt, and a light-coloured shirt. In the dimness of the room I cannot say for certain the exact colour of either the shirt or trousers, but that was what they appeared to me to be. The shirt was short-sleeved for I could see his lower arms as they hung idly at his side. The complexion of his skin appeared light and somewhat freckled, something I would not normally associate with Saudi Arabians; the same could be said for short-sleeved shirts. On his right wrist was a watch with a metallic band and on his left hand was a wedding ring. All these things were unusual. The wristwatch told me he was left-handed, the ring that he was married and probably Christian. The fact that he wore a watch on his right wrist made me think that he was not Saudi, for I had met few Saudis who would admit to being left-handed and had never seen them wear a watch anywhere other than on the left wrist. As for the ring, I had never seen a Saudi Arabian or any Muslim male wearing a wedding ring. In general, the wearing of jewellery by men is frowned on in Saudi society, and even wearing a watch is considered inappropriate by some.

Told by Khaled to repeat what he and I had gone over moments before, I began to recount the fantasy that was the new addition to my confession. Those before me listened silently while I stated that I was employed as a British spy, acting under orders in participating in the bombings. The stated purpose of these events was to embarrass the Saudi Arabian government and to drive a wedge

between the western expatriate community and the local Saudi Arabians in order to prevent too great a familiarity to develop between the communities. As I said these words, I wondered what my listeners would think of them. Was this sequence of events and the putative motivations for them were believable? Yes, apparently. Nothing was said to me then, and the substance of my statement would change little over the ensuing weeks. When I finished, those before me moved away to the door, where they huddled together forming a whispering conclave. Their muffled voices prevented me from hearing anything distinctly, which I found odd. To date all conversations that my captors held in front of me in Arabic were conducted at normal conversational level, for they seemed to be comfortable in their belief that I spoke no Arabic (which was at least true). So why were they now whispering? Were they speaking in Arabic or in another language, one that I might understand? I felt, rather than saw with my restricted vision, them turn toward me, and the whispering stopped. The group left the room, but they remained in the corridor just outside as I was able to hear their shuffling movements and the odd indistinct snatch of conversation through the door.

What was it that they did not want me to hear? What was it that they did not want me to see? Who was the fifth man in their group? These were questions that I asked myself repeatedly during my incarceration and still ask even now. Before I could ponder them when first I posed them to myself, the door opened and Khaled entered the room to accompany me back to the interrogation office. Once there, the blindfold was removed, as were the handcuffs, and I was allowed to sit. Ibrahim was already there, exercise books and pens at the ready. I knew what I had to without being told though Khaled gave me the obvious instruction that I was now to write down everything I had just said. So began my life as a spy, sitting there writing my new confession with odd thoughts highlighting the absurdity of my situation. I tried not a smile as I wondered if my new career had a good pension and medical coverage, though doubtless I would never find out anyway. When finally I had completed my statement, it was whisked away and I was allowed a few moments alone to consider the new directions that things might take. Within five or ten minutes, my tormentors returned, pronouncing themselves satisfied, allowing me to be returned to my cell.

That night's session had not been long, nor had it left me as devastated as the previous night had, regardless of what had been done to me. I returned to my established ritual of going to the cell-block toilet and washing myself as carefully as I could. While I washed and wiped my backside, I inspected myself for further bleeding and was heartened that it seemed to be minor. Back in my cell, I began slowly and carefully to go over that night's events. I came to various conclusions about the profile of the fifth man. I concluded that he was not Saudi Arabian, nor even probably Muslim. From the minor indications that his physical appearance provided, I concluded that he was a western expatriate. But what exactly was his role in all of this? Was he a western expatriate working for the Saudi Arabian Ministry of the Interior as either agent or informer? Was he a member of a western intelligence or police organization working in collaboration with the Saudi Arabians? I knew that as a result of the recent bombings, members of London's Metropolitan Police had visited Saudi Arabia. The fact that the conversations that occurred after my verbal presentation were conducted initially in whispers and then outside the room told me that he did not speak Arabic with the necessary fluency. This made me think that he probably was not a British or French operative, for their services seem to have a sufficiency of such personnel, whereas the Americans are noted for their deficiency in this regard. If this was the case, were the Americans involved because of the arrest of Michael Sedlak? I assumed, correctly as it turned out, that the American government would not tolerate such accusations

against one of their nationals, but would they go so far as assisting the Saudis in fitting these crimes to other western nationals? To this day I do not have an adequate answer, but given the intrigue that surrounds our case, it is not beyond the realm of possibility. Certainly, I believed then that someone within the western diplomatic or intelligence community knew what was being done to us, and information that I have gathered since my release confirms this position.

When the breakfast tray arrived, I sat again on the edge of my mattress wrapped in my blanket eating only the pita bread and drinking the tea and water. I attended to my rice diary before leaning back and allowing myself to drift off while I awaited the collection of the tray. When this was done, and I was once again standing chained to my door, I cast my mind back over the events of the night before and wondered what would be done with my confession. What would be the reaction of the British and the Canadian governments when they would inevitably be faced with the Saudi Arabian government's accusations about my role in the recent bombings? I could only smile at the prospect of the incredulity with which these charges would be met and wondered if they would be made public. I wondered also what purpose would be served by this confession. For what reason was it necessary to have me confess to being a spy? Whom did it serve to create a situation that would cause the diplomatic confrontation that could be provoked by airing these accusations? I came to no definite conclusions then, though it seemed to me that I was now a pawn in an internal political struggle within Saudi Arabia, and was not just a convenient scapegoat providing cover for the true cause of the events for which I was accused. At that moment I did not know that I would have years to contemplate these questions, questions that to this day cannot be comprehensively answered.

I was surprised when I heard the midday call to prayer, for I had expected to be taken for a perfunctory visit with the doctor.

Instead, I had spent the morning hours going over and over the questions that I had posed myself. Sometime after the prayer call, the cell door was opened and I was released briefly before the guards replaced the handcuffs and shackles. No blindfold was used and it was indicated to me that I had to collect my shoes, so I was somewhat confused, not knowing whether I was on my way for interrogation or a medical examination. I was led out of the cellblock into the entranceway where I could see in front of me the small room with all the television monitors. The two guards who accompanied me milled around, shouting questions at the guards still in the cellblock and at that those sitting in front of the monitors. From where I stood I was able to glimpse one or two of the screens, hoping for some reason to catch sight of a fellow detainee. This was not to be, for all I saw were the backs of two men in thobes, chained to their cell doors in the manner I had been.

I could see out of the door into the courtyard beyond, noticing the high white wall with the automated white-painted metal gate in its centre. The gate rumbled open, and a white police van drove through, pulling up just in front of the doorway by which I stood. When the van stopped, the guards beside me were galvanized into action, and quickly hustled me out of the building and around to the rear of the vehicle. I was placed in the back and sat down on one of the benches, whereupon my companions departed and locked the door behind them. I sat there alone for a few minutes before the door opened and Khaled, clutching some papers and an inkpad in his hand, climbed into the back with me. I asked him what was happening and was met with the lamest of explanations.

"We are going to be repairing the cells over the next few days, so you will be kept somewhere else until it is finished, but we will bring you back" was his answer to my entreaties.

I hardly could believe such a statement, and it crossed my mind that maybe this was it, my last journey. Before this thought had fully registered, Khaled began waving his papers in front of me. I was told that I had to sign them as they were a record of all my property that had been confiscated from me. Listed on the top page was nothing other than an account of the money that they claimed had been in my possession at the time of my arrest. I did not get a chance to see the other pages, though their contents would have been as inaccurate as what I saw before me. The page I was required to sign stated that I had 8,600 riyals (about $2,700) in my possession at the time of my arrest. This was far from the truth, for at that time 2,500 riyals (about $795) had been in my pocket, and in my briefcase were 12,500 riyals (about $3,985) in an envelope with the word "watch" scrawled on the outside. I questioned Khaled about the discrepancy between what was stated on the paper and what I knew I had had in my possession. Khaled simply reiterated that I should sign and he would look into my query. Like all such promises, it was just another of his lies, but I was in no position to argue or make demands. Anyway, I had expected this. It was a normal aspect of being arrested in Saudi Arabia that various police officers would help themselves to whatever they found on you. I had known too many ex-patriates who had had their wallets emptied even when held briefly for the most minor of offences. On top of which I had seen the blatant theft of some of my property when my house was searched. Still it irritated me, for I did not want them gaining any greater benefit from my demise than they already had.

One might consider that the amount of cash I had been carrying was suspiciously large, but my captors did not seem to think so for I was never questioned about it. The money in my pocket was a relatively normal amount for me to carry, and the money in the briefcase, while more than I would normally carry around, was for a specific purpose. Later on the day I was arrested, I was supposed to have collected a watch that would have been a present for my father's seventieth birthday; it would have cost me 10,000 riyals (about $3,190). Most such purchases in Saudi Arabia were best done in cash for it allowed for some haggling to take place over price, and it was not unusual even in the most expensive shops to see transactions done in cash rather than by credit card. The rest of the cash was for the purchase of a return ticket to London, which I was also supposed to collect that day. I had planned to spend the Ramadan holiday period, which that year corresponded fairly closely to Christmas time, in Britain visiting friends and family. Needless to say, I did not get the opportunity to collect these items, nor did I make my trip.

With the document signed, Khaled climbed out of the van before turning to address me again.

"We will come and see you in a couple of days. We have a holiday now. You may get some sleep now."

With that the door to the van was closed and locked and I was left alone. If this last statement was meant to reassure me, it did not. Although he had tried to keep his demeanour friendly, I had no interest in his friendship nor in seeing either him or his partner again.

His mention of a holiday reminded me that the Eid celebrations were almost upon us, for the month of Ramadan was drawing to a close. The date was now December 28, and I should have been on leave from my job at the Fund from the twenty-seventh. Instead I was enduring the eleventh sleepless day of captivity, sitting in the back of a police van, signing another fictitious document, and anointing it with my thumbprint. I was exhausted, battered, bruised, and violated. I was also filthy and stinking, despite my earnest attempts to keep clean. This was certainly not how I had envisioned spending my holiday.

XXX ///

I felt the vehicle begin to move, reversing from its parked position to head out through the gate, which now rumbled open. I tried as best I could to calculate where we were headed by assessing all the twists and turns of our journey. It was to no avail. I did not know where I was from the outset. My part of the van had no windows, and it was impossible for me to accurately calculate distance, direction, or time. All I was able to calculate was based on the sounds that the vehicle made while travelling, and by certain of its movements. I am certain that we re-entered one part of Riyadh, for on two or three occasions we came to a stop as if waiting at traffic lights. I am also certain that we passed through a tunnel or underpass and over a motorway overpass because of the changing sounds of the tires on the tarmac and the echoes of the engine.

Where we were headed I did not know. Was I was being taken for execution or disposal? Logic dictated that having given them the confessions they wanted, a Stalinist show trial would be in order before my ultimate demise. For some reason during this journey, my mind stayed active with these thoughts even though I was starved of sleep. I remained awake throughout the journey, and thus was aware of our coming to a halt. I heard the driver's door open, accompanied by various shouts in Arabic. Then I heard a series of automated gates opening, and we went through them. Eventually we stopped; the driver and guard alighted and came around to open the rear of the vehicle.

Before me was a large modern building in reasonable repair. The vehicle had parked close in to its shadow and I was unable to see any further structures. I was taken from the van through a doorway and found myself in what I now know was the reception area for this part of the prison system. I was given a small bundle of items and led to a cubicle where I was told to change. I inspected the bundle and discovered that it contained two thobes, two T-shirts, two pairs of boxer shorts, a pair of sandals, a towel, a bar of soap, a toothbrush, and a small tube of toothpaste. I quietly changed into these cleaner items, leaving my own clothes in a heap on the bench, and then walked out of the cubicle. The uniformed guards who now attended me brought over a plastic bag indicating that I should put all my discarded personal belongings into it. When I'd done that, I was led into another room, a bare-walled office with a desk, a couple of chairs, a digital camera mounted on a tripod, a computer, and a printer. Here I had my mug shot taken, and various pieces of paperwork were completed to which I affixed my signature and thumbprint, though I had no idea what I was signing. I now had a new prison number, 357/3, by which I would be identified over the coming years.

I was in one of the prisons in Al Ha'ir, fifty or so kilometres south of Riyadh. Al Ha'ir is a small town around which are located a number of prisons, ranging from the modern one used for political prisoners that I now found myself in through to two smaller, older, and more decrepit prisons that housed, for want of a better expression, normal criminals. The complex that I was in was huge, and though I did develop a sense of the scale of the section I was in and that it was just a part of this prison complex, I never developed a complete appreciation of the full scope of the place. The only other thing of note in the Al Ha'ir area was an air force base due south at Al Karj, where USAF personnel had been stationed, and now had employees of British Aerospace along with a few seconded members of the RAF. After my release, when I came to know where I had been held, I realized that my excursions into the deserts to the south of Riyadh had brought me close to what was now my new home.

As my processing was completed, I was handcuffed and blindfolded and was led into the prison itself. I tried to count and measure my paces to give myself some sense of size and direction. I would walk through this area countless times blindfolded, each time performing the same exercise. When finally I did so without my vision being compromised, I was surprised at how accurate was the mental picture I had constructed. We walked for some distance, through a number of electrically and pneumatically controlled gateways before I was delivered to my new cell and the blindfold was removed. The door was locked behind me, and I was alone.

My new accommodation was a slight improvement over my previous residence. Most noticeably, it was clean. The cell measured two metres wide by three and a half metres long. The walls were covered in a layer of rubberized paint to a height of three or four metres, and the whole cell was a sickly off-white yellowish colour. All the other surfaces within reach were covered in the same manner. The floor was covered with grey linoleum. Down the cell to my left was a raised bed plinth, the top of which was just below knee height. It measured about one and a half metres by three-quarters of a metre wide. To my immediate right was a waist-high shelf in front of which was a stainless steel stool mounted directly into the floor. Beyond that was a partially enclosed cubicle that contained the toilet, sink, and shower unit, the first two of which were also in steel and stamped with their country of origin: Canada.

I turned and looked at the door to my cell, noting the glass viewing slot with external cover inserted at about head height. To one end of the shelf was a small recess with a metal door. It was like an over-large mailing slot, and it was through this that my meals and other items would be delivered. On the other side of the door, mounted through the wall, was a television screen, which made me smile as I wondered if they got cable. Looking upward I noted an opaque Plexiglas skylight at the highest point in the ceiling of the cell, and saw that the roof sloped downward from the wall in which the door was housed to the back of the cell. At its highest, it must have measured twelve or fifteen metres high and at its lowest about four metres. The skylight had metal bars across it, and though these were an obvious security feature, they seemed redundant, given the insurmountable difficulty of climbing to that point in the cell. Finally, there was the CCTV camera, mounted in the top corner of the cell above the mailing slot, protected by a Plexiglas screen and a metal enclosure. Next to that was the ventilation grill for the air-conditioning system, running across most of the width of the cell.

My prison-issued items had been placed on the shelf, and on the bed plinth were a mattress, blanket, and pillow. All these items were at least clean. With that in mind, I removed what I had recently donned, grabbed the soap, and went into the shower cubicle. The water was tepid but still refreshing. I washed off the accumulated dirt and grime of the past eleven days, dealing with the external manifestation of my treatment. Inside I still felt dirty and somewhat ashamed, something the shower could not attend to, but which I would gradually come to terms with during my incarceration.

Having completed my shower, I dried off, carefully inspecting myself. A substantial part of my body had turned into a virtual rainbow of colour. From about my kidneys to the backs of my knees was a mixture of colours ranging from black through to blue and red. My lower abdomen and pelvic area was a mixture of black and purple. My swollen penis looked like an overcooked sausage. My testicles had swollen to the size of oranges, and their tenderness made walking difficult. With each step I received a piercing reminder of their condition. My feet were also swollen and tender, making the wearing of the prison-issue sandals uncomfortable. I went barefoot even though this too was painful. The top of my feet and part of the way up my calves were a bright red colour interspersed with an occasional patch of blue; the skin was stretched and taut. The soles were a single colour, a flaming red, and were hot to the touch, feeling as if they had been grilled. My body was hardly an edifying sight.

I began then to brush my teeth, but had to do so gently for they were also damaged and sensitive. Inspecting them, I saw that at least three of them had been badly damaged. One each in the lower jaw on the left and right sides of my mouth were cracked and loose; one on the upper left side of my jaw had already disintegrated to a spiky stub. Eating was now difficult and uncomfortable. It would remain like this throughout my incarceration, regardless of the crude dental treatment that would be provided in the prison system.

Having completed my now ritualized cleansing and inspection, I dressed, putting on a T-shirt, boxer shorts, and thobe, and climbed onto the mattress, wrapping myself in the blanket. I found the air in the prison cell cold; it was, after all, December and the temperature could not have been much more than nine or ten degrees. The clothing I was wearing provided little warmth in the circumstances. Furthermore, the cold that I felt seemed also to emanate from within me, as if the brutality had induced a feverish chill. I lay back in my blanket and, shivering, drifted off into sleep.

I was awakened by a double-clicking sound originating in the door. This was a sound that I would become familiar with, and one that I would learn to dread, for it was the sound of the electronically controlled locks in my cell door being sprung. I do not know how long I had slept then, but through the skylight I noticed that it was still daylight, so it cannot have been more than an hour or two at the most. Through my grogginess I discerned the sound of multiple footsteps approaching my cell, before the door was opened. Two uniformed guards and a be-thobed officer entered the cell. A single word was said to me, "Doctor," and I raised myself from the bed. I was surprised that no restraints were used nor blindfold applied as I was led from the cell. I noted that I was on the far end of a twenty-metre-wide corridor with cells on either side, in the middle of which was a sunken area filled with green shrubbery and plants. (The purpose of this garden still baffles me.) To my left the corridor stretched away to what looked like a central control station from which three other corridors radiated. To the right of my cell, which was the last on my row, were two doors set in a wall about three metres high. At the apex of the wall, a flat roof reached back another two to three metres, ending at the exterior wall of this cellblock, which reached up to a height of about fifteen metres. Behind the nearest door was a small doctor's office into which I was now led. It contained a desk, a couple of chairs, a small filing cabinet, and a large set of scales.

When I entered this office, the doctor, a slim bearded man of Indian or Pakistani origin, spoke to me in English, telling me to stand on the scales. I was not a little shocked to note my body weight, for at the time of my arrest I had weighed about ninety-six kilograms, and I now weighed eighty-nine kilograms. I knew that I had been badly overweight, and that I would not miss a few kilograms, but I had lost those six or seven kilograms within a very short time. I was then told to take the seat next to his desk and roll up my sleeve. Another perfunctory medical examination had been undertaken, with nothing more than my weight, pulse, blood pressure, and temperature recorded. I went through the routine of answering another list of questions concerning my medical history. My comments on the treatment I had received, and the damage I had suffered, were blithely ignored. The only response I got was when I asked to see a dentist and was told that he would ask permission for this. I had also noted that on his desk was an old paperback novel by Louis L'Amour. I attempted a more personal communication by asking him if he enjoyed westerns and if when he was finished with the book he could pass it on to me. His response was to look down at the floor to avoid my gaze.

With the medical exam over, I walked back to my cell, climbed onto the mattress, and drifted off to sleep once again. When next I awoke I saw that night had fallen as the skylight was dark. Sitting on the shelf by the mailing slot was a food tray covered by a pita bread – the food was now cold – a cup of tea, an orange, and a small bottle of water. I had not heard the intervening prayer calls or the arrival of the food, such was my tiredness. I sat down on the stool and ravenously consumed the chicken and rice that the tray contained. As I did so I remembered that my rice diary had been left behind, and I wondered if it would be discovered and its significance understood. I put the orange to one side of the shelf, collected the requisite number of grains of rice, and restarted my rice diary. It seemed a futile act but I knew that I must establish a routine, which in itself would help preserve my dignity and sanity. While part of me wallowed in cynicism, another continued to tell me to record everything and remember everything just in case it would ever be useful. With my diary done and my competing thoughts dealt with, I climbed back onto my mattress and rapidly sank into unconsciousness.

I awoke the next day sometime in the morning to discover that the food tray had been removed and replaced with another. It contained the usual breakfast fare, but at least it contained a couple of hard-boiled eggs, which I consumed with relish. I was a little surprised that the tray had been left for so long considering it was now daylight. During Ramadan, food was served only twice a day, just before dawn and in the evening after sunset prayer. Although the evening food tray had been left on occasion to await my return, the morning one was usually collected quite quickly, lest my eating during daylight hours offend their delicate sensibilities. Now for some reason, I was being allowed to eat at my leisure; maybe the conditions of my imprisonment were improving. It was a faint hope that I allowed myself, letting down my guard slightly and mistakenly.

During the rest of this and the next day, I received numerous visits from various be-thobed officers who asked general questions about my needs. The first of these was a tall bearded individual in his early thirties who entered my cell alone. I later discovered his exact role in the prison hierarchy and realized that his visit to me then was somewhat out of the ordinary, but occurred because he was one of the few officers available at the time of my admission who was fluent in English. He was followed in quick succession by various others, until just after nightfall when a group of five officers entered my cell led by a tall long-faced man with a thin neatly trimmed moustache. This was Colonel Mohammed Said, deputy governor of the prison, to whom I gave the nickname "Smiling Knife" for his surreptitious role in our mistreatment. During our incarceration, he would be promoted to the rank of brigadier and head of the prison as a reward for containing us.

With these visits over, I was allowed to drift back to sleep. Throughout the next day I drifted in and out of consciousness, my mind and body trying desperately to catch up on the sleep I had missed at the interrogation centre. Not that it could, but when I awoke on the morning of my fourteenth day of captivity, New Year's eve, I felt substantially refreshed. My sleep over the preceding nights had been deep and dreamless, a descent into total oblivion that I needed. I had half-convinced myself that the torture must now be over and all I could do was wait for the disposition of my case. I began to muse over all the incidents of my captivity so far, trying to make sense of them, before finally giving up and turning my mind once again to more pleasant memories.

At some point in the morning, the double click of the door sounded and footsteps approached, the door opened and two guards walked in, one of them carrying a blindfold, the other telling me that I was to see the doctor again. Soon after the medical consultation, if it could be called that, back in my cell I heard the prayer call announced loudly and distortedly across the prison public address system. This was followed by the food being delivered, and given that it was still light, I thought that it must be early afternoon, which indicated that Ramadan had ended. Somehow the night before I had slept through the prayers announcing the end of the fasting, as well as those during the preceding couple of days. It was a measure of my exhaustion that I had not been disturbed by the distorted racket broadcast regularly throughout the prison.

However, this period of relative tranquility was soon disrupted. A little after the last prayer of the evening, the guards again appeared at my cell door. This time they had handcuffs and shackles as well as a blindfold, and they said a single word that chilled me instantly: "Investigation." I was placed in the restraints and led from my cell toward something that filled me with dread. My vision was restricted, but not completely, for through the bottom margin of the blindfold I could see my feet, and by slightly canting my head could snatch a few details of my new surroundings. This I did surreptitiously so as not to alert my guards and provoke a readjustment of the blindfold.

It seemed that Khaled and Ibrahim were fulfilling their promise of paying a visit. Naïvely I had hoped that I would not see them again, and naïvely I had hoped that the brutality had ended, even though my perverse understanding of my situation told me that it had not. So as we walked, I tried to distract myself by counting off the paces as I shuffled on. We turned right of what I assumed was the control station, proceeding onward for a similar distance until we stopped. I heard a minor electronic tune and a voice emanating as if from an intercom. One of my guards responded and was rewarded with the double-click sound of an electronic lock being released. We proceeded, and I heard the sound of a pneumatically controlled gate being opened. We seemed to walk around in an arc, before stopping at an office where I was asked my number. Once this was duly recorded, we headed out again along a long corridor through some sort of metal detector such as those found in airports, then another door before turning left and entering an elevator. When we left the elevator, we turned right and began walking down another corridor, then we stopped and entered a room. I was guided over to a chair and told to sit, which I did. Once more I was filled with the sense of anticipation that I had experienced in the interrogation centre; the cycle had begun again.

I sensed rather than knew that someone was in the room with me and had this confirmed when the door opened for someone to breeze in and remove my blindfold. It was Khaled, and he did not look amused as he dismissed the guards who silently had stayed in the room with me. Behind him followed Ibrahim, carrying in his hands two rattan canes and the metal pipe, which he dumped unceremoniously just inside the door against the wall before disappearing. Khaled had stayed with me, glaring angrily and speaking aggressively. For whatever reason, I knew that I was in for it and that something more was required from me. I was disappointed but neither shocked nor crestfallen as I might have been. Some part of me had steeled myself against the inevitability of such an outcome, tempering my earlier naïve hope.

Khaled stood in front of me, the stench of his halitosis making me mildly nauseous, while he told me what they intended to do to me. It was a litany of all the threats that had been previously made. It would be repeated ad infinitum. I was told that my story was fine as far as it went, but they wanted to know about the involvement of Raf and Sandy, to whom they had made little reference during the latter days at the interrogation centre. Obviously, having betrayed myself and my country, I was now to be required to betray my friends. Khaled then left me, having delivered his dire warnings, so once again I sat there in anticipation of what was to come. Eventually, a guard entered the room and sat down to keep me company.

When Khaled returned, he had with him Ibrahim, who began shouting and glaring at me with great but overacted ferocity. He continued his performance, with Khaled struggling to keep up the translation, when suddenly a mobile phone rang. Ibrahim reached into his pocket, grabbed his phone, and answered it. Immediately his voice changed, the tone becoming softer, gentler, and to a certain extent almost cowed; I knew he must be speaking to his wife. Without thinking I innocently looked at Khaled and asked, "His wife?"

The look of surprise on Khaled's face was a picture as he replied, "How did you know? You speak Arabic?"

By accident I had impressed on him that I had a skill not within my repertoire. Not sure that he would now believe me I said, "No, I don't, but I don't need to. He is hardly going to speak to his brother in that tone of voice."

It was strange to see the look of consternation on Khaled's face, for I seemed to have done something unexpected or at least uncovered something that I should not have. Why should he have been so surprised to discover that men have a habit of changing their tone of voice when speaking with women, particularly their wives, lovers, or daughters? Surely he was observant enough to have noticed this, or at least I thought he should be, given his chosen profession. But then again I had spotted a number of cracks or flaws in their façades, so maybe they were not as infallible as they thought, only brutal.

With the end of the phone call, Ibrahim once again turned his attentions to me, roaring and thundering at me, demanding that I confess to the roles played by Raf and Sandy, and demanding to know the names of my contacts in the British Embassy. I found it curious that they had not tried to get this information from me before getting me to confess to being a spy. It was a question that was ridiculously easy for me to answer, for I had dealt directly with only one British Embassy official, Simon Lovat, the first consul, who had left Saudi Arabia on health grounds earlier in 2000. The only other individual whom I knew of at that time was Ian Wilson, the then current first consul, but I had not dealt directly with him. I told Ibrahim their names, knowing full well that had the Ministry of the Interior been watching the embassy or watching me they would have few records of my comings and goings, and none within the last two or three months. It made the task of creating evidence against me even more difficult for them. For once my solitary nature was paying unexpected dividends in creating problems for my captors.

Ibrahim was not pleased with this and began slapping and punching me across the side of the head and in the chest and stomach, screaming at me the single English word "liar." I reiterated that I was not lying and that their own surveillance of the British Embassy would show this to be true. I pointed out to them that I confessed to being a spy at their insistence, but they knew the truth. It was another of my unfortunate verbal gaffes for it only infuriated both Ibrahim and Khaled, who were working hard to convince themselves of the truth of the lies that they were perpetrating.

Having easily convinced me of the seriousness of their threats, they left me in the company of a uniformed guard. They were not gone too long before returning to tell me that I was being sent back to my cell. They also told me that if I did not change my story and begin cooperating with them fully, they would make me regret my stupidity and stubbornness. I wondered how inventive I would have to be with them to prevent the brutality they so enjoyed inflicting. Could my imagination stay one step ahead of them in the convoluted conspiracy they had concocted? It was going to be a strange time, as if it was not strange enough already.

On the way back to my cell, we took a detour once we left the elevator. I was taken through another electronically controlled gate and into an office, where I was introduced to another doctor, a fat, bespectacled man of late middle age and Indian or Pakistani origin. Another cursory examination was undertaken before I was dismissed and returned to my cell. It was not late, nor was I particularly tired, so I lay down on the bed and tried to work out once again what it was they wanted and what I could do to delay the process. I was caught up in my thoughts when I heard the cell door unlock, causing my heart to race. It was a Pavlovian response, one that stayed with me throughout my imprisonment and is with me yet whenever I hear a sound similar to that.

Into my cell walked a short, very stocky, dark-skinned Saudi Arabian, someone I would have instinctively referred to as a black Saudi, not in the pejorative sense that is conveyed when pronounced by Saudi Arabians, but simply because that was what he was, a Saudi of African origin.

There is a sizeable minority of Saudi Arabians whose ethnic and racial heritage is African. The reason for this is simple; the slave trade was abolished in Saudi Arabia only in the early 1960s. Some of the former slaves and their families have prospered alongside the families that originally owned them, for many continued in the employ of their old masters, and as their former masters prospered so did they. Most of what were referred to as black Saudis existed almost outside the normal function of Saudi society, for they were without the tribal allegiances and family ties that bind Saudi Arabia together; in the eyes of their fellow citizens they were regarded as second-class. However, those black Saudis who end up as functionaries in organizations such as the police force are actually held by other Saudis to be more honest or easy to deal with for they have no calls on their integrity because of their allegiance to a tribe. It was something I would come to notice, for of the Saudi Arabians within the Ministry of the Interior who treated me with decency and humanity, those who always treated me well and often acted against the orders they were given were black

Saudis. It was certainly the case the night my house was searched, for the guard who treated me well could easily have been the cousin of the man now before me.

It turned out that he was the dispenser of medicine, doing his nightly rounds. In response to my requests concerning my various injuries, the doctor had prescribed some aspirin and an anti-inflammatory cream with which I was now being provided. Realizing that I had to apply the ointment immediately, I removed my thobe and boxer shorts. The sight of my naked and abused body caused the guards accompanying the dispenser to turn away. He just sadly shook his head and fitted disposable plastic gloves over his hands, indicating that I should turn around. When I did so, he gently coated my lower back, buttocks, and thighs with the ointment. He handed the tube to me, and I went about gingerly and liberally coating the damaged areas of my abdomen, groin, legs, and feet. It seemed to me that the main benefit from this ministration was not physical but psychological. I felt less isolated in this sea of inhumanity. For this I will always be in this man's debt, for his small kindnesses and for his humanity were manifest throughout my imprisonment.

Eventually, they departed, the door was locked, and I returned to my bed. I turned my mind away from the things that had been said to me that night, thinking instead of time spent skiing in Switzerland with an old girlfriend. These pleasant memories slowed my pounding heart and gentled me to sleep.

$\cancel{||||}$ $|||$

When I awoke it was to a new year, but not one filled with hope or promise. What I had feared had begun again, grinding along in its inexorable manner. For the next two weeks each day would be much as it had been at the interrogation centre, with a few exceptions.

From my sixteenth night I was deprived of sleep until after an interrogation session nearly two weeks later. This presented some difficulties for the guards in my new home, for my cell had nothing to which I could be chained in an upright position. All the items I had been presented with on entering this place were confiscated, leaving me with only a thobe, T-shirt, and boxer shorts. My mattress, blanket, and pillow were removed. I had nothing on which to rest and nothing in which to wrap myself to keep warm. During this period, the guards would frequently come into my cell to ensure my compliance with the regime of sleep deprivation they had been instructed to enforce. I was not allowed to rest, or for that matter get warm. All I could do was stand or, when permission was given, sit on the end of the bed plinth and lean into the wall. My bouts of sitting were what normally precipitated the entry of the guards into my cell, for as I sat, I deliberately tried to snatch as many moments of sleep as possible by leaning on the wall, letting myself slump briefly into unconsciousness.

These moments would be few because I was being constantly monitored by the CCTV cameras. Thus, whenever I began to doze off those viewing me on their black and white television screens would send some underling down to force me to stand. I entered a slightly bizarre game of trying to estimate how long each standing and sitting session lasted. Thankfully, I was at least free to walk about the cell, stretching and massaging myself to alleviate the cramps that my injuries and fatigue induced on an all too regular basis.

The hallucinations began again after a couple of days and continued throughout this time. They no longer induced the strained sense of paranoia that they did initially. During the time I spent either alone in my cell or waiting between sessions of beatings and questions, I dredged my memory for snatches of poetry and lyrics, both to occupy my mind and to fortify myself. That one poem, which had come to me days earlier, became a chant, mumbled under my breath for hours on end. It came to have a hypnotic effect on me in much the same way that a mantra does for meditating devouts. It did not drive away my suffering but somehow gave me just enough emotional strength to prevent a complete breakdown.

When I was taken for interrogation on the fifteenth night, I wondered how it would start. Would they try sweet reason and friendly persuasion or would they launch immediately into brutality? I knew what my money was on, and I was not disappointed. Having been taken to the interrogation rooms sometime in the afternoon, I sat waiting for what seemed an exceedingly long time. I learned this was the standard in this prison. I would be collected sometime after noon prayer and usually before midafternoon prayer, and would then wait blindfolded, handcuffed, and shackled in an interrogation room until well after the fourth prayer of the day. Calculated by the intervals between the prayers, the duration of which was affected by the shortness of the daylight hours, I used to wait in this limbo for between three and five hours before the arrival of Khaled and Ibrahim, and the interrogation would begin. This would then last well into the early hours of the morning, often ending only with the dawn prayer call.

During the first few months of my residence at Al Ha'ir, whenever I was taken outside of the cellblock, I was kept blindfolded. I tried to work out the structure of this interrogation area by the educated guesswork of pacing. When I later entered this area with unrestricted vision, I felt a perverse pleasure in being able to note that my blindfolded estimations were quite close to the reality.

When one left the elevator, one stood in a large foyer replete with easy chairs, sofas, and rugs. Two corridors stretched off from either side of this atrium. One of them went to the main offices and monitoring suites of this prison block, the other led to the interrogation rooms. There were three of these small, nearly identical rooms on each side of the corridor. The three rooms on the left were separated by a small kitchen. The rooms on the right were separated by a toilet area. Each of these offices had a desk and a few chairs and was carpeted with the same rough material that I had seen at the interrogation centre. At either end of the exterior walls in each of these rooms were narrow windows running from the floor to ceiling filled with an opaque safety glass through which the faint outline of bars could be seen. Lodged in a corner where the walls and the ceiling met was a CCTV camera mounted and protected in the same way as in the prison cells.

The last two offices, one on either side of the corridor, were a different affair altogether. These were plushly decorated and appointed, each with a large capacious desk, sofas, and a low coffee table. They were connected by a doorway that led into what I came to believe was either a toilet or equipment room. I got to spend time in these rooms only when, satisfied with my output and having finished beating me, my interrogators took me there for a special treat and friendly relaxed chat.

When on this day Khaled and Ibrahim arrived, I noted that again The Spiv was not with them, and thankfully I would not see him throughout the rest of my incarceration. My blindfold was removed and I was told to sit on the floor. I was immediately prepared for falanga – suspended from the bar and placed across two office chairs that were in the room. These items of furniture were the type that had a central pedestal, and thus did not make a particularly stable platform for the purpose they were now being used for.

As the beating started, my spasms and jerks caused the chairs to move, flexing and creaking under the strain. The beating had not gone on for more than a cycle or so when I heard a loud crack and fell to the floor. The chair to my left had broken, resulting in a definite failure of sense of humour on the part of Khaled and Ibrahim. To the accompaniment of their angry screams, I was dragged from the wreckage, the bar was removed, and I had a few moments' respite from being beaten before I was placed in the hog-tied position for the flogging to recommence. Over the next few weeks I would not be submitted to falanga. I was spared the extra distress caused by being hung upside down.

Again everything I went through was much as I had come to expect, though there were some differences. Once the daily inter-rogation sessions began, when I was between questioning and beating sessions, it became normal for me to be made to face a wall and stand on one leg with my arms raised above my head, or made to squat down on my haunches with my arms outstretched. Both positions were painful because of my battered and weakened con-dition. Standing on one leg strained my ankles, and the state of my feet made my balance poor, causing me to wobble. The squatting position was even more uncomfortable. The beatings had exacer-bated a longstanding injury to my right knee. I would find myself in one of these positions for up to an hour at a time. This might not sound like either a great duration or punishment, but under the circumstances I found it so.

The guards who were left to watch over me during these periods had been instructed to punish me if I moved from the position, and some of them took to this responsibility with alacrity. From the way they responded when I moved out of the position, I learned quite rapidly which were the thugs who took pleasure from what was being done to me, and which were the ones who found the job difficult and distasteful.

A couple of the younger guards relished any transgression I displayed, for this provided them with an excuse to kick or punch me, and one in particular would make use of a cane as a means of disciplining me should Ibrahim have left one in the room. This individual bore a striking resemblance to a young Saddam Hussein, with much the same predilections. I was amused, for want of a better word, that this guard had a brother (or at least a close relative) among the guards who looked to be his twin, and who was even more brutal. These two I nicknamed the Saddam Twins. They would have a prominent role in a number of other violent incidents during my incarceration.

One or two guards, though, seemed quite happy just to let me stand on both feet as they leaned against the door, using their position as an early warning system for me to resume mine whenever someone tried to enter the room. I was then and am still thankful to them for their insubordination, for both Khaled and Ibrahim were quite happy to subject the guards to physical remonstrations for any perceived disobedience or error.

Fortunately this game did not form part of the initial period of anticipation that occurred in the interrogation offices. It was started only once Khaled and Ibrahim had arrived, and the interrogation session had formally begun.

The questioning sessions seemed longer now, with more effort being put in by Khaled to befriend me. I acted out my role of kind friend, asking personal questions and wondering if the answers that he gave were true. As a result, I discovered that Khaled was married and his wife was pregnant with their first child. Such a revelation gave me pause for thought, as I wondered exactly how he would discipline his offspring. He also told me that he had been to Toronto, where he had taken English courses. If this were true, it was an odd coincidence, for I had friends in that city who worked as teachers of English to foreign students.

I also gleaned from him that Ibrahim had just taken (taken being the operative word) a second wife, and it was she who frequently phoned during the interrogation process, breaking Ibrahim's rhythm. The interludes that her telephone calls produced had a strange quality that never lessened. To be lying there trembling with pain only to hear one's torturer break off to answer a call, his voice instantly assuming the conciliatory tone of the henpecked husband, was extremely strange.

Night in and night out for the next thirteen days, that is how things went. The beatings comprised a mix of the usual punching, kicking, and slapping; the liberal use of the rattan cane; or Ibrahim standing on my testicles. When the cane was involved, it was applied across my buttocks while I stood, or across my feet when I was hog-tied. I have made copious notes filled with details of the beatings and punishments that I was subjected to, but these notes show only the sheer repetitiveness of the brutality, in which each day could almost be exchanged for any other such was the immutable nature of their pattern. Only the small oddities broke the awful tedium.

At the end of each interrogation session, I was not led directly back to my prison cell, but taken on a slight detour. When leaving the elevator that took one down from the interrogation offices, instead of turning right and heading into the cellblock, I was turned left through 180 degrees, passing by a pneumatically controlled gate and then into a small doctor's office where my blindfold and restraints were removed. On one of the nights, the office door remained slightly ajar, allowing me a view of the area that I was now in. From my estimations, I was just below the interrogation offices or control rooms, in what was a secure medical facility, which was on the opposite side of the atrium to the reception area for this cellblock. Outside this doctor's office I could see individual cells, each enclosed not by a solid door but by floor-to-ceiling barred gates of a more traditional type, affording a view into the cells. The cells I could see were unoccupied, each containing only a hospital bed.

There were three prison doctors. All of them deemed me fit for punishment. On my first post-interrogation detour to this area, I met the third of the prison doctors. He was a short, spindly individual with a full beard, who spoke almost unaccented English. I was not able to make any accurate estimation of his origins from either his physical characteristics or his speech, but have since been told that he was Palestinian. Thus within my first few days I had met the entire medical staff. On the occasional times that my pain and frustration would override my common sense, I managed to ask each one of them in turn how their medical training prepared them for the current role.

On one of those occasions, about the twentieth night in captivity, when I challenged the older, chubby bespectacled doctor on this point, I was given this simple justification: "If you tell them what they want to know, I would not have to treat you. This is your fault, not mine."

I learned from this particular encounter that each statement I made had the potential to be reported to my interrogators, for at my next session my interrogators remonstrated with me in all too painful fashion for my insolence in challenging a member of their medical staff. It made me aware then that in all probability reports on all aspects of my behaviour were being given by the prison officials to those who questioned me. It was a realization that was reinforced by later incidents, one of which in my own way I would use to discomfit my guards and senior prison officers.

I began cooperating again on the sixteenth day, confessing to being involved in the bombing that occurred on November 22, the one for which Raf had been arrested. I also rewrote the confessions concerning the first bombing, this time to implicate Sandy Mitchell.

Not that these new drafts satisfied them, for they were written again and again over the next ten or twelve days. On about the twenty-fourth day of my captivity, it was demanded of me that I write a supplemental confession detailing my activities on each day for the months of October, November, and December of 2000. The activities I described were an amalgam of actual events mixed with the fantasies of my captors.

Through writing and rewriting I accounted for each of my waking hours, ascribing timings to the exact minute for each of my activities. Outside of my attendance at my place of employment, I apparently spent every evening for up to three hours at a time planning the bombing campaign with my co-conspirators.

What makes this aspect of my confessions particularly risible are two factors, the primary of which was the comical manner in which the bombing campaign was conducted. When one reads the basic details of my confession, which I shall go into, one can only wonder at how someone could have spent so long planning an operation that reads like a farce by Tom Sharpe. Just as important, though, was my interrogators' expectation that any individual would be able to write a detailed confession that could give an almost minute-by-minute account of a period of eighty days.

Try the following exercise. Starting on the day that you read this, select a date two months in the past. Going from then to the present, write down to the exact minute everything that you did on each of the days. While I am sure that there are some individuals whose memories are so accurate that they could give a complete accounting, for nearly everyone else this is an impossibility. Unless an event has a particular reason for your noting the time, you will be hard-pressed to be as exact as the confessions of my captors required. Such a point might seem minor, but, given the difficulty of the exercise I have asked you to perform, the notebooks containing my confessions should provoke questions concerning the authenticity and veracity of the contents.

Finally on the twenty-seventh day of my captivity, January 13, 2001, Khaled and Ibrahim pronounced themselves satisfied with my confessions. I was allowed to sleep the whole night, and all items that had been confiscated from me were returned. Until then, I had also not showered for I had found it too cold to do so. I thus relaxed by prolonged attention to my personal hygiene, followed by wrapping myself up in my blanket and hungrily drifting off to sleep.

On that day and the next, Ibrahim, Khaled, and I undertook the tedious task of translating my confessions into Arabic. I read my words, Khaled translated, and Ibrahim wrote out the Arabic in fresh exercise books. At the completion of each page, I went through the ritual of dignifying this nonsense by placing my initials and thumbprint on the page. This task was done in the more luxurious surroundings of one or other of the offices at the far end of the corridor. If I had been able to view the scene as it presented itself, I would find it hard to connect it to the brutality of the preceding month. The atmosphere was for all intents and purposes friendly. My interrogators had laid on shawarmas and fruit cocktail from a restaurant in Riyadh. They offered to provide me with cigarettes, which I declined for I then did not need or want them. The best picture I can give of these two sessions is to paint a scenario of three business colleagues working long into the night to complete a much-needed management report.

The "confession" that seemed to satisfy them made little sense to me, and I could not believe that it would make sense to anyone outside of Saudi Arabia should ever it be released in full. What I stated was that on November 16, Sandy had called at my house and dropped off two bombs, which I stored under my kitchen sink. The next day at 11 a.m. Sandy collected me in his car, which I drove to a street junction from which we could observe the Rodways' villa. Sandy then planted the bomb on Christopher Rodway's car, returned to his car, and waited with me in plain sight for more than an hour for the Rodways to depart.

When they did so, Sandy and I followed them from their villa onto Ouruba Road. As they pulled away from some traffic lights and the T-junction, I broke off the tail by turning left, and at the same time detonating the remote-control switch that I had in my possession. From there, we returned to my house by a particularly convoluted route, where Sandy and I parted company.

What is strange about the scenario is the over-elaborate series of actions involved. First, Sandy's car was a GMC Jimmy with a manual gearbox. Thus, I would have had to execute a left-hand turn, shifting gears while pulling away from a traffic light, and at the same time with my spare hand detonate a bomb. What spare hand, I hear you ask? Moreover, Sandy and I had spent a ridiculous amount of time in an exposed position sitting in a vehicle watching someone's house. Finally, the exit route that we took was unbelievably complicated, and the car we were supposed to be driving was in fact off the road in a GMC dealership having its gas pump replaced (Mitchell has a receipt to prove this).

If that confession does not sound strange enough, then one detail in my involvement in the second bombing is even stranger, the rest being just as ludicrous. For the first bombing, Sandy and I had been working as a pair, but now we had a third partner in crime. What my confessions stated was that Raf became involved because he had overheard a conversation between Sandy and me the day after the first incident, in which we discussed the operation, and as a result became aware that we were the terrorists that everyone was now talking about.

Because Sandy and I had been ordered to plant a second bomb, he and I decided to involve Raf in order to ensure that he kept his mouth shut. Thus we revised our plans, so that Raf would be the one to plant the next bomb. On the day concerned, I arrived home after work and collected the remaining bomb and a dummy bomb that Sandy had dropped off the day before. I then drove around to Sandy's villa, where I was due to meet him and Raf. When I arrived there, I summoned Raf out to my car, and in broad daylight in the middle of street handed Raf a dummy bomb wrapped in a plastic shopping bag. The real bomb remained in my vehicle under the passenger seat. A few minutes later, I departed and went on home.

The plan was supposed to be that Raf would go to the Al Fallah compound, where he would await my instructions. I would then drive over to the Al Fallah compound, spot the target vehicle, and call Raf on his mobile, describing to him the vehicle on which he was to plant the bomb. After doing this, Raf was to return to the compound and wait for the driver of the target vehicle to depart. He would then follow the vehicle, as would I. I would detonate the bomb and drive by, while Raf would pull over to provide emergency assistance, in order to ensure that there were no fatalities.

How was I to detonate a bomb that I had stated was a dummy bomb? Simple!

Once Raf had planted his device and left the scene, I went and planted the real device. The reason for Raf planting a dummy bomb without his knowledge was supposed to be a form of insurance. If he refused to go through with it, then I would have been able to see it through without him, for supposedly Sandy and I did not trust him to perform his assigned tasks.

As for the selection of the vehicle, I was supposed to be on the lookout for the vehicle belonging to Steve Ford-Hutchinson, a British expatriate whom we knew and who worked at the National Guard hospital, and a regular patron of the bars on the Al Fallah compound. Upon sighting his vehicle, I was supposed to call Raf; however, Steve did not show up, and with time pressing on, I called Raf and had him plant his bomb (a dummy) on the vehicle parked immediately next to his before I replaced the dummy bomb with the live one. All this was conducted within fifty metres of the two or three guards who manned the entrance of a Saudi Arabian Air Force facility situated next to the Al Fallah compound.

When it was closing time at the bar and everyone began to depart, Raf followed the vehicle with the attached bomb, and I followed Raf. Finally detonating the bomb, I drove off, leaving Raf to minister to the injured.

What purpose did it serve to have Raf stay behind given his putative involvement? That is answered by the next part of the confessions provided. Supposedly Mitchell and I were operatives of MI6, under the command of Ian Wilson and Simon MacDonald, senior officials in the British Embassy who were our controllers. Our orders had been to set off a series of non-lethal explosions targeting British expatriates that would embarrass the Saudi government, in order to shake them into greater intelligence cooperation with the British security services, and to drive a wedge between the expatriate and Saudi Arabian communities in order to prevent over-familiarity. They were not happy that we had caused a death, and so instructed Sandy to find a means of preventing this. Thus for the next explosion one of us was to plant and detonate the bomb, while the other was to arrive like a knight in shining armour to minister to the wounded. Therefore Raf fitted nicely into this part of our supposed instructions and plans.

I do not know about anyone else, but I find the details provided in my confession concerning the second bombing to be even more ludicrous than those in the first. Nevertheless, that would not be the end of it. I would have to rewrite my confession about the second bombing incident again at a later date. However, at that moment Khaled and Ibrahim were satisfied with the story they had constructed, beaten into me, and had me regurgitate. The nature and contents of my confessions would not bear scrutiny and there was no other real proof of my involvement (or of the others) in these incidents, something that gave me some small sense of pleasure.

In one thing, though, I had been successful. As they built their scenario, I was able to convince them that I would have been the one to detonate the bombs. During the preceding couple of weeks, it had occurred to me that it might be argued the only person guilty of murder was the one who detonated the bombs. The others might be seen then simply as unwitting accomplices and therefore not as culpable in the face of any show trial, with the possibility that they would not have to face the death penalty. This went some way toward assuaging my lingering feelings of guilt for having implicated my friends. It was not much to take solace from, but it helped.

On the night that I began this round of confessions, just after I had been given a beating, Khaled blindfolded me, instructing me to be silent and not say a word. I was guided from the interrogation room toward the far end of the corridor, into the last office on the right-hand side, which I saw for the first time once the blindfold was removed. Khaled was now standing beside me, gesturing with his index finger for me to remain silent. In front of me was Sandy Mitchell, eyes covered by a blindfold, standing and trembling, his voice cracking from the pain as Ibrahim beat him across the buttocks and lower back.

I was forced to watch as Sandy was struck five or six times before Khaled asked him a series of questions concerning his involvement with the second bombing, and his position as a spy. I did not have the courage to speak to Sandy, to try to offer him some moral support or utter my acceptance of what he was doing as necessary (for I was doing the same). I just stood there, dreading a return to the same treatment, tears slowly filling my eyes, for in some ways I found watching his pain as emotionally difficult as experiencing my own.

With this little demonstration finished, I was once again blindfolded and taken back to an interrogation office to await the return of my interrogators. I wondered if Sandy realized that I or another prisoner had been standing so close to him. As the blindfolds used were held in place by Velcro, there was no chance of their being removed silently. So I wonder if he had heard the distinctive sound of my blindfold's removal? Funny, I don't think I have ever asked him that question since the opportunity has been there to do so. What I felt then was a return of the sense of guilt I felt for having confessed in the first place, implicating those I knew, as I was pushed back into my allotted office.

As I think back on this incident now it causes me more difficulty emotionally than thinking back on any incident that occurred directly to me. It is strange how at times I can be coldly cynical and accepting about my own fate, but find more distressing the pain and suffering of others. From where stems my lack of concern for my own safety and comfort I do not know exactly, though I am sure it has its roots in my childhood, when I had to deal with the vicissitudes of my parents' failing marriage and the demands this placed on me, developing a marked level of stoicism that is one of my more prominent characteristics.

About six days after witnessing the torture of my friend, I sat anticipating another beating session, when Ibrahim and Khaled returned to the room. I was made to stand up, a blindfold was placed on me, and I was told to speak only when asked questions. I assumed that it was Ibrahim who left the room for I could no longer smell his cologne so strongly. All that remained was the halitosis of Khaled, who stood there slapping me across the head and between my legs. A few moments later the door opened and someone shuffled in, just as I finished reiterating again their statement concerning my knowledge of the British Embassy officials that I knew. I then heard the voice of Sandy Mitchell saying to me to tell them what they wanted to hear. I noted his choice of words, yet my captors did not. He used the word "hear" not "know," a distinction apparently lost in translation.

After his brief statement, the door opened and Sandy was ushered out. I can only surmise that these two acts were done to demonstrate to each of us the betrayals of the other, in the hope that this would lead to further cooperation and compliance. Not that I was not compliant, just that my imagination could not keep pace with theirs. One wonders if it is a necessity that secret police-men have an innate ability to construct and believe in Byzantine conspiracy theories well beyond that of sane and normal members of society.

On the eighteenth day of my captivity, I saw something that I have yet to understand, but that has an odd significance. I had been taken to the interrogations offices, and had asked to go to the toilet after about an hour or so of waiting for Khaled and Ibrahim. As I left the toilet and was being returned to the office, my interroga-tors arrived, barking something at the guards. I was immediately hustled into the closest office, which I knew not to be the one in which I had been originally installed. For some reason – nervous-ness provoked by the aggressiveness of his superiors or just lack of comprehension of his orders – the guard accompanying me removed my blindfold, letting me see the office that I was now in.

In general details it differed little from any of the other inter-rogation suites, except that it contained one curious item. Placed upon one of the two desks that this room contained was a rather dusty scale model of a cityscape, replete with buildings, parks, and roads, even showing various traffic features. On one edge of the model was a small expanse painted blue, which indicated a water feature. It looked like something one might find as part of an oper-ational planning room used by the military. For a moment I stared uncomprehendingly at what I saw before me, before seeing what it was. It hit me like a thunderbolt.

The cityscape was of the Al Khobar area, and as I continued to look at the model I began to recognize its features. My eyes were then drawn to one particular point, where I saw a two- to three-centimetre-long model of a car beside which was painted on the surface of the city model a coloured cartoon-like sketch of flames indicating an explosion.

This was obviously the third explosion that had been men-tioned in passing in the first days of my incarceration and that had occurred two days prior to my arrest. Why in hell was such a detailed model present in Al Ha'ir prison? How long had it been there and when had it been constructed? The incident that it was a reference for had occurred barely a month previously and, given the model's grimy state, it had been sitting in its current location for a good few days. It was an eerie feeling, taking in the detail of this model and its obvious early preparation. Even though I was then (and still am) certain that the Mabaheth of the Ministry of the Interior knew who was responsible for the bombings of which I was accused, the possibility that occurred to me then was that they might have been more directly involved. I have not yet been able to explain my chance discovery of this planning model or its full significance.

One thing I am sure of, I was not meant to see it. For as I stood there staring at it, Khaled burst into the room, shouting imprecations in Arabic at my guard, who nearly jumped out of his skin in response to the invective that battered him. Hastily the blindfold was replaced and I was hurriedly dragged into another office. Khaled then removed the blindfold and immediately tried to ascertain if I had recognized what I had just seen. I tried to give every indication I did not. After about half an hour he decided that my dumb act was genuine and he departed, leaving me to squat on my haunches under the watchful eye of the now-chastened guard. For the rest of my incarceration, this remained an incident that I returned to time and time again as I tried to fit it into my attempts to understand my situation.

One of the curious little games that I played during the periods waiting in the interrogation offices derived from the tactics that I was developing to help me relax. I have, like my father, the annoying habit of fidgeting or fiddling as we would call it in the Sampson family, though I am not nearly so bad as my father. If there is a scrap of paper, a small cotton thread, or piece of string lying within reach of my father's hands, he will sit there for hours rolling them into balls and unrolling them. Wherever he goes he leaves in his wake small piles of spherical detritus, as he fidgets away happily. I too do the same thing but not nearly to the same aggravating levels of my parental mentor. For one reason or another, we seem to do this unconsciously, deriving some sort of relaxation in the distraction this activity provides.

What I found was that the seams of my thobe and T-shirt seemed to be an almost endless supply of small threads. These I unravelled, keeping a steady supply of them in the pockets of my thobe, which I would then surreptitiously wind and unwind around my fingers. When first I engaged in this activity in the interrogation offices, it provoked the entrance of guard officers into the room where I was held for the purpose of emptying pockets and removing my distraction. It was obvious that someone was monitoring me fairly constantly via the CCTV camera, so now began the game of trying to conceal my fidgeting activities. I am not sure whether I was successful or whether those who monitored me had given up, but within five or six days I was able to engage in my surreptitious pocket activities without interruption. Another small victory, but this was what my days were to be made of, constantly seeking for some advantage or some small angle.

When first I had arrived at the prison, I had asked for toilet paper and been given a small roll, but this was confiscated once the interrogation started. I rapidly learned to wash myself using the floor spigot next to the toilet in my cell. Not that I was happy with this, but it at least allowed me to keep clean, even if, without soap, I was unable to thoroughly clean my hands. However I found another source of this essential commodity, making my life a little easier.

On the second day of this period of interrogation, I had asked to go to the toilet. Once delivered there and removed from my restraints, I discovered that the cubicles had toilet paper. I saw an opportunity, I unwound a substantial part of the roll, splitting my acquisition in two. One part I stuffed in the pocket of my thobe; the other I spread as thinly as possible and tucked into the waistband of my boxer shorts. When I returned from the toilet and began again to fiddle with my cotton strings, provoking a search of my pockets, the tissue there was discovered and confiscated, but that in my waistband was not. Even at the end of the evening when I passed through the metal detector and was given a cursory patdown search, my guards failed to find my hidden treasure. Thus began my career as a jailhouse smuggler of toilet paper.

As for its purpose, the toilet paper performed two functions, beyond the sense of victory that its discovery and theft conveyed. First, it performed its usual function of wiping and drying my arse, as I still continued to use the water spigot for cleansing that part of my anatomy. I also found that it provided good fidgeting material. The balls of clean paper provided me with something to chew, another minor distraction and thus an alleviator of stress. My tactic in this was that if I were searched, any paper in my pocket would be confiscated. So I requested at least two trips to the toilet during the interrogation sessions, one as I arrived in the interrogation offices and another partway through the night. During each of these respites, I would take the opportunity to make a number of small wads of paper that I would wedge into my upper gums, and upon which I would grind slowly for the duration of the sessions. Not that my mandibular activities went unnoticed, but I was always able to swallow the evidence and persuade the guards that I was chewing my tongue.

As for my rice diary, begun in Al Ulaysha interrogation centre, that in itself proved a little problematic, for I was accumulating a noticeable pile of rice, given that I was collecting three grains a day. In this cell, I had no mattress in which to hide it. Initially I concealed the rice behind a couple of oranges that I retained from my meals. Even so, I was concerned that the pile would be discovered and removed. My solution was to wrap the grains of rice in tissue paper and carry them with me, clamped between the cheeks of my arse while in transit to and from the interrogation offices, and held in place by the waistband of my shorts during the sessions themselves. I performed the transfer of these packets of my diary, from buttocks to waistband and back, in the toilet cubicles in the interrogation offices while I collected my day's ration of toilet paper, preventing their discovery during the routine pat-down searches that occurred each time I went to and from the cellblock to the offices.

I had initially prepared these little parcels in my prison cell, managing to do so without being discovered for I had found a minor blind spot in the surveillance system. The shower and toilet area of my cell was enclosed by a wall of about head height. When seated on the toilet, one was partially obscured from the gaze of the CCTV camera and could engage in small activities without arousing suspicion. I had noted that during my period of sleep deprivation if I spent too long seated on the toilet, the guards would investigate. However the time required for the wrapping and rewrapping of my rice grains was not long enough to cause me a problem. I was in effect making myself absurdly occupied with minutiae, but I needed to be occupied with something, and this was at least constructive in its own way.

Small and insignificant though these activities of mine might seem, they had a purpose: to help me endure, to help give me some minor sense of control, to create a small area of privacy in the physical world. In each of these purposes, these activities were successful and should not be dismissed as frivolous or foolish. When stripped of all normal reference points and all normal comforts, one's mind desperately needs to find ways of occupying itself and distracting itself during periods of such high stress and debilitation. Any little activity that provides comfort, provides a sense of self-control, or helps anchor one in time and place needs to be engaged in, in order to preserve one's sanity and sense of self. Your captors want you and need you to become completely dependent on them so that they can manipulate you emotionally, controlling all aspects of your mental state. If you are not to succumb to this Stockholm syndrome, you need to find some way of observing, of monitoring, of remembering and keeping small things hidden.

So it was that I arrived at the twenty-ninth day of my captivity. The beatings seemed to have stopped, and my interrogators seemed happy with what they had achieved. I lay on my mattress pondering what would come next, wondering how long I would have to lie there in isolation and effective sensory deprivation before the final disposition of my case. At least some things had improved. I had had two nights' sleep and two days without beatings of any description. I had my mattress back and managed to open a small hole in its seam, where my rice diary now resided. For the moment I no longer had to carry it around between the cheeks of my arse. I was passably clean, and almost warm. Frankly I felt I was due a vacation, though I honestly didn't expect one.

In my first twenty-eight days, I had experienced twenty-three days of sleep deprivation and twenty-one days of physical abuse. I had come to know intimately the sounds that occurred immediately beyond the walls of my cell, dreading what they signalled. The sound of the prayer calls marked the passage of time. The double-click of my cell door indicated a visit from prison officials or if it occurred in the afternoon it signalled the impending brutality of an interrogation session. The distant high-pitched electronic ping-pong sound with an immediate echoing click-clack followed by the air-pressure release of pneumatically controlled gates indicated someone leaving my cellblock; its reverse indicated someone's arrival. The rumbling noise of the food trolley, added to the opening and closing of gates, signalled mealtimes.

I had come to know and associate each of these sounds that occurred at specific times of day with different levels of expectation, anxiety, and fear. As I was always collected between noon and six o'clock for interrogation, I listened intently to the nature of the

movements and sounds occurring during those hours. The indoctrination I had endured meant that for months to come my anxiety
would build from soon after the noon prayer until I heard the last
prayer call of the day, when at last I would relax, believing that I
had survived another day without brutality, and had at least twelve
to fourteen hours before it would possibly occur again.

My emotional state at that time could best be described as
fragile, dominated by fear and dread, but the degree of desperation
that I had experienced at Al Ulaysha interrogation centre did not
recur. I had managed to accept, albeit reluctantly, the inevitability
of being tortured and brutalized. While the anticipation of interrogation still filled me with dread, and each day produced a cycle
of mounting anxiety as I awaited the inevitable, I had managed to
develop some means of both distraction and relaxation that prevented a descent into hysteria.

I did whatever was necessary to keep the brutality to a minimum for I did not have the physical or emotional strength to continuously endure the abuse. To some this might seem that I lacked
the courage or moral fibre to provide the necessary resistance. However, one thing I was aware of before this process began, and came
to understand both intellectually and viscerally, is that the will to
resist is finite. You can resist for a time, but eventually you will
succumb. The time it takes will vary between individuals, but eventually you will try to give your captors what they want to hear. So
I focused during this phase on giving my captors what they wanted
to hear, while at the same time trying to build into their scenario
elements that would add to its absurdity. Surviving each day with
as little pain as possible was one objective, but so too was maintaining my distance from my captors while convincing them of my
emotional compliance.

This aspect of my performance was particularly difficult
because the degree of disorientation caused by the physical punishment, sleep deprivation, and isolation was severe. It was difficult

to maintain an emotional distance from Khaled and Ibrahim, despite the transparent nature of their attempts to form an emotional bond. Your own mind does play tricks, so much so that while you are aware that you are innocent, you begin to wonder about the innocence of your co-accused. All that I heard is what I was told by the interrogators, who reiterated ad nauseam the details of my confession and those of my friends until their fantasies started to seem like a reality in my confused mind. Thus the only reality I faced was in fact the fantasy of my captors.

When such doubts creep into your mind, it is very hard not to become convinced, if not of your own guilt, of the guilt of those arrested with you. If you succumb to this distortion of reality, you begin to blame your own friends for your circumstances, breaking your emotional bond with them, making the emotional overtures of your captors even more enticing. I suffered from these creeping doubts because of the hypnotic nature of writing and rewriting my confessions, of listening to the constant reiterations of my captors, while in the vulnerable state that the interrogation induced.

Even though I saw through the hypocrisy of my interrogators' entreaties, managing to keep an emotional distance from them, I still found myself questioning whether my friends could have been involved with the events of which we were accused. Somehow, I managed to dispel these doubts, constantly grounding myself with the falseness of the accusations. While alone in my cell, I would review what I could remember of my own activities during the preceding months, along with what I knew of the activities of my friends, demonstrating to myself their innocence, and thus dispelling what my interrogators were trying to induce. It was not an easy process, and I can understand all too well how some would succumb to these implanted doubts.

It was in this state of anxiety, fear, guilt, and doubt that I arrived at the end of this first major period of interrogation. As I was led back to my cell that night, not long before the dawn prayer was intoned, I wondered if these two days without brutality marked the end, or whether it would all start again. My interrogators had completed the translation of my confessions, and this seemed to me the end of their requirements. They had what they wanted, my handwritten statements implicating me and my friends in two bombings. I tried not to hope that the relative tranquility of this last session and the one preceding marked the end of torture, for I had seen my hopes dashed all too frequently in the previous days and weeks. Still there was a small glimmer of hope, not much of one I grant you, that the worst was over. It might seem strange to consider the worst being over when I was expecting to face the death penalty, but as I said, death seemed like a small price to pay for an end to the pain, both mental and physical. I limped back to my cell, collapsed onto my mattress, and drifted off to sleep.

Ⅷ Ⅷ

I awoke on the twenty-ninth day of my cap-
tivity sometime after breakfast had been delivered, for the tray was
still there. I wondered what was coming next, in nervous and
anxious anticipation. I listened and interpreted every sound that
occurred beyond the confines of my cell. It was a hellish existence,
but it was better than sitting in an interrogation room with even
higher levels of anxiety and apprehension. That day and the next
six were spent in exactly the same way, tensely awaiting removal
for interrogation during daylight hours, followed by an easing of
tension once the last prayer call of the day was intoned. I was taken
to the doctor every second day, each departure from the cell being
conducted with the full complement of restraints and blindfold.
There was even a blood sample taken, the purpose of which was
to determine if I had any infectious diseases, and it was performed
more for their peace of mind than it was for my health. The aches
and pains that seemed to emanate from all corners of my body
began to abate; the bruising began to become less vivid – hues of
yellow and green crept into the mosaic as the discolourations dif-
fused and spread – but this was of concern only to me.

I received a couple of visits from English-speaking officers,
including the Smiling Knife, Colonel Mohammed Said, who made
perfunctory inquiries as to my condition and asked more detailed
questions about my religious beliefs. Their curiosity made me feel
like a prize exhibit in the zoo, and although on the surface their
manner was friendly, I did not trust them. I cannot but imagine
that they sensed my unease; however, they made every effort within
their narrow repertoire to develop a rapport. I was just too wary

and, thankfully, too full of hatred to respond. Quite rightly, I saw it as just another attempt to create emotional dependency.

The day after the fifth week of my imprisonment arrived, I experienced a minor change in my fortunes, if it could be called that. The door to my cell opened and one of the English-speaking guard sergeants entered. He was a short, extremely stocky man, bald with a neatly trimmed black beard, whom for some reason I labelled Orson. As I would come to see over the ensuing years, he was one of the decently behaved members of my guards.

He seemed overjoyed. "You are moving – the investigation is finished."

As other guards collected my mattress, spare clothes, and toiletries, Orson took me by the hand, leading me away from this part of the prison. The pleasure he derived from his brief statement seemed to be real. The word "investigation" was used as a euphemism for the process of torture that was the stock in trade of the secret police, and his pleasure that this treatment of me had finished seemed sincere. Without restraints or blindfold, I was led from my cell, past the control centre of the cellblock, and out into the main hub of this prison area, and then led into another cellblock off the hub, laid out in the same radial pattern as the one from which I had come.

My eventual destination was a cell designed for ten men. It was a cavernous room eight or nine metres from the cell door to the opposite wall, and fifteen to sixteen metres across. The internal wall, in which the cell door was housed, was at least ten metres high, and the roof sloped down to the external wall, which had a height of two and a half to three metres. On one side of the room was the sleeping area containing ten bed plinths, separated from the rest of the room by a dividing wall about chest height. On the opposite side of the room lined against the walls were three toilet cubicles with wooden doors, then three stainless steel sinks with steel mirror plates above them, and then three shower cubicles with wooden doors. In the middle of the floor of this part of the cell was a large waist-high dining plinth, with steel stools mounted into the floor, four on each side of the plinth and one at each end. The floor was covered in cheap linoleum over reinforced concrete. The plinths and walls, including the dividing and cubicle walls, were covered in the same yellowish rubberized paint as my previous cell. At both ends of the cell, mounted on the internal wall at its junction with the roof, were two CCTV cameras, protected by the same style of Plexiglas and steel housing as elsewhere in the prison. My delivery into this more spacious abode – in which I was the sole inhabitant – apparently signalled that the interrogation phase of my detention was now over, and the disposition of my case was about to begin.

The following day, I was collected from this new cell, blindfolded, handcuffed, and shackled, and delivered to the interrogation offices. The manner of my delivery increased my level of fear and anxiety, as I believed that the previous day was another false dawn of hope. My tension eased when Khaled entered the room in which I was held, having the restraints removed in the process. He informed me that I would be meeting officials of the court. I was instructed by him to say only that what I had written was in my own hand without assistance from either him or Ibrahim. Then I was taken into an office where I was shown my passports and made to confirm my identity. Finally, I was taken to one of the better appointed offices at the end of the hall. Waiting for me there were Ibrahim and Khaled, along with two people dressed in the usual attire of thobes and ghutras, but wearing thin formal black bhishts. These were judges or officials of the court, and before them I stated what I had been told to. Satisfied with my answers, they dismissed me, and I was taken over to another of the offices where Khaled, smiling resplendently, joined me and said that my case would now be processed quickly and that things should go well as I had been cooperative. Well for him I was sure, but I trusted his assurances as much as a turkey should trust the assurances of a farmer just before Christmas. With this over, I was returned to my cell, and the ennui of solitary confinement.

I spent the next week sitting in the hangar-like space of my cell, alone and without any distraction. When any of the senior prison authorities visited and asked if there was anything that I needed, I requested books, but none were delivered. I spent my time in reflection, trying to find the meditative means to still my anxiety. For a brief period, I was able to clear my mind and think of nothing. At other times my mind roamed over memories of more pleasant times, and I began to project the outcomes of imagined activities. I was having to learn to occupy my mind against the numbing boredom of being alone without intellectual or social stimulation, and was fortunate that the solitary performance of my old hobbies of climbing and trekking had provided some training for this.

Two days after arriving in this new cell and after repeated requests to the medical officer, I was finally granted a visit to the prison dentist. The only treatment he was able to provide for my three broken teeth was to fill the stumps with dental amalgam as best he could. It was at best a temporary repair, providing me with only a minor improvement in my ability to chew the rubbery prison food. The repair did at least reduce the pain caused by drinking warm tea or the occasional cold fruit juice delivered with my meals. That was the extent of the restorative work available for the damage that my mouth had suffered.

From the count of the days provided by my rice diary, I arrived at January 28, 2001, a Sunday. The guards entered my cell in the morning just after breakfast, bringing with them the clothes I had been wearing on the day of my arrest. Told to get dressed, I heard the one word that could cause me fear: investigation. Blindfolded and shackled, I was taken to the interrogation offices, where I met Khaled, who told me only that I was being returned to Al Ulaysha, the interrogation centre.

Because I could not fathom that there was any more confession they needed, I immediately believed that I was to be executed. I was both nervous and calm at the same time. I did not doubt their ability to terminate my life and was not particularly afraid of dying, but only afraid of not dying well. This may seem to be a ridiculous piece of machismo, but it was in fact resigned stoicism. Death is something that comes to us all, and in my particular situation it loomed large on the horizon. Either you come to terms with it, or its presence will destroy you mentally and emotionally. Your captors might have your physical being, and even your conscious cooperation (as in my case they did), but a part of you remains hidden to all but yourself. That is the part that only fear of death can overcome or destroy. As death is an inevitability no matter what your circumstances, there is no point in fearing it.

Led from the interrogation offices to a loading bay located near the main hub of this prison area, I was placed in the back of a prison transport and taken to Al Ulaysha. During the journey I recited aloud the small part of John Donne's metaphysical poem on death that I was able to recall. Once again, I looked to the words of others to give me solace and abate my tension.

When I arrived at the interrogation centre, I was led up to one of the offices, where both Khaled and Ibrahim waited. I was informed that I was about to receive a visit from officials of the Canadian Embassy. I was instructed what to say and told in no uncertain terms what would happen if I did not comply. Then, without restraints or blindfold, I was led out of the building, through the security gate, and into another office block to await my appointment.

Eventually I was taken into a large well-appointed office, at the end of which was someone operating a large commercial video camera; the interview area was bathed with the brightness of his camera lights. Moments after I was seated in the company of Ibrahim and Khaled, the representatives from the Canadian Embassy arrived. One was Omar El Soury, the other was the consul of the embassy. I had met Omar El Soury at the embassy and at a police station. I had met the consul at the embassy when visiting there to make a report about my earlier arrest. The consul of the embassy had not impressed me. When we had first met, he had tried to impress me with his worldliness and insights into the character of Saudi Arabia. He admitted that he had not been in the Kingdom for very long. His last assignment was Rwanda. His next pronouncement was that Saudi Arabia was just like Africa. I remember my sense of incredulity. I was amazed that someone in a supposedly professional position could utter such a piece of errant nonsense and that someone with a complete lack of understanding of the character of Saudi Arabia had ascended to this position of responsibility. To use the vernacular, he was and is a Muppet, hardly the sort of person that one needs as one's representative. I would have issues with him later in my imprisonment, resulting in my final refusal to deal with the time-servers of the Canadian Department of Foreign Affairs.

After the introductions were over, the consul proceeded to read in a stilted manner a series of questions on a piece of paper he grasped nervously in his hand. These were the usual questions that would be asked as a matter of course in such situations; most were meaningless for me or any other prisoner, serving only the bureaucrats who asked them, allowing them to say they did their duty. I was asked if I had been treated well, if I had been physically mistreated or tortured, and if there was anything I needed. The last question I was able to answer truthfully, asking for some books, toothpaste, and soap. As for the questions on my treatment, I answered as I had been instructed to, saying that all was well.

Responding as instructed was a mistake. I should have taken the opportunity to tell of the abuse that I had suffered even though the interview would have been terminated, and I would probably have been abused as a result. As the abuse had stopped only two weeks previously, I had no wish for its return so I answered as instructed.

One should take the earliest opportunity to tell of the abuse, regardless of the consequences.

My torturers were going to abuse me, regardless of how I complied with their instructions, as I was to soon find out. Speaking of the abuse then would not have made my treatment any worse than it was going to be. I live with the regret that I did not have either the courage or the insight to defy the instructions I had been given.

As for the consul who asked these questions, I wonder why he bothered, other than so he could say that he had asked. The entire meeting was conducted in the presence of my torturers, as were all subsequent meetings that I had with embassy officials. Though the consul was not to know that the officials before him were those who tortured me, he would have known that the lack of privacy in this interview was in violation of agreed diplomatic norms. The interview should have been a private affair between me and representatives of either the British or Canadian governments. It was not, nor were any other similar interviews. Yet no protest was made. Surely it should have dawned on all the Canadian officials present at this and subsequent interviews that the presence of Saudi Arabian officials constrained my ability to speak freely. Quite possibly it did. Quite possibly it was more important to appease my Saudi captors than it was to understand what was being done to me. No wonder certain Canadian officials found it easy to believe I was guilty.

When the interview was finally over, I was taken from this office block back to the one containing the cells and the interrogation offices. There I was left in an office room with a single young guard corporal, whom I would come to respect at a later date. From the window I was able to see the recently completed towers of the Kingdom Centre and another landmark, located in the Oleya area of Riyadh. Using these two landmarks as triangulation points, I was able to determine the approximate location of this interrogation centre. I had little else to occupy either my mind or my time. It was another piece of information that should have been denied me, so I took some pleasure in knowing it.

By now it was the early afternoon, and I heard the prayer call telling me that the time was after three o'clock. It was obvious to me, given all the preparations and delays involved, that I was not the only one being seen that day, and I wondered if my friends had fared any better with their embassies. What I subsequently learned after my release was that the behaviour of the British officials was then and at other interviews more supportive of the morale of those they visited. Finally I was collected, blindfolded, and shackled, and returned to Al Ha'ir prison. Mistakenly, I felt the emergence of some small hope as I believed that if the officials of an embassy had access to me, at least the torture was at an end. I still had no hope for the final outcome, but at least the pain was over. I was wrong.

Two days later, guards arrived at my cell carrying my western clothes, issuing the same instructions. When I arrived in the interrogation offices, I was informed by Khaled that this time I was required to make a video of my confessions, the purpose of which was to allow senior members of the Royal family to be informed of what I had said. This was an obvious lie, as transparent as all the other ones that he told, and I sensed an opportunity. Instinctively I knew that these videos would be broadcast for propaganda purposes, used by the Al Saud dictatorship to justify their arrests and to embarrass and pressure the countries to which the prisoners belonged. Khaled told me the nature of what I was to say, but I was able to persuade him that it would be best to give me pen and paper so that I could write my own script. I persuaded him that my command of the English language was such that for the video confession to be believable it was necessary for me to do it. My idea was that if I could prepare something that sounded stilted and disjointed enough someone, a family member at least, would pick up on the subtext and understand that I had been coerced or forced into this.

So it was that I found myself, after my frantic scribbling, taken into another office that had been prepared as a temporary studio, with all the necessary accoutrements. I delivered my confession through a number of takes, some with the script at my elbow, some without. After more than an hour of this tedious performance, and during which I delivered my performance in as forced a manner as possible, I was taken to another office to wait. It was obvious that Raf and Sandy were going through exactly the same process as I had, and that I was waiting for the cameraman and my interrogators to pronounce themselves satisfied with all our performances.

Back in my cell, I spent the next forty-eight hours wondering how exactly the tape would be used. Obviously, my captors needed a better performance, for I was again collected from my cell in the early evening and taken back to the interrogation offices for the next session of video confessions. The process was repeated, though this time the script I prepared and recited dealt with a description of the devices that we were supposed to have planted and with our reasons for conducting the bombing campaign. Thus it was that I looked into a camera and said that I was a spy acting on the orders of the British government. I could barely stop myself from laughing. The thought that the Ministry of the Interior might broadcast such an obvious fabrication was absurd to the point of hilarity. Even in my difficult circumstances, I could see the humour in it.

With my part finished, I was ushered into another office. Khaled and Ibrahim duly arrived, bearing a tray of fruit, fruit juice, and tea. They were inordinately happy, exaggeratedly serving me from their own hand in the custom of their culture. Oddly, they asked me a series of questions that were in fact a little disturbing. They asked why my phone had not been working on the night of the second bombing and asked who it was that had phoned Raf while he was at the Al Fallah compound that night. The answer to the first was simple – my battery needed charging. As for the second question, I had no idea, but they kept asking it in such a manner that it caused me grave concern. I could not understand why it was so important, given the number of lies that they had beaten into me already. At times, understanding the perversity of my captors' psychology was impossible.

As for the dates that I performed these videos sessions, they would have occurred on January 30 and February 1, 2001. On the fifth of February, the edited highlights of our collective confessions were first broadcast, as I suspected they would be. Though only the edited highlights were shown, and our direct statements that we were spies were discreetly left out, Prince Naif made his own contribution at the end, stating that the orders and material for the conduct of our bombing campaign had come from a country related to our nationalities, and that the Saudi Arabian government would fiercely resist attempts by external agencies to interfere with the governance of the country. Our videos and his statement served as the first confrontational salvo fired in the diplomatic mess that would surround our case.

卌 卌 /

For the next few days after the second video session, life slipped into a routine that thankfully did not involve any brutality. Food was delivered three times a day, which along with the prayer calls provided me with a rudimentary sense of time. I kept up my rice diary to mark the passage of the days. Every other day I was taken to the doctor and was presented to the dentist once again, for some of the temporary repairs that he had earlier effected had failed. I was taken to the prison barber, where my hair and beard were made presentable. It seemed that there was a barber shop in each of the cellblocks, and in mine it was located near my cell at the end of the corridor. As with everything else, surface appearance was important to my captors. The more presentable they made me, the more believable would be my coerced testimony and their claims concerning my treatment in their hands.

On my visit to the dentist, I saw just how assiduously they were keeping all information from me. While I sat in a waiting room with a couple of guards for company, I noted a few out-of-date medical journals on the table before me. To pass the time, I picked up one. It was snatched from my hands by one of the guards.

"No newspapers," he said in English.

I was amused and tried to explain to him that these were not newspapers. My companions gave me blank stares as they collected all the reading material, holding them on their laps as if they were some great treasure. What my captors imagined I would have gleaned from articles on dental reconstructive surgery, I am not sure. Mind you, I still hadn't been allowed any reading material, so anything of that nature might have ameliorated the sensory deprivation to which I was being subjected and was thus forbidden.

Even after such a short time in prison, my ability to judge the passage of time would have disappeared if I had not kept my rice diary. If you are able to see daylight, as I was able to through the opacity of the skylight, then you can tell when one day passes another, though the fact that the cell was illuminated by fluorescent lights for every minute of the day and night can cause confusion. Without the other signals by which one normally counts the days, it is easy to lose track. I also recited every day what had happened since my incarceration. This practice has allowed me to be reasonably accurate in my recollection of dates. Even so, I expect there will be discrepancies between my recollections and those of officials who had a more usual means of keeping track.

On the fifty-ninth day, February 14, after twelve days of being left alone and nine days after the world saw me confess to being a terrorist, guards entered my cell just after lunch had been served. They were carrying my western clothes, though in their hands were someone else's shoes. They told me that I had a visit from the embassy and told me to get dressed. This I did, once I had persuaded them to locate the footwear that actually belonged to me. Blindfolded, handcuffed, and shackled, I was taken to the interrogation offices for briefing by Khaled. I was instructed not to talk about my case or any personal matters. I was to tell my visitors that I had received the books that had been sent and was shown a pile of books whose titles I was told to memorize. I was also told that the visit would take place in the prison's visitor centre, and that I would travel there underground. I sensed that Khaled was tense and irritated by something, but I dismissed this intuition because I could see no reason for his agitation.

With this preliminary interview over, I was once again wrapped up in the usual restraints and led away. Although I could not see where I was going, I worked out that I had been led to the prison reception area before being taken down a number of flights of steps. At the bottom of steps, I was guided to sit down on the rear-facing seat of an electric cart of the type seen in airports. All this I confirmed later in my incarceration when I was not blindfolded in transit. The journey we now embarked upon lasted ten or more minutes. We travelled along a subterranean passage off which were a number of other stairways, leading I assumed to other areas of the prison, for a distance of more than a kilometre.

A conversation with Khaled a couple of weeks later, in which he mocked my predicament, stating that no one could break me out of this prison and no one knew exactly where I was within the prison, explained the reason for this covert means of movement. I realized from his words that this prison must be spread out over a large area, and that movement from one section to another could be done covertly so that no outside observer could determine the exact location of a prisoner within the complex and so that no prisoner could determine his relative position in the complex (and thus pinpoint those he might leave behind upon release). The paranoia inherent in the prison's design was interesting.

The ride terminated at the end of the passageway, and I was led up into the visitor centre. My restraints and blindfold were removed, and I found myself standing in a rectangular atrium, off which numerous doors led to rooms used for visiting. Some of the rooms were well appointed, some were not. I was led into one of the smaller, grubbier offices, before being collected and taken before the officials of the embassy who were seated in one of the larger rooms. It was ringed by large plush sofas with a desk and bookcase at one end and a couple of small low tables in the seating area. Khaled and Ibrahim led me into the presence of the Canadian consul, the Muppet, and another member of the embassy, a chubby gentleman with a Vandyke beard. The conversation was meretricious and trivial, and I answered in the affirmative when asked if I had received the books. The only departure I made from my instructions was to mention that someone would need to dispose of my personal property, particularly as the rent on my house was soon to be due. This drew a fierce look from Khaled, telling me that I was in for it. There then ensued a silly conversation about power of attorney. I requested that someone from the embassy be appointed in this capacity. (The officials of the Canadian Embassy refused to assume this responsibility. This form of assistance was provided by the other embassies.)

The whole thing lasted maybe fifteen or twenty minutes before the interview was called to a close by my captors. Once again, as always, there was no privacy, not that that concerned anyone but me. I was led back the way I had come. I expected to be returned to my prison cell. Instead, I was delivered to the interrogation offices. As I sat there in the late afternoon, awaiting the arrival of my tormentors, I expected to be disciplined for my minor transgression. I anticipated a beating. Unfortunately, I was not disappointed.

Just after the fourth prayer call, Khaled and Ibrahim arrived and my blindfold was removed. I was told to take off my shoes, which I did. I knew what was coming and I could feel my legs turning to jelly. My hands were released and re-clasped behind my back. Then it began. Ibrahim slapped me across the head and pushed me into one of the walls. I stood there trying not to tremble as he moved in close to me. Pushing me back against the wall with one hand, he started to punch me repeatedly in the testicles. I began gasping for breath due to the pain, which produced only laughter from them both. Then the punches stopped and they departed.

I stood there and tried to work out what they wanted. What new crimes did they want to ascribe to me?

When they returned, Ibrahim was carrying a rattan cane. Before I had even a moment to panic, I was pushed to the floor and my feet and wrists joined together in the hog-tied position. Then the strokes started, and the pain that I had tried to forget coursed through my body again. No questions were asked nor statements made by Khaled – the only noises were those of my screams and the impact of the rattan on my stockinged feet. There were a number of pauses during the beating that seemed to be to a pattern. After ten or twelve strokes my tormentors would rest briefly. This pattern was punctuated by longer breaks during which the two of them departed and left me lying on the floor in agony.

How long did this session last? I am not sure, but the last prayer call of the day had long since passed. Suddenly during the middle of a cycle of strokes the cane broke, sending Ibrahim into paroxysms of hysterical rage, as if I had conspired to wreck his favourite toy. He immediately began kicking me in the hips and the ribs. His fury intensified. Kicking me hurt his feet. The linking set of handcuffs was released, allowing my legs to drop to the floor. Now instead of kicking me, he began to stamp with all his weight on my lower back. I felt the bones of my hips and lower spine shift and the joints crack. This was one of the most prolonged and ferocious attacks I suffered. I believe Ibrahim actually wanted to beat me to death.

Eventually the punishment stopped, and I was left alone. The guard left to watch over me removed the restraints and I was allowed to sit up. I remained on the floor, dazed and confused, my back propped up against the wall, rather than trying to gain one of the seats. My legs just felt too weak to stand upon, even briefly.

After a while, as my thoughts began to become more coherent, I realized that there had been a new development in the case that was causing my captors problems. I wondered if more bombings had occurred or if the video confessions had been shown to any officials from the British, Belgian, or Canadian governments. One thing was certain, the fact that I was receiving embassy visits did not protect me from torture as I had hoped it would.

Ibrahim and Khaled returned. Khaled was holding a clear plastic bag in which was a round black object. Ibrahim immediately approached me, kicked my legs part, and placed his foot on my testicles, pressing down with all his weight. While he did this,

Khaled leaned over, peeling the bag away from the black object, and ordered me to take it.

I saw the object more clearly now, thrust as it was in my face. It was circular, about twenty centimetres in diameter and seven or eight centimetres thick, covered in thick black tape, looking like an over-sized hockey puck. I asked what it was and received further pressure on my testicles and a slap across the head for my curiosity. Taking it in my hands, I found that it weighed about a kilogram, and felt hard and metallic underneath the tape. Khaled told me it was a bomb that had not gone off. My fingerprints were now all over it. This would have given them some forensic evidence of the claims against me, if presented as having been collected from my house. Just as these thoughts passed through my mind, Khaled retrieved the object with his bare hands, an action that contrasted sharply with his earlier handling of the device and that left me even more confused. With his prize collected, both he and Ibrahim left the room.

When they returned, the testicle crushing recommenced. Khaled produced another of the black discs (or at least I assume it was), and he casually dismantled it before my eyes, first unwrapping the tape, then opening the metal cylinder that it covered. He removed a jumble of electrical parts, one of which Khaled claimed was the detonator, and a bag full of a granular substance that looked like finely crushed brick. Each of the components was given to me to handle, before being collected (bare-handed) by Khaled and dumped into another bag.

Meanwhile, Ibrahim enjoyed passing various insults, translated by Khaled, about the state and stature of my genitals and thus impugning my masculinity. As for the insults, they had no effect; my captors' opinion of me held little importance, and their insults had all the intelligence of those bandied about by bad-mannered four-year-olds.

When eventually they finished their little game, I was taken back to my cell, via a visit to the doctor. I lay there hoping for sleep to come but it did not till some time after I heard the dawn prayer intoned. I was worried and was trying to figure out the significance of what happened that night. If they were trying to get my finger-prints on items to be used as evidence, then they were certainly doing it in the most unprofessional manner imaginable. As for there being a detonator or explosives in what I handled, the manner of my torturers seemed to be just a bit too casual for that to be believable.

I passed the next week in a state of anxiety and suspense. I had begun to overcome the anxious Pavlovian responses to the sounds outside my cell because I believed the torture was over. Now, each day was again characterized by mounting tension that spiked in response to the sounds of certain gateways in the cellblock opening and closing.

||||| ||||| //

A week of uneasy anticipation ended on Wednesday, February 21, just after the noon prayer when guards entered my cell carrying my western clothes, telling me that I had another visit from the officials at the Canadian Embassy. During their last visit the consul had said they would be returning on a weekly basis. I accepted my clothes from the guards and got dressed.

I was placed in restraints and led up to the interrogation offices to await what I expected would be the usual briefing from Khaled. When Khaled and Ibrahim arrived, my blindfold was removed and my heart sank. In Ibrahim's greasy little hand was a brand-new rattan cane. I was told to remove my shoes, then I was forced to the floor, placed in the hog-tied position, and beaten over the feet. When the beating stopped, the verbal abuse began.

"You thought you would see your embassy? You will never see your embassy again. We have the power to do anything we want to you, and I tell you that you will die here if we want it. We can beat you until you are dead, it is our right. Your government cannot do anything for you, they will not challenge us, and we are too powerful."

In the midst of this tirade my world crashed in upon itself. I had been thrown a lifeline in the form of embassy visits, and I believed that they would offer some protection. This hope was torn from me, leaving me to drown in a welter of pain and fear. The whole act of having me dress for a visit was just that, an act or façade to help throw me off balance, to make the shock of the coming brutality even worse psychologically. Only the application of different techniques could have possibly made the physical pain any worse, and they thankfully had not changed their repertoire. When the beating stopped, I was told that my confessions were wrong and that I would have to rewrite them.

As I lay on the floor, I wondered what new twists and turns had yet to be added to the convoluted and implausible fable.

If I took one lesson from this, it was not to depend on any visits for sustenance or protection. The visits served the governments concerned. They made it possible for like-minded bureaucrats to pat each other on the back and tick the boxes on their annual assessment forms. They were nothing more than a propaganda exercise. Since these visits now had no value whatsoever for me, if I was going to survive it would have to be from whatever resources I could draw on from inside myself or recreate from whatever sources of inspiration came to mind. I could not afford any more false hope; it was too destructive emotionally. I had to shut down, smile when told to, laugh when ordered, cry when I could hold it back no longer, tell them what they wanted to hear without too much willingness, endure the beatings for as long as possible, and hide in the only place left to me, the dim recesses of my memory. I was terrified again, but I now knew that whatever was happening to bring about the renewed abuse, torture would be a permanent feature of my imprisonment. I had not yet managed to formulate a strategy to fight back, for I was not yet ready or able. Everything was a matter of existing with a minimum of pain, and I could only try to calculate what was necessary for this objective.

The pain and beatings continued through that night into the early hours of the morning, repeated in the same pattern over the next four nights. In all but a couple of the interludes between the beatings, my restraints would be removed and I was made to adopt stress positions, sometimes standing on one leg with my arms held above my head or in a crouch with my arms outstretched at my sides.

During the beatings, Ibrahim and Khaled chanted questions about my mobile phone. Why was it not working? Why had I not called Raf on the night of the second bombing? Who had called Raf that night? Hours earlier, during the first interlude on this, the sixty-seventh day, Raf had been led blindfolded into the interrogation room in which I was being questioned and was made to recite to me some of the new details the torturers demanded that I recite or confess to. It was my only sighting of my friend during our entire time in prison; he looked terrible. His recital was mechanical and his voice was numb. I knew the scenario had changed and I would be beaten until my story conformed to the "official" version of events.

An essential of the conspiracy story was that I had called Raf to give him final instructions. Neither of our phone records show this because no such call was made. Yet for my captors, having Raf receive instructions by phone was central to their construction of the sequence of events. If someone had phoned Raf that night while he was at the Celtic Corner, they were going to find themselves in a welter of pain. My tormentors wanted more names.

They began asking me questions about Les Walker and Carlos Duran, a Filipino who worked as a mechanic at one of the main car dealerships in Riyadh. It appeared that my statements about my whereabouts on the night of the bombing were being used to ensnare my friend, Les. Now they hoped I would implicate Carlos. I had met Carlos on only one occasion, when he had examined Sandy's car, and that was only a brief introduction before Carlos disappeared underneath Sandy's car. Carlos also worked freelance in his spare time to earn extra cash. Carlos serviced Raf's car, and I knew that he had called Raf on the day of the bombing to arrange servicing for it.

I was accused over and over again of working with these newly claimed co-conspirators to plant the bombs, of having an affair with Carlos's wife, of having an affair with Aida, Les's wife, of having an affair with Noy, Sandy's wife, and of being homosexual. I will admit that hearing that accusation again delivered immediately after accusations of adultery forced me to restrain a smile that tried to form despite my pain. I must be a rather odd homosexual if the only intimate acts I could be accused of were heterosexual in nature. I was tempted to point this out, but the abuse meant I could only scream and endure.

I assumed that some of these claims would be used against my fellow inmates. As step-by-step information was imparted to me with each swing of the cane, I discovered that the questions and accusations were actually central to the new twists in the plot formulation. Gradually I began to see the form of the new story that I was to relate. The revised confessions would require me to betray another friend, someone I had met only in passing. I was as loath to do this as I had been to betray either Sandy or Raf, so I tried to hang on, denying my captors any new confessions. I knew that I could not resist forever, but for my own peace of mind I had to endure for as long as I was able. It may have been foolish, but it was necessary for me in order to retain a semblance of personal integrity.

Shortly before the dawn prayer of the sixty-eighth day, I was returned to my cell where my meagre possessions were collected. I changed into my prison clothes and was taken back to the cellblock with the smaller one-man cells. I was left in a cold cell with only the clothes in which I was clad: a thobe, a T-shirt, and a pair of boxer shorts. Even my prison sandals had been taken. The doctor then visited, pronouncing me fit to be tortured, as was his duty. Not that he specifically stated this, but his function was obviously aligned with the needs of the abusers, not the abused. With that over, the guards left me alone, informing me as they departed that I had to remain standing. For the rest of what was now morning I stood there, occasionally shivering in the coldness of the cell. I was tired but not so tired that I would fall asleep on my feet and fall over; however, since the cell did not have anything to which I could be chained in an upright position, I wondered what would happen if they intended to keep me awake for a prolonged period. I found out soon enough.

After the second night of sleep deprivation, I fell asleep on my feet, collapsing into the door through exhaustion, and I was granted the concession of being allowed to sit on the end of the bed plinth. I was made to stand again only when it was noticed that I might be about to fall asleep. I will admit that having been allowed to sit, I immediately snugged myself up against the wall, leaned my head over, and promptly tried to grab a few moments of unconsciousness. Thus began the game of my standing till I fell (sometimes deliberately), followed by being allowed to sit, then my abusing the privilege by trying to sleep, and finally being made to stand again. This went on for eighteen sleep-deprived nights before I was again collected for the investigation just after noon prayer. Much as I had anticipated, the cycle of torture began again.

The torture went on in the same old way, using the hog-tied position, my feet turning into inflamed lumps. Between the beatings, the guards supervised my being put in one or another stress position, intensifying the agony. The same accusations and the same demands were repeated over and over. Interestingly, at no time did Khaled act out the pretence of trying to help me. Was the effort required to feign friendship beyond his professional abilities, now that he was showing more and more pleasure in demonstrating his power over me? The process of torture and interrogation continued into the next day for more than twenty-four hours, sleep being denied me.

Several times during the first few days I was subjected to lectures from Khaled. On the second night, during an interlude in the torture, Khaled revealed that he and Ibrahim were part of an investigation that would prove the Americans had been working to destabilize the Kingdom. At the outset, I did not find such paranoia astonishing, and his basic premise was fine as far as it went, for the American government has frequently worked to discredit or overthrow regimes that are not to its taste or that are out of favour (Cuba, Chile, Nicaragua, Iraq, Iran to name a few). It is not beyond possibility that the American government would prefer a different regime in Saudi Arabia, but how likely was it? Given the lengths to which the American government has gone to support the Al Sauds, and the involvement of American companies in the defence and development of the Kingdom, Khaled's initial statement was one that did not bear deep examination.

While I sat on my haunches, he wove a web of conspiracy theories. According to Khaled, he and his colleagues were soon going to prove that the suicide bombing directed against the USS *Cole* in the Yemen was conducted by the CIA and Mossad, undertaken to reinforce American demands for a greater troop presence in the Kingdom. Further to this, the terrorist bombings that occurred in Riyadh in 1995 and Al Khobar in 1996, initially attributed to Iran by both the Saudi and the American governments, then later attributed more correctly to Bin Laden, were in fact the work of American intelligence with the assistance of Saddam Hussein. As I first heard these claims, I searched Khaled's face for any sign that he was joking. All I saw were the burning eyes and vehemence of a true believer.

During his tirade, I asked him a number of questions, following them up with a couple of ad hoc conspiracy theories of my own concerning the Clinton-Lewinsky scandal, in order to try to keep him talking. For all the difficulties of my situation, I found his delusional claims fascinating, and they did in fact provide me with a picture of his warped intellect. As he fleshed out the detail of his claims, it dawned on me that this could in part be why it was necessary to have me confess to being a spy, to show that western governments were indeed their enemies. If this was to be the case, then it gave me another reason for believing that some if not all of us would not get out of this alive.

On the third night, during another of the interludes, Ibrahim left and I was allowed to sit down, albeit awkwardly as my wrists were still cuffed behind my back. Thankful for small mercies, I positioned myself in front of Khaled, wondering if an attempt to build emotional dependency would take place. I watched as he pulled from the pocket of his thobe a small number of photographs, the uppermost of which I immediately recognized. It was one of the set recording a trip down the Hejaz railway with my father. He had sent me these as he knew I had no camera of my own. Now a selection of them was being displayed before my eyes. They had been carefully chosen, being only those in which my father was the subject. As each one was placed before me, Khaled made a barrage of threats and promises, telling me how my father must be worried about me, how disappointing it would be for him never to see me again, how he never would if I did not cooperate. His entreaties fell on deaf ears until the last photograph appeared.

It was not a photograph my father had sent me, nor was he its subject, but I recognized it nonetheless. It was a photograph of the front of the apartment building in which he lived. As recognition took hold, I felt a rising sense of shock and disorientation that I was unable to hide or disguise, and I am sure my reaction did not go unnoticed.

"We know everything about you," Khaled said as he toyed with the photograph. "We can do anything we want to you or your father. If we wanted, we could bring him here any time we want to."

As I heard those words, my heart sank, and I felt a new fear: dread for the danger that my father might now face. One might think that this was all an elaborate mind game on the part of my captors, and that my father was in no real danger. In this one would be partially right; it was a mind game, but it was certainly possible that my father could be at risk. The photograph had to have come from somewhere. It did not belong to me. It could only have been taken by someone acting under instruction to obtain it. If they could get close enough to take a photograph from the street outside his residence, they could get close enough to take other actions. Would they do something like that? Certainly, the intelligence service of the Saudi government is not above taking violent action against its own citizens resident overseas, and with the seriousness of what they had so far done to me, it was not beyond the realms of possibility to my feverish mind then (nor to my more considered opinion now) that they might involve my father. As the shock brought on by these realizations began to dissipate, I felt sick, but I also felt a rising anger. This feeling was so intense that had my hands not been manacled behind my back, I would have reached over to throttle the life out of the bastard before me.

They had finally found an emotional lever, one that could provoke a reaction and be used, so they thought, to manipulate me. Though it did affect me, filling me with alarm and shame at the potential risk to my father that their threats implied, my overriding emotions were of hatred and anger. What it stirred inside me buoyed up my sinking resistance for at least another night. All I could hope for was that my father would watch his back, as I knew full well that nothing I did or did not do here could guarantee his safety.

By the fourth day I was finding it difficult to walk, for all the attention had been focused on my feet, and there had been hours of beatings. From the knee downwards my legs had become incredibly swollen, worse than at any time during the first period of torture. Probably the vascular damage that had occurred at that time had not fully healed, and thus my body had entered this stage of punishment in a substantially less healthy condition. When I arrived in the late afternoon for that day's beating, the room in which I was placed had a pair of robust-looking armchairs, and along the wall was the metal pipe. I knew what was coming, almost grateful for the fact that my feet would be spared some of the attention meted out during the coming assault; however, this was counteracted by the knowledge that my scrotum would again become a target. My testicles had only just returned to their normal size from when Ibrahim had worked them over the week before. They had still been slightly discoloured as the result of the first period of interrogation and had become again slightly swollen and sensitive as a result of his most recent ministrations. With my feet acting as an indicator, having deteriorated as rapidly as they had done this time, I anticipated problems if my scrotum was attacked as it had been in the early days.

The Midget and Acne arrived. I was immediately suspended in the falanga position and the new session began. As the beating proceeded, Khaled repeated what was needed to stop it. Confess to what we want, tell us that Les was involved, tell us that Carlos was involved, the pain will only stop when you do. I knew that the pain would stop only temporarily even if I did confess, but I had hung on for three days and knew that I could not hang on for much longer. I prayed that Les and Carlos had left the country, so that when I finally confessed as demanded they would be beyond the reach of my tormentors; however, that was not to be. Why should they have left? They were innocent of any wrongdoing.

Sometime in the morning after four or five periods of beating, I could take no more. I was as sore and burning with pain as ever I had been, from my feet to my crotch through to my shoulder joints. I agreed to confess to what they wanted at that moment. Thus it was that I implicated Les Walker and Carlos Duran on the morning of February 25, 2001. After my release, I discovered that the day before both of them had been arrested and were residing at Al Ulaysha, the interrogation centre. They were already in the frame, so my confession was needed to keep them in it. For about the next hour, I wrote my new confession, incorporating the new details, and in so doing this made it seem even more ludicrous and fantastic. This would not be the end of their demands for new confessions but it was the last confession I was required to write.

When I was finished and they were satisfied, I was taken to one of the plush offices at the end of the corridor. There I was plied with the remains of a tray of somewhat stale sandwiches, tea, and fruit juice. Their faux hospitality was all the more disgusting for the contrast it made with their brutality of little more than an hour ago; it made me want to vomit. As I sat there being regaled by Ibrahim's claims of power and influence, the dawn prayer sounded, bringing the session to an end.

I returned to my cell where I began the routine of standing, falling, sitting, standing, falling, over and over. Just after noon prayer call, I was collected and taken to the offices. My lunch was delivered to me there, as was the evening meal. Khaled and Ibrahim finally showed up as the last prayer of the day was being called, which delayed for a moment the implementation of their intentions. When the interrogation began, I was placed in the hog-tied position. They said nothing concerning my confessions. They screamed at me to keep still as Ibrahim beat me. For my part, I found it impossible to keep still, much to their annoyance. Guards were brought in to hold me while my feet were struck. One began an angry discussion with Ibrahim before storming out of the room and slamming the door. Someone else stepped forward to fill his shoes.

Some time later, when Khaled and Ibrahim had gone and left me to the care of the guards, they still had not made clear the purpose of this session, though I expect it was just part of the maintenance and control routine prescribed in their manual.

Between each session of beating, I had been made to adopt a stress position, finding them increasingly difficult to maintain as the days and nights wore on. Putting weight on my feet was becoming more difficult and my balance was shot. When that night was finished and I was allowed to return to my cell, I found that I could no longer trust my own legs to carry me. After two or three steps toward the door, I collapsed, dislodging the blindfold.

"Stand!" my tormentors screamed.

I screamed back that I could not. A guard kicked my rib cage. As this happened, the door to the room opened and the guard who had refused to help my abusers stepped in. I noted that he was a corporal and therefore outranked the others in the room. He was also a black Saudi. He demonstrated the greatest humanity under the circumstances.

His angry words were directed at the other guards as he reached down and helped me to my feet. The pain was excruciating and I felt my knees go weak, as he helped me lean against the desk while he removed my handcuffs and shackles. Then gently he put his arm around my waist, to which I responded by putting my arm around his shoulders, leaning into him. In this manner, with my companion taking most of my body weight, I was guided gently back to my cell. There were frequent interruptions to our progress, for each time I gave vent to my pain, he paused to lift me almost off my feet. This must have been a struggle for although he was about my height, he was considerably slimmer than I. During this journey, I got my first clear view of the layout of this section of the prison. I took no immediate pleasure in the accuracy of my predictions made during my blindfolded peregrinations.

Back in the cell, I was laid down on the bed plinth, and both the doctor and the black Saudi dispenser were ushered in. My thobe was raised for a cursory inspection, exposing me from my buttocks downward, after which the doctor left. The dispenser and my helper then began their ministrations, gently massaging my exposed areas with an anti-inflammatory ointment. Given the natural body modesty they would have learned as part of their culture, this act was quite touching to me even at that time. When they were done they departed, leaving me prone on the plinth, longing for sleep. I do not know how long I lay there, but at some point, the door opened and another guard entered to demand that I sit up, assisting me as I stiffly assumed the position at the end of the plinth and leaned into the wall. Though not allowed to sleep, for the next two days I was allowed to sit rather than stand, so in that position I remained except for the few minutes accorded for meal times and for going to the toilet. After one of the daily visits by the doctor I expect I was passed fit to stand, and this I was ordered to do.

By now I was sufficiently sleep-deprived that the hallucinations had begun again, and I desperately strove to drive them off. I was now fully immersed in the nightmare realm. Mumbling mantras of half-remembered pieces of Lovelace, Donne, and Nelson as I retreated in to daydreams, I grasped for every ounce of sanity that I possessed. I counted out the days, attending to my new rice diary, for I had lost the last one when my mattress was confiscated on my transfer to this smaller cell. I had immediately restarted it at the first meal served with rice, and during the hours spent alone in my cell had recited over and over again the litany of abuse that I had endured while extracting the grains necessary to maintain my rudimentary record.

I had been able to get some toilet paper by the same means as I had developed earlier, and once again used some of it to hold the new diary; however, concealing the diary was more problematic. I simply kept a couple of oranges from my meals, using them to weigh down my clean paper, hiding the wrapped rice grains behind them. It was all I could do and was surprised to discover that this simple subterfuge was never checked when I was out of the cell, nor was it checked when the guards inspected my cell in my presence. So it was that I spent from the seventy-second until the eighty-seventh day, alone and effectively sleepless in my cell. I now realize that this respite was because Khaled and Ibrahim were interrogating their new captives, Les and Carlos.

In the early hours of the morning of Tuesday, March 13, 2001, the eighty-seventh day, events happened that could be construed as both good and bad depending on one's perspective. For me, I view them as positive regardless of the permanent damage I suffered as a result. Sometime after dawn prayer, not long before breakfast was served, I began to get a cramp in my left forearm. I had no idea what had caused this, though I thought that it might have resulted from my leaning heavily on that arm while seated at the end of the bed plinth. The pain was sufficient to rouse me to a fully conscious state, so I stood and walked while massaging the affected area. Within a minute or two, the pain faded away, and I thought nothing of it.

Soon it was back, and it had spread, encompassing both my forearm and the lateral margin of the biceps and triceps muscles on my upper arm. Alarm bells went off in my head, as it dawned on me that this could be the first stage of a heart attack. I pushed the alarm or call button at the side of the door and awaited the response of the guards. When they arrived I asked to see the doctor. I was told, "After investigation."

I was about to be interrogated again. The pain faded away, and I began to relax. Had I overreacted? When the morning repast arrived, I ate what I could, before going back to sitting on the bed plinth to await being told to stand. After at least an hour had passed, the pain returned but had now spread, flaring up in my forearm, upper arm, and now under my left shoulder blade. I was in no doubt now; I was in the early stages of a heart attack. Again I pressed the call button, again I was told "After investigation." The pain faded away. I was perplexed and not a little worried.

Just after the noon prayer call, the pain returned and had spread. Appearing in all the old familiar places, it was present in my chest, along the lower margin of my left pectoral muscle. Once again I lodged a request to see the doctor, and once again I was refused. I thought to myself that if I was right, I might not see the day out. Under the circumstances, the thought brought me some measure of relief. Dead though I might be as a result of the combined lack of medical attention and the surfeit of brutality, the pain would be over, and my captors would face a major problem in explaining how I came to be in that condition. It might even result in the rapid resolution of my friends' incarceration. These thoughts calmed me, providing me with a degree of resignation and comfort.

As I heard the lunch trolley being wheeled around the cell block, the pain came on again, along my pectoral muscle and in the centre of my chest at the bottom of the sternum. The severity of it left me gasping for breath. A cold sweat broke out on my face. This is *it*, I thought, sitting down on the stool by the service hatch, but these pains also faded away as the hatch opened and lunch was served. I went through the now tried and tested ritual of asking for the doctor. I received the same response. Not long afterward, while the lunch trays were being removed, I was collected for interrogation. My anticipation was more curiosity than fear. Would I die while being tortured?

As I sat waiting for Khaled and Ibrahim to arrive, pain came and went in my chest, my arm and shoulder blade no longer showing the symptoms. None of it was as severe as the last attack. When they arrived, I immediately made it known to Khaled that I was having pain in my chest, and that I suspected I was having a heart attack.

He told me I did not know what I was talking about. I was trying to fake my way out of what was to come. For the first time in my interrogation I responded angrily and aggressively, screaming at the top of my voice that given my postgraduate qualification in this field, I had forgotten more than they had ever known. Their response was initially one of surprise and fear. They actually stood back defensively, even though I was still handcuffed and shackled and posed no immediate threat to them. It was my first indication of their underlying cowardice, though I am sure there must have been easier ways for me to discover this aspect of their characters.

I was told to sit and that I would see the doctor after they had questioned me. For a while I was left with a solitary guard, not even being required to assume a stress position. When they returned, I was hauled to my feet and Ibrahim began to beat me across my buttocks. Painful though this was, after all that I had been through it seemed almost mild in comparison; however, in the midst of the beating, something reached inside my chest and squeezed with an almighty force. I no longer noticed the pain in my backside, as the thumping pain in my chest told me that my heart was being crushed. My lungs did not seem to be able to find enough oxygen as I gasped desperately to fill them. Then I collapsed, legs giving way as my body dropped like a stone. How hard was my contact with the floor I do not know for all I could sense was the pain in my chest. As I lay there, Khaled demanded that I stand up while Ibrahim reinforced these orders with kicks to my midriff. There was nothing I could do besides clutch my chest and try to breathe deeply. The pain pulsed through me with each beat, and all I could do was lie there squirming. Finally, my torturers began to sense that this could be serious, and Ibrahim left the room to summon a doctor and Khaled remained to comfort and reassure me, though a less likely nurse than he I cannot think of.

Two perverse thoughts crossed my mind at that moment, the first being a scene from the film *Alien*, where the first character to have an alien hatch from within his body bounced around on an examination table as the newborn creature fought its way through his rib cage. That is exactly what it felt like, as if some wild animal were hammering with all its might to tear its way out of my chest cavity. The second was a quotation from the early career of Richard Nixon, thirty-seventh president of the United States. Hell, I was dying so what more could they do to me?

"You won't have William Sampson to kick around any more."

I doubt Khaled recognized the quote, though he did recognize the fatalism of such a statement and he immediately redoubled his efforts at reassurance. The look on his face was a picture – nothing but rampant fear adorned his features, and he was not the one dying, or maybe he would be if things continued to go pear-shaped, as they gave every indication of doing.

The pain began to subside to a dull roar by the time the doctor arrived. He began his examination, taking my pulse and blood pressure, assuming some measure of responsibility for me, much to my nurse's relief. The results of this cursory assessment were quite astonishing: pulse 84, blood pressure 130/85. While slightly elevated above the medical establishment's ideas of average health (pulse 72, blood pressure 120/80) and above those recorded during my regular medical inspections (typically, pulse 76, blood pressure 120/75), my vital statistics could hardly be called hypertensive, life-threatening, or even indicative of a heart attack. It was perverse to say the least, and by this time the pain had finally gone, although I still felt weak and shaky. The doctor's resultant diagnosis was direct and to the point.

"You are suffering from bad flatulence," he pronounced.

If his need to curry favour with my tormentors was not so cruelly dangerous, it would have been the stuff of comedy.

"How did you get your degree, by mail order?" I asked.

Khaled demanded that I stand up. This I did, though somewhat slowly and hesitatingly, until I stood before these Three Stooges. The three of them then left the room, leaving me to my own devices, as no guard was ushered in to keep an eye on me. When Khaled returned, he told me to sit down, for I worryingly (at least to him, I suspect) wandered close to one of the room's windows. There we remained, seated, glaring across the desk at each other in silence until the arrival of Ibrahim.

They started again with their demands concerning my involvements with the wives of my co-accused and my other sexual proclivities, until I snapped and asked them to make up their minds. I was either a rampant homosexual as they claimed or I was a rampant womanizer, I could not be both. Though technically not true, for one could be both, I guess, my statement gave them pause for thought for within the tiny realm of their experience and prejudice what I said was to them correct. For some reason this did stymie them, and they left the room for some considerable time, during which the pains in my chest visited intermittently and briefly but without their previous severity.

When they returned, Ibrahim had his favourite toy in his hand, and I was dragged to my feet. Again the strokes rained down on my buttocks and lower back. Again I could feel my pulse quicken and my blood pressure rise in response to the pain until in due course the alien fought to free itself from my rib cage. The pain was just as debilitating as before and had the same result: I crashed to the floor in agony. No matter how many kicks Ibrahim delivered, I did not respond. He could have kicked me to death and I would not have moved. I could not. I just lay there.

"Go fuck yourselves royally," I groaned.

Oddly, it felt good to berate them with obscenities. I could not but help to let out the odd strangled laugh, which probably sounded more like my choking on my tongue. I was fighting for air, sweating profusely, with my skin adopting an unhealthy pallor (this latter feature I have assumed, as I literally felt the blood drain from my face, and my skin grow cold). Even to such as they, I must have presented a worrying picture. Ibrahim departed to fetch what passed for a doctor, while Khaled resumed his role of nurse. Frankly, I wish he had left too, for listening to his whining hardly comforted me.

"Shut the fuck up, you hypocrite."

Funnily enough, he obeyed, causing me some amusement through my pain.

When the doctor arrived for the second time, my pain had not subsided, and the alien was working overtime. My pulse was now 130 and my blood pressure was 165/120. This was more like it; the putz before me had to issue a diagnosis something other than flatulence, which he did, though he characterized my problem as mild angina. If that was mild angina, then my backside is a frying pan. Since that time I have experienced episodes of mild angina, so I know from personal experience that what was happening on that night was anything but mild; I was having a myocardial infarction, a bloody heart attack.

My body had had enough, and was saying so, and I craved complete collapse and the freedom it could give me from my tormentors. That night reinforced the lessons gained climbing; death was a price worth paying for one's freedom, for it was in itself a form of freedom.

So I lay there on the floor trying to calm my body by force of will in order to dull the pain, while my observers stood over me trying to decide what they were going to do. Finally, it was decided that I had to be taken to hospital, and the doctor left to summon an ambulance. While we waited for his return, I scrutinized the faces of my tormentors. The same fear that I had seen before was present on Khaled's face. Ibrahim's face, however, showed nothing but disdain and contempt. I was cheating him of his fun, preventing him from dotting the i's and crossing the t's of the perverse fantasy to which he wanted me to confess.

Khaled began to talk to me as I lay there, the timbre of his voice indicating that he was distressed by events. Frankly, I hoped this situation would give *him* a heart attack, bringing him to his knees, but it didn't. He continued to try to persuade me to confess to having affairs with the wives of my friends, in particular with Noy Mitchell. I was mute as I listened to his obsequious attempts at persuasion. He told me how much easier things would be if I would just cooperate; his promises were as transparently false as his emotions. My silence and the removal of his ability to subject me to more brutal persuasion seemed to give him verbal diarrhea, and he began to run off at the mouth, going over the new confession that I had signed, trying to have me plug certain gaps, until finally filling them in himself.

During the days that I had been required to rewrite my confession to the second bombing, I incorporated Les and Carlos into the plot, so that it was now even more convoluted. The early part of the confession remained the same up until the point that I arrived at Sandy Mitchell's and delivered the fake bomb to Raf. After that I now went over to Les Walker's house and waited until about eight o'clock before going over to the Al Fallah compound to try to spot the target vehicle. When it did not arrive as expected, I switched target vehicles, selecting the one parked next to Raf's. So far so good; however, when I checked my mobile phone I realized it was not working. As a result of this I was forced to leave the scene, drive over to Les's house and ask him to phone Raf and deliver the instructions. Les had thus become a member of a cell of covert operatives working for the British government.

After I had done this I went back to the parking area and waited for Raf to plant the dummy bomb on the revised target with everything continuing as previously stated, until just after my departure from the scene of the explosion. Instead of going home, I drove back to Les's house via a circuitous and complex route, where I dropped off the now operational dummy bomb for storage, then waited until the wee hours of the morning before going home. These were the new additions that implicated Les; there was little else for me to add, though Khaled and Ibrahim had introduced impossible complications for others to confess to, as I now found out.

In the early days of this period of torture they had wanted me to confess to going around to Carlos's apartment to give him the instructions, instead of going to see Les. However, it gradually dawned on them that I knew little about Carlos, being unable to recognize a photo of him shown to me on the second day of the recommencement of torture. In fact, it was only as I was lying on the floor having my heart attack that I realized that Carlos's picture must have been among the various photographs of Filipino nationals I was shown. These had been placed before me without any names being mentioned and I was asked if I recognized the faces, being beaten every time I said no. I managed to convince them of the truth that I knew none of the faces, sabotaging the carefully prepared scenario.

Why it was important to them that I know Carlos, I do not know, particularly as all the rest of my confessions were a fabrication of their making. Somehow, within the confines of their logic, they needed a real personal connection between him and me to sell their lies. Because they did not have this, they had changed the scenario so that when I left Les's house after dropping off the request to make the phone call to Raf, Les, accompanied by our acquaintance Peter Brandon, then drove to Carlos's apartment and had him make the call, before driving back to their starting point.

I had been required to add to my confession that I found out after the fact Les had used Carlos to make the call, thus adding them both to the list of those I was forced to implicate. Oddly, my confessions contained no statement that Peter Brandon was at Les's house or was involved in any way, yet here he was being drawn in as Khaled spun their web. And then there were six. How much further could this ridiculous conspiracy theory expand? I was just beginning to learn how much, as the final twist to the saga of the second bomb was revealed. It made all the earlier complications contrived earlier seem mundane by comparison.

What I now heard was that the dummy bomb was not in fact a dummy but an operational explosive device (apparently used in another bombing, but this was something I discovered after my release). Having performed the swap of the bombs, instead of carrying a dummy device, I was thus carrying an active device, rigged to explode to the same signal as the bomb attached to the GMC, meaning that when I used the remote control to detonate the real bomb, the now operational dummy bomb would explode in my car killing me. Why in hell was that supposed to be part of the plot?

The reason was simple, at least in the eyes of my captors. It was supposed to lead the authorities to me and they would conclude that I was a lone mad bomber who had died as a result of his perverse art. I was to be sacrificed because Sandy Mitchell had discovered that I was having an affair with Noy, his wife, as well as with the wives of other of my friends. False sacrifice and revenge were the motivations. It read like an unlikely plot by Ed Wood. I had first met Noy when she was seven and a half months pregnant. I pointed this out to them that night, enjoying the look of disappointment that crossed their faces. It is obvious to me now that the more complex the plot, the more believable it was to my captors.

My mind was assailed by this unabashed nonsense. When the prison guards assigned to drive the ambulance arrived with their stretcher, I was loaded up and wheeled out to the elevator. It was then discovered that the stretcher with me aboard would not fit. The crew had only just managed to get it in the elevator on the way up by fully collapsing it and raising it vertically. The day had long since turned into a farce.

I said to Khaled, "You bastards could not organize a fuck in a brothel."

Strictly speaking this is not true, for if anything the one thing the House of Saud is more than capable of is just that.

I was released from the stretcher and stood up, my heart still trying to break free, as I walked down the steps while the ambulance crew fitted the stretcher into the elevator. They had spent a frantic few minutes trying to figure out how to get the stretcher down the stairs so I could take the elevator, but the exercise in geometry was beyond their initiative or imagination. I made the decision for them, walking gingerly toward the stairwell, cursing them for the clowns they were. By the time I limped into the back of the ambulance, whatever goodwill the guards or the drivers might have had for me would have disappeared, but I did not care.

I was dying, at least by my reckoning, and I just wanted to get it over with.

As I lay in the ambulance, propped up on my elbow and leaning over to the left, having discovered that the position minimized my discomfort, I felt somewhat disconnected from my body. I could feel all the pain, but I felt detached from the sensation of my body slowly dying underneath me. I was not afraid. I was filled with an almost natural calm consideration of my condition. I was staring oblivion in the face; there was nothing more that could be done to me, the pain would now be transitory so it no longer had the power to control me in the way that it had. Thus it was that my captors lost control of me temporarily. These realizations were strangely empowering, and I found that even in the face of what was now before me, I felt more alive than I had done in the preceding weeks, my sense of self returned more strongly than ever. I was no longer an anonymous member of the living dead, I was alive again, even if only briefly. It felt good.

four

IF

‖‖ ‖‖ ∕∕∕

The prison ambulance pulled into Shamasi hospital, and I was unloaded onto a wheelchair and pushed into the emergency room. I noted from a wall clock that it was now eight-thirty in the evening. By my estimation, the first bouts of pain had started around eight that morning, and I had first collapsed during interrogation at three in the afternoon. From noting the time on the wristwatch of the prison doctor, I knew that it was four-thirty when he finally decided that I needed to be hospitalized. It had taken them four hours to make the arrangements and deliver me to the hospital; it had been nearly twelve hours since I first asked for medical attention. The response of the prison authorities could hardly be called rapid or concerned, though that is how it has been portrayed.

The emergency room was filthy, dilapidated, and chaotic. This was one of the Kingdom's lower-grade facilities, for the use of the ordinary citizenry. As I was wheeled from examination room to examination room, I saw the victims of violent crime, crime that supposedly did not occur in Felix Arabia. Among the patients were a couple of people being treated for stabbings, one man with a gunshot wound, and people suffering head wounds from fights. My guards, who by now had been joined by an English-speaking officer, did not seem to mind the questions I was asking the nursing staff who confirmed what I saw. This changed later.

Eventually I was wheeled onto what passed for the cardiac intensive care ward. It was a long open-plan room with about thirty beds lining the walls. In the centre of the ward by the main door was the nurses' station, staffed by three nurses and a doctor.

A few other ancillary workers milled around, making deliveries or collections. I was put on a bed immediately opposite the door, and my guards took up station there, watching me. The medical staff then began the process of pumping me full of the medication deemed necessary for my condition; it was a cocktail of everything from anticoagulants to vasodilators. Nothing alleviated my condition, my heart painfully continuing its attempt to break out of my chest. Perversely, I had a severe reaction to one compound that was being fed into me by intravenous drip, a nitrate used to dilate my blood vessels. It increased my discomfort by giving me a headache as severe as the pain in my chest, a common side effect of that drug.

After these ministrations, I lay back and tried to sleep, but the pain would not let me. It sustained the conditions of sleep deprivation that I had endured for so many days already. I spent the next few days, until Thursday morning, wracked with pain, waiting for the end. The nurses were as attentive as conditions in an understaffed hospital allowed. To be treated, I would need to be moved to one of the more sophisticated hospitals open only to the more senior members of the Saudi state. The decision to do that was beyond the remit of those attending me; it had to be made by officials of the Ministry of the Interior. Though it was known within an hour or two of my admission to the Shamasi that the facility there did not have the means to help me, I spent thirty-six hours there. The doctor who attended me that first night told me that he had already recommended that I be referred onward if they were serious about treating me, but was told to mind his own business.

As I had entered the ward, a corpse was being wheeled away from the bed to the right of the one where I was placed. That bed's new occupant arrived a few hours later, only to die within a few hours, amid the usual flurry of resuscitative activity on the part of the ward staff. My neighbour on the left eventually died also. I wondered when it would be my time. I watched death come to those around me with detached calm. It is not that I had given up, but more that I had accepted my fate, and knew that there was little I could do. Imagining the difficulties my death would cause helped me pass the time. I knew my death would be worse than inconvenient. I also knew all the governments involved would cover up its causes. Still for a brief period of time, sinecured civil servants would be running around trying to protect their reputations. In death I would be an even bigger nuisance, and this amused me.

Just before midday on Wednesday, I was removed from the ward and wheeled out to a prison ambulance. I was told that I was being returned to the prison and was loaded into the back, and the vehicle began to manoeuvre out of the hospital driveway before coming to an abrupt halt. I could hear a shouted discussion occurring before the vehicle reversed back to its starting point. I was then unloaded and returned to the ward. The same happened again later in the evening of that day or in the very early hours of the next morning. I am not sure of the time for I had only just awoken from a drug-induced sleep. Again, I was wheeled from the ward to a waiting prison ambulance and told that I was returning to the prison, a piece of information that drove away the last of my wooziness. However, before they managed to get me loaded into the vehicle, I was taken back to the ward once more. Someone was either playing a malicious game, or there was a conflict going on among the officials responsible for my detention. My guards exhibited no concern for my life. They stood at the doorway of the ward smiling viciously. Whenever they noticed me looking at them, they made slicing motions across their throats.

I managed to sleep briefly during my stay on this ward through the prescription of medical cosh. The first thing that was tried, sometime early on Wednesday morning, about six, was an intravenous shot of Valium. This did relax me but did nothing for the pain, so sleep did not come. What did come was sexual arousal. Of all the most inappropriate sensations to arise under the circumstances was the awakening of my libido. Maybe the Valium unleashed an atavistic instinct for procreation that came to the fore because I was dying, driven by the subconscious belief that I had no chance but the present to attend to such matters; or maybe my conscious and subconscious were so battered that, having had the first truly pleasant experience for weeks, my body had no idea how to respond appropriately. I have no adequate explanation for it, but I do know that it was ludicrous to be lying there in the midst of a cardiac crisis, sweating, in agony, half covered by the blanket, and fully erect.

While this reaction to the injection took hold, one of the nurses was leaning over my bed, going through routine checks and trying to make me more comfortable. In my drug-induced haze, I reached over with my hand and began caressing her buttocks. She did not seem surprised at my behaviour, more amused as she gently tucked my arm back under the blanket. Maybe my response to the medication was normal given the dose and the circumstances. She smiled and I giggled inanely.

Sometime Wednesday night I was given a shot of morphine. My response was almost an immediate descent into oblivion. As the drug was injected through one of the catheter lines, I felt its cool trace as it flowed up the vein in my arm, followed within seconds by what I can only describe as being wrapped in a warm, wet blanket of sensuality. For a brief instant before I passed out, I felt no pain at all, only an unreal state of bliss. I concur with Coleridge that the opiates are just too good to try. When I look back on the feelings that the morphine induced, I find them frightening because of their seductiveness and understand why such a substance is so addictive. It is not something that I want to touch again.

Finally at nine o'clock on Thursday morning, there was a commotion in the corridor outside the ward, and in swept a large number of be-thobed individuals, the leader of whom identified himself as a surgeon. He informed me that I was to be moved to another hospital where I was to undergo surgery, and that everything was going to be done to alleviate my medical problems.

"You took your bloody time making up your minds, didn't you?"

His expression turned in flash from one of feigned concern to one of anger, and I could see that he restrained himself from replying just as vehemently. Three hours later I was once again bundled out of the ward and into an ambulance and driven to the Security Forces Hospital in central Riyadh. I was delivered into a private room in the hospital, one of a group of rooms normally used for VIP patients located discreetly near the main entrance. Over the course of my detention and subsequent hospital visits, these rooms would be converted to contain VIP prisoners by the addition of CCTV cameras and the addition of supplementary doors to further isolate the area from the rest of the hospital.

As I lay on my new bed, more blood samples were taken, and I was introduced to the surgeon who would treat me, an Iraqi who told me he had trained in the United States and was a member of the American College of Surgeons. I have no reason to doubt him. In the hospitals that service the upper echelons of the Saudi government, only the best are hired. I noticed that Colonel Said, the Smiling Knife, had also arrived and now engaged me conversationally, trying to outline how well I was being treated. I refrained from telling him that I would not be in need of this treatment if I had not been so abused.

By now it was four-thirty in the afternoon. The plan was to move me to the King Khaled Military Hospital for the operation, and then I would return here. I was told we were waiting for members of the Canadian Embassy. They were to observe the sterling medical treatment that I was receiving. While I was being told this, the results of the blood tests came back. My heart was giving up the ghost – I had to be operated on immediately. The Smiling Knife pulled out his mobile phone and spoke to the embassy officials again. They were still demanding that everything await their arrival. Apparently they were out on a picnic in the desert and had not foreseen the necessity of cutting it short. I demanded to speak to them, and surprisingly Said handed me his phone. The voice I heard was one I recognized, that of the consul whom I had met previously. He asked if it was necessary for me to be operated on so soon, and I curtly informed him that as I was having a heart attack, it was necessary only if the doctor did not want to operate on a corpse. This seemed to change his demeanour somewhat, for when he spoke again to Said, new arrangements were made and another embassy member was sent along to observe.

So once again I was on the move, placed into the back of an ambulance with Said and a Canadian Embassy official, who I believe was a military attaché – at least I assume he was for in conversation he informed me of his long service in the Canadian military even though he did not inform me of his official function. While I was being loaded into the ambulance, he delivered another piece of news that I did not need to hear at that moment. He told me that my father had been informed of my situation and moves were afoot to get permission for him to visit me. My response was immediate, telling him that I did not want my father to visit me as I feared for his safety. As I told him that my captors had threatened my father, Said joined in our conversation demanding to know what I had said and thus effectively terminating my first almost private conversation.

The operation was performed in one of the cardiac catheter labs of King Khaled Military Hospital. The room was outfitted with a viewing booth that allowed members of the prison service and the sole embassy representative to observe the procedure. The theatre staff in attendance were all westerners, and among them were faces I knew from the bar scene, our mutual recognition giving them a sense of unease before their professionalism took over. The operation itself proceeded routinely enough, with all the machinery necessary being inserted into my femoral artery while I lay flat on my back. It was discovered that one of the branches of my left coronary artery was occluded and required the placement of a stent (metal pipe) to keep it open. I also had an 85 percent occlusion of another branch of the artery and was informed by the surgeon, Dr. Gosaib, that I would be returning in six weeks for that to be attended to.

I was able to watch the progress of the operation on the monitors arrayed to one side of the operating table. As I witnessed the arterial branch being opened, the chest pain immediately disappeared. While the stent was manoeuvred into position, I could tell when the branch was closed by the instantaneous return of the pain. Oddly, I felt no sense of relief when the exact nature of the problem was discovered and I realized that I was not going to die just then. I was not going to be allowed to die as the result of the administration of torture. That would be too embarrassing for all concerned, but would I be executed for the crimes that I had been forced to confess to? Would I still be tortured?

After the operation, I was taken to the critical care unit of the Security Forces Hospital, shackled to the bed (as was standard procedure during all the time I spent in hospital), and kept there for three days of post-operative recovery before being taken back to the VIP rooms a few floors below, where I remained for the rest of the week. The nursing staff that took care of me could not have been more attentive, for although they were under instruction not to talk to me, nor even allowed to know my identity, they had realized who I was and saw also the condition I was in. Within the constraints placed on them, they indulged my every request, even giving the most thorough bed-baths that one could imagine. What I remember most of that first night in their care was one of them leaning over me as he prepared me for cleaning and saying quietly: "We will make you as comfortable as possible. You can relax while you are here. I know what you have been going through."

The statement touched me, bringing tears to my eyes and causing the nurse to pause, wondering if his movements were hurting me. I recovered myself quickly, explaining that I was experiencing pain at the incision point in my groin. It was not the last time that tenderness and consideration in the midst of the barbarity of my incarceration caused me to explain away my emotions due to the aches that my body gave off on a more or less permanent basis.

The desire to conceal my identity caused a farcical incident just before I was taken to surgery. I had been required to sign a surgical consent form, but was initially prevented from doing so by the Smiling Knife, Mohammed Said. He permitted me to enter my prison number, 357/3. Dr. Gosaib then refused to operate, and there followed an argument between him and the Smiling Knife, with the occasional interjection by me, letting it be known that I was quite happy if the operation was cancelled as long as I could have some more pain killers to make my passing less excruciating.

The surgeon won the argument and I was allowed to sign in my own name. I doubt that he insisted out of concern for me. I am sure he wanted to cover his own backside in case I died on the operating table and my family challenged his competence in an American court. He was at least open about his concerns, which was somewhat refreshing after the hypocrisy of the declarations of concern made by Said.

Said kept up a litany of how well I was being cared for, of how the facilities that were being used were available only to the most important of their people, of how this showed how I was a much honoured guest. Honoured guest? One could wonder as to the fate of one less honoured, though I know the answer to that all too well. Had I not been a western passport holder, I would have died in the Shamasi hospital – if indeed I had ever been allowed to reach its doors.

I would occasionally be attended to by western nurses (but by the time I was on my third visit, only Filipino nurses were allowed to attend me). No doubt there was worry that the western staff would pass messages or information to me, or on to the outside

world. The thugs of the Ministry of the Interior did everything possible to keep me isolated. Snippets of information were passed to
me by the medical staff when the Saudi guards could not be bothered supervising their ministrations. While grateful for the consideration shown and the risks taken, I was just as happy to remain in
ignorance. A few brief words were not enough to convey significant
information, and they put the bearer in danger of a lot worse than
dismissal from their job. I did not want that on my conscience, not
with my failure to resist still weighing heavily upon me.

The day after the operation, my captors mounted their charm
offensive with such forcefulness one would have thought they were
storming the beaches at Normandy. It was an obvious exercise at
brainwashing, and when conducted in front of members of the
embassy, it was done to deflect from the obvious question as to how
I came to be in the state I was then in. That was a question no one
raised directly in my presence, least of all the Canadian Embassy
officials or their superiors at Foreign Affairs. The Smiling Knife
presented me with a list of books available from Jarir Bookstore,
and I was now allowed to select some from the list, which would
then be purchased from my prison wages, if there was enough
available to meet the costs. Said continued his propaganda lectures,
going over and over the fact that I was receiving such special treatment, and how I could have no bad opinion of him or his officers.
Unfortunately, my tongue got the better of me and I angrily
pointed out to him that I would not have so nearly died if I had not
been falsely arrested and tortured, the latter happening with the
collusion of the officers of his prison. My outburst at least shut him
up, but I would learn that everything I said to him was being faithfully reported to Ibrahim and Khaled. Not that this was a surprise
to me, for he was after all part of their system of putting people in
the right way.

I received two other visits that day, the first from Khaled and
Ibrahim, who presented me with a large tin of Quality Street

chocolates. Using my heart condition as an excuse, I refused their gift, passing it on to the nurses. Unfortunately, I was unable to keep hidden my displeasure at seeing the two who had almost murdered me for the sake of a cover-up. Being hooked up to various monitors, I noted that my pulse rate had increased significantly on their arrival, something noted also by Khaled, who pointed this out to Ibrahim. I had tried to keep my voice level and show no hint of emotion but was betrayed by my own damaged heart. Our conversation danced around how all my problems must be due to my prior medical history, making me aware that a cover-up within the cover-up had begun.

Both Khaled and Ibrahim took my increased heart rate to be a sign of my fear of them. Only days before they would have been right, but now the increase in my pulse was due solely to hatred. With the knowledge that my body would in its own way spare me prolonged pain, the fear that they had previously inspired was gone. All I felt was hatred, sharp, pure, and reviving. I was not in the position to take action against them, and at that moment it did not cross my mind, but the sustained loathing that I felt for them would drive me in that direction. They departed to leave me in peace, a smug self-satisfied grin on the face of Ibrahim.

When I next saw them, about ten days later back at the prison, Ibrahim would inform me, through Khaled's inestimable translation, "I know you fear me, but you do not need to be afraid as long as you behave and do what I tell you. If you help me, I will make your life so easy."

What an ignorant egotistical fool he was and is. He continued in this vein for some time, telling me of all those he had interrogated who now viewed him as a brother. I felt the urge to tell him not to turn his back on such new-found friends, but resisted. I also learned during this conversation that they were unhappy with my comments to Said, which had been relayed to them. I was told that my condition was my own fault for not cooperating, that my sickness was due to my life before my imprisonment, and that any claims to the contrary would be met by punishment. I was also told in no uncertain terms that if I said anything different to the embassy staff, it would not just be me that suffered. It was interesting that they now tried to control me through threats against the other prisoners, even though they had earlier informed me that these same people had tried to kill me. The twisted nature of their thinking was something to behold.

In the second visit of that day, officials from the Canadian Embassy arrived, the first consul among them. His greeting was followed by an expression of surprise that I would be sitting in bed reading Tolstoy's *War and Peace*. I pointed out that as it was available, why should I not be reading it? His response helped me form an idea of his opinion of me and my situation, for it would seem that he considered that such a tome was something someone like me would not bother with and something too intellectually demanding under the circumstances. One could visibly see his thought processes grinding out their incorrect conclusion that perhaps things were not so bad if I could read a book like that. It was obvious to me that he viewed me through the lens of his own intellectual limitations and the severely prejudiced opinion he had formed of my guilt. I learned that this individual actually considered me to be guilty of the crimes of which the Saudis had accused me. It took me some time to understand what he based his conclusions on, but that was months in the future. Right now in the hospital room, I wondered how long I would have to be polite to the civil service Muppet who strutted before me. If nothing else, it provided me with the opportunity to tell my visitors to keep my father from visiting me, a demand that I would reiterate on all but one occasion.

With these visits over, I spent the next few days convalescing. I was able to shower and clean myself, amusing myself with the limited selection of reading material with which I had been provided.

Despite the fact that I was in hospital due to a heart attack, I felt quite relaxed and content. I knew that even if torture loomed on the horizon, I would not have to endure it for long. As it was, the regimen of my incarceration had become slightly more humane, with many people expressing insincere concern for my condition. There was no one I could trust, but that did not bother me. This situation had the makings of a long siege, and only I could provide the means to keep myself together. These things I had known instinctively from the first day, but events had shown me to be right. I still did not expect to experience ever again another day of freedom, but at that moment I was concerned purely with surviving and not exacerbating the situation, so freedom was not a luxury to be entertained.

Too soon, I was returned to the prison on the ninety-ninth day of my imprisonment, put back into an empty ten-man cell, and began again the daily routine of incarceration. My conditions had improved somewhat, and I was no longer moved around the prison wearing restraints or a blindfold, so I could confirm the accuracy of my sightless estimations. Now I was allowed to order reading material from a list provided, I was given access to the prison commissary, I had a daily visit to the doctor, and I was permitted one hour every day in an exercise yard. I gladly availed myself of these opportunities to break the monotony of solitary confinement. I placed regular orders for fruit juice and for bran flakes and began to build up a small collection of books, among which was a copy of the Koran, something that I had not ordered, but that I was exhorted to read on numerous occasions. Physically, my body seemed to be repairing. I still had aches and pains in my feet and several of my joints, but these decreased sufficiently to allow me to exercise. I experienced the occasional jolt of angina, telling me that I still had problems to be fixed, but that concerned the prison officials more than it did me. Overall the situation was tolerable.

It was during this time that the propaganda lectures started in earnest and I had my first visit with a prison psychiatrist. The propaganda lectures were now a regular feature of my imprisonment. They occurred once every week or two weeks depending on the availability of Mohammed Said, the Smiling Knife. Into my cell he would waft, full of false bonhomie and bullshit. He would always begin his talks the same way with exhortations as to the righteousness of Islam and Sharia law, followed by criticism of the western way of life, of the behaviour of westerners in Saudi Arabia, of my own way of life. One constant in these exhortations was Said's reiteration of the claim that if I had suffered in prison, it was not at the hands of his prison officers. For the first couple of months of these lectures, I lay on my bed plinth and listened, providing none of the obvious rebuttals. When he attempted to probe my knowledge of Islam, he discovered I had a surprising understanding of the five pillars and the Koran for an infidel. I had read the Koran and the Haddith years previously, as I had done the other major religious works, and found all of them severely lacking intellectually and spiritually. I did not state this immediately, letting Said believe that my knowledge came from the more recent provision of the Koran, thus making me ripe for conversion.

My first visit with a prison psychiatrist was an amusing occasion, one that further reinforced just how closely I was being monitored by my torturers. Taken to the prison medical centre, where my teeth had been patched up, I was ushered into the presence of a member of the Mutawa, who I was told was a psychiatrist there to help me understand the reasons for my harming myself. I then found myself subjected to a lecture on the wisdom of converting to Islam, followed by statements that my current medical condition was due entirely to the sins of my imperfect life. It was all I could do to stop myself from laughing in his face. When finally he asked me why I had wanted to die, I could only ask what I had done that showed that such was my desire. I knew the answer before he uttered it, so it was no surprise to hear that my heart attack was the proof of my self-harm. My response was simple: if he wanted to test my suicidal nature, he should give me a revolver with a single-chambered round, then he would get his answer.

For some reason he did not avail himself of my offer. I have often wondered what I would have done if he had. As the Smiling Knife was sitting next to me, I am fairly certain of what my actions would have been, but I never did get the opportunity to put this to the test. The conversation was then steered toward how I had felt during my heart attack and how I felt when I'd received the pain-killers I had been given. Now came my chance to really upset the fool before me. Given his overt religiosity, I regaled him with the sexual arousal that resulted from the administration of the Valium. As I expected, he was shocked and disgusted that I would have behaved so, let alone talked to him about such a subject. The inter-view was terminated with him telling me that medication would be prescribed that I was to take, and that I should start reading the Koran every day to purge me of my impure thoughts. I have no idea about the professional credentials of this individual, but what could one think of a psychiatrist who denies the presence of sex in the psyche of his patients?

Two days later, I found myself being escorted to the interroga-tion offices, but without the customary blindfold or other restraints. There I was greeted by Khaled alone, who it turned out was not pleased to see me. He expressed his indignation that I would dare insult the psychiatrist by describing the perverted fantasies of my immoral and diseased mind. It was both laughable and disgusting at the same time to be given a lecture on sexual morality by a man who had raped me only short weeks before. I reminded him of his prior actions and was awarded a slap across the face, while he called in the guards to place me in handcuffs. I was made to under-stand by the punctuation of his sentences with the flat of his hand that I was never again to be so insolent. It would take only a simple phone call for Ibrahim to return with his sticks. From the look of malevolence in his eyes, I could see that was what he in fact desired.

The threat and the minor brutality were further reinforcement of the fact that my every statement was being faithfully reported to my torturers. Those such as Colonel Mohammed Said actively colluded in the process of my torture through these reports and by their orders that made me available for these beatings. Though he and others could try to hide behind the fact that they did not actually take part in the interrogations, in fact they had an active and compliant part in the process that indulged in torture. Thus, it was that I came to call Said the Smiling Knife.

For the next couple of weeks, prison life proceeded in the milder routine that had been established since my hospitalization. I now had books and began to devise a new means of keeping track of time and recording the principal events of my incarceration. I chose to use for this purpose some Discworld novels of Terry Pratchett that were part of my meagre possessions, as their length was sufficient to record a single year each. I had no idea how long I would remain in prison, but I assumed it would be at least a couple of years before my final disposition. I folded over the top corner of a page each day, then folded the bottom corner to mark the passage of a week, and unfolded the top corners. I put a small tear in the centre of a page to mark an interrogation session or visit with Khaled and Ibrahim, folding the tear over to record if torture occurred. I put a tear in the upper quarter of a page to mark periods of sleep deprivation and put a tear in the bottom quarter to mark embassy visits or periods of hospitalization. Thus I was able to keep track of the timing of events by reference to this *aide-mémoire*. It was a more efficient, flexible, and accurate method than that provided by my rice diaries. The page numbers gave me an accurate record of the number of days spent in prison, from which I could perform a mental calculation to estimate the date.

The tears allowed me to look at a day or period and remember sequentially what had taken place. In conjunction with the mantra of remembrance that I performed while marching around my prison cell, the books helped me maintain a detailed sequential recollection of the time spent as a hostage.

I received another visit from embassy officials, which followed the stringent protocols established by my captors; the conversation was anodyne and unimportant. Not wanting to cause further problems for myself or my fellow inmates, I was maintaining my compliant behaviour. It was at that visit that I came to visually understand the scope of the prison complex, for having been led to the visitor centre without a blindfold, I could better gauge the distance travelled in the underground passageway and develop a sense of the scale of the Al Ha'ir complex.

The cellblock in the part of the prison where I was housed contained 32 ten-man cells and was one of two such blocks, along with two cellblocks of 120 one-man cells each that radiated off the main hub. Over all, I estimate this area of the prison could accommodate 880 prisoners. When I was taken to the visitor centre, I was able to see that the underground tunnel stretched away toward the visitor centre and in the opposite direction for what looked to be the same distance. Along the passageway to the visitor centre I noted that there were four alcoves with stairs leading upward. If as I suspect these led to other cellblocks, then there would be another four prison areas between where I was held and the visitor centre.

Although I never travelled along the passageway to the other end, looking down it I discerned that it probably replicated what I was able to see in the other direction, giving the prison complex a further four detention areas, and a total holding capacity of between 7,500 and 8,000 prisoners. Since this prison was used to hold political prisoners and was the most secure facility of its sort in the Kingdom, it gives one a measure of how much more concern political dissent causes in Saudi Arabia than does serious or violent criminal activity. Admittedly, some political dissent did take the form of violent terrorist attacks, as was the case for the crimes of which I was accused; however, those who called for reform through more peaceful means were just as likely, if not more likely, to find themselves housed at Al Ha'ir.

On the 122nd day of my captivity, my heart began to act up again. I had had intermittent mild angina attacks during the previous couple of weeks, which had subsided upon administration of appropriate medication. On that night, April 17, 2001, the first attack subsided as expected, but the second did not. It was a hell of a birthday present, and I wondered how long it would take for me to receive treatment or if the prison medical staff would once again diagnose an intestinal complaint. I need not have been concerned, for I was immediately taken to the cardiac ward in the Shamasi hospital where I spent the night trying to predict which of my ward mates would die during the night.

In the morning I was transferred to the Security Forces Hospital, and what had now become the Prisoner Care Centre within it, where I was visited by Dr. Gosaib and the Smiling Knife. By this time, as my angina had subsided, I was hardly in a cooperative mood, so I refused to accept the operation proposed. My reasoning had been that the occlusion that still needed to be fixed was bad but tolerable for the moment. Though it did make my physical state more vulnerable, it had certain acceptable ramifications if any physical abuse were to occur in the future. My more fragile condition offered me either protection from abuse or a means to escape (via death) should abuse occur. Thus I decided that I would have the necessary operation when released from prison or not at all, stating this fact to my audience. As I still believed that my release was unlikely, the operation would not have occurred at all, but this was not a matter that concerned me. To say that Gosaib and Said were annoyed is an understatement; both of them vented their frustrations verbally in response to my refusals. My only reply was directed at the Smiling Knife. I asked if he was supposed to be my friend, why was he so angry with me? Both men became silent and then left me alone, shackled to the bed, chuckling inwardly at them.

About four days later, while still lying chained to the bed, I received an entourage comprising three members of the embassy, the Smiling Knife, Ibrahim, Khaled, and Dr. Gosaib. Once again the medical facts concerning the precarious state of my heart were laid before me, alongside nagging complaints that my refusal was causing concern to all involved in my case, most of all to my father. I capitulated, agreeing to undergo further surgery. Though I was not in a wholly compliant psychological state, I was still susceptible to coercion and a desire to ease the conditions of my incarceration. Thus, it was not too difficult for them to persuade me to change my mind. The seeds of rebellion had been sown by the realizations that my initial heart attack provoked, but had not firmly taken root, so I signed the necessary forms and permitted the surgery to go ahead.

I was also beginning to find lying in a hospital bed quite tedious, more so than being in the prison. At least in my prison cell, I had the freedom to go to the toilet and to shower as I saw fit, whereas at the hospital I was dependent on the guards releasing me from my shackles to indulge in even that. If being in solitary was boring, this was even more boring for I had no freedom of movement whatsoever. While the first period spent in hospital was a relief, now I was happy to think of being returned to my cell. However, Dr. Gosaid and the Smiling Knife concluded that I would have to remain in hospital under permanent observation until I agreed to surgery. This threat, allied with the nagging and hectoring of the embassy officials, worked on me. Frankly, I wish I had not conceded. This regret crept up on me sometime later during the long days of isolation.

As it was, I spent another few days lying in my bed while I waited to be taken for surgery. When this finally happened, on the 129th day of my incarceration, things went smoothly enough. The same theatre staff had requested that they be part of the surgical team in order that I have a few familiar friendly faces present. Consideration such as this once again touched me, and I am thankful to them. They were less nervous of my presence this time around, speaking to me during the procedure, acting against their orders. From them I learned that Sandy Mitchell had also been subjected to an angiogram, just after my first operation had occurred. Fortunately, he had shown no irregularities in his coronary arteries and was found to be suffering from an irregularity in his heart rhythm, probably brought about by both the interrogation procedures and the maladministration of tenormin, a medication he had been taking for some time for a pre-existing cardiac problem.

After the operation I spent the next six days at the Security Forces Hospital, first in the Critical Care Unit, then in the Prisoner Control Unit. Boring though it was, at least I was disturbed by only the nursing and medical staff, being spared any propaganda or anodyne commentaries that other visitors would have subjected me to. I still got feelings of discomfort in my chest, but these seemed to be artifactual in nature and were not accompanied by any symptoms other than the odd pricking sensation along the margin of my left pectoral muscle. I mentioned these sensations to Dr. Gosaib during his last visit before I was returned to prison.

On that day, he swept into the room in the grandiose manner that seems to be adopted by so many of the medical profession, and he proceeded to ask a series of questions concerning my condition. I mentioned the continuing odd sensations in my chest, about which I was curious rather than concerned, for I had already come to the conclusion that they were not of physiological significance. Dr. Gosaib responded, "They are not significant. You will go back to prison; there is nothing wrong with you now. You are lucky that I operated on you, you filthy Jew."

Momentarily at a loss for words, I struggled to reply to his angry outburst, but before I managed a response he departed, leaving me with my initial confusion. I will admit that I was surprised not by the racism inherent in his remarks but by their specific nature. First, I was registered as a Christian on my work permit, and second I am not in fact Jewish (though being one would not cause me any concern). Either someone had told him that I was Jewish or he had jumped to that conclusion having seen me naked on the operating table, and thus observed that I am circumcised. Whatever the reason for his conclusions, this very minor aspect of my anatomy had led other captors to the same conclusion. While I silently mused over the slur, my guards wheeled me out to a waiting ambulance and I was returned to my prison cell.

XXX XXX III

A week later, about the 142nd day of my captivity, I was again collected for an interview in the medical centre. One of the English-speaking officers in charge of my escort became the next person to cast aspersions on my supposed religion. As we waited in the loading bay for the transport, he looked me straight in the eye, studying my reactions, and said one word: "Jew."

I smiled and asked, "Why do you believe me to be Jewish?"

"It is obvious" was his reply, as he averted his eyes from my gaze, giving me the clue as to his reasons. Yes, in his limited world view only two types of men are circumcised: Muslims and Jews. As I was not a Muslim then I must be a Jew. I tried to explain, but to no avail. He continued to repeat what was for him a monosyllabic slur. I was not insulted. I was amused by his insistence. As I thought about this and the other racist abuse, I realized that my captors' belief provided both a threat and an opportunity. A threat in that the obvious disgust with which my supposed religion was regarded could have an impact upon my handling by the guards and thus the conditions of my imprisonment. However, it was also something that I could and would use against them, playing on their insecurities by turning their xenophobia and racism against them, though doing so meant that I would have to pay a price.

When I arrived at the medical centre, it turned out that I was to have another interview with another psychiatrist. This time it was someone sent in from the Security Forces Hospital, so there was a remote possibility that this would be a more professional encounter. Just prior to this session, I was introduced to the governor of the prison, an avuncular gentleman who held the rank of general. He was not well pleased with my enquiries concerning his involvement in the torture of inmates; still, he managed to appear concerned, which oddly enough seemed genuine. Maybe he was a very good actor.

When my meeting with the shrink occurred, it was conducted in the presence of the Smiling Knife. I refused to discuss my personal life. I tried to engage the shrink in discussions on the psychological ramifications of torture. He found this disconcerting. Said repeatedly steered the discussion away from the topic. He kept up a litany of interjections and seemed to become more and more annoyed. The meeting drew to a close with an argument over the addictive qualities of various pharmaceutical compounds, including hallucinogens such as LSD. I managed to discover that the professional before me had no idea about the side effects of the compounds he wanted to prescribe or any idea concerning the addiction/habituation index of any compound that I mentioned. I angered my companions because I had questioned their professional competence. It was an amusing engagement, but I suspected that my insolence would mean that Khaled and Ibrahim would be paying me a visit.

I was not wrong. A couple of days later, The Midget and his sidekick summoned me to the interrogation offices, and I once again spent an evening being threatened with severe punishments while receiving the occasional slap or punch. I said nothing, as they pointed out that if I did not behave things would not go well for me at my trial. It was stated more than once that I faced the death penalty, and that it was in Ibrahim's power to recommend either the application of the full penalty or leniency. They failed to perceive that death was no longer a threat. The only threat that could coerce me was a return to the full barbarity of what had gone before.

During this time, things remained relatively quiet, and stultifyingly boring. My time in the cell was spent walking or reading, the monotony broken only by daily visits to the doctor and the exercise yard, along with the delivery of meals. My diet, now restricted to boiled chicken and plain rice at the main meal due to my heart condition, was supplemented from the commissary by the purchase of fruit juice and bran flakes. I received a couple of visits from officials of the Canadian Embassy, preceded by the usual briefing from the thugs, during which I managed (to the displeasure of my captors) to get a supply of multivitamins provided. The only thing of note from these interviews was the recurrent mention of an impending visit from my father, something I did not want.

Weeks before when this had been raised during a visit while I was in hospital, Khaled and Ibrahim seemed to be against it. I found their reticence in this matter surprising, considering their attempt to use this relationship as a means of pressure. As it was, on my return to the prison I had been instructed to write a letter to my father telling him not to come to Saudi Arabia. I did this without any hesitation. I had no desire for him to show up in the Kingdom; I needed him to remain as far away from this place as possible.

The missive that I wrote, using my own fountain pen sneeringly provided by Khaled, contained a couple of coded references to Joyce and Wodehouse, an attempt to dissuade him from becoming a pawn in the propaganda efforts of either the Saudi or Canadian governments. Unfortunately, this letter was never delivered to him. A few days later, the desires of my captors changed, and so during a visit from the embassy, at which the officials rejected absolutely my repeated request to assume my power of attorney, I finally conceded that my father should come to the Kingdom. They, both the embassy officials and my captors, reiterated time and again during the meeting that the only person who could assume such a role for me was my father, and that unless my personal affairs were dealt with there could be no progress on my case. Whatever the truth of their statements (and I believed them to be patent lies), I capitulated and wrote another missive (which was never delivered) asking my father to come. I did not know that at the same time I was agreeing to their demands, my father was on his way to the Kingdom.

For the next few days I lived in fear and anticipation of his arrival. I did not want him to visit. I consented to it because I knew from the statements of my captors that I could expect physical punishment if I did not write the letter. I was flippant and even argumentative on occasion but I retained too much of the fear instilled during the torture to be openly hostile or confrontational. Basically, I remained compliant. Occasionally, I experienced a surge of anger or frustration that shook me from that state, but these surges were quelled by fear. I had not developed any particular strategy for my behaviour and was only too glad for easement in the conditions that were now part of my captivity.

It was a Wednesday, just after lunch, the 150th day of captivity, that I was given my western clothes and told of an impending visit. At the interrogation offices, Khaled took a rather perverse pleasure in announcing that my father had arrived. While he instructed me in what I was allowed to say, he made frequent reference to the fact that my behaviour should not cause my father any problems, leaving the nature of the problems unsaid, the implications hanging heavily in the air. Thus I proceeded to the visitor centre filled with a sense of dread and of shame for having involved my father in this debacle.

When I was finally led into his presence, the picture I presented must have caused him no end of concern. A few days earlier, I had had my head shaved for I found it more comfortable in the summer heat. I had also lost a lot of weight through the stress of my incarceration, and I was very pale and haggard. It must have been evident that I had been going through hell. Though his face did not show it, I saw in his eyes the momentary shock that the change in me inspired.

He was sitting in a room with the first consul of the Canadian Embassy, another embassy official, and Khaled and Ibrahim, who sat either side of him. As I approached him we greeted each other, trying to keep the emotion from our voices. It was not for us. We would not give any displays that would amuse or inform my captors. We both fought hard not to give them anything at all.

As I shook his hand, my first words to him were "I'm sorry about this."

"Don't be" was his immediate response, as we stared hard into each other's eyes, trying to convey silently that which we were either not permitted to say or would not say. It was a moment redolent with emotion, and I could see him fighting down his feeling, as I am sure he could see the same in me.

When we sat, our conversation was kept to acceptable topics, as he told me of messages from friends, letting me know in his way that a fight had been engaged in. For my part, I made light of my heart attack, making reference to the wonderful weight loss and exercise program available in my current abode. The flippancy and sarcasm of our conversation caused the others in the room to look askance at us, for obviously they expected or hoped for something more obviously emotional. We did not satisfy them, and I know that my father and I took pleasure in so denying them.

I found it extremely difficult to watch Khaled and Ibrahim fawning over my father, telling him how well they were taking care of me. As they promised to show him the delights of the local souks, my heart sank as the thought of him alone in their company played across my mind. The visit ended with my providing my father with a written power of attorney and requesting a couple of items of clothing, including a pair of running shoes to help me exercise. As he and the embassy officials were escorted out of the room by my interrogators, I managed to say one last thing to him, a single word: "If."

Weeks earlier when asked by embassy officials if I had a message for him, I had said just that, perplexing them with the brevity of my statement. When it had been passed along to my father, he was questioned as to its import, being horrified that they did not know the poem of which it is the title. Casting aspersions on their education, he provided a none too brief sarcastic and pointed synopsis of the works of Rudyard Kipling. I guess the piece is no longer part of the school curriculum, being a little old-fashioned for today's tastes even though the message it conveys is not. If one wonders where I garnered my sharp tongue, one does not have to look too far.

What I did not know at the time of this visit was that my father was having a difficult time with the Canadian government and the first consul of the embassy. When my father had not heard from me during what should have been my Christmas break, he began trying to track me down, to no avail. He learned of my arrest only weeks after the event when he managed to speak to a work colleague of mine. He had no idea of the accusations that were being made of me until the broadcast of my video confession on February 5, his seventieth birthday. He also had to contend with discovering that officials of the embassy and thus the Canadian government had adopted an official stance that accepted my guilt without question.

He had found this out during his first visit to the Kingdom when, while speaking to the first consul in the corridor outside his office at the embassy, my father remarked on how ridiculous the Saudi accusations of my being involved in a "bootleggers war" were. The reply he received shocked him.

The first consul stated, "Those guys in Montreal, the Hells Angels, they are fighting for their turf too!"

If the consul expected my father to accept such a statement at face value, he was very much mistaken, for he had only a few minutes earlier overheard a conversation concerning the increased level of security that was in response to another attempted car bombing. If this was a turf war, then why was the embassy adopting security arrangements for dealing with terrorism? The same official later gave me pause for thought, as I too was confronted by his official acceptance of my guilt.

I had been informed during the visit that I would see my father again after the weekend, four or five days later. With this to look forward to, I returned to my prison cell, wondering how I could communicate more effectively with him. I formulated a brief statement that I hoped my father would understand, and that would give him some idea of my plight, in order that he could pass this on to the relevant authorities. Not that I thought this would help my situation, but it would at least provide some confirmation for what I assumed the diplomats would have already worked out. I was not aware until after my release of the culture of denial engaged in by all the western governments concerned, British, Belgian, and Canadian, who still refuse to accept the fact that their citizens were tortured.

Thus, the next visit, a less formal affair that involved only my father, Khaled, and another Saudi prison official, started a rather horrendous chain of events. The conversation had initially been as lightweight as our first meeting, until I asked my father to pass along a message to my friends.

"Tell the guys from St. Stephen's that it is just like being back in boarding school, the mattresses are lumpy, the food is no better, and there is plenty of attention from Dr. Birching. Tell my friends in Rosyth that it is just like being in the navy – although there is no rum, there is plenty of the other."

I had never attended a school called St. Stephen's, I had never been a boarder, nor did I know anyone at Rosyth Naval Shipyard. These deliberate mistakes were there to let my father know that a subtext was being conveyed. The reference to Dr. Birching was a thinly disguised reference to the practice of corporal punishment known in some circles as birching (beating with a birch cane), and the naval allusion was to the saying "Rum, Sodomy, and the Lash," which referred to the conditions that had prevailed in that service many years ago. What this statement meant was that I had been tortured and raped. My father understood exactly what I was saying, but much to my consternation as the import of the words registered he showed a reaction that Khaled noticed, though Khaled said nothing at the time.

With the visit over, I returned to the prison, but not to my cell. I was taken instead to an interrogation office, the only one that comprised a small anteroom and a main room, where I awaited the arrival of Khaled and Ibrahim. I sat there in anticipation for a few hours, for prayer calls came and went and night had fallen before they arrived. As they walked through the door, they set about demanding to know what I had said to my father, starting with the message conveyed by "If." This was easy enough for me to answer, so I gave them a rather long-winded account of the poem. It did not soften their mood. Khaled began by providing a garbled version of my statement made at the visit's end. He demanded that I tell him what it meant. My protestations fell on deaf ears, so I was placed in shackles and forced onto the floor. My feet were raised and I was delivered of four or five strokes with the rattan, while they continued with their questions. They described their future intentions and then departed from the room, leaving me lying on the floor contemplating what was to come.

When finally they came back to continue their ministrations, they began to subject me to a series of threats that started with the usual statements of the power that they had over me, progressing through to the level of brutality to which I could be subjected. Interspersed with the threats was a litany of questions about my conversations with my father. As I lay there listening to their ranting, it was all I could do not to respond. I wanted them to get on with it, knowing full well that my condition was fragile. I mused as to the consequences of a full-scale beating given that I was now taking anticoagulants as part of my post-operative medication.

As my thoughts swirled around what I viewed as an interesting opportunity, Khaled declared, "We have your father in the next room. When we are finished with you, we will do the same to him."

With that one statement, my worst fears were realized. They were using the only emotional lever that might elicit a response. However, the response was not what they expected. As the import of the words sunk in, I felt a rage boiling up inside me, the like of which I had never felt before. Anger surged through me instead of the fear that they hoped to provoke. To this day I do not know how I managed it, but one second I was on the floor and the next I was on my feet, even though my ankles were shackled. All that coursed through my mind was one feeling, one desire: to kill the bastards. Khaled and Ibrahim were visibly shocked and stepped back from me in surprise. For my part, I let out an incoherent primeval roar as I lunged toward them.

Instead of trying to subdue me, they ran out of the office into the small anteroom beyond, with me following just behind them. I had little chance of getting my hands on them, but still I tried. I had only one objective – to kill them. I know that if I had laid hands on either of them, the Saudi Arabian government would have been able legitimately to charge me with a murder. I had no desire to harm or punish, just a naked atavistic lust for their blood. Whatever I would have done had the opportunity arrived, it would have been brutal, uncontrolled, and savage. All I sought was to bathe myself in their blood as I snuffed out their misbegotten existence. Never in my life have I felt such rage. Never in my life have I felt such a need to kill. I hope that I never do again, regardless of the circumstances.

Would I have been justified in doing what I desired? Yes, given what they had done to me and what they now threatened my father with. Was I foolish to believe that they would arrest and torture my father? Yes and no. Yes, because it was such an obvious tactic to employ this kind of threat, and for them to arrest my father would have risked further diplomatic problems. No, because problems of a diplomatic nature did not bother them too much, given the level of brutality to which I had been subjected, and because my captors had shown me evidence that surveillance of my family in Canada had been undertaken.

Once into the anteroom, I continued my pursuit, with Khaled and Ibrahim well beyond my reach. Standing in the doorway to the corridor were four guards, who looked up in surprise as my tormentors raced past them barking orders. For a second they remained immobilized by shock, long enough for me to reach the doorway, before finally reacting and tackling me to the floor. Now my wrath was directed against them and I struck out with my hands, landing blows that angered my guards. Within another couple of seconds more guards joined in and I was completely overwhelmed. As they struggled to restrain me and place me in handcuffs, I managed to stab my hand into the face of a guard, directing my thumb into his eye. I was in part successful, for he fell back, but given the intention of that strike, it fell short. Punches and kicks rained down on me, as I fought with all my strength to break free. My efforts were in vain as eventually my hands were cuffed and then the handcuffs were further handcuffed to the ankle shackles. Still I struggled, cursing and screaming obscenities; nothing could still my rage. Months of brutalization had brought me to this, a writhing mass of rage that wanted only to fight to the death. Reason was no longer part of my thinking.

Trussed up like a turkey, I could do little as the guards now began to haul me back to my cell. Bounced down the stairs and dragged along the corridors, I felt my rage subside just a little, and I struggled less. The guards kept putting the boot in as they pulled me along, angered as they were by my attack. When eventually the journey ended and I was back in my cell, I was left in the restraints for quite a few minutes before one of the senior NCOs entered and instructed that I be released. This was done with a great degree of caution, and once I was freed the guards sped from my cell, slamming the door behind them. For my part, I was still furious though more controlled, rage colouring my every thought. I pulled off my shirt and trousers, leaving me wearing only a pair of boxer shorts, and stuffed the clothing into the cell's mailing slot. I began pacing the cell, fists balled, spoiling for a confrontation. I directed my anger at the doors on the toilet cubicles, tearing them from their hinges.

Then it dawned on me, here was a source of weaponry that would even up the odds. Someone was going to die that night, and if it was to be me, then someone was going to join me on the ride to hell. If they wanted to hold me in their prison, then a price was to be paid by these bastards. I began to use one door against the other, smashing off the lathing that bounded them. I found myself in possession of jagged strips of wood about a metre long, sturdy enough in their other dimensions to make improvised spears. As I was fashioning my armoury I failed to hear the double-click of the door because of the noise I was making. The door opened, and guards poured in, ten or fifteen of them, and pounced on me. I had no time to deploy my makeshift spears or time to do any harm. Still, I struggled as the handcuffs and shackles were placed on me. I managed only to sink my teeth into the hand of one of them, who yowled in pain. Fists battered my head as the guards tried to break the hold that my teeth had gained. When finally my grip was broken, I noticed that I had managed to draw blood. I hoped the wound would leave a scar.

I was once again completely constrained, with my wrists handcuffed to my ankle shackles, lying on my back in a folded position. The floor of my cell was littered with pieces of broken wood and was awash with liquid from the twenty-litre water container that had been upturned in the fight. Two guards then proceeded to drag me backward and forward across the cell, while their companions delivered kicks and occasionally stooped to throw a punch. I was lifted off the floor and almost thrown onto one of the bed plinths. Instead of my landing on the plinth, my back collided with the edge, and I felt a sharp crack in one of my vertebrae before making contact with the floor. While I lay there, finally subdued by the pain that now radiated from my back, someone pulled my boxer shorts down (or in this instance up) to my knees. I then heard half-stifled giggles from the guards as they inspected my penis. A couple of them looked at me and spat in my face while vehemently expressing their contempt with the single word "Jew." Another poked me in the scrotum with the toe of his shoe. I exerted as much pressure on my bowels as I could and defecated, narrowly missing the foot of my tormentor. My action had at least one beneficial effect – all the guards backed away, repulsed by the smell, obviously having no desire to be contaminated by my faeces.

It was at about this point that one of the more senior officers on duty arrived and put an end to the fun. This was Major Zharani, one of the more humane of my captors, who immediately began to try to assess any injury that I might have suffered. By then I was exhausted and the fight had left me for the moment, making his task easier. Thus I found myself once again taken back to the Security Forces Hospital for a medical investigation; this time at least I did not end up in the Shamasi hospital first. Medical examinations over the next couple of days ascertained that I had suffered multiple contusions, exacerbated by the fact that I was taking ticlodipine, an anticoagulant. The result was that most of my body from my neck to my ankles turned green, as I became a singular mobile bruise. I also suffered a broken toe and, more seriously, my back was broken again. I say "again" for the injury occurred to the same vertebrae that I had broken in a climbing accident years earlier. It seemed that hitting the bed plinth caused a wedge fracture at almost the same place as the earlier injury. It made life bloody uncomfortable for a couple of weeks or so, but provided few complications beyond that, though it remains a permanent source of discomfort.

I spent nearly two weeks in the hospital while the bruising diminished. Toward the end of the first week I was supposed to receive an embassy visit, but this was postponed for a few days to allow my highly coloured state to become less vivid and shocking. As usual, when the first consul was allowed to see me, Khaled and Ibrahim were present. All of them sat around my bedside feigning concern. The conversation was anodyne, with Khaled explaining my condition to have been caused by my falling and "cricking" my back. This seemed to satisfy everyone present, though I suspect they were looking for the easiest explanation. Given how this incident was reported to my family, and the statements made to them by members of the Department of Foreign Affairs and International Trade and the consular staff, they seemed to be more than happy to assist in any cover-up.

A few days after my return to prison, I was ushered over to the visitor centre, where everybody and their dog seemed to have come to see me. Apart from Khaled and Ibrahim, Colonel Said and the prison governor were there. The embassy party included the ambassador, Melvin MacDonald, and a doctor whom I recognized. He was one of the GPs who worked for the medical practice at which I was registered. I do not think he was too pleased when I apprised him of the fact, and I do not blame him, given the number of people with whom I was associated that had by then ended up in the hands of the Ministry of the Interior.

Prior to the meeting I had been briefed by Khaled that I was to be given a medical in the presence of my embassy and that I was to inform them that my recent hospitalization was due to an attempted suicide. I wondered how I was supposed to have accomplished this. I also wondered if I would be granted a private audience. I hoped that I would but I did not expect it. The idea flashed through my mind that I had attempted suicide by standing on the dividing walls of the shower stalls and had tried to head-butt the floor – the image caused me to smile. My reverie was broken by

Khaled describing how I had tried to use screws extracted from the door of the cell's toilets to slash my wrists. An interesting scenario that, and one that should have been particularly unbelievable given that wood screws are rarely hardly large enough or sharp enough for the purpose. More importantly, the doors were held in place with bolts that had no sharp edges. I wondered if my visitors would believe this bullshit, expecting that they probably would unless I could find some way of disabusing them.

The visit was the sort of farce in which everyone tries to better their neighbour with their effusive compliments toward each other. This might just have been the nicety of diplomatic discourse, but it was enough to turn my stomach and try my patience. The examination was conducted in full view of everyone in room, providing me with no opportunity to speak privately with the doctor. Even so, I tried to apprise him through sarcasm of the inaccuracy of the claims that my captors were now making. When he asked me about the longitudinal scratches on my wrists, my response was simply that it was rather convenient that the marks ran in that direction. From my understanding of such things, longitudinal cuts are indicative of a serious attempt at suicide while lateral cuts are indicative of self-harm but not suicide. Thus, my sarcastic reference to the convenient positioning of these marks was derived from this belief and intended to warn the doctor not to take everything he saw or heard at face value. I also stated that the scratches were "apparently caused by the bolts from the door and were self-inflicted." Unfortunately, the doctor missed or ignored my oblique references either through his nervousness or inability to understand me.

When I was asked directly by the ambassador what had happened on the night in question, I said simply that I had "wigged out" and been injured when the guards restrained me. That simple statement was not far from the truth, for I had "wigged out" – not to hurt myself but to hurt others; however that was not how it was interpreted. After my release, I was able to read the doctor's report of that medical examination and no reference was made to my comments to him; however, the word "suicide" featured prominently. It also featured prominently in the report of the others present. In both, it was recorded that I had said that I had attempted suicide, a word that I did not utter even though I had been instructed to do so. I was not direct enough, much to my shame. Once again, I should have taken the opportunity, with all its inherent risk, to make it plain that I had been tortured.

When the visit was brought to a close, the embassy party departed, leaving me alone in the interview room for a brief period. Khaled and Ibrahim eventually returned, and I experienced the usual post-visit debriefing where my every statement was analyzed. Both of them were annoyed that I had not confirmed the claims that obviously had already been made about that night. They made threats that I would be punished if I continued to defy them and not do as I was told. They said that my lack of compliance would result in Ibrahim asking for the death penalty, something it was reiterated that he wanted to do but that he was willing to forgo out of mercy.

All I did was shrug my shoulders at their comments. I was not in the mood for a confrontation and did not feel up to provoking their more sadistic behaviour. I was then still swithering between compliance and resistance, without an exact plan of campaign upon which to focus. One thing I had determined was that from then on I would never allow myself to be beaten or abused without trying to fight back; beyond that I did not have any reason to confront my captors and make the conditions of my imprisonment deteriorate. I did recognize that by having prevented me from dying when I first collapsed and on other occasions by quickly admitting me to hospital, my captors did not want me to expire as a result of any physical abuse suffered at their hands. I knew that my body might not last through another period of prolonged torture, and my captors knew this also. Therefore any abuse could not last beyond a few days without risking my death. Thus their threats did not chill me as they once did, for I knew that I could endure any abridged periods of torture. However, the threat of execution rang true. I knew full well what they were capable of and was certain that one of us would die in Dira Square, a blood sacrifice to the political needs of the Al Sauds. Therefore, in the intervening time before such an appointment there was little reason for me to make life any worse than it already was.

Since the beginning of June 2001, when I had arrived back at the prison from hospital, conditions seemed to have improved. A stack of new books and some playing cards awaited me, along with socks and a pair of running shoes with Velcro fasteners sent in by my father (shoelaces were not permitted). I was allowed my allotted hour in the exercise court and began the process of building up my fitness. I started first by walking, and as my strength and fitness improved over the next few weeks I began running. Given the small perimeter of the enclosed yard (estimated at seventy-five metres), I needed to switch the direction of my running every few laps so as not to precipitate a repetitive strain injury in either my hips or ankles. In order to keep track of the number of laps, I carried a batch of small drinking straws extracted from the juice cartons delivered with my meals. After every ten laps I would drop one and change direction. In this way I was able to keep track of the distance travelled. By the end of September, when this privilege was withdrawn as punishment, I was able to run continuously for the entire hour, covering a distance of about thirteen or fourteen kilometres. Given what I had been through, I was astonished by this progress. My feet still hurt, as did my back and many of my other major joints, but I had become used to the pain by then, focusing instead on the relief such exercise gave me.

The days passed, varying little, and I developed a routine to fill them. On rising I would walk for an hour, pacing my cell, switching direction after so many laps, keeping track of my progress here by the use of one of my books and a playing card. When this was complete, I would perform a round of calisthenics before settling down with a book and reading. After reading for a few hours, I would take up one of the mathematics texts that I then had, trying to solve the problems in my head without use of pen or paper (which I did not have). Sometimes I would play various games of solitaire or use the cards to lay out the floor plans of houses that I would design in my imagination. At some point, I would sit back and try to meditate, clearing my mind of all thought. At first I found this hard, but over the years of my imprisonment, it became second nature to me. I found that I could fix my eyes at spot or blemish on the wall, looking at it until, due to the tricks that one's visual cortex can play, it would begin to move. I would then relax myself into a state where the spot would become still again, exerting conscious control over a subconscious neural accommodation. When this stage was reached, my mind would be devoid of thought, my body immobile, my breathing measured and rhythmic, and my pulse slow. I would spend hours every day in this way, having managed to reach a state of near tranquility even though my circumstances were anything but. Interspersed with these activities was the now daily trip to the doctor and to the exercise court, and the occasional visit to the prison barber.

One thing that I must explain here is that what I refer to as a day is a little different from what one might expect, for my day became longer than normal caused by changes that occurred to my biological clock. Throughout my imprisonment the lights remained on in my cell at all times, bathing me in the constant slightly flickering illumination of fluorescent strip lights. I noticed the flickering not because the lights were functioning improperly but because my vision is sensitive enough to notice such fluctuations. The results of being kept under such conditions were for me twofold. First, the flickering occasionally induced headaches. When this phenomenon first occurred, it was not difficult to deal with it. The simple administration of aspirin or other such pain killer would drive away the headache. However, when I later indulged in my medical strike and refused all medication, I would not and could not avail myself of this remedy. The headaches thus assumed horrendous proportions lasting for three or four days at time (a few lasted for a week), and being so severe as to interfere with my sight, causing tunnel vision. Exercise, reading, or other similar pursuits would be impossible during those times, and I would have to fall back on meditation and relaxation techniques.

The second problem wrought by being kept under constant light was that my body adjust to a different length of day. I was not aware of this until sometime in August 2001, when during an embassy visit I discovered that my calculation of the date was wrong. I had noticed that I had developed a sleeping pattern that consisted of two distinct periods: one of six or seven hours and the other of one or two hours. Furthermore, I noted periods of sleep occurred at a later time each day, going right round the clock. If I began my longer period of sleep at eight in the evening, I would wake in the early hours of the morning, and the short period would then occur at about eleven the next morning. On that night my longer period of sleep would start at nine o'clock. Thus, my body had adjusted to a day of twenty-five hours in length, causing my own estimation of the passing of time to fall behind by one day in every twenty-five actual days. I was able to confirm this and ascertain the exact figures only in March 2003 when I received a calculator with a time and date function. Up to that point, I was able to roughly estimate this time slippage only by asking the date of the first issue of every visit I received or every discussion I had with medical staff, for these were the only people who would answer such a question. (The guards had obviously been briefed to give me no information whatsoever, even something as basic as the date.)

The odd thing about this change in my biological rhythm was its regularity. When I was able to make an accurate assessment during the last few months of my incarceration, I found that it varied not at all. I did not have one day of twenty-four hours and another of twenty-six; every biological day was twenty-five hours long. If my long sleep was seven hours, then my nap would last only for an hour. If my long sleep was only six hours, then my nap would be two hours long. Regardless of how tired I was from the variations in my exercise routines or how stressed I was by confrontations with my captors, I slept for eight hours in every twenty-five. Moreover every period of sleep was deep, refreshing, and free of nightmares, even the naps. Frequently I would be amused and annoyed that my body was dragging me to wakefulness in the midst of a particularly pleasant or erotic dream. It was obvious to me that while my conscious thoughts might be troubled, forced to deal with the unpleasant reality of my imprisonment, my subconscious was remarkably untroubled. If this told me one thing it told me that I had adapted well to my circumstances and that however close the torture had driven me to the edge of insanity, I had not fallen off. Others might see it differently, in that my untroubled accommodation to the abuse and deprivation was in fact the product of a damaged psyche, for only someone so subconsciously damaged could be so untroubled by such circumstances. Effectively only the insane are unaffected by insane conditions. Certainly I have heard such statements repeatedly since my release, but I can only laugh at them. They are expressed by those with little or no understanding of my situation or those holding to an ill-found belief regardless of the evidence.

In what were my evenings, I would spend time either reading or daydreaming, often laughing at myself for the fantasies that I would construct. The dreams would vary from time to time, but I found that certain ones recurred, aided over the years by some of the books I received that had similar themes. I would dream of walking the streets of Edinburgh, shrouded in mist as I wended my way through my favourite haunts, ending with my looking down from the summit of Arthur's Seat. I would dream of wandering in London from Fulham to King's Cross, meandering in its parks or strolling along the Regent's Canal. I would recollect days spent climbing or skiing alone in the Alps, and then try to project these reminiscences into visualizations about climbs that I never managed to get around to. I would dream of building a boat and sailing single-handed around the world – even though I did not know how to sail!

These particular fantasies never failed to make me laugh at myself, for there I was, sitting alone in a prison cell, starved of human contact, and where did my mind take me but back into a form of self-imposed solitary confinement? If ever there was evidence of my eccentricity and absurdity, that must surely be it. Even now the memories of these fantasies bring a smile to my face, causing me once again to laugh at the fool that I am and always will be.

When finally I could sense that my body was telling me that another day was over, my mind would slide into memories of someone whom I had held close during my life. I would gentle myself to sleep remembering the love and the passion that I had experienced from a woman whom I had loved, but had left behind years ago. The memories of the sound of her voice, the softness of her touch, and the tenderness of her embrace would fill me with a certain warmth that let me fade into unconsciousness in a manner both relaxed and erotic. Thus, every night I fell asleep, I walked out of my prison cell into the arms of Siobhan. For those few sweet hours, I was a free man again and learned all too well that Lovelace was right.

At the beginning of July 2001, my situation again began to change. I had been spared for a brief few weeks both the presence of my torturers and the propaganda lectures of Mohammed Said. It was too good to last, so when the Smiling Knife arrived in my cell one day and delivered me a lecture on the fairness of Saudi Arabia's justice system, I wondered what would be next. I lay on my bed plinth listening to his sermon, finally putting forward a polite rebuttal concerning the obvious lack of due process. He was not best pleased with my attitude, and I was certain that within a day or two a visit with Dopey and Acne was on the cards once he had written his report.

The next day what I received instead was another psychiatric consultation, if one can call it that. I had been given my western clothes and told that I was receiving a visit, so I partly expected to first go to the interrogation offices for instruction. I was led into the reception area past the stairs to the offices and into the small medical ward situated directly underneath. I was puzzled by this, wondering what it heralded; however, it became clear when I was led into a small office on one side of the ward. There I saw a group of officers seated in chairs that ringed the walls. The Smiling Knife sat at the far end of room, and near him sitting behind a desk was a short be-thobed Saudi with a neatly trimmed beard and moustache. As I was led into his presence, Said stood and introduced him as a psychiatrist brought to the prison to interview me.

The psychiatrist's name, as I discovered after my release, was Hussein Al Humaid and he had completed some of his training in Canada. As the introduction ended, Al Humaid stood and reached out to shake my hand. With an idiotic insincere ear-to-ear smile plastered across his face, he spoke to me, saying in a voice that reminded me of Pee Wee Herman, "Hello, Bill. I want to be your friend."

It was all I could do not to burst out laughing. He did not even know me but he wanted to be my friend? Whoever provided him with his training should have told him that the use of such false sentiment is hardly going to inspire trust in a prospective patient, particularly not one in my position. I have never heard of such an unprofessional greeting as that, particularly given the circumstances. I sat down without being invited to, ignoring his outstretched hand, saying as I did so, "What makes you think I want friends such as you?"

The smile left his face as rapidly as if he had been slapped. Maybe he was used to more compliant patients, and not pointed insolence. At any rate, his displeasure was apparent. As he began to explain what he was going to help me with, I interrupted him, pointing out that I had no intention of discussing anything with him, and that the only way he would get my cooperation would be if he was to return me for torture. This statement prompted from him a moronic question.

"What do you mean by torture?"

Maybe this was his gambit to get me talking, I do not know; however, I did not answer his question. Instead I regaled him with a story, relating to him a report that had appeared in the *New England Journal of Medicine*. I informed him that the article had analyzed the patient profiles of a number of psychiatric and psychological practices, finding that the social group with greatest representation among the patients were mental health practitioners and their families. I suggested that given the nature of such findings, he was more in need of his own services than ever I was.

I have no idea if such a piece of research has ever been published or even undertaken, having made it up on the spur of the moment. I will admit that to my ears, I sounded convincing. Certainly my story had an effect, for whatever patience Al Humaid had left deserted him. He turned away from me and in annoyed tones addressed Said. I managed to irritate him when I pointed out that as his prospective patient spoke only English, it was rude of him to speak about me in another language. From the look on his face and the sharpness of his response to my latest rejoinder, I almost expected him to slap me. I was amused that I was able to quickly get under the skin of someone whose professional training should have let him see my game.

We sat in silence for a few moments before Said addressed me, asking me if there was a psychiatrist or doctor with whom I would speak. I answered I would gladly speak to a psychiatrist, but only to one who was western educated, western trained and experienced, and Christian, and then only in private. I knew that my response would irritate them both, and it did. I knew also that I would pay for my insolence, but wondered when.

I got my answer about two days later when I was taken for an embassy visit. It followed the usual routine with me being briefed by Khaled in one of the spare rooms of the visitor centre before being paraded in front of the first consul. The meeting took a strange turn because of a comment I made that resulted in my being rebuked for my lack of political correctness. I had been listening to the consul deliver greetings from several of my friends, including some from ex-lovers. I noticed that Khaled was listening intently to the names mentioned, so I became somewhat dismissive, saying that "they seem to becoming out of the woodwork. Well, you know what they say, women are like streetcars, there's one coming along every five minutes. However, the bus service is actually pretty lousy here."

"You are very sexist," the first consul said sniffily. He followed up with a brief remonstrance suggesting that I not be so rude and change my attitudes. When he finally got this off his chest, he asked me if I would let my father visit me again.

I was trying to give as little personal information as possible to my tormentors. And I was admonished for being insensitive. I had told my father not to visit me again and reiterated this instruction to the embassy officials on numerous occasions, and this infuriating, patronizing clown was asking again if I would let my father visit.

I said, "I do not want a visit from that old fool."

With that remark, the meeting degenerated into a farce, with the first consul siding with Khaled and Ibrahim as they angrily denounced my poor attitude and bad manners.

When it was all over, I found myself taken to the interrogation offices and placed in restraints. I awaited their arrival with nervous anticipation, knowing full well that I had overstepped the mark (at least in the eyes of my tormentors), wondering how long this session would last. Mercifully it lasted for only a couple of hours, and the beating I received, while painful, was bearable, just. Placed into the hog-tied position, I was assailed by both the rattan and a litany of threats, heard so often now that they were meaningless. While the cane descended, Ibrahim ranted and Khaled translated. I was told that at the next interview with the embassy I was to request that my father be allowed to visit. I was censured for my behaviour toward Dr. Humaid and instructed that I was to do as he wanted. The only statement that elicited a reply from me was when I was threatened with the death penalty, telling them quite simply to get it over with. They mocked my show of desperate bravado, not convinced and not capable of understanding that my response had been sincere. Eventually they tired of "putting me in the right way" and I was allowed to limp back to my cell.

Two days later I found myself taken into the presence of Dr. Humaid, who again acted affable and friendly. I was unresponsive, stating only that I would not cooperate with him. His frustration clear, the interview was terminated. His parting statement was that I would eventually cooperate, which I knew was well within the bounds of possibility if sufficient torture was applied. Till then I was determined to leave him frustrated. I did expect some sort of physical punishment to follow, but was pleasantly disappointed. What did follow was the start of the mind games, centred on the few privileges that I had been afforded.

These punishments began about 210 days into my incarceration in the middle of July 2001. They were designed to demonstrate to me the power my captors had over me. Because I was kept under an information blackout, I was unaware that more bombings had occurred, that the Saudi authorities continued to round up westerners, and that among these westerners were people I knew.

The situation was grave for all of us, as Naif and his minions were doing everything in their power to hide the very real problems of insurgency. My captors were now careful to ensure that I was fully cuffed and shackled before every abusive session because I was beginning to fight back.

$\cancel{||||}$ $\cancel{||||}$ $\cancel{||||}$

The collection of dirty laundry occurred on a weekly basis, with the freshly cleaned clothing being delivered at the same time. When the mailing slot door opened, I was required to deliver my laundry. On this particular Saturday, in return for my dirty laundry, I received only two thobes, and none of the T-shirts, boxer shorts, or socks that I had sent out the week before. I was left with only the T-shirt and boxer shorts that I was wearing. I complained to the guard captain. He shrugged his shoulders and told me to wear the thobe. I had no intention of doing this.

When I was in the cell, visiting the doctor or the barber, or going to the exercise yard, it had been sufficient that I wore just a T-shirt and boxer shorts, but now I was in a situation where I had to wear the thobe for I had nothing else that was clean. I asked the Smiling Knife the reason for this during his next propaganda lecture two days later. I was told simply that the prison rules required that I be properly dressed at all times, and if all I had was the thobe then that was what I must wear. Any other action would be met with punishment.

I let his statement on the matter pass without comment, but thought to myself that hell would freeze over before I would wear the thobe. What I was wearing was not a little on the sweaty side, so I did the sensible thing. When the lecture was over, I stripped off, wrapped a towel around myself, and did my *dhobi*. I plugged the outlets of two sinks with wads of toilet paper and then half-filled them, using one sink to scrub my clothes, massaging them with a bar of soap. The other sink was the rinsing basin. The arrangement was more than adequate, and given the temperature of the cell, my single shirt, shorts, and pair of socks dried rapidly, allowing me to put on fresh garments before the afternoon was out. Thus, I was, in my eyes at least, properly dressed and clean. When the laundry was again called for the following Saturday, I gave them nothing for there was nothing to give. For their part, another two thobes were delivered, but none of my other items were returned.

As this game was playing itself out, I had another embassy visit. I had arrived at the visitor centre to be informed by Khaled that my father was here to see me and that I was to behave myself or else. I nodded in acquiescence, and my father, along with the first consul and another embassy member, was led into the room. I uttered no words of pleasure at the sight of my father. I angrily criticized his stubbornness and refusal to listen to my last request. I told him in no uncertain terms that he was never to visit me again, and if he did I would disown him. At the same time, my torturers and the embassy staff kept trying to interrupt me, denouncing me for my bad manners.

When my father was finally led out of the room and the situation was calmer, the first consul lectured me on my behaviour. He told me that it was making life difficult for everyone, including the other prisoners. I had already begun to wonder what his agenda was, but it was strange to listen to my representative speaking on behalf of my captors, delivering very similar admonishments and threats. This meeting marked the beginning of a rapid deterioration in my relations with the Canadian Embassy and Canadian government. It appeared to me at the time that the embassy officials were more concerned with accommodating my captors than providing assistance to my family or me.

I told him that if ever they asked that my father visit or if they ever brought him here again, I would withdraw all cooperation. I stated pointedly that I needed nothing from them and would meet my fate without their assistance. My words fell upon deaf ears.

Once the visit ended, I expected to be taken to see Khaled and Ibrahim for readjustment, but I had some small luck for this did not occur. However, the next day, while I was reclining on my mattress just after having washed my clothes, a guard officer came into my cell and collected my soap, toothbrush, and toothpaste, stripping me of the means to keep myself clean. I was then collected for an interview with Khaled and Ibrahim, where I was informed that until I conformed to their requirements, neither my clothes nor my cleaning materials would be returned to me. Their words were reinforced with a few harsh slaps and a couple of punches to my testicles, but nothing more. I said nothing. I had the pleasure of realizing that my behaviour was causing them problems, as was the apparently fragile condition of my body. I could barely keep from smiling.

Up to this point my relations with the prison guards had in the main been based on indifferent tolerance, except for the occasions when they had been required to subdue me for one reason or another. In fact, more than a few of them had tried to be genuinely considerate. I can think of the two black Saudis – the dispenser and the young corporal – to whose company I would add Moussa, a very religious individual whom I would often see leading prayer; Zapata, so nicknamed because of his long moustache; Huey, a chubby individual with slight crossed eyes who reminded me of someone I knew in Glasgow; and Santa, a balding barrel-shaped man, who had taken great pleasure when he was able to escort me to the ten-man cells when the investigation was supposed to have finished. Santa would show a great deal of courage and consideration during one of my more violent outbursts, and I will always respect him for this small kindness. Now as I began to ramp up my protests, my behaviour was going to try everyone's patience, even theirs.

Thus, the early phase of my dirty protest began. If they were trying to make me conform by withdrawing such privileges as laundry and soap, then I would not wash or wear clean clothes. I knew I would get used to my smell, but would they? I began to stink within days.

Before a week was out, I was informed that my soap and other toiletries would be kept outside the cell, but would be given to me as I requested them. Moreover, my laundry was returned, and I now had fresh T-shirts, shorts, and socks should I wish to wear them. I was mildly amused, believing they had capitulated quickly, but it turned out that I had an embassy visit the next day, and they hardly wanted me presenting myself in a filthy state. However, I had decided that once a privilege was withdrawn, I would not accept its return, so I simply pushed the clean laundry back into the mailing slot, holding back the thobes. These I gave special attention, tearing them into shreds and stuffing the pieces into the toilets. I knew my actions would be observed on the CCTV cameras.

I was once again taken to the interrogation offices and made to await the arrival of Khaled and Ibrahim. When they arrived, they confronted me over my lack of cleanliness. I was told that all this would go badly for me at my trial, and that Ibrahim was more than happy to ask that I be executed. This threat had been repeated so many times it was boring.

When I had the chance to speak, I said, "Get on with it then. Take me to trial and execute me. I have had enough of your bullshit."

"You will not be so brave when we take you to Dira Square," Khaled said with the usual punctuation of slaps across my face. "You will cry like a little baby."

I responded by spitting at him. I missed, and the session deteriorated rapidly as a result. I was pushed to the floor, placed in the hog-tied position, and struck across the feet with a cane. It was well past midnight when I limped back to my cell, returning my western clothes to the guards in the usual routine. I was in a lot of pain and in a foul temper, having been through one of the longest sessions of beating since my heart attack. I found a tray of food waiting for me, which I threw against the wall, spraying the food across the cell in rage and frustration.

I decided there and then if it was cleanliness they wanted, then they were going to get exactly the opposite. I stripped off my T-shirt and boxer shorts, leaving myself naked, though only those viewing me on the CCTV cameras would notice. I knew that my nakedness was culturally unacceptable to my captors, many of whom would find it insulting if not an outright sin against God. From that day forward, I never wore clothes while in my cell. Next, I walked over to the door and proceeded to urinate on the floor, adding my waste to the now spoiled food. If they wanted to gain access to the cell, they would have to step through my filth. Finally, I squatted and tried to defecate, but was unable to. That would have to wait. My anger abated. I surveyed my handiwork and began laughing gently.

The next morning when the dispenser and the guards entered my cell to deliver my medication, I remained prone on my mattress instead of going to the door to collect my daily dose of aspirin and vitamins. I could not help but smile on hearing their curses as they walked through the mess I had made. When finally I got up, I was confronted by their glares, making me wonder how long it would be before I was called for another correctional session. It did not come, and I was left to decorate my cell with my food and urine for the next couple of weeks.

My cell gradually began to smell of rotting food and stale urine. My body also had begun to stink. I became used to it, but my guards did not. As the smell worsened, they would enter my cell holding their berets or their ghutras over their noses, in vain attempts to ward off the noxious vapours. I felt a fleeting sense of guilt. I was causing problems for them all, not just those who deserved it. Nevertheless, I knew that the prison authorities and my torturers would respond, and their response would not be pleasant.

My cell was not allowed to remain in that filthy state. It was cleaned once every two weeks. Usually while I was out in the exercise yard or with the doctor, the prison cleaners, a crew of Pakistanis or Bengalis, would enter my cell and scrub it clean. For them I did feel a sense of remorse. I knew they were often badly treated, and they had to deal most directly with my detritus. The guards would go to great lengths to prevent us from seeing one another. The authorities seemed desperate to ensure that no one could identify me and thus be able to provide the location of my internment. Whenever I would pass by these crews, they would be commanded to face the walls and close their eyes. Those who were not swift to obey were slapped or punched to make them comply more quickly. It always angered me when I saw them treated in this way. On occasions, it led me to verbally abuse my guards, provoking minor physical altercations.

About a week after I had begun my augmented dirty protest, while I was out in the exercise yard, the cleaners descended on my prison cell, scrubbing away my filth, applying an all too liberal amount of bleach. When I re-entered the cell with the guards, I felt my eyes smarting from the chlorinated fumes. I looked over at the guards while I peeled off my clothes, returning myself to the insulting state of being naked. I could see that the be-thobed officer with them was smirking at me.

I said, "See something you like?"

His smile disappeared. He attempted to ignore the implications of my remark and said, "See, the cell is clean."

Maybe he thought they had won a great victory, or maybe he thought I would see the futility of my gesture, I do not know. It did not dawn on him that I would take this as a challenge that affirmed the rectitude of my dirty protest.

"Good, I can redecorate my cell. It gives me something to do," I replied.

That was true enough. It was not as if I had a busy social calendar. Somewhere in my day I could easily find the time to attend to messing up my cell. It took less time to do than it did for the cell to be cleaned. If nothing else, it cost them some extra cleaning materials.

The officer looked at me in disgust, mumbling something under his breath, and then spit out, "You are dirty Jew."

He was right in the use of the adjective but wrong in the use of the noun. It had long since become clear to me that part of the enmity that was directed toward me resulted from my captors' mistaken belief concerning my religious and ethnic heritage. Without giving any thought to the consequences, I instantly decided to turn their racism against them. I said, "There are three million of us Jews in Israel. There are 150 million of you niggers in the rest of the Middle East. We are still kicking your arse, so tell me which one of us is God's chosen people."

Turning his own prejudices against him was one of the few weapons that I had; even so it was the only one of my actions I have ever truly regretted. I knew that they called me a Jew as an insult to identify me with a group they obviously considered their enemy. However, I also knew that in the inherent racism of their society, those of African nationality were not considered deserving of respect, not even the enmity they held for Jews. I believed that addressing him in this way got right inside his insecurities and prejudices.

With eyes bulging in anger, the officer barked out something in Arabic. I assume it was a translation accompanied with orders. As he did so, he stepped forward and punched me in the face. Before I had a chance to respond, the other guards were upon me. I tried to fight back, but they had swarmed over me, preventing me from landing a single blow. Knocked to the ground, I felt their feet thud into me, ranging over the whole of my body. As I lay there, curled up protectively, I could not stop giggling through the pain. Truly my observations were correct; I had another weapon.

When finally they had vented all their anger and left the cell, I picked myself up. I examined my body for any visible damage, but there was nothing more than a few red marks. The beating was minor, and it had been worth it. I walked over to the door and urinated all over it, directing the stream up to where I could see the hand marks left when the door had been pulled shut. Redecoration had started and would continue in the same manner every time my cell was cleaned in the future.

A week or so later, the eighteenth of August, day 245, I had just finished filling one of my toilets with the remnants of my lunch, when I was summoned for an embassy visit. I ignored the guard who delivered the news. A few minutes later, while I was reclining on my mattress and reading a book, a be-thobed officer entered my cell accompanied by four or five guards, and demanded that I get up and get dressed for a visit. I peered over the edge of my book, sniffed the air a couple of times, and returned to my reading. My guests milled around for a couple of minutes, repeating the request, before finally giving up and leaving the cell.

I was sure that this would not be the end of it, and I could feel my adrenaline surging as I braced myself for a more physical confrontation. I could not concentrate on my reading, so I tried to meditate myself into a calmer state. While I was doing this, another officer entered the cell carrying a pen and paper. He demanded that I write down my reason for refusing the embassy visit. I was happy to comply. I wrote out two brief statements, signing and dating them both after I had ascertained the date. I stated I would refuse all visits from the Canadian Embassy, and I renounced my Canadian citizenship. These were fairly drastic statements, but I felt justified in making them.

The embassy officials had been determined to make me accept visits from my father, contrary to my stated wishes. I had also found that whenever I had spoken out of turn in the visits, the first consul had always sided with my torturers, reprimanding me for my bad manners or my sexism or my state of dress. Whatever his agenda may have been or whatever the agenda of the Canadian government may have been, it was not mine. It had become obvious to me that the matter of most concern was the avoidance of a diplomatic incident and the maintenance of the propaganda that my father's visits helped provide. I was not of the view that cooperating with the hypocrisy of the Saudi government was the best means of resolving the situation (and in this I have been proven right), nor did I wish to see my father placed in danger by entering the Kingdom or be used as a tool in either government providing a veneer of respectability to my incarceration. The only weapon at my disposal was withdrawal from contact, even though I knew it would cause my family and friends some concern. I had just had to do what I knew to be right.

In the early evening my cell door opened and in walked Khaled and Ibrahim. I was practically delighted to see them. They and Said had frequently told me that the prison regulations forbade interrogators from entering the cell area, demonstrating the independence of the prison service. It did not take much provocation to show this was a lie, and exposing them amused me. They were furious because I had refused the visit and they demanded to know why. I ignored them as best I could, and my casual behaviour infuriated them. Ibrahim barked orders in Arabic, and the guards pounced on me, placing me in handcuffs and shackles. Commanded to get up, I refused even though I was being punched. I remained motionless, doing everything I could to keep my temper in check. Eventually, I was lifted on to a blanket made into an impromptu stretcher, carried up to the interrogation offices, and placed in the hog-tied position.

I knew what was next and wondered how long it would last. The answer to my question – hours. I was beaten, then left in my trussed-up position, then beaten again. All the while my list of sins was chanted at me. My nakedness, my filthiness, my refusal to cooperate, my rudeness, all were recited as the rattan descended. I did as I always did, I screamed in agony. It went on through the night till I heard the dawn prayer call and was returned to my cell in the same manner I had left it. Even in the face of threats of continued beating, I had refused to stand.

The cell had been cleaned during my absence, so defiantly I went about redecorating it, for the first time adding my faeces to the mess that I made. The cell stank as a result, but it made me feel a little better. Sometime later that morning, the black Saudi dispenser came into my cell, holding in his hands a tube of anti-inflammatory ointment. I looked up at him and shook my head, refusing his attention. There was a pained expression on his face as he silently tried to urge me to reconsider, but I did not accept his entreaties. When a few moments later the doctor paid his respects, I was a little more voluble in response to his inquiries, telling him that I was uninterested in his services. I did not leave my cell that day; instead I spent time on my back, sparing my aching feet. Just after the last prayer call, I was collected again and hauled to the interrogation offices, where the activities of the previous night were re-enacted. With a defiance that I did not wholly feel, I told my interrogators to keep it up, for soon they would give me what I wanted: my freedom.

After it was over, and I was back in my cell, I lay there trying to think clearly through my rage and my pain. The threat of execution had featured prominently during the night, and I was more than ever certain that one of us would meet that fate. As I took stock of my life and of my situation, I understood that my interrogators had focused on me as being the leader in their fantasy. I also knew that of the prisoners I was aware of, I was the only one who had not been married and who had no children. I reviewed the conclusions I'd come to earlier. There was no one waiting for me outside the four walls of my cell who was dependent on me. If as I suspected, one of us would be sacrificed to the needs of the regime, while the others would be freed to demonstrate the regime's mercy, I decided that I was the obvious candidate, and should do everything to ensure that the others were spared.

Later that morning, when the door of my cell opened to admit the dispenser and a couple of guards, I raised myself from my slumber and picked up the first book that the authorities had given me: the Koran. With that in one hand, I collected my medication and walked over to a toilet cubicle. Once there, I popped the tablets into my mouth, while with a flourish I opened the book, tore out a couple of pages, wiped my arse with them, and dropped them into the toilet. The three interlopers stared at me in disbelief that rapidly mutated to anger, as the enormity of my actions hit home. I stood, staring them down, Koran in hand, awaiting their response. Would they confiscate the tome? They mumbled a few curses, and then they left me alone. I knew full well that they would faithfully report my first act of apostasy. It pleased me to imagine the displeasure it would cause.

With the visit over, I tore out another couple of pages and placed them on the floor of the cubicle. Squatting down, I defecated onto the paper and then worked the resulting turds into an amorphous paste that I began smearing over my body. I concentrated on my wrists and ankles initially, the first place the guards would reach for when placing me in restraints, working the remainder over my arms, legs, and shoulders. I stank so badly, it was all I could do to stop from retching, but within a few minutes my sense of smell began to accommodate my new perfume. As my cell was quite hot and the air lacked any humidity, my faeces dried to a flaky crust within minutes, leaving me looking dirty but not as grotesque as I thought it would.

The next disciplinary withdrawal occurred at the beginning of September 2001. It was in part a response to my refusal to wash and in part to my refusing to accept an embassy visit. Prison regulations saw to it that prisoners were paid an allowance of ten riyals a day, given to the prisoner in a lump sum once a month during a visit to the cells by the prison bookkeeper. The bookkeeper accompanied by a couple of guards would arrive in the cell, hand over the cash, requiring me to sign on a rather large ledger sheet for its receipt. This along with money sent in to the prison by my father meant that I had sufficient funds to avail myself of the commissary and the purchase of books. The commissary service consisted of a prison staffer coming around to the cell every couple of days, taking an order for food items, newspapers (not allowed to me), cigarettes, toiletries, etc., and then delivering the items at the next visit, while collecting the next order.

One morning as I walked around my cell, getting part of my daily exercise, I could hear the prison commissary officer doing his rounds, and I began to anticipate what I would order. When the door of my cell finally opened, two guards stepped in and went directly to my sleeping area, where I kept my books and cash. They rifled through the various volumes until they found what they were seeking and collected all the money that was kept there. I stood and watched with surprise. At the same time I willed myself not to confront them. I knew that the confiscation of my cash meant that I was being denied access to the commissary and to the purchase of books, and I was enraged. As they walked past me toward the door, the one holding the money turned and said something to me in Arabic with a laugh. I have no idea what he said, but it was mocking at best. I felt my gorge rise at the petty amusement his putative power gave him, so I did the only thing that came to mind. I spat in his face.

It was their turn to be surprised. They turned on me with menace, looking to revenge themselves. I stood my ground, balled my fists, and called them on. My bellowing cowed them and they backed toward the door. I followed, daring them to confront me. I spent the rest of the morning, pacing my cell waiting for another confrontation or explanation, trying to work off my anger. None came until the next day, when an English-speaking officer informed me that if I showered and wore clean clothes, my privileges would be returned. My only response was to spit on him as well. He was not best pleased, but made no further issue of the matter.

At the beginning of September I was informed of another visit from the embassy and decided to accept it, for no other reason than it would break the monotony and would give me the opportunity to bait my interrogators. The visit passed like all the others, with further admonishments from both Khaled and Ibrahim about my behaviour, and similar complaints arising from the first consul. The only thing of interest was his statement that the Canadian government could not, given my current circumstances, accept the renunciation of my Canadian citizenship. I found this curious. The written power of attorney, gained from me under duress, was readily accepted by the embassy. Moreover, as I found out later, my confession was also readily accepted, and it was gained with significantly more duress. Did the acceptance of my renunciation cause a degree of diplomatic embarrassment that the acceptance of my guilt did not?

The consul was a bit more conciliatory than usual, and when I rebuked him for his criticisms, he backed off. He also assured me that the message not to visit had been delivered, and I would hear no more about it. Not that I believed his assurances, but my refusal of the last visit did at least have some effect. Nothing more resulted from this meeting, not even a session of correction from the thugs, and I found myself back in my cell, spared further meretricious persiflage.

On the evening of the third of September, day 261, I was awoken from my nap by a group of guards telling me to get dressed for the investigation. I lay back ignoring them, wondering if they would appreciate my new skin treatment, for I had no intention of going voluntarily. When finally I arrived in the interrogation offices, carried there by a nauseated and angry coterie, I was informed by

Khaled and Ibrahim that I was going to have my trial the following day, and further instructed that I was to plead guilty and beg for mercy. As the sermon wound on its tiresome way, it was punctuated by Ibrahim delivering slaps and punches. I wonder if he knew just what his hands were touching as he made contact with my abdomen. I also thought about the statement that I had formulated. I spent the rest of the evening in my cell, in nervous anticipation of my day in court, hoping that I would have the emotional strength and presence of mind to deliver it. Eventually, I drifted off to sleep, awoken only by the delivery of the breakfast tray. A little later, just as my medication was delivered, a group of guards appeared in my cell carrying my clothes. Without a word being spoken, I dressed immediately, and was then placed in handcuffs and shackles and blindfolded. I was taken to the interrogation offices where the blindfold was removed and Khaled repeated the warnings of the night before, while I stared blankly at the wall behind him. My silence was impudence and it raised his ire. He concluded with direct threats about the death penalty. I just kept looking at the wall.

With this over, I was led down to the loading bay, without the blindfold in place. I was put into the back of a transport vehicle and taken to the court building. The first I saw of it was from the covered delivery area at the back of the building as I stepped down from the vehicle. My escort, now numbering six guards, two of whom were armed with revolvers, took me through the entrance into a narrow corridor and then to an elevator. That produced the first piece of comedy of the morning, as it was too small to accommodate the entire party, something they discovered only after trying to fit everyone in at once. Eventually we arrived on the floor of the court in which I was to appear, where I was kept in a segregated waiting area. I was at the edge of the southeast quadrant of the city, as I could see through a window only a few buildings before intervening wasteland and desert stretched out to the Industrial City.

After about forty-five minutes, I was told to stand, my restraints were removed, and I was taken into a courtroom. In the front of the room was a raised bench at which sat the three judges. Immediately in front of this and slightly to the right was an individual sitting at a low desk, writing in a bound volume; this was the court recorder. Standing beside him was the court translator. Then came rows of benches for the spectators and the accused. Seated on a bench to my left were Khaled and Ibrahim, and I was led over to it to sit beside them. As it turned out, Ibrahim was not only the arresting officer, chief interrogator, and torturer, but he was also the prosecutor.

Now that I was seated, the farce began. First, I was required to identify myself by stating my name, religion, and nationality. Then, when he was invited by one of the judges to do so, Ibrahim stood and began his recitation. While this was going on, the court translator approached me and began to do his job. I know that not everything Ibrahim said was translated, for two or three minutes of his speech would result in only about twenty seconds of translation. Frankly, I had no need of the translator, for what was being said was irrelevant to me. I had my own agenda.

As Ibrahim performed his duties, he called no witnesses, introduced no forensic evidence, all that was supplied was one single book of my confessions. Not even my co-accused were present. This was the standard format of the judicial process; no wonder every trial resulted in a conviction. The book containing my confession was passed to me so that I could confirm it was my writing and that it was freely given without coercion. As I looked at it, I felt like asking what happened to the other volumes, but I bit my tongue, instead refusing to acknowledge the book or my part in writing it. This drew angry glances from both Khaled and Ibrahim, as well as the judges.

After Ibrahim had finished, I was invited to make a statement. Throughout the intervening period prior to this, I had felt a mounting tension as I grew more and more nervous. My stomach had tied itself in knots, and I could feel my mouth going dry from fear. When I stood to make my contribution, I felt an urgent need for the toilet, and my legs seemed barely able to hold me up. Silently, I had kept reciting my recently remembered mantra while waiting. Now I said what I had prepared.

"I refuse to acknowledge this court, deriving, as it does, its legitimacy from the teachings and precepts of a false prophet and a false god; and deriving as it does its authority from a country and culture that is politically corrupt, socially regressive, morally bankrupt, and genetically degenerate."

With those words, I had just roundly insulted the culture of Saudi Arabia and more importantly committed the crime of apostasy in front of judges of a supposed Sharia court. As apostasy is punishable by death according to their code, I had given them a real reason to execute me, rather than just the falsified charges for which I was appearing. I had thrown down the gauntlet, feeling my tension ease as I did so.

The court translator looked at me dumbfounded before he began to interpret my words. He seemed to do so with an accuracy he had not applied to his earlier translation of the case against me delivered by Ibrahim. Again he need not have bothered, as one of the judges obviously spoke English, for I noticed him growing apoplectic as I delivered my statement. I noted that once I had finished, he had leaned over to the other judges, providing them with a translation in advance of the truncated version nervously provided by the court translator. With this over, I was required to sign the court record before being led away.

I arrived back at the prison a little after noon; my entire trip, including the trial, had taken less than three hours. I was fortunate to be in time to be allowed out to the exercise yard, where I worked off the last of my nervous tension by running laps in the noonday sun. Later that evening, much as I had expected, I was taken to the interrogation centre. I expected to be beaten, but was somewhat taken aback when I was presented with sheet after sheet containing passport-size photographs and required to identify the faces that I saw. As I looked over the sheets of paper, my eyes were drawn to the symbols at the head of a couple of the pages. They were in a script that I did not recognize. It was certainly not Roman, Cyrillic, or Arabic, and it was not until I was back in my cell that I recognized it; the script was Hebrew, a realization that posed more questions than it answered. I did recognize a couple of the faces that I was shown, but pretended I did not, even though I wondered how and why the photographs of two Canadian nurses had appeared on those sheets. With this duty over, Khaled escorted me into another office where Ibrahim awaited, and where for a brief hour or two my attitude was corrected. It was apparent that my performance in court had caused quite a stir, as I was constantly told that I would never leave Saudi Arabia alive.

The day of my trial had been a Tuesday, leaving only three days before Friday, the day on which executions are held, rolled around. Having committed myself to the strategy that I had, and insulted the court, I was sure of the outcome and awaited the arrival of Friday with some anxiety. I spent hours telling myself that I had to show them how to die, that that was my objective. When Friday arrived, ten or eleven guards entered my cell prior to the delivery of breakfast. Once dressed, placed in restraints, and blindfolded, I was taken to the interrogation offices where I was greeted by Khaled telling me that I was being taken for execution. It was funny but his words did not disturb me; instead I became calmer, more resigned. It was all over bar the applause – I was soon to gain my release.

Still in restraints and blindfolded, I was led out to the loading bay and placed in a transport. We departed, driving for what I estimated was nearly an hour, during which I prepared myself for what was to come, telling myself not to give the bastards the satisfaction. All my senses were attuned to pick up the slightest thing, and I

tried to interpret everything I heard or smelt. As the vehicle came to a halt, I was guided from the rear of the vehicle, through a door into an air-conditioned hallway. I tried to deduce if I was in the buildings at the back of Dira Square. As my escorts and I moved forward, I began to sense something familiar about my surroundings, so many of the sounds seemed known to me. It was when we passed through the second set of pneumatically controlled gates, it began to dawn on me that I was not at Dira Square, but was back in Al Ha'ir prison.

When the blindfold was finally removed, I was not surprised to discover that I was back in my cell. I was the victim of a rather cruel and sadistic joke, something novel to add to the repertoire of brutality that I had so far faced. Pacing the cell, I gradually calmed from the anger I had felt when I realized the nature of this game. I walked for hours, before I tired myself out enough to sit and meditate, and finally fall asleep.

日本 日本 日本 /

When I woke the next morning, just before the dawn prayer call, I found that I had slept well despite the psychological distress caused by the previous day's events. I felt calm in an almost surreal fashion. As the new day unfolded, progressing through its usual routine, I seemed to go through the motions as if disconnected from my surroundings. Despite the occasional comments from one or two of the less pleasant of the guards, I could not be bothered responding. I did not even bother to add to the mess in my cell. It was only with passing into the next day that my mood returned to normal, shaking off my zombie-like state and renewing my protests.

The first real piece of news that I received about the outside world came during my next embassy visit on September 12, day 270. Just prior to the visit I was given the usual briefing by Khaled, being told not to mention the trial. When I was led into the presence of the first consul, Ibrahim produced an Arabic-language newspaper and showed me its front page. The cover photo made me realize, at the same time it was described to me, that a major terrorist attack had occurred in the United States. Since so far I had been deprived of any news, I wondered why I was being shown what was now before me. My questions took on an even stranger form, as I listened to the information being imparted. The first pieces made perfect sense to me, as I heard that a series of hijackings had occurred in the United States, with the aircraft being used as guided missiles against their targets, one of which was the World Trade Center, and that the attacks had probably been inspired by Osama bin Laden. That much I had deduced from the front-page photograph. What was strange to hear was that I was told that I had to be patient, for my situation would now take a long time to resolve. I wondered why my situation had now become entangled with terrorist events thousands of miles away. Fleetingly, I wondered if my captors would somehow try to link me to those faraway events. While such a thought might seem far-fetched, it was no more far-fetched than the scenarios painted in the confessions that I had been forced to provide. Certainly my captors became agitated at the mention of Osama bin Laden's name, going so far as to state that he was not involved. I later learned upon my release of the attempts by the Saudi Arabian government to deny the involvement of any of their citizens in this attack. An indication of their desperation to eradicate any involvement was the government's suggestion that my fellow detainees and I were somehow involved.

Nearly the entire visit was taken up with what had happened in New York and Washington, until near the end when I committed my by now usual social faux pas and spoiled the tea party. I mentioned that I had been to taken to trial eight days earlier. This provoked both Khaled and Ibrahim to raise their voices in annoyance. Concomitantly, there was a look of shock on the consul's face as my words sank in, and he was then bombarded with denials by my interrogators. My statement brought matters to a close on a rather sour note, but that was now par for the course. I expected but did not receive some form of immediate punishment for my audacity, and so found myself back in my cell, attending to my restricted means of existence.

The day after the visit, when lunch had been served and I was sitting at the dining plinth chewing on a piece of rubbery chicken, I noticed out of the corner of my eye something moving on the floor. As my eyes focused on the point where I saw movement, I saw a creature with eight straw-yellow legs and a pale white body, waving its yellow claws and tail as it scuttled purposefully across the floor. I had encountered scorpions when out in the desert and treated them with caution, for those common to Arabia are fairly poisonous, though their sting is not usually fatal – except on occasion to small children or people with certain weaknesses like a heart condition. When it got to about two metres from the dining plinth, I was better able to assess its size and appearance. It was fairly large, about six or seven centimetres long, though frankly it looked anaemic in comparison to the ones I had seen in the wilderness. Certainly I had never seen one with so pale a body colour.

As I sat contemplating my new companion, the thought crossed my mind that its diet was about as nutritionally challenged as was mine, bringing a smile to my lips. It was also just my luck that in having a mild phobia for spiders and other such arachnids as I do, one of the more unpleasant examples would decide to pay a call. I pondered what to do about the curiosity in front of me. It was when I considered calling the guards that it struck me that the scorpion would make an ideal present. Keeping my eyes on it, I reached over the central dividing wall to collect a book, and I tore its cover off. Then I collected one of my plastic drinking cups. As I looked at it, I could see it would be a tight fit for the wee beastie, so I ran a reasonable chance of being stung. Slowly and cautiously, I edged toward the scorpion, which had thankfully decided to remain still. Deftly, and with no small sense of trepidation (the damn thing gave me the creeps), I trapped it in the cup, sliding the book cover underneath.

For a few moments, it thrashed around fiercely, surprising me with the force its restricted writhing produced. When I was satisfied that it had calmed down sufficiently, I lifted it onto my food tray, keeping it trapped in its plastic prison. When I heard the noise of the food trolley coming to collect the tray, I moved over to the mailing slot with my present. Once there, I removed the cup, swiftly covering the scorpion with a leathery pita bread, hoping that its stinger could not penetrate it. I waited for what seemed an interminable time – mind you, two seconds is an age when you are holding down an irate scorpion – before the mailing slot opened.

I rapidly slid the tray out into the waiting hands of a guard, while at the same time lifting off the pita bread. The pandemonium that ensued as the scorpion was released and the guards now had to face its ire was more than a little amusing. Screams and shouts emanated from the other side of the cell wall, food trays clattered to the ground, and a brief period of frenetic activity ensued. I am sure my guards had never moved as quickly as they did. I just stood back and howled with laughter, awaiting their response. It was not long in coming, for a couple of minutes later the cell door opened and it seemed like the entire shift of guards poured into my cell. I managed to get in a couple of punches before their mass over-whelmed me and I was knocked to the floor. I managed to latch onto one of the legs that kicked me and with gusto sank my teeth in, being rewarded with howls of pain from my tormentor. My head was kicked and punched until finally my hold was broken and the guards disengaged and left the cell. Yes, I received another kicking, but it was worth it. Just the memory of that day provided hours of childish amusement as I wended my way through my solitary confinement.

Now on my own again, I decided to continue the day's amuse-ments and look for something in my cell to destroy. A couple of months before when I had ripped off the doors of the toilet and shower cubicles, they had not been replaced, so were not available for my pleasure. I climbed on top of the steel sink units and jumped up and down in an attempt to dislodge them – to no avail. I then inspected the steel stools that surrounded the dining plinth, trying to see if I could exert enough force to rip one from its mountings. This proved to be a hard task, but after a couple of hours I felt the seat disc of one of the stools begin to flex. Inspecting the underside of the plate, I saw that the welded joint between the stem and the disc had begun to crack, so I redoubled my efforts and after another hour or so was rewarded by the disc coming away.

I now held in my hands a stainless steel disc of about thirty centimetres in diameter and weighing about three or four kilograms.
With this heavy blunt instrument, I went to work on the sink units
and the surrounding plasterwork, succeeding only in making a few
dents. When I tired of bashing the sink units, I turned my attention
to the hinges of the cell door, making little impression on them.
The noise I was making was horrendous, the hollow chamber of
my cell resounding to each strike like a bass drum. Eventually the
guards tired of my antics and came to confiscate my new toy. I did
think of putting up a fight, but then realized that if I hit someone
with the disc, I would probably kill them, and while many of my
guards deserved contempt, they did not deserve being bludgeoned
to death. I lobbed the disc at their feet and watched as they scuttled out of the way, the angry look in their eyes showing that they
thought I had tried to hit them with it. I was definitely succeeding
in annoying my captors.

A couple of hours later, my evening meditation was disturbed
by a second group of guards entering my cell to inform me that I
was to be moved into new quarters. As was my wont, I had to be
dragged out of the cell, towed along the floor on my blanket, and
deposited in a new cell. This one, I noticed, had a complete set of
doors on the cubicles, something for me to make use of, I thought,
but not for that night. I had had my fun. Instead I indulged in a
little redecoration, before turning in for the night.

Ten days later, when it was time for my new cell to be cleaned,
I refused to leave. The group of guards that had been sent into my
cell were not in the mood for the constant stream of verbal abuse
that I directed at them, nor was their mood made better by the filth
and stench they encountered. They tried to persuade me to move
by pulling the mattress upon which I lay off its plinth and onto the
floor, where they proceeded to kick me to make me stand. When
this failed, they placed a set of shackles on my ankles and attached
a set of handcuffs as an extension, then dragged me out of the cell

into another vacant cell. When the cell had been cleaned, I was dragged back and unceremoniously deposited inside the door. Throughout this procedure I had managed to keep my temper, managing to provide just passive resistance to their demands and inducements.

Now that I was alone, I vented my frustrations on the cubicle doors, tearing each one from its hinges, smashing off the lathing around the edges. These smaller pieces of wood I jammed into the gaps around the door, effectively locking the door in place. Obviously I could not get out, but the guards could not get in. With that task done, I continued to work on the remainder of the cubicle doors, providing even more wood fragments, which I wedged into the door frame. The guards monitoring me on the CCTV cameras had taken their time in understanding what I was doing. When they arrived at my cell door, I redoubled my efforts to secure it, amused by their orders telling me to behave. I then retired to my mattress and took to reading while they pounded on the door. After a couple of hours of attempting to gain access, they retired briefly. When they returned they must have had some sort of heavy mallet with which they pounded the door. Gradually my wooden wedges began to compress and splinter, allowing the door to move centimetre by centimetre. It opened just wide enough for a single guard to enter, then refused to budge. Had I been truly in the mood for violence, I would have held them back at that slim entranceway with the plethora of sharp pointed pieces of wood that were now in my possession. I suspect that thought also crossed the minds of the guards, for it was some minutes before any of them slid into the cell and began properly to clear the door frame.

Once the obstacles were removed, the door opened farther. More of my captors poured in and then proceeded to drag me back to my original cell. Once deposited there, I inspected my surroundings and noted that in addition to there no longer being any cubicle doors, the stools around the dining plinth had been removed. My captors had removed all the fixtures and fittings that I might use to cause problems, or so they thought. My eyes fixed on a small plumbing feature, which I discovered could be taken apart with relative ease. I smiled to myself at their lack of attention to detail, filing my discovery away for future use. Then it was time to redecorate, exercise, and meditate, to prepare and maintain myself for the long days of harassment and interdiction ahead. Given the hateful glares I received from so many of my guards, and the occasional abuse that I suffered at the hands of those who could not restrain their frustration and enmity, I knew that I was getting to them. In turn, I knew this would be communicated to my torturers and to the court. I could not see any leniency being granted, nor did I want any. In a rather perverse manner, things had started to go my way, making my imprisonment more tolerable if not exactly idyllic.

By this time the privilege to visit the exercise yard was also withdrawn. I was told it would be reinstated only when I washed and cleaned myself. The withdrawal of this privilege was not only a punishment for my filthy state. It was also for my behaviour during my first court appearance. This new restriction was reinforced by the confiscation of my running shoes. I now had no means to exercise except within the cell, and even that was hampered by the fact that the sandals I still had could not be used to jog in and afforded no protection to my feet or shins while I pounded out my laps on the reinforced concrete of the cell floor. I learned to walk barefoot.

I now re-established my daily routine to incorporate all my exercise within the confines of my cell, leaving it only to see the doctor every second or third day.

My steady pacing made my bare feet develop hard leathery calluses, so thick that days after my release when a small tack became embedded in the front pad of my left foot, I did not notice it immediately. I was not, however, able to walk without discomfort. I found that my feet could endure only a little less than three hours of walking, which I equated (quite accurately as it turned out) to a distance of about ten miles. Then I would have to stop and rest, my feet hot and sore from the friction and hard contact. I would then bathe my feet in the coolish running water from one of the spigots in the toilet cubicles, making my feet temporarily the cleanest part of my anatomy. After a period of about an hour or so, the pain in my feet would subside enough for me to engage in another session of walking. In this way, I completed between ten and twenty miles a day, pacing like a caged animal, a creature I was beginning to resemble.

In early October, they chose to reinstate the privilege to visit the exercise yard; however, I was not having any part of their concession. Again returning clean clothes and also returning my running shoes, a guard officer asked if I wanted to exercise. I ignored him. When he left, I swabbed the floor with the clean clothes before placing them back in the mailing slot; however, I again extracted the thobes and shredded them in a most theatrical fashion for the benefit of my watchers. The running shoes remained in a corner of my cell, untouched for the rest of my incarceration. I no longer had need of them.

A couple of days later, the authorities tried to reinstate my commissary privileges. When the guards accompanied the bookkeeper into my cell and announced that I could collect my prison wages and do "shopping" again, I appeared to acquiesce. I walked up to the shelf by the mailing slot where they all stood, smiling at them as they waited at my leisure, and received my 300 riyals (thirty days' allowance). Being naked, as I always was in my cell by then, and also unwashed, my physical presence and my smell made them shy away as I made to sign the ledger sheet. However, instead of signing it, I took both the cash and the ledger sheet, folded them together, and proceed to wipe my backside with them. The parties in my cell were stunned. Before they had a chance to react, I raced over to the toilet where I tore the paper and the cash into pieces and dropped them into the awaiting receptacle. When my task was complete, I turned to them and smiled. They cursed me as they departed.

That was the last time that privilege was ever offered, though a couple of weeks later, the prison authorities began to try to entice me to buy books. For a couple of weeks, I would almost politely ignore the officer who came in waving the booklist at me, until one day I decided to again demonstrate my contempt. Accepting the offer of the list, I repeated my performance with the ledger sheet, and promptly deposited the remnants of the book list into the toilet. Once again, this would be the last time they tried to reinstate that privilege.

So things went for about four weeks, which were almost blissful in their boredom, for I was spared the company of my interrogators. This imperfect idyll was shattered on the evening of October 9, day 297, when I was collected and carried to the interrogation offices to meet with Dopey and Acne. They had arrived a few minutes earlier to instruct me in my behaviour, so for once I did not have to wait. As my torturers talked, I remained mute, but fixed my eyes on Ibrahim with a look that could have given only one message, one of absolute malicious hatred. I know that I unsettled them both, for Khaled frequently told me to stop staring. I did not, enjoying the feeling that I could unsettle those who wanted to unsettle me. I had had more than adequate proof of their cowardice. They were diminished in my eyes, and never would they again exert the same level of authority or power.

When finally Ibrahim's temper broke, I was forced into the hog-tied position and subjected to a few minutes' reintroduction to the rattan. All the while, I was told what my next performance should be. I was informed that I was being given a second chance, that I was to appear in court again, and that I was to plead guilty and beg for mercy. While I screamed accompaniment to the strokes, one crude thought repeated itself over and over in my mind: "Like fuck I will." When Ibrahim exhausted himself, he released me and hauled my filthy form upright. As I stood with my back against the wall, he punched and slapped me while the consequences of any disobedience or departure from the next day's script were outlined by Khaled. If I misbehaved in any way, it would guarantee my execution and the execution of my fellow detainees. When the slaps stopped and Khaled ran out of threats, I spoke, staring directly at Dopey with as much malevolence as I could muster.

"You had better execute me. If you do not, you will always live in fear, for if one day I am free, I will hunt down you and your family. I will first kill your children while you watch. Then I will kill your wives. Then I will castrate you and break your back, leaving you alive, alone, and powerless, to bear witness to my handiwork."

As my words were delivered, I could hear the change in Khaled's voice as he translated. A tone of incredulity crept into his speech, and when the last of my words were interpreted, silence fell between us. Both he and Ibrahim stared at me with a look of curiosity mixed with disgust. They seemed unable to believe what they had just heard, and as they struggled with it, their apprehension showed, giving me all that I wanted. Before they had a chance to say anything further, I spat in Ibrahim's face. His reaction was almost a reflex as he struck out at me with the rattan that he still held in his hand. The cane whipped across the side of my face, causing them both to spring forward to inspect the damage. They were worried that I would now bear visible marks and thus disturb the protocol of the following day's farce. Their close proximity resulted in my being able to spray them both with my saliva. Whatever was intended in this interview, it was not going according to their well-thought-out plan. Without any further comment to me, they called the guards and had me returned to my cell.

If you find my threat to Ibrahim disturbing and wonder if ever I would carry it out, I can answer you with surety that I would not. It was formulated to disturb my interrogators, to tap into the concept of the blood feud, even now a common occurrence in the Kingdom. I made my war and my hatred to be more than a matter of business, I made it something personal, something of the blood, an attempt to get inside their heads and twist the knife, as they had tried to do to me. Did such actions and statements work or did they just serve to let me vent my fury and frustration? They worked to serve both purposes. When I later spoke with one of my fellow detainees about this, he said that Khaled had told him of my threat and asked him if I would carry out such a vendetta. His reply to Khaled's question was simple – he said yes. He confirmed Khaled's suspicions not because he believed me capable of such a thing, but because he could sense Khaled's fear.

I slept well that night, despite the pain in my feet, looking forward to the morning. When it dawned, I was already awake, pacing my cell, doing my morning constitutional, whistling the tune of the *Great Escape* as I walked (and laughing at myself for whistling such a ridiculous theme). While my clothes were being delivered by the guards, I took the time for one more show of defiance. I turned my back on them, walking over to my sleeping area where I collected the Koran. I slowly sauntered to the toilet, tore out a couple of pages of the book, and then dropped them into the pan. I then took the opportunity to squat over them and defecate, completing my act by cleaning myself with the torn sheets. Then I collected my clothes and dressed, observing the looks of anger that the guards directed toward me.

The trip to the court was uneventful. I was not nervous, as I had been the first time. I needed no mantras to fix my mind on my purpose. I had been there before and knew there was nothing for me to fear either from the process or from my own weakness. I knew what I had to do and what I wanted to do. It was a different courtroom this time, but the players and the stage were the same. Again Ibrahim ranted, and again I received a foreshortened translation of his pithy statements. Again, I refused to acknowledge the book containing my confession. The only thing different came when asked to state my name and I replied Lord Lucan, restating the same answer when the question was repeated. Finally it was time for me to make my statement, so I stood and said what I had said in my first trial: "I refuse to acknowledge this court, deriving, as it does, its legitimacy from the teachings and precepts of a false prophet and a false god; and deriving as it does its authority from a country and culture that is politically corrupt, socially regressive, morally bankrupt, and genetically degenerate."

As I stood to deliver those words, there was none of the anxiety that I had felt on the previous occasion. I was firm in my resolve to metaphorically spit in their faces. I no longer felt like their prisoner, for I was free in the only place that one could be free. It had taken such a long time and been such a complicated journey for me to come to feel what I knew intellectually, but everything from my rape through my heart attack had prepared me for this defiance. So as I stood insolently before those who would sentence me, before those who knew full well that I was innocent, I savoured the moment, looking at the anger on the faces of all those around, save one: the court translator. The poor fellow looked like he would sooner slit his wrists than translate my words.

Ibrahim glared at me, and Khaled whispered in my ear, "We will see you later."

"Can we do a little last man standing?" I asked quietly. Khaled did not get the inference and was bemused, but his glare was malevolent.

After signing the court record, I was led away, passing in front of the judges, one of whom leaned forward to address me, the one I suspected spoke English. The words he spewed at me confirmed to me the nature of the court and all who served it.

"Don't you know what we can do to you? Don't you know what we can do to you? Where is Christopher Rodway? Don't you know what we will do to you?"

"He is where you put him," I replied, staring down the corrupt thug that dared to call himself a judge.

"It is where we will put *you*" was his rejoinder, as I passed out of the room and into the corridor.

This time my performance did not merit a mock execution, but it did result in the usual brutality. When I arrived back at the prison, I was taken straight to the interrogation offices, where I was asked to review more passport-size photographs printed on paper with the same strange letterhead. I recognized none of the faces that I saw, despite Khaled's insistence that I must know some of them. I was telling him the truth, but I was curious about why I was shown the photographs. I never did find out what purpose this served or what language the words on the pages were written in.

With this job done, Khaled left the room, sending in a guard to watch over me. Not that I could go anywhere, as I was still hand-cuffed and shackled. I sat out the rest of the afternoon, thankfully dozing off to help time pass. When Khaled returned, he was accom-panied by Ibrahim, and I was subjected to another evening of beat-ings. When finally I was returned to my cell, I was in a foul temper, having had to be carried back, spitting and thrashing about. Once released from the restraints, I calmed myself down by pacing the cell on my already sore feet. For the next two days I was hauled back to the interrogation offices, to receive silent beatings inter-mittently throughout the night. As the last session drew to a close, I was told that I would be seeing someone from the embassy in a couple of days and threatened with further punishment if I men-tioned anything concerning my most recent trial.

When I was led to the visitor centre after lunch on October 15, day 303, I had decided to disobey Khaled and mention more than just my trial. Not that I expected to be listened to or believed by the embassy officials, but at least I would discomfit the overly friendly and passive relationship that the embassy staff had devel-oped with my torturers. What surprised me was that the first consul immediately informed me that we could now discuss my case. He then went on to reiterate that I was to be provided with a lawyer. I then informed him that I had been taken to trial for the second time the previous week. To my face, he simply discounted this as my total inability to understand the process of law in Saudi Arabia. I found this a bit rich coming from a man who thought Saudi Arabia was just like Rwanda, but demurred to his beliefs, inspired as they were by his willingness to accept at face value the statements of my captors. I further reiterated the position I had adopted on legal representation – that I had no intention of dignifying the corrupt judicial process of the Kingdom by my willing participation. I had stated this during previous visits, each time receiving remonstrations from both the embassy staff and the thugs. It had become obvious to me from these encounters that the Canadian government had little interest in the justice of my case, only in the superficial forms that would make it technically acceptable. This was driven home by the consul's response to my saying, "It is good to see that you are at least trying to establish my innocence."

He replied, "We are not interested that you are guilty; we are only interested in you receiving a fair trial."

"You are a little late to ensure that" was my riposte, which he chose to ignore.

Up to this point, my captors had remained silent, only glaring at me for having overstepped the mark. Now Ibrahim stood and proceeded to the doorway of the room, from where he called a guard. Sensing that he was going to forcibly terminate the interview (my mistake – he was instructing a guard to fetch some tea), I threw in my next gambit, staring at Khaled as I did so.

"So we can talk about my case, can we? So shall we talk about the torture that these two delivered?" and I indicated both Ibrahim and Khaled as I posed my question.

The responses were immediate; Khaled bade me to shut up, and the first consul told me such comments were neither relevant nor helpful. Somehow, I would have thought that the use of torture was materially relevant to both the legality of the proceedings taken against me and the admissibility of any confessions, but then I must also remember that within intergovernmental relations the recognition of such things are in fact hindrances to the smooth running of affairs. Certainly, this has been shown to be so by the behaviour of all the governments involved in this case.

When Ibrahim rejoined us, Khaled translated my comments, and Ibrahim angrily denounced me for lying and playing games. I smiled as he passed his remarks, wondering if he truly believed what he was saying. Certainly, his acting was getting better. Yes, I was playing my games, but at least in doing so, I was not trying to murder someone for crimes that they did not commit. My games were the only way of my fighting back against the tyranny of the situation. The games of my captors, involving the sacrifice of whoever was available, were simply to maintain the hypocritical façade that the problems in their country were caused by the corrupting influences of khawajas and that their judicial system was independent and uncorrupted. As for the other governments involved, Saudi Arabia was too important a client state for them to ever challenge on these matters. So much for an ethical foreign policy.

The last words of the meeting came from the first consul, informing me that the embassy would find a lawyer and that I would soon receive a visit from a Canadian psychiatrist. I said nothing, refusing to even shake his hand as he left, his earlier statements having left a rather poor impression on me. Immediately he was out of the room, I was put in handcuffs and then slapped across the face. Khaled and Ibrahim had at least learned to take the necessary precautions when dealing with me in that manner. Their remonstrations were brief and to the point: my behaviour had guaranteed that I would never again be free, that I would die screaming like a little girl. Spitting at them, as was my wont, I simply responded as aggressively as possible, restating my position that they had "better ensure that I die, for if you do not I will find you and teach you how to beg."

I could barely prevent myself from laughing at the foolish bravado of my statement, bringing to mind as it did the moronic scripts of Hollywood blockbusters. However, it had its effect, for the pair of them stopped talking to me, avoiding my eyes as they called instead for the guard. I was surprised to find myself taken straight back to my cell, and additionally surprised that I was not called again into the presence of my torturers until just before the next visit, ten days later.

During the long intervening period I had plenty of time to contemplate the remarks the first consul had made. I understood that the Canadian government, either because of political expediency or genuine acceptance of the Saudi Arabian propaganda, was operating from the premise that I, and by extension my fellow detainees, were guilty. Under those conditions, the only relevant function that the embassy (and the Canadian government) provided was as a rather paltry point of contact for myself and my family. In anything else – representation to the Saudi government or provision of legal counsel – I could not trust them and knew I must rely solely on my own judgement and wits. Even though neither was infallible, they were the least likely to betray me. Cooperation with the diplomatic stooges would be maintained only as long as I considered it necessary, and that would not be for much longer.

Months earlier, another attempt to get my mind right had made me refuse to take my medication. I also refused to accept any more medical consultation. A temporary repair to a damaged molar in the left side of my mouth had failed and the tooth had split down to the root, resulting in inflammation and minor swelling. Treatment for this ailment was undertaken at the Security Forces Hospital, with the tooth having to be extracted. While residing in the hospital's prisoner control centre, I was subjected to a visit from the embassy, during which my medical condition was discussed.

I had at that time stopped taking the antihypertensive medication prescribed after my heart surgery, though I continued to take the aspirin as prescribed and included a daily multivitamin as part of my medical regimen. I had decided to stop taking the antihypertensive because I felt that it was unnecessary. My blood pressure with the antihypertensive was routinely 95/60, causing me to suffer postural hypotension – if I stood up too rapidly, I would become dizzy and had on a couple of occasions blacked out as a result. Without the medication my blood pressure was 105/68, very low and hardly indicative of hypertension. However, both the medical staff and the embassy officials had nagged me for a couple of months to resume taking it, though no one could give me a cogent reason for doing so. I had also decided to refuse all embassy visits. Nevertheless, once again, here in the hospital I was subjected to the wheedling of the embassy staff whom I had recently determined to have nothing to do with. It hardly put me in a pleasant frame of mind and I was glad when their visit was over, and glad to be returned to the relative freedom of my prison cell.

The day following my return to my cell, my vitamin supply ran out. The vitamins had originally been deemed unnecessary, but they had become a regular feature when I had asked the embassy to provide a supply. Embarrassed by my request, for which I received the wrath of Khaled and Ibrahim, the prison authorities began to supply them. I had considered them vital because the food was extremely bland and overcooked. They had become even more essential once my commissary privileges had been withdrawn. So for a couple of days I did without them; such an interruption in their supply (or the supply of any medication) was not abnormal, so it caused me no concern.

On the day that the vitamin supply started again, I looked at what was being offered to me with some suspicion. Instead of the typical rounded oblong shape that I expected, I was presented with a white hexagonal tablet that would have been ovoid in its cross-section. Though wary, I had no reason to doubt its provenance, so promptly swallowed it along with the aspirin that was offered. Within a few minutes, I began to regret my decision. I felt light-headed and confused; every movement of my body felt strange, as if the air had suddenly become dense, requiring me to force my way through it. I lay down on my mattress oblivious to all that was happening around me, unable to order my thoughts for more than a few seconds at a time. I even failed to notice the arrival of the Smiling Knife, who sat down near where I lay.

For the next few minutes I was subjected to another propaganda lecture, but I was powerless to respond. I heard the words spoken to me as from the end of a long tunnel. It was a bizarre experience, and none too pleasant. When Said finally departed I remained motionless in a strange state of suspension. I felt unable to do anything, even sleep. I remained in this state of lassitude until sometime after nightfall, when I struggled to my feet and began pacing the cell in an attempt to revive myself. It seemed like hours before I began to drive off the fog that assailed my senses.

The next morning, when one of the medical dispensers arrived at my cell, I refused to take the vitamin pill on offer, indicating that I would only take the aspirin. It was promptly indicated to me that unless I took all the tablets offered, I would get none. So I chose none, asking instead to see the doctor. Once in his presence, I asked to see the packaging that the vitamin tablet had arrived in, but my request was denied. I aggressively denounced the doctor, telling him that the practice of medicating me under false pretences would in any civilized country result in his being the prisoner, not me. I had obviously been administered some form of hypnotic or tranquilizer, and he, as well as his superiors, were complicit in its administration.

I left his office and returned to my cell, resolving that I would no longer accept any medical treatment, no matter what the necessity, and thus began my medical strike, adding to my list of protests by refusal. Over the next few days, medication was brought to my cell and I declined it, as I declined each request that I see the doctor. After a week of this the doctor himself visited me in my cell.

I informed him in no uncertain terms, "If you lay a hand on me, I will rip out your fucking throat."

Somehow, I think that he and his colleagues got the message. No more medical visits occurred, and no more requests were made for me to attend a checkup. My new recalcitrance did result in a visit from Khaled and Ibrahim, whose threats and arguments influenced me not, for they could not get around the logic that if they wished to sentence me to death, there was hardly any necessity for me to accept treatment, and if they were trying to subdue me with a chemical cosh why should I cooperate? No physical punishment was meted out at that meeting, nor were any further restrictions imposed. In some ways they had little left to withdraw.

I no longer washed, wore clothes, went to the barber, spent time in the exercise court, bought things from the commissary, or requested books (I did continue to receive some new books sent to me by friends via the embassy, though I later discovered that fewer than one in five reached me).

When I was next taken to the visitor centre, on October 24, day 312, it was for an audience with a Canadian psychiatrist whose presence there had been arranged by the Department of Foreign Affairs and International Trade. Preliminary instructions for my behaviour, as outlined by Khaled just before the interview started, were that I was not to mention the means by which I had been "put in the right way" and that I was to confirm that I had attempted suicide. I listened to the instructions with amusement. I found it comical that my tormentors would lecture me on the legitimate and righteous use of physical brutality but were afraid to describe it for what it is and were afraid for it to be mentioned at all to the representatives of a foreign government.

When the audience was finally underway, the party consisted of Dr. Neil Oliver from the Department of Corrections in Canada; Dr. Al Humaid, the Saudi Arabian psychiatrist whose reports on my uncooperative behaviour had resulted in further physical correction being administered; and Khaled and Ibrahim. This was hardly an appropriate forum for me to unburden myself, for every personal revelation that I might make would then be used against me. I answered the questions put before me as best I could, but remained guarded in my responses, revealing as little about myself as possible.

Throughout this interview, and the subsequent one held three days later, the only questions put before me that I answered in any detail were ones through which I was able to reinforce my solitary nature and my lack of regard for my own safety. Many of the references that I made to my early life were in fact allegorical referrals to my current situation. I knew that if I were to speak too directly, the interview would be terminated by Ibrahim, so I resorted as best I could to colouring the information I provided on my early life with my present situation, hoping that Dr. Oliver would cross-reference my statements with members of my family and thus comprehend the subtext. I recounted conflicts that I had with a teacher of rather fundamentalist religious beliefs. Given that I had no such teacher, I hoped the shrink would take the hint that part of my behaviour in prison was in response to the religious preju-dice and indoctrination to which my captors were subjecting me. Throughout these interviews, I was constantly disparaging of the business and government institutions in Saudi Arabia, much to the annoyance of Khaled, Ibrahim, and Al Humaid, though initially at least they did not try to silence me.

Conflict came when at the end of both interviews I brought up contentious issues. When Dr. Oliver asked about my suicide attempt, I reiterated that no such thing occurred, recounting at length the abuse that I suffered at the hands of the guards on the night in question. When interrupted by Ibrahim and Khaled, I con-tinued to talk despite their protestations, branding them both liars as they attempted to contradict me. Dr. Oliver managed to calm down the confrontation and changed the subject, but I wondered how he would interpret my captors' attempt to prevent me from speaking freely. This confrontation was repeated at the end of the second interview, when I accused my captors of the torture that had resulted in my near death. Again I wondered what would be made of my statements. Certainly, I saw no value in those psychi-atric interviews, given the conditions under which they were con-ducted and given the information that was conveyed. When I was finally parting from Dr. Oliver, I told him to pass this message to my father: "Tell him my race is run; it is all over for me now. Tell him to take care of his wife and forget about me." As I said those words, I suspected that their fatalism would count against me in any analysis of my mental condition. But the flawed and erroneous analyses of a state-appointed psychiatrist were the least of my problems then.

I have, subsequent to my release, been able to review the report filed on those interviews and am not surprised to find them as valueless as I suspected. Effectively, I was described as depressed at the time of the interviews, despite my protestations to the contrary. My statements were not cross-referenced, so none of the subtexts were noticed. Furthermore, the statements by my torturers and Dr. Al Humaid concerning the nature of my behaviour were included in the report and accepted at face value. My dirty protest, my obscenities, my violent behaviour were all presented to Dr. Oliver as if arising without cause or provocation.

Just over a week later, I was escorted to the interrogation offices, where Khaled told me that I would have another embassy visit the following day, at which I would meet the lawyer assigned to my case. My full cooperation was expected or it would go badly for me, I was once again warned. Nothing further was said by Khaled and no reinforcement was delivered, so I returned to my cell. At a previous embassy visit when the matter of legal representation had been raised, I was told that I would be represented by either Sheik Salah Al Hejailan or Dr. Ahmed Al Tuwaijeri. I was not interested in legal representation, for I felt it served only to legitimize the corruption and inhumanity inherent in the judicial process of the Kingdom. However, I knew that I would have to play a part in the next evening's farce, so I thought carefully about what I would say to the lawyer and what I would ask him.

The next evening, I was led over to the visitor centre and into one of the rooms, where the first consul and another embassy official were waiting. With them was a tall distinguished-looking Saudi Arabian, wearing his finest bisht as well as the de rigueur thobe and gutra. He was introduced to me as Dr. Al Tuwaijeri, and we politely shook hands before being seated and the meeting commenced. As with all other meetings, both Khaled and Ibrahim were present, so the prospect of client-attorney confidentiality was non-existent. I had in fact hoped to meet Sheikh Al Hejailan, for I had had business dealings with members of his family, finding them relatively honest in their transactions, and thus he presented a more known quantity to me. The Saudi Arabian lawyer sitting before me was an unknown entity, and I was immediately on my guard.

I know that my physical appearance, with my matted hair and beard and my filthy T-shirt, along with the odour that I must have exuded, did not make a favourable impression on either the embassy officials or the lawyer. I expressed, quite determinedly, my views on the corruption and lack of impartiality of the judicial system, describing the court members and my interrogators as criminal clowns and stooges, little better in their behaviour than animals, an opinion to which I still adhere. I also informed all those present of the statements that I had made at my two court appearances. These words that I had spoken before the court amounted to the crime of apostasy. While I related this information, I could see the looks of concern grow on the faces of my audience as the import of my words sank in. Toward the end of my harangue, I was met by remonstrations from both my interrogators and the first consul, while the lawyer sat silently.

When I had finished, the lawyer addressed me, stating that he was willing to represent me in any forthcoming proceedings and that Sheik Salah Al Hejailan was to represent the British detainees. Finally, he asked if I had any questions. I asked him about the nature of my first two trials, and why I was denied legal representation. He told me that those were not trials, just preliminary hearings. I knew that he was lying, for my court appearances were conducted in exactly the manner that I knew trials were conducted in Saudi Arabia. I knew also that the preliminary meeting with officials of the Sharia court had occurred in January 2001, having taken place at Al Ha'ir prison in the interrogation offices, though I did not enlighten my audience with this piece of information. I therefore declined Dr. Al Tuwaijeri's services, much to the consternation of the first consul, who continued to demand that I reconsider my decision. I know it was reported at this meeting that I claimed to have greater knowledge of Sharia law than the attorney, but that was not how I put across my refusal. I stated simply that the lawyer knew that my court appearances were not preliminary hearings, and that he knew this as well as I did, thus basing my refusal to accept his services on what I saw as his deceit. The meeting that night ended with the lawyer departing first, followed by the embassy officials. I told them if they ever appeared again with such a lawyer in tow, I would refuse to see them.

It is interesting to note that in April 2002, Dr. Al Tuwaijeri was quoted in the press as having informed the Canadian government that I had been convicted and sentenced to death at the trial occurring in October 2000, with a subsequent appeal in January 2001 (at which I was not present) upholding the verdict. The death sentence was ratified in March 2001 and the Canadian government was finally informed of these results on April 17, 2001, my forty-second birthday. One can only wonder why Dr. Al Tuwaijeri, when speaking with me for the first and only time in November 2001, would deny that my court appearances had in fact been my trials, when later he would have to publicly contradict his earlier pronouncement to me.

A couple of days later, I was informed of another impending embassy visit. Khaled and Ibrahim's brutality was limited and brief, as I was told that I had no choice but to accept Dr. Al Tuwaijeri as my lawyer. My initial thoughts, left unspoken, were that hell would freeze over before I followed their instructions, though I was curious why my interrogators were insisting that I accept Al Tuwaijeri rather than be represented by Al Hejailan, as the other detainees were. I wondered if I was reading too much into this matter, but have subsequently learned that different lawyers represented each of the different national groups of the detainees, and this did seem to be part of the strategy of the Ministry of the Interior to play off against each other the different interests of the Belgian, Canadian, and British governments.

When, on the evening of November 12, day 331, I was taken for another embassy visit, I found myself in the presence of the first consul, with only Ibrahim and Khaled as the other people present, a fact I found somewhat suspicious. As the visit progressed, I was admonished by both my interrogators and the first consul for my refusal to engage legal representation. I listened attentively as I was urged from all sides to accept Al Tuwaijeri. It was strange to hear a representative of the Canadian government singing the praises of the Saudi Arabian judicial system, castigating me for my rudeness to the prison officials, and demanding that I conform to the perfectly fair requirements of my captors. Eventually, he ended his harangue with the statement, "Bill, I am disappointed in you. If you do not accept Dr. Al Tuwaijeri, there is nothing further the Canadian government will do for you."

So there it was, a threat to withdraw assistance, something I would normally have welcomed given my experience with the representatives of his government, but it did represent my only effective means of communication with my family. I capitulated. To this day I do not have an adequate explanation for my response, given my track record till then. I know that at the time of the visit, my resolve was at a low ebb. Throughout the process of resistance, the futility of my position was always apparent. I was still aware of the deceit that surrounded my meetings with the lawyer. Yet for all my conscious realizations, in my then more emotionally susceptible condition I agreed to the demands of the first consul. Both my interrogators looked on in obvious surprise, as I briefly wrote out a statement appointing Al Tuwaijeri as my lawyer. I was just too tired, too alone, too battered, and too bruised to do otherwise; I failed in my purpose, much to my eternal shame, and gave my captors another victory. With my surrender freshly inked on a piece of paper, the interview was ended, and I returned to my cell.

At some point during my journey through the underground labyrinth to my cell, a sense of rage began to fill my being. Rage directed not at my captors but at myself, for my weakness and stupidity, as I had agreed to be represented by someone who had failed to be honest with me, and I had wavered and capitulated to the demands of at least two political systems that were doing everything in their power to destroy innocent people in the name of political expediency. It was then and still remains one of my greatest betrayals of myself that occurred while I was in prison. The first betrayal was more understandable, for confession was inevitable under the circumstances. This time it was not. I could have prevented the collapse of my resolve had I shown the strength of character necessary. I berated myself for my stupidity and lack of moral fibre. By the time I arrived back at my cell, I had decided to refuse to cooperate or even meet with Al Tuwaijeri. I just hoped that I would live up to this new resolution, though only time would tell. In fact, I managed to adhere to this commitment right up to my release, refusing every entreaty to meet with Dr. Al Tuwaijeri or cooperate with any part of the hypocritical legal proceedings through which the case was dragged over the ensuing years.

During the next couple of weeks, while pacing my cell and while meditating, I went over and over the statements that had been made by the first consul, concluding that somehow the Canadian government was either convinced of my guilt or was at least happy to accept at face value the version of events put forward by the Ministry of the Interior. I was not fully able to fathom the reasons for such perfidy and did not come to any firm conclusion until some time after my release, though I was convinced that I was being sacrificed in the interests of diplomatic relations.

I entertained two more visits at which the first consul was the sole representative of the embassy. At the first of these, occurring about November 19, day 338, I was confronted with the usual admonishments to behave and cooperate, at the end of which he made a statement that I made a point of remembering.

"Considering what you have done, you must cooperate fully with the Saudi Arabian authorities, or there is nothing that we can do to help you."

Once again, I was faced with the de facto acceptance of my guilt and a threat of withdrawal of assistance. It was hardly credible to me that I had been provided with any effective assistance. I can accept that during the first days of my imprisonment there was not a lot that could have been done for me, but after that initial period no amount of involvement of the western governments had prevented the torture that had resulted in my heart attack nor prevented the ongoing brutality. So what exactly had been done or would be done?

The next visit provided even more evidence of the perfidy and naïveté of the first consul. The initial discussions during that visit were between the consul and Khaled and Ibrahim, while I sat to one side as a bemused spectator. The first consul congratulated my interrogators and himself on developing such a good relationship. He talked about the confrontations that had occurred between members of the British Embassy and my interrogators during their visits to my fellow detainees. I was tempted to point out to him that such confrontations were better for the morale of my fellow prisoners than were his all too obvious arse kissing of those who had tortured me, but I bit my tongue, allowing him to talk without interruption.

Obviously carried away with his perspective on the difficulties faced by the British legation and by his apparent success in getting me to be more compliant, he bragged how comfortable life had become for him and his spouse since arriving in the Kingdom, adding that his spouse had obtained the position of head of marketing at the Specialist Hospital. As he said this, I could barely contain my surprise, for I had more knowledge about this than he would have been aware of.

During my tenure at the Fund, a Canadian co-worker had handed me a copy of the resumé of the first consul's wife, saying that I should help a fellow Canadian find employment in Saudi Arabia. Given the nature of the employment she was seeking, a senior position in the health care or pharmaceutical sectors, I saw little prospect of her gaining a position normally given only to men and rarely if ever to expatriates, so I filed the resumé with the promise to look into things and promptly did nothing. This was not long before my earlier arrest in October 2000; at the time, I had been working on an analysis of the viability of developing a central laboratory reference facility within the Specialist Hospital as a commercial entity that would provide its services at a fee to all other hospitals in the public and private sectors. At the time I was preparing my report, certain medical diagnostic tests were being provided at labs outside the Kingdom at considerable expense, and it was thought that an economic opportunity existed to consolidate such work within a single facility in the Kingdom. My report was positive, indicating that such a development would probably prove necessary in the long run as the health care sector within the Kingdom expanded and became more sophisticated. However, at the time of my arrest, the project had not gone beyond the proposal stage. Now, as I sat being regaled by the effusive first consul, I learned that the hospital in question had a new position, that of head of marketing, something that had not existed in December 2000. Not only had such a position not existed at that time, but because of how such posts are staffed, it would normally have been given to a well-connected Saudi Arabian male, with a male western expatriate in the position of deputy head doing all the actual work. Added to this was the regulation in existence at the time that spouses of diplomats were not permitted to work in Saudi Arabia (except as part of the legation staff), further making such an appointment highly suspect (since then the Saudi government has changed this regulation). I was hearing something that involved at best a major conflict of interest if not out and out corruption, and at once the pronouncements concerning my guilt began to make sense. It was not until I became aware of the case, months after my release, of *Marc Lemieux vs. the Department of Foreign Affairs*, which alleges a degree of corrupt practices occurring within the Riyadh embassy, that I understood that the handling of my case was possibly affected by a deep malaise within the Canadian Embassy.

At the end of the visit I was once again met with a memorable statement, one that had an immediate effect on me, particularly when considered with the inadvertent revelations that preceded it. "We know things have been difficult, but we have managed to get your conditions improved, so cooperate. As you are guilty, you must completely cooperate or we cannot help you."

As the words were delivered, my mind was made up. I would no longer accept any assistance from individuals such as the first consul or the government for which he worked. If that meant my family had no means of communicating with me, even in the restricted manner that was allowed, then so be it. I knew what I had to do, and they would just have to bear the strain of my doing the right thing. It was time to fight completely alone, for my interests were not being served by those who professed to be providing assistance. Their tacit acceptance of my guilt was hardly what I needed, regardless of their political need to cooperate with the corrupt government of Saudi Arabia. Thus, the cumulative effect of this and previous statements by the first consul, along with the other revelations, led me to conclude that the Canadian government was just as much my enemy as was the Saudi Arabian government. I knew that the only person upon whom I could rely was the one who stared back at me from the polished steel plates mounted over the sinks in my cell.

Although you could say that this conclusion was the product of an incipient arrogance, as well as the creeping paranoia that can result from treatment such as I received, it was not. I constantly questioned and examined my every thought and feeling, trying to determine if there were benign explanations for what I had observed, and trying to determine if any of my conclusions were the product of the emotional effects of torture and solitary confinement. I could come up with none, and as I reflect on my experience I believe that I was correct in my assessment that the western governments involved worked not in the best interests of their citizens, but in the best interests of their relationship with Saudi Arabia, regardless of the cost to those incarcerated. I have also become aware that by the time I had come to these conclusions, so too had members of my family and some of my friends, who were in constant contact with the governments involved and who were shocked by the statements with which they were confronted.

My situation now was one of full-scale protest that brought me into constant conflict with the prison authorities, as strategies were employed to maintain their dominance over me. I have already discussed the various stages of my protests. By December 2001 I no longer washed or showered, no longer wore clothes, no longer left my cell for exercise, no longer used the commissary, and no longer visited the doctor or took my medication. I must add that further restrictions had also been imposed as a result of my behaviour.

The normal facilities provided in the prison cell included a twenty-litre plastic bottle that contained drinking water and a thermos-style cooler for the storage of food purchases. Blocks of ice were delivered daily for use with the cooler, allowing the fresh produce or fruit juices to remain fresh for longer than would normally be the case given the ambient temperature in the cell, which in the summers was rarely below 35 degrees. By this stage the air conditioning in my cell had been turned off and was never again turned on, so temperatures would come fairly close to that of the external environment, meaning baking heat of 45 degrees during the summer, and cooler temperatures of 8 to 10 degrees during the depths of winter. For a brief couple of months in spring and autumn, the temperatures in my cell would be comfortable for someone who had chosen to be naked. At the other times, I dripped sweat even when lying still or had to wrap myself in my blanket to keep warm. However, I got used to these extremes, particularly as the transition between them involved a period of months during which my body seemed partially to adapt to the change of the seasons. If this denial of heating or air conditioning was meant as punishment, it was one of the most ineffective, for I did not miss it, unlike the withdrawal of other privileges.

As for my cooler, it had long since been confiscated. When my commissary privileges had been revoked, I had no use for the cooler, so I began to leave the delivered ice in the mailing slot, letting it melt through the gaps and making a mess in the corridor outside. After a few days of this game, the guards got fed up, and the cooler went the way of all good things. What did surprise me was that my water container was replaced as necessary without protest, even though I had occasionally up-ended it into the mailing slot, causing a minor torrent to pour from my cell. I did wonder if this privilege would be maintained, but assumed it would be as they did have to provide me with food and drinkable water.

Small 250-millilitre cartons of fruit juice were usually delivered with the midday meal along with fresh fruit, primarily apples and oranges, and at breakfast small 125-millilitre cartons of UHT milk were also provided every couple of days. For a period of time during the late summer and autumn, once my dirty protest was in full swing, I made particular use of the empty cartons, opening them fully in order to refill them with my urine and faeces, then shaking vigorously to make rather unpleasant slurry. I would then pour the slurry through the mailing slot, spreading my filth beyond the confines of my cell. The guards tolerated this for some time, until I put the cartons to another use.

I had been hauled out of my cell for it to be cleaned, and in the process had received a few punches and kicks to encourage me into compliance, not that it did. When I was returned to the cell, I was dragged to the low wall that divided the cell, and the handcuffs and shackles were removed. When I stood, cursing at the guards as they headed for the door, I noticed that two open reeking fruit juice cartons had been left on the shelf of the dividing wall. How or why they were overlooked during the cleaning process, I do not know. However, I immediately made use of them, hurling them at the backs of the retreating guards. I had targeted two guards in particular, because of the glee with which they had tried to encourage my compliance, and I was rewarded by seeing the cartons strike home, soaking the backs and shoulders of the respective targets and spraying their neighbours. I expected to be descended on for my actions, but instead saw only that the guards increased the pace at which they left the cell, slamming the door shut behind them. A few moments later, before I had a chance to refill the containers, the guards returned, and one of them, wearing disposable plastic gloves, confiscated the offending items. From then until my release, I no longer received any more fruit juice, though a few months prior to my release UHT milk once again appeared with the breakfast tray.

As for the fruit, I put that to another use. While I was happy enough to eat the oranges, the apples slowly accumulated in my cell, for I have never had a taste for them. By the time I had collected about two dozen of them, I wondered what use I could put them to, though the answer was obvious. Once again, after another confrontation concerning the cleaning of my cell, I managed to hit one guard rather forcefully in the back of the head. When one of his companions turned and made to approach me, he received a direct hit just above the bridge of the nose, while another that I threw exploded against the wall beside the door. Standing at the far end of the dining plinth, with the ammunition close at hand, I would have been able to get off three or four more well-aimed shots before being overpowered, so the guards once again beat a hasty retreat from the cell.

While I surveyed the pattern produced on the wall by the explosion of my impromptu missile, it dawned on me that there was another use to which the apples could be put before they could be confiscated, as I was sure they would be. I picked up a couple of them and threw them at one of the CCTV camera housings located over ten metres above the floor, watching as they burst on it. After half a dozen apples had been launched, I had managed to cover the camera housing, obscuring its view of the cell. I then went to work on the other one, eventually covering it in a film of apple pulp. Needless to say, two days later I was hauled out of my cell once again. As I was dragged along the floor toward the end of the corridor, I saw a partially assembled wheeled gantry obviously brought in to gain access to the CCTV cameras to make any necessary repairs. Its presence explained the delay in the response to my effectively shutting down their means of observation, for such an item would have had to have been dismantled before being brought into the cell block and then reassembled. That was the last I saw of any fresh fruit.

My sleeping arrangements were the source of another battle of wills between the authorities and myself during December 2001. According to their requirement, my mattress was to be placed on a particular bed plinth, one that was visible to both CCTV cameras. I chose instead to place my mattress on the floor between the two plinths closest to the exterior wall. I also rearranged my books on one of the plinths to make a small wall. The overall effect of this was that when I was lying on my mattress, I could not be seen by one of the cameras, and only my feet, poking out from the end of the plinths, could be seen by the other. This afforded me some privacy, and I would have thought my captors would have been pleased not to have to look at my naked form. However, this was not the case, for immediately I had set up this arrangement, the guards raced down to my cell, dragged me out from between the plinths, and hauled me back onto the prescribed plinth. My response was just as immediate, returning everything to the way I wanted it. This went on throughout the first night of my rearranging my furniture, until sometime after dawn prayer I fell asleep lying between the plinths. When I awoke just as lunch was being delivered, I found that I had not been moved. I wondered if I would be allowed to continue sleeping in this more private arrangement, receiving an answer early that evening when the game began again. This went on for about ten or twelve days, before finally the guards gave up and left me to make my sleeping arrangements as I saw fit, for they were at least able to see my feet moving even if the rest of me was not so visible.

Over time the number of books in my cell increased, and so too did the height of the wall they formed. I found that by lying tightly against the bed plinth and drawing up my knees, I could completely hide myself from view. Whenever I did this, a group of guards would be sent to my cell to confirm my presence and that I was still breathing (though I am sure they would have been quite happy if I was not). This was a source of amusement to me, for this simple action meant that the guards would have come all the way into my cell, traipsing through all the detritus that I had strewn around, just to confirm that I was still there. I played this game only at night, during the times when my sleep cycle had me sleeping during the day. The reason for this was that most of the guards pulling the night duty would normally be asleep in the control centre, with only one or two of them awake to monitor the cameras. Therefore I knew that my actions would not only force them to enter the stinking hole that I had made of my cell, but also that they would have to be roused from their slumber to do so. I was thus able to create two sources of irritation for the price of one rather minor action. This never failed to amuse me, but at that time I was easily amused.

The biggest area of contention between the guards and me centred on my refusal to leave the cell for any reason. Whenever the guards would enter the cell to request that I attend a visit or interrogation or leave the cell so that it could be cleaned, I would refuse to acknowledge them, only raising my head from my book or my pack of playing cards to acknowledge that a new and more unpleasant smell was now apparent in my cell. If they became verbally abusive, I would reply in kind, irritating them more than they irritated me. Their frustration at my refusal to submit to what they saw as their legitimate authority, visible in their faces, made the prospect of direct confrontation all the more likely, particularly when a certain guard officer was in command of the detail. If they were determined to remove me from the cell, then handcuffs and shackles would be placed on me and I would be dragged out. I tried during this procedure to engage in passive resistance, forcing them to handle directly my filthy form. I managed to maintain my composure when the guards simply carried me out; however, on more than one occasion the officer in charge would order the guards to force me to stand and walk, which they would try to do with punches and kicks.

For some reason, these confrontations always occurred when the cell needed to be cleaned, and always when one particular officer was in charge. Removal from my cell to attend visits with embassy staff developed a specific ritual. Attendance in the interrogation offices now became rare, but when necessary it seemed that particular officers were sent in to handle taking me to Khaled and Ibrahim with a minimum of confrontation. However, cell cleaning remained another matter.

The period of time between each cleansing grew longer over my incarceration, increasing from two to four weeks by the spring of 2002, probably because my captors could not be bothered with the problems my removal caused. By the end of 2002, I was no longer removed from my cell for that purpose; instead, a cleaning crew would be admitted and the guards would form a human barrier, isolating me in my sleeping area. The policy of strict isolation from any of the prison's foreign workers had obviously been waived, allowing for a less confrontational means of trying to maintain some semblance of hygiene in my accommodation. Until that time arrived, however, this exercise was one fraught with difficulty for the prison authorities.

In particular, two such confrontations spring to mind. It was in mid-February 2002, during the morning. The guards had entered my cell under the control of a be-thobed officer, a rotund bespectacled individual with a thin moustache and evil slitty eyes. Whenever this particular officer was in charge of the guards, physical brutality was always administered. On this occasion, handcuffs and shackles were placed on me, and my mattress (with me riding on it) was dragged out from between the plinths and lifted onto one of them. At the officer's signal, the guard on my right grabbed my hair, lifting my torso upright. He was one of the Saddam twins, both of whom were nasty individuals. If any violence was to be directed toward me, they were always present and always eager.

As the Saddam twin held me up with one hand, he proceeded to slap me across the face with the other, while another guard shouted at me to stand up. The rest of them, numbering a dozen or so, just stood around watching and wondering what would happen next. My temper snapped and with an aggressive scream, I lunged at the twin. Just as I did so, the guard I nicknamed Zapata interceded, pushing the twin out of the way. That meant that my target had moved, and I now sunk my teeth into the arm of one of the more decent of the guards. With my teeth sinking into Zapata's flesh, I hung on with all my strength; it made no difference to me who I was biting, all that interested me was giving back some of what I had been served. Pandemonium broke out among the guards, with the Saddam twins and others raining blows on my head and neck in their attempts to break my hold. Eventually they succeeded, and I was rolled onto my stomach and pressed into the plinth. Somehow during the struggle, the mattress was dislodged, leaving me on the bare surface of the plinth, when my hair was again grabbed and my head turned to one side. At this point the officer stepped forward, and with all his might began punching me in the ear. Six or seven blows hit their target, driving my head into the hard surface. I felt something pop inside my ear, followed by a sharp pain. All semblance of resistance left me as I became dizzy and stunned as a result of the punches. As I was no longer capable of fighting back, I was pulled off the plinth, banging my head on the floor in the process, and dragged from the cell into the barber's office for the duration.

When I was returned to my cell, I still felt somewhat disoriented and it dawned on me that I had nearly been knocked out. There was a roaring sound inside my left ear, and everything that I heard seemed distorted. I ran my fingers over my head, probing for sore spots and swellings, and my fingers felt something crusty around my ear. On closer inspection, at the wall-mounted steel plates by the sinks, I saw that my ear had been bleeding. I knew my eardrum had been perforated and wondered if any further injury had been done. Fortunately, the bleeding seemed to be minor, though I suffered from hearing impairment in that ear for some months. Eventually the injury healed, but I have been left with some minor hearing loss on that side.

Months later, during August of 2002, another such confrontation occurred. Once again it was the squat bespectacled officer who was in charge. No brutality was directed toward me during the extraction, though I was rolled onto my stomach and dragged by the ankle shackles face down along the floor. This time instead of being taken into the barber's office, I was dragged all the way out to the exercise yard, bouncing down the few steps at its entrance. As I was being pulled from the cell, I had managed to grab one of my blankets, for I had every intention of making myself passably comfortable wherever they stored me. I was glad that I had done so, for as my body came into contact with the concrete surface of the yard, I felt the searing heat that it radiated and the sensation of my skin burning at the contact. This being August, any surface under prolonged exposure would have been hot enough to fry an egg.

When the guards released their grip on the shackles, I made to stand, gathering in the blanket to place under my feet. As I did so, it was snatched away from me. While my feet were smouldering as I stood there, the officer appeared and dropped a thobe in front of me. A guard who had appeared with him held a pair of sandals and told me that I could have them once I was dressed. It was a tempting offer, for the heat was becoming excruciating. I promptly picked up the thobe, making those before me smile, but their smiles disappeared as I tore the thobe to pieces and stepped out into the centre of the yard. I knew that my feet were burning, not just from the pain that I could feel, but also from the smell of my flesh as it was cooked by the heat of the concrete. It was an odd smell, not unpleasant, but disconcerting nonetheless. I stood there and stared aggressively at the officer, who turned on his heel and departed. The guard with the sandals looked on bemusedly for a few more seconds before leaving as well. The guards who remained behind to supervise me muttered among themselves, as my actions seemed to confirm to them that I must be mad. A few more minutes passed, then finally one of the guards broke from the others, gathered my blanket, and threw it at my feet. I picked it up and dropped it behind me, keeping my feet in intimate contact with the concrete. I was adjusting to the pain and had become curious to see how long I could endure this trial.

After about twenty minutes, I was summoned to return to my cell. I astonished the guards by deciding to walk, collecting the blanket and limping along on my now blistered feet. Back in my accommodation, I immediately entered one of the toilet cubicles, using the floor spigot to bathe my feet in cool water, before retiring to my mattress. A cursory inspection showed that my feet had been burned across most of their soles, with blisters forming in a number of places, but thanks to the thick layers of callus that my barefoot walking had created, the damage was not irreparable. A little while later, the doctor entered my cell and asked to inspect my feet, but I rudely refused his request, sending him away shaking his head in disbelief at my foolish stubbornness. It was more than a week before I resumed my exercise routine, and for the first couple of days afterwards, I lay on my mattress stirring myself only to collect food and go to the toilet.

With my refusal to accept embassy visits or visits with my lawyer came other odd occurrences. The guards, normally led by an English-speaking officer, would enter my cell and announce that I had to attend a visit, and I in turn would ignore them. This resulted in the guards leaving the cell for a few minutes, only to return a little later bearing various faxes or notes that usually contained entreaties for me to accept the visit. Sometimes the note was waved in front of me, being offered for my perusal on the condition that I get dressed and leave the cell. Needless to say I refused such offers and invitations. On other occasions the notes were given to me, but I simply tore them up and wiped my arse with them, eliciting the usual looks of disgust. Whenever notes were waved at me or handed over to me, it was done in an overly theatrical manner. At first, this did not strike me as curious, until one day, not only was a note delivered but so too was someone's necktie, dangled in front of me with the not particularly tempting offer that if I wanted to find out who it belonged to, I should get dressed and leave the cell. As the tie was presented, I watched the officer, finding his actions comical, until it dawned on me that he was acting this way for the benefit of the CCTV cameras. I understood then that my captors were recording my actions, making me wonder for whose benefit this was being done. I was fairly certain that the embassy officials would be the primary audience, particularly given some of the comments on my behaviour that had been delivered during the last of the visits I had accepted. Pity that my captors chose only to provide such a selected record of my incarceration, for it would be of much greater educational value to the diplomats who were involved to have been shown videos of my interrogation, not that they would have had the stomach to sit through them.

On the evening of February 25, day 436, the television mounted in the wall of my cell sprang to life, waking me from my slumber. It was the first time that it had been turned on, confirming, if nothing else, that it worked. The volume was obviously at the maximum setting, for the noise that emanated from it was both distorted and deafening. I was certainly not going to get back to sleep, and what was being broadcast was hardly something I was interested in. The annual hajj holiday was in full swing, and Saudi television was broadcasting long prayer sessions, with which I was now being assailed. I pressed the button next to the cell door to summon the guards. When they arrived and opened the mailing slot to enquire what I wanted, I asked them to turn off the noise. I was met by a simple denial of my request. Whoever was in charge of the guard detail had obviously decided that I needed a session of enforced religious education.

Being fully awake, and the noise level gave little chance of being anything else, I scoured the cell to try to find something with which to persuade the guards to turn off the noise. As I inspected the toilets, I discovered that I could unscrew part of the foot pedal that operated the water spigot, giving me a small stainless steel disk about five centimetres in diameter. With this new implement in hand, I walked over to the other side of the cell and began throwing it at the protective screen of toughened glass behind which the television was placed. After about five attempts, the glass began to crack, until a few minutes later the screen was a mass of fracture lines.

As I continued with my attempt to break the glass, the television was turned off as suddenly as it had been turned on. Satisfied, I began to walk back to my sleeping place, when the cell door opened and the cell filled with guards led by one of the least obnoxious of the officers. He politely asked me for the disk. I complied with his request, lobbing the disk into the throng, throwing it without any force or at anyone in particular. Still, my action scattered the guards, providing me with further light relief. Collecting the disk, the officer and the guards departed, only to return a few minutes later to demand that I vacate my cell. By that time I was lying on my mattress, forcing them to carry me out. When I was returned, the television and its protective screen had gone, and in its place was a simple sheet of plywood. At least now my sleep could not be disturbed by that means. Unfortunately, about two weeks later, the damn thing was replaced, though at least in future it was never used to bombard me with the caterwauling of Saudi television.

On March 15, day 454, I was lying down with a mathematics book in my hand, trying to solve a rather sticky problem without benefit of pen and paper, when the television sprang into life again. This time I was regaled with the curious site of an ESPN broadcast of a stadium dirt bike event. I was wondering what this portended, when the cell door opened and the usual gang of fifteen or so guards, led by an English-speaking officer, entered the cell. As I tried to ignore them, I was informed that I could now move from my cell to be rehoused with some of my fellow detainees. As the offer was repeated over and over again, I stubbornly refused to acknowledge it. Exasperated, the contingent left my cell and a few minutes later, the television fell silent. I pondered what was going to come next, and the ensuing state of anticipation left me unable to focus on my reading, so I indulged myself in a long walk round and round the cell to work off my anxiety. Thankfully, nothing further occurred on that issue for nearly two weeks, giving me plenty of time to consider my options should it be raised again.

On the morning of March 27, day 466, the television once again burst into life, and given what had happened on the previous occasion, I sat back and awaited the arrival of the guards. I was not disappointed, for a few minutes later they arrived with Mohammed Said, the Smiling Knife, leading the way. This time I was not asked if I wanted to join the other prisoners; the Smiling Knife bluntly told me that regardless of my opinion on the matter, I was to be moved in with the other detainees. In the face of this statement I could not continue to ignore his presence. I responded by pointing out that I was powerless to prevent them carrying out what was proposed; however, I would kill whoever my new cellmate was. Were they willing to take such a risk, I asked. I received my answer as they departed my cell, leaving me alone again. Within minutes the television fell silent, denying me even its background noise for company. Later that evening, I was collected from my cell and taken to the hospital, though initially I thought my bluff was being called and I would find myself with a new roommate.

I had been in solitary confinement for well over a year by that stage, so one would have thought I would have welcomed some company. In truth, I found the offer extremely tempting and hard to resist. My regime of protest was difficult to maintain, as was the solitary confinement difficult to endure, and my resolve did waiver in the face of their entreaties. I knew, though, that if I had to share a cell with another inmate either I would have to stop my protests, for I could not subject another inmate to such conditions, or my fellow inmate would have to join me in the various protests. Neither scenario was what I wanted, for I was trying to provoke the Saudis to bring their wrath down on me, so that should they need a scapegoat, they would automatically select me. To terminate these protests would possibly defeat that objective, just as having some-one join me in them would do. So it was that I decided my only course of action was to remain alone. It was not an easy decision to reach, but it was one that I found necessary, even though the thought of company was at times just too seductive for my tired and stretched condition.

After the first couple of months of my refusing to accept visits from embassy officials, my captors finally hit on a solution to that problem, one that was quite obvious. The guards would appear in my cell in force and place me in restraints, then a collapsible gurney would be wheeled in and I would be placed on it. Using various straps and belts, I would then be further restrained. Finally, a white sheet would be draped over me and I would be ready for transporting. Then, immobile and anonymous like a corpse on its way to the morgue, I would be wheeled out to an ambulance, taken to the Security Forces Hospital, eventually ending up in one of the rooms of the section reserved for prison-ers and shackled to a bed. Thus the Saudi authorities could main-tain the façade that I was undergoing a routine medical checkup, and by coincidence it would be convenient for the embassy offi-cials to visit me. The fact was that doctors made an appearance only when the embassy officials were present, and then only to demonstrate the fact that I was refusing medical attention. It was just another part of the dog and pony show that my imprisonment had become.

The first of these visits occurred just after the second attempt to remove me from solitary confinement. That evening I was collected in the manner described and taken to the hospital, where the fol-lowing day, officials from the embassy were trooped in to see me. At their head was a new face, introduced to me as the new first consul. I should have known that would be his post, given his appearance. He was an exact carbon copy of the previous first consul, short, slender, and follicularly challenged, dressed in a checked jacket and striped tie. Everything from his physical appearance to his manners to his poor taste was so similar that it crossed my mind that there must be a secret government laboratory hidden away producing clones.

Our meeting was hardly auspicious, for he started in by lecturing me in an aggressive and demanding manner. I chose to ignore him. I was told quite plainly that my situation was my fault and that my current behaviour, particularly my refusal to meet with my lawyer, was causing problems for the disposition of the case, adversely affecting not just me but also the other prisoners. I was also roundly condemned for the stupidity of my medical strike, and informed that I had no idea about the consequences of such an action. I wondered if he thought his show of force was going to gain anything other than my responding in kind with my own verbal abuse, which I saved for the time being. I first began by re-iterating that I had no interest in his government intervening in my case, and that I had no intention of meeting with a lawyer whom I considered nothing more than a puppet of Naif's henchmen. Finally, I informed him that I knew full well the consequences of my medical strike, which was why I had engaged in it. As the consul began to try to rebut my statements, I cut him off with a loudly exclaimed "Fuck off." This halted his speech and he terminated the meeting, leaving the room for a private discussion with his seeming new friends, Ibrahim and Khaled. I use that term advisedly, considering that all the embassy officials seemed to get along better with my torturers than they ever did with me. When their discussion was over, everyone involved re-entered the room, and the consul once again launched into further demands that I allow the doctors to examine me. I replied simply, "You can kiss my Irish arse."

This stopped his tirade and the meeting was brought to a close by my being informed that I would be visited in a couple of days by a prominent Canadian MP. Everyone, it seemed, was getting in on the act, and all the governments involved were trying to exploit this situation for whatever propaganda value they could milk out of it, or so it seemed to me.

Two days later, just after the breakfast tray had been removed, a flurry of activity began to take place. Uniformed guards began entering and leaving my room with regular monotony, bringing in items of furniture, then taking them away, then bringing them back. First a circular carpet emblazoned with the logo of the Kingdom was brought in and then removed, then some armchairs appeared along with the carpet, then the carpet was removed, then it was brought back along with a potted palm tree and the chairs were removed, and then the chairs were brought back and the potted palm was removed. The ceaseless activity was as annoying as it was amusing. Finally, it was time for lunch, and it struck me that it would be a good idea to add to the decorations. Thus, when the furniture arrangements had been finalized and lunch had been brought in to me, I scattered the food around and urinated all over the chairs. When a guard returned to collect the food tray, his discovery of my additions to the décor resulted in the rapid removal of all that had been placed in the room, and a cursory attempt was made to remove some of the scattered food, though the puddle of urine remained untouched, drying out as a broad veneer of yellow on the floor.

When the embassy team arrived, with the visiting dignitary in tow, they were greeted by the sight of my none-too-clean hospital room, though they showed no surprise as complaints had been made by my captors before their entry. Apart from the four members of the embassy team, it seemed that every dignitary from the prison and the hospital, along with Khaled and Ibrahim, were in attendance. The opening gambit of this forced audience was made by the consul, who brought up the fact that I had refused the offer of being housed with the other prisoners and was refusing all medical attention, confirming that these things had been offered but that my recalcitrance was in fact the real problem.

I was then introduced to the visiting dignitary, Stéphane Bergeron, Bloc Québécois MP for Verchères-Les Patriotes. It turned out that some of his constituents, friends from some time past, had alerted him to my plight and insisted that he get involved in my case. Being a member of the Canadian Parliamentary Foreign Affairs Committee, he managed to have a visit to Saudi Arabia included in the last leg of an overseas trip and was granted permission to see me. I must admit that I was surprised to hear the names of the friends that he mentioned. My public reaction was one of dismissive laughter. However, the effect that the simple message from friends had on me was profound. The words burrowed deep into me, directly and immediately strengthening my resolve. I felt as if my spine had become encased in steel. I became even more determined to pursue what I saw as the right path, regardless of its consequences. This meant continuing my protests.

In some respects, I am sure the words delivered were to show me that there were those outside the restricted world of my imprisonment who cared deeply about me and hoped I would do nothing that would cause me further harm. I had no intention of directly harming myself, but for the benefit of my captors I stated that my friends should forget about me, that for all intents and purposes I was dead.

There then followed a series of discussions concerning my health, led by one of the hospital's cardiologists, which were all a bit surreal, for he posed his questions to the embassy contingent, who then repeated the questions to me. When finally I got fed up with this stupidity, I pointed out that as the doctor was standing within a metre of the bed, he could just as easily address me directly. In response to the various questions put to me about my understanding of my medical condition, I left no one in any doubt that I understood the potential consequences of my medical strike, and that I had no intention of changing my mind. I explained quite clearly that my condition was a result of what had happened during my incarceration.

"What caused my first heart attack was the torture that those two did to me to get me to confess; those two there." I pointed at Khaled and Ibrahim as I made the statement.

The effect this had on my torturers was as could be expected, with Ibrahim, once my words were translated, angrily barking out, "Halas."

As he said this, he waved at the contingent to direct them from the room.

One of the embassy staff barked back, "No. No, the meeting is not finished."

I was a little surprised by this sudden display of resistance on the part of one of the diplomats, but as I thought about it, it did make some sense. It was done not for my benefit but for the benefit of the visiting politician, a cynical attempt to demonstrate how well they were fighting for my rights.

Even so, the meeting was adjourned. Everyone departed to discuss the unpleasant turn that my mentioning the forbidden word "torture" had caused. To my surprise, my visitors trooped back into the room for round two. I was now given a letter, brought by Stéphane Bergeron from one of my friends. It was handed to me in a rather showy fashion by Ibrahim, who made an overt display of his "serving me by his own hand," an attempt to demonstrate the care and respect he supposedly showed toward me. Nonetheless, as I read the words contained in the letter, the feeling that I had felt earlier coursed through me again. I put the letter back in its envelope and handed it to one of the embassy staff, indicating that it had no meaning for me, though privately I felt anything but dismissive.

Another round of medical questions ensued, and I finally agreed to undergo a thorough medical examination later that day. With the cursory initial examination over, and everyone satisfied with my apparently more cooperative attitude, the visit drew to a close and briefly I returned to my solitary gazing at the ceiling.

A few minutes after everyone had left, Khaled and Ibrahim returned to the room. As they approached the bed, they began admonishing me for having mentioned that I had been tortured. To begin with I ignored their comments, but then they changed tack and began making personal insults about my friends who had delivered the messages of support, casting aspersions on their western morality. At these latter words, I reached over to the bedside table and retrieved an orange that was sitting there, immediately hurling it at Ibrahim, managing to hit him in the forehead. As I launched this projectile, I jumped from the bed and raced toward them, for though my ankles were shackled, someone had forgotten to attach them to the bedstead. Initially stunned by the rapidity of my movements and by the accuracy with which the orange found its target, the two of them now sprang into action. Turning to flee, they raced for the door, with me hobbling behind them as rapidly as I could. I almost managed to get my hands on Ibrahim just as he pulled the door closed behind him, locking it to ensure his own safety. Once again, I had seen a demonstration of their cowardice, and as I returned to the bed with an overly large smile on my face, I wondered what price I would have to pay for my latest piece of effrontery.

When the door opened, a few guards entered cautiously and came over to the bed, to secure my shackles to its frame before departing. So I was to remain until I was returned to the prison two days later. There was no change in my regimen there, and no new restrictions were added. When the doctor returned in the early evening, I refused to allow him to examine me, saying that my earlier cooperation had been for the purpose of ending the discussion about my health. I did have the usual interview with Khaled and Ibrahim, under circumstances that made them feel a lot safer – me fully restrained with a coterie of guards holding me down. That was over soon enough, and I was returned to my cell to contemplate the error of my ways, and to try to anticipate what was next on the agenda.

||||| ||||| ||||| |||

About five months later, around September 10, 2002, day 633, I was hauled off to the hospital in the established manner and informed that I would have an audience with another visiting dignitary. As with the last such enforced visit, the hospital room was meticulously prepared. I had noticed one change in the decor, that being the addition of a CCTV camera. Slowly over the period of my incarceration, my Saudi captors had adapted their medical facility to the presence of such high-profile guests as my fellow detainees and me. When all the furniture in the room had been arranged, and the necessary additions made, I was left alone to await my special treat. I had not been served any food that day, so I was unable to add that to the décor. Obviously, the guest was too important for my captors to allow such a demonstration. The only refreshment that I managed to consume was tap water, acquired during a couple of supervised trips to the toilet. When I was certain that no further alterations to the room were to be made, I half stood off the bed, one foot on the floor and the other knee on the edge of the mattress. From this position I was able to empty my bladder onto the chairs that had been placed next to my bed. If nothing else my puckish sense of humour would be tickled when someone placed their unsuspecting backsides on the sodden foam of the seats.

Eventually, I heard a commotion outside, the sound of numerous footsteps and voices penetrating the closed door; the visit was imminent. When the door opened, the first people through were members of the prison staff, including my torturers, the governor of the prison, and the Smiling Knife, Mohammed Said. I turned my head to them and said quite crudely, "Fuck off."

No one obeyed my command. The embassy party followed the Saudis, looking dour and serious. Among them was a single face that I did not recognize. When everyone had finished arranging themselves around the edge of my bed, the introductions began, and I was informed that I was fortunate to have such a prominent guest. This was Don Boudria, a senior member of the ruling Liberal party. It was not a name that I recognized, nor quite frankly was it one that I wished to recognize. With the initial introduction over, Boudria sat and began to address me, and for my part, I could barely contain my amusement at the thought of what he sat himself upon. The initial part of his speech sounded more like an election address than what I considered germane to the matters at hand, and I wondered who he was trying to impress. I listened as he told me of my good fortune to have so many people working on my behalf, of having such a fine lawyer as Dr. Al Tuwaijeri representing me, and at having my case being taken so seriously at such high levels of government. He went on to state that my case was now being heard at the highest court in the land, and he was hopeful that the situation would soon be resolved.

"I am a British citizen," I said forcefully. "I will not be dealt with by representatives of an ersatz mongrel state."

For a few seconds Mr. Boudria seemed at a loss for words – something quite unusual in a politician. After a moment he said he would see what he could do about handing my case over to the British. With that, the visit was drawn to a close, and everyone began to depart, the embassy party being herded away by their hosts. While the last of them began to leave the room, I flung out one last parting shot, "What have you done to stop the torture?" As I uttered these words, the only person to visibly respond to them was Khaled, who was standing just inside the doorway ushering out the last of the dignitaries before closing the door. With the room emptied, I lay back thankful that it was over, and looked forward to returning to my prison cell, where at least I could get some exercise.

When the door opened again, only minutes later, it was a young officer of the prison guards who entered. As with all those in uniform who had attended the visit, he was attired with all the belts and buckles of full dress, with a holstered revolver at his hip. He removed the chairs, pushing them into the hallway, then returned to inspect the room, looking for what, I do not know. For a moment he ceased his activity, standing with his back to me, seemingly deep in thought. I noticed that the restraining clip of his holster was undone, the revolver invitingly close and just beyond the limit of my reach. As I focused on that object, I realized that with a lunge I might be able to snag it, but the risk of failure would be high.

The mere thought of attempting to escape was attractive to me. I had examined the possibility from every angle and come to the simple conclusion that my only chances of effecting an escape would occur during transit or while I was in hospital, and here was as close an opportunity as I would ever be presented with. Capture the revolver and try to shoot my way out was as good as I could expect, and the chance of a lethal failure would be high. It was not that I expected to get very far, but the simple fact of such an attempt even with its associated risks would create a major distur- bance and a major embarrassment. Frankly, if, as I believed, I was going to die then maybe it would be better to die in a manner that would cause the greatest difficulty. As I weighed these thoughts and calculated what would be necessary for me to make my grab, the officer was called from the room by another guard.

Three days later, I was returned to my cell and found that the mattress and drinking water container had been removed. Only two blankets had been left for me. When I made the guards aware of these deficiencies, they shrugged their shoulders. One said that "Captain" had ordered their removal. I realized that by "Captain" they meant Ibrahim, and this was another punishment. So, I had been wrong, there was something further that could be confiscated to make my imprisonment more uncomfortable. Now I would sleep directly on the hard floor and have to drink the tap water. The floor as my mattress presented little concern to me, and I adapted to it without any problem. The water was another matter.

The sinks in the cell had a central tap with a water-fountain–style feature. The water tasted strongly of rust, and I wondered whether it was safe to drink. My only other source of fluids was the tea served with the meals, and given that it was strong enough to dissolve a spoon, it was more likely to act as a diuretic than as a source of refreshment, adding to the problem of dehydration. While the taste of the tap water was tolerable, its effects on my digestive tract were worrying. For the first few days, I suffered from diarrhoea. Fortunately, this seemed to be from the high mineral content. By the end of a week my stomach had settled down.

As I grew used to these new restrictions, I wondered what more could be done to make my life unpleasant. As I sat reading, it dawned on me. I was dependent on this activity, savouring the infrequent delivery of new reading material sent in by friends and well-wishers. I would be devastated if this privilege was denied me. I thought I would not be able to cope. Instinctively I knew what I needed to do. I stacked all my books together into an over-large wall beyond my casual reach and I stopped reading. With the exception of keeping up my book diary to mark the passage of time, for the next few weeks I did not pick up or handle any of the books, and I read nothing.

This was the most difficult deprivation I had to endure. The books that I had on hand were my companions. Reading helped me get through the long days and also provided a landscape through which I would let my mind roam. Effectively, they were my primary means of external emotional support, as they had been during some of the more difficult times of my childhood. Now, I rejected them, making myself live completely in my mind, dependent upon only my innate imagination and the meditative abilities developed through the imprisonment. It was a strange but edifying experience, and by the end of the third week it no longer required a constant act of will to keep from straying from my purpose.

During the fourth week, at the end of which I had planned to terminate this self-imposed trial, I received another delivery of books. Usually, I would begin to devour such reading material as soon as it arrived. Now, however, I put them to one side, feeling no temptation as I did so. When the time came to end this piece of silliness, I instead extended it by a week for no other reason than I could, reinforcing my discovery that I could live completely in my mind dependent only on my own memories and my own imagination. Perversely, I began to look forward to the time when Ibrahim might order the confiscation of my books.

One evening, not long after I had begun to read again, guards entered the cell carrying in a mattress and twenty litres of drinking water, depositing them just inside the door. Obviously, the punishment was over, to which I had only one response. I shredded the mattress and then urinated on the resultant pile of foam. As for the water, I poured it through the mailing slot before stuffing the plastic container into one of the toilets. My jobs done, I resumed my position between the bed plinths and went back to reading. No more attempts were made to deliver either another mattress or drinking water to my cell for the duration of my imprisonment. Apart from denying me reading material or subjecting me to full-scale torture, there was nothing left that could be used to discipline me.

I spent the following few months in anticipation of the next enforced visit, for I was sure there would be others. I turned down entreaties to accept embassy visits or consultation with my supposed lawyer Dr. Al Tuwaijeri, as per the established ritual. The New Year came and went, and I entered the third year of my imprisonment. Everything had quietened down to a dull roar. The only changes to the regimen under which I was kept pertained to my diet. Every couple of days at breakfast, a box of cereal, usually a locally manufactured version of bran flakes, would be included.

Once a week, I would be provided with roast beef and rice with gravy heavily spiced with peppers, and on two separate evenings hamburgers and pizza would be delivered. While the roast beef was a welcome addition to my diet, the hamburger and pizza were not. Both these latter items were mass-manufactured freezer products, reheated prior to serving, and tasted like poorly flavoured cardboard, but they were a change.

Collected on day 808, March 4, 2003, I found myself once again shackled to a bed in the Security Forces Hospital, wondering whose presence I would be subjected to this time. Two days later, I got my answer. The door opened and the visiting party began to enter the room. As expected, Khaled, Ibrahim, and Mohammed Said were among them. Slightly surprising was the presence of my lawyer, Dr. Al Tuwaijeri, and of the Canadian ambassador, Melvin MacDonald. However, what really shocked and angered me was the presence of my father. Just as stubbornly as I had demanded that he not visit the Kingdom, he stubbornly ignored me. To say that I was furious with him would be an understatement. I was incandescent with rage at what I saw as his stupidity, understandable though his actions were. As he drew closer to the bed, with the rest of the party spreading out around him, he greeted me.

"Hello, Bill."

"Leave. Leave now" was my terse reply.

"No, I will not. We need to talk."

As he now stood immediately beside me, I directed a punch at his chest, knowing full well that with all the wallets and passports that would be in his jacket, I would do him little harm, though the action would shock him and the rest of the audience and hopefully terminate the interview. That did not happen, as my father stood his ground and various members of the party demanded that I calm down, approaching the bed to restrain me.

Calm down. I was calm even if angry, but if it was going to take something more to bring this to a close and deliver my message to my father, then I would give them a demonstration of absolute fury, the like of which they had never before seen. I sprang from the bed, planting my unshackled foot on the floor, the other hanging suspended from the bed frame. I pushed my father toward the door, bellowing as I did so, "Get the fuck out now."

Unfortunately, as he backed up he moved away from rather than toward the door. Dragging the bed behind me, I continued to move toward him, as pandemonium broke out among the rest of the party. It seemed as if everyone raced for the door at once, none of them trying to restrain my movements, not the guards that were present, not my torturers, not my lawyer, nor even Mohammed Said. They all ran in one direction, toward the exit. It was something straight out of a cartoon, as each literally tried to climb over the others to get away. Bumping into each other and almost wedging themselves into the door space, the first to leave the room were Khaled, Ibrahim, and the ambassador, who I noticed jammed his finger against the door as he grabbed at it in his desperation to get out. The others were close behind, trying to distance themselves from me. The only exception was a guard whom I had nicknamed Santa, one of the decent members of staff, who placed himself protectively between my father and me and began to usher him out of the room. I found then, and still do, his concern for my father's safety to be touching, but I had no intention of expressing such sentiments in the midst of giving vent to my fury.

I grabbed the bedside table, hurling it to the ground, breaking off its collapsible wing in the process. This I threw at the retreating figures. I then turned my attention to the bed frame and my ankle shackle. I had long ago realized that the tubular bar to which I was normally attached was simply slotted into the main body of the frame and therefore removable. I grabbed it, pulling it from its mountings, releasing the ankle shackle in the process. I was free of the bed, holding a hollow seventy-five-centimetre-long stainless steel tube, one ankle still wearing the shackle, the other end of which was now attached to nothing. I advanced toward the last of the retreating figures, brandishing the tube, smashing it into the walls as I went. As the last person left the room, the door slammed shut and was locked.

I was alone again, free from restraint, with the ability to create as much damage as possible. I proceeded to destroy the fixtures and fittings of the room, attacking the television suspended from the ceiling and the CCTV camera, breaking apart the remains of the bedside table and the bed frame, pummelling the walls and the door, leaving dents in the latter as I did so. Finally, there was nothing left for me to ruin. As I let my fury subside, I could not help but smile; I had just caused a few thousand dollars of damage, demonstrated the cowardice of my captors to their foreign guests, and given everyone an exhibition of the depths of my anger. Damn, it felt good, childish and immature though such a feeling is. I knew that I would not be left alone for very long; I wondered how they would try to restrain me and what punishment was in store for me. I knew full well that this incident would be described as evidence of either mental instability or at least of my extreme recalcitrance. Had I really been as out of control as has subsequently been suggested, more than just a few items of furniture and electronics would have been harmed.

I was standing in the centre of the room surveying the wreckage when the door finally opened. The first to enter was Mohammed Said, brandishing a chair in front of him like a lion tamer. Behind him others cautiously followed. I waved the tube at him, as he demanded that I drop it. When he was within striking distance, I directed a blow at the chair, forcing him to take a step back. It would have been easy to hit him directly, and though such a blow would have been deserved, that did not form part of the purpose of my demonstration. Again, the Smiling Knife demanded that I put down my weapon, and this time I complied. As I did so, the Smiling Knife and the guards with him rushed to grab me, forcing me to the floor, and placing me in handcuffs and shackles. Following in their wake was Dr. Al Tuwaijeri, a look of contempt on his face.

"You are a filthy animal; you deserve what we have done to you," he said and then he turned away.

"Look in the mirror if you want to see a filthy animal," I shouted at his retreating back.

At last I had seen his true face. I was right not to deal with him. After my release, through correspondence with my father, I learned of a conversation he had with Al Tuwaijeri as they walked through the hospital toward their appointment with me. To quote my father, "Walking through the hospital corridors al Tuwaijeri turned to me and remarked: 'Of course, we don't know that he didn't commit these crimes.' He then went on to complain of Bill's behaviour in the prison. I realised then that he had been working on behalf of the Saudi Royal Family, not my son, and he could now foresee the release of the prisoners. He was about to lose face and did not like it. He also recounted some of Bill's antics that were intended to annoy the guards. From the stories he told me it was not surprising that Bill succeeded. Unless they are mentally subnormal it must also have been obvious to the Canadian Ambassador, and other staff members, that al Tuwaijeri had not had any interest in helping Bill, but had been solely intent in helping the Saudi authorities. The hypocrisy, downright dishonesty and treachery of the Canadian Department of Foreign Affairs is appalling. They must have known the lawyer's agenda but did nothing to replace him or even complain of his perfidy."

I was not the only one who suspected Al Tuwaijeri's motives. In conversations with James Lee, a fellow detainee, I discovered that Al Tuwaijeri had been instrumental in getting James to reinstate his confession and change his plea back to one of guilty. By the end of 2001, all the detainees, having met with their appointed lawyers, retracted their confessions, changing their pleas from guilty to not guilty. In fact I was the only one who did not do this, for I had refused to meet with my lawyer; however, it was assumed that my refusal to recognize the legal system was an effective plea of not guilty. In the summer of 2002, a number of the detainees were taken from Al Ha'ir prison back to the Al Ulaysha interrogation centre. There they were subjected to rounds of interrogation that while they did not involve physical torture saw the detainees once again subjected to sleep deprivation over a period of about ten days. The purpose of these interrogations was to get at least one detainee from each group to change their plea back to guilty in order to guarantee convictions for all those involved (the detainees were effectively considered as two groups by our captors, those responsible for the first two bombings – Mitchell, Schyvens, and myself – and those responsible for the later bombings – Brandon, Cottle, Lee, and Walker, with Ballard being the final addition).

During these renewed interrogations, James Lee was one of those put under pressure to reinstate his confessions. Threats were made against James Lee's girlfriend, Gillian Barton, who had remained to work in the Kingdom and was providing support to those imprisoned. Khaled and Ibrahim threatened to imprison and rape her, and given what had so far transpired, such threats were highly credible and extremely worrying for James.

As it turned out, James's lawyer was Al Tuwaijeri, who between sessions of the interrogations had visited Lee and questioned him concerning the honesty of his pleading not guilty. Finally, when James was unable to take any more pressure, he gave in to Khaled and Ibrahim and agreed to reinstate his confessions. There then followed a series of ridiculous attempts by the two thugs to have James rewrite his confessions in full in front of Al Tuwaijeri. Given that James could barely remember what he had been made to write more than a year previously, this idea was abandoned. Instead James wrote an apology to the Saudi government and rewrote his confession in its entirety under Khaled's supervision, except for the last couple of sentences. Later, Al Tuwaijeri was shown into the office, to witness Lee writing the last couple of sentences of his new confession without apparent duress. Thus was Al Tuwaijeri able to state that the confession was freely given. At the next meeting, Al Tuwaijeri informed James that he had been to the Ministry of the Interior and checked the facts of his confession, and he now knew that James was guilty and he could properly begin his defence. Had I bothered to deal with al Tuwaijeri, I would have been under pressure from him to plead guilty. So much for the provision of proper legal counsel.

With Al Tuwaijeri now gone, I sat back against one of the walls, watching as the room was cleaned and all the broken glass removed. Once that was finished, I was dragged into another room and dumped onto a bed to which I was then chained. This time the guards made sure I was attached to a more secure part of the frame, and the following day I was returned to the prison.

I expected that some form of interview with The Midget and Acne would ensue, or that some form of punishment would be meted out, but none came. Over the next couple of days I waited in anticipation, until the guards once again streamed into my cell and prepared me for transportation to the hospital and another enforced audience. I did not know it then, but this would be the last time I would leave the prison before my release. As I lay in my hospital bed, in the same room that I had destroyed only days previously, but which was now fully repaired, I did not have long to wait for my visitors. Their arrival was presaged by a be-thobed English-speaking officer, one who had studied in the United Kingdom, entering the room to place me in what would be termed four-point restraint, with both my wrists and ankles being securely affixed to the bed frame. This time at least I was not going to get the opportunity of terrorizing my guests. When the party finally entered, it comprised Dr. Oliver, the Canadian psychiatrist whom I had met previously; Dr. Al Humaid, the Saudi psychiatrist; and Khaled and Ibrahim.

F

As Dr. Oliver spoke to me, he tried to convince me that my actions were not appropriate, questioning me as to my motives for behaving as I had done. I replied to his question, trying to get under his skin as I did so, explaining my motivation as being the product of personal integrity – "Not something you would know about or be capable of understanding."

Dr. Oliver was too much the professional to be bothered by the rather deliberate insult in my words, though I did see flashes of anger in the eyes of Dr. Al Humaid and the others. I gave up on trying to anger Dr. Oliver and instead listened to what he had to say. From the way he expressed himself, stating that I had made my point and that my protests were no longer necessary, I was sure that there was a subtext in his comments, but I chose to ignore it. I pointed out that I had been tortured by Khaled and Ibrahim, and that Dr. Al Humaid was aware of this. Expecting my torturers to irately interrupt the proceedings, I was surprised when all I got were angry glares. The meeting did not last much longer, with Dr. Oliver wishing me well and further reiterating that my protests were no longer necessary.

After they had departed, the be-thobed officer returned, removing some of the restraints, leaving me with a single point of attachment to the bed. As he went about his work, he spoke to me, ridiculing me for the stupidity of my behaviour. I interrupted him.

"What would you do if you had been tortured into confessing to crimes that you did not commit?" I asked.

"You should talk to the investigators about that. I had nothing to do with it," he replied.

"Yes, you did. You were responsible on many occasions for delivering me to and collecting me from the interrogation offices, where you knew I was being tortured."

"So? I was only doing my job. I did not take part in any of the torture that you say happened," he said.

"Just because you did not swing the sticks does not mean you are not responsible. You assisted the torturers by ensuring that I was delivered to them for that purpose. It is a long-established principle in international law that following orders is no defence for performing or assisting in the performance of an illegal act. Torture is illegal, and your acts of complicity are just as illegal as those of the investigators."

The smile on his face disappeared, and he stared at me with something akin to revulsion. I drove my point home by saying, "You had better hope that I do not get out of here, for I will find a way of bringing you to justice. I know your name and I know where you studied; I will be able to identify you properly."

This last statement was a bluff, for I had no idea about his name or any of the details of his exact place of study. Nonetheless, it had its effect, for without another word he turned on his heel and left the room.

Early the next morning, I was returned to the prison. Later that same day, sometime after lunch, while I contemplated what further acts of defiance I could engage in, the cell door opened and the guards trooped in bearing gifts. I was somewhat surprised by the treasure that they now delivered. There were copies of *Wired* magazine, and a few out-of-date copies of *The Economist* (sent by Gillian Barton, who was still in the Kingdom to provide James Lee and the rest of the detainees with local support – a courageous act on her part), more than double the usual number of books, pads of paper, a couple of pens, half a dozen pencils, and a calculator. This latter item was for me the most useful, for it had a date function and a clock, so I now had the means to mark the actual passage of time. It was with this that I was able to determine how my sleeping patterns and sense of the length of a day had been affected by the conditions of my imprisonment, and it provided me with the only means to monitor one specific aspect of my physical condition, my pulse. In itself such a health check would tell me little. However, by logging my resting pulse over time, I might have been forewarned of any deterioration in my cardiovascular system.

After my release, I discovered that all these items were supposed to have been delivered more than a year previously, and that the Saudis had been claiming that they had done so. At the time, I wondered what had brought about this show of generosity, but came up with no answer. A couple of minutes after I had inspected everything, the mailing slot opened and a copy of the *Arab News* was pushed through. This was an English-language daily published in the Kingdom. I asked the guards whether the paper was current, and was told that it was. The date on its masthead was March 12, 2003. After 817 days of captivity, I was finally being given news of the outside world. I wondered what new developments in relation to our imprisonment had made this possible.

The *Arab News* published reports by local journalists as well as articles culled from newspapers published the previous day in the United Kingdom, the United States, India, and the Philippines. The news was heavily censored and contained nothing that had not been approved by the Ministry of the Interior. On more than one occasion the newspaper was delivered with articles cut out. I surmised that they related to our imprisonment or to ongoing terrorist activity in the Kingdom, and I was right in my musings. Speculating on what news may have been cut out of the paper helped me pass the time.

For the rest of my imprisonment, this paper was delivered daily from Saturday through to Wednesday. The weekend editions, those published on Thursday and Friday, arrived with Saturday's paper. However, there was a brief hiatus in the delivery. I had received the paper on Wednesday, May 7, and as the weekend was about to start I did not expect to receive the next delivery until the Saturday. This did not occur, and it was not until May 19 that delivery started again. Again I assumed that delivery had been suspended because something quite catastrophic had occurred in the Kingdom. In fact on May 10, three explosive devices, placed at separate exits of a shopping mall in Jeddah, had been discovered and dealt with. The paper, during the next couple of days, contained articles on the hunt for those responsible. Then on the night of May 12, four separate suicide bombings hit Riyadh, and the newspaper was full of articles on the government's pledge to hunt down those responsible. My captors would not want me to see this news, and it was easier for them not to provide the paper than to cut out the copious articles on the subject. Still, in the ensuing weeks, despite the extra censorship that the paper was subjected to, I was able to read a number of articles that had missed the censors' scissors and I was able to piece together the fact that a major terrorist incident had occurred.

Probably the most amusement that the paper provided came about on June 5. There on the front page, complete with his smiling picture, was an interview with one of the Kingdom's official executioners. The thought crossed my mind that only in Saudi Arabia would such an item merit the front page of a daily newspaper. At least the authorities did not try to hide their predilection for the death penalty, even if they did hide their predilection for torture.

The article contained these gems: "Me? I sleep very well. . . . [My sword] is very sharp. People are amazed how fast it can separate the head from the body. . . . I successfully trained my son Musaed, 22, as an executioner and he was approved and chosen. . . . I deal with my family with kindness and love. They aren't afraid when I come back from an execution. Sometimes they help me clean my sword."

The article appealed to my gallows humour and made me laugh. I also wondered if it had a purpose. Maybe it was meant as a threat to the active terrorist cells, though why publish the article in an English-language daily? Maybe it was meant to reassure the western expatriate community, to show them the nature of Saudi justice in order to allay their fears concerning the ongoing terrorist threat? Maybe it was meant for my fellow detainees and me, along with the diplomats involved, again acting as a threat or warning. Maybe it was just a normal article that was published at an opportune moment. Frankly, I have no idea which is correct, but I managed to be amused.

One evening, four days after the first delivery of the newspaper, I was lying down reading an article on cooking, when my thoughts on the next stage of my protests coalesced. I had done just about everything that I had imagined possible, but realized there was at least one thing left in which I had not indulged – a hunger strike. As I thought about it, it hit me that to proceed with one would be extremely difficult. I was unsure if I had the discipline to embark on this course. If I announced my intention and then failed in its execution, it would serve my captors more than it would me. Death did not worry me for I had long ago come to the conclusion that it was just another form of freedom; what worried me was my ability to control my appetite. Thus I struck a bargain with myself. First, I would attempt to stop eating for a period of five weeks, not announcing what my intention was. If I was successful in that, then when the third anniversary of my arrest approached, I would accept an embassy visit and inform my hapless guests that I was about to pursue my freedom by the only option left to me.

The next morning, having foregone breakfast, I asked to see the doctor. This surprised the guards, who repeatedly returned to the mailing slot to confirm my request. Eventually, having dressed myself in the solitary filthy pair of boxer shorts that remained in my cell, my request was granted. When I entered the doctor's office, he beckoned me to sit, while he set up his sphygmomanometer. Ignoring him, I stood on the scales and checked my weight, discovering that it had crept up to seventy-two kilograms. With that done, I indicated to the guards my intention of returning to my cell, leaving the doctor looking somewhat perplexed.

So it began. For the next five weeks I ate nothing, not even bothering with the sugarless tea that I was normally served, choosing to drink only tap water. Each time a meal was delivered, I would immediately go to the mailing slot, pushing it straight back into the hands of the guards. If I was asleep when food was delivered and the tray was still there when I awoke, I immediately emptied it into the toilets. It was hard for the guards not to notice my apparent lack of appetite, and on a couple of occasions, the more concerned among them led a delegation to my cell to ask why I was not eating. Even the doctor was brought into the cell to question me. I answered them with muteness, continuing as I intended to.

At first I noticed little change in myself, but over the coming days, my urine became almost colourless. Within weeks both my sweat and my urine developed a slightly aromatic scent, which I took to be signs of ketosis. Eventually, I began to notice that my face was becoming more gaunt and that the bony protuberances of my body were much more prominent. The first day or so it was not too difficult to ignore my hunger. However, by the third day it was a struggle to maintain my commitment to this trial for two reasons. First, hunger is a strong driving force, and I was not immune from its call. My stomach rumbled, even cramping on a couple of occasions, and thoughts of food permeated my thinking. Second, being as I was in an environment that deprived me of so much of what could be called normal sensation, the mere fact of eating was something that I looked forward to not just to satisfy my hunger, but also for the sensual pleasure that it brought, breaking up the monotony of my existence. Thus I found myself having to fight on two fronts my urge to eat, the physical and the psychological, for distinct and different reasons. What surprised me was that after about ten days, the hunger pangs began to lessen, disappearing altogether by the end of two weeks, alongside the disappearance of my emotional need to eat. My self-imposed trial of not reading had been more difficult to maintain than this had been.

A few days after my forty-second birthday, on the morning of April 21, the date I had set for the resumption of eating, I asked to see the doctor. As in my last visit five weeks previously, I weighed myself, but did not allow him to examine me. I returned to my cell to my calculations and to the anticipation of lunch, from which I left no scraps. My weight had dropped to 54 kilograms, my body having shed 18 kilograms over the period, a rate of 3.6 kilograms per week. I calculated that if over the next few months I allowed my weight to climb back to about 65 kilograms, at that rate of weight loss, it would take between eight and nine weeks before the onset of serious medical problems, and that with my damaged cardiovascular system, complete physiological collapse would not be far behind.

I knew from this experiment that I had the self-discipline to undertake a hunger strike, and I began to deliberate how to get the most theatrical effect from my final statement. If, as I planned, on December 17, 2003, I announced my intentions and carried them through, outrage would be followed by panic and deep embarrassment on the part of the diplomats and my captors. I contemplated the embarrassment I would cause as I saw the relief of my captors when I began to eat again. It was in this frame of mind and in circumstances that had become easier to bear that I contemplated the upcoming anniversary of my imprisonment, just a few months away.

five

RELEASE

One evening at about eight-thirty I was aroused by the double-click of the door mechanism that told me someone was about to enter my cell. I remember the time because I had checked it only moments before on the clock function of my calculator. I had gone through my nightly ritual of checking my pulse before making myself as comfortable as possible. Then, half covered in a blanket, I lay on the floor between the bed plinths, book in hand ready to drift off to sleep. I wondered what was on the agenda for this evening.

In the preceding few days, the guards had come into my cell to inform me of visits that they said were from the embassy and from my lawyers. I had refused to attend. Huey, the senior guard sergeant, stepped into the cell. He was on his own, and that was unusual, for all other entries into my territory usually required a minimum of six guards for a conversation and fifteen or more if I was to be moved.

I raised myself and watched as he silently approached me. His progress was direct, as he did not have to avoid the usual detritus. My cell had been cleaned two days previously, and with the exception of a few food stains on the walls and the unflushed toilets, I had not begun the process of redecoration. When he was about a metre from where I lay, he addressed me.

"Get dressed, you see doctor."

I lay back and began reading my book again, studiously ignoring him. I had not obeyed a request to see the doctor for more than eighteen months, and I was not about to start.

"Get up, get dressed, go to see doctor," he said again.

Again I ignored him, though by now I was beginning to feel a mounting tension and wondered if a full-scale confrontation was soon to begin.

"Get up, get dressed, go to see doctor," he said for the third time with exasperation and resignation.

I did not even bother to look up from my book, playing the game by the rules that I had set myself. Huey said nothing further, turning away to leave the cell. I heard the door close, the electronic double-click confirming that it was locked. Whatever had been going on, I had won round one and now began again to prepare myself for sleep. Ten or fifteen minutes passed, by which time drowsiness had returned, when the double-click yet again impinged itself upon me.

This time it roused me fully from my stupor, as I felt my pulse rate and thus my blood pressure climb. I was sure now that a full-scale confrontation would occur and began to prepare myself mentally for the onslaught. However, rather than the usual gang, Huey alone entered my cell, this time carrying a small cardboard box.

Once again he approached to within a metre of my prone form before saying anything. His words put me on edge instantly, for I thought that the last of the possible sanctions or confiscations was about to take place. I had prepared myself for this, but also I knew that it would make my survival harder in a way that nothing else had been able to. Adrenaline began to course through my body, making it difficult to keep my anger in check.

"Get dressed, put books in box, go see doctor," he said.

It was as I feared – they were about to confiscate the one thing that they had not confiscated before: my books. Yes, I had prepared myself for this, but I also dreaded it. My clothes had gone. My medication was a thing of the past. I had not been in the exercise yard since September 2001. I slept on concrete without a mattress. Items for personal hygiene were absent, and I had to drink the metallic-tasting water from the sink taps. However, none of those things had affected me; I had taken them in my stride, knowing that my refusals in those matters would bother them more than me. My books were another matter, for they were the only external stimulation that I had and upon which I had some dependency. It seemed that the test I had assigned myself months earlier had been a sensible strategy, for now I was going to have to live solely on my own intellectual stimulation.

"No, I am not going to see the doctor," I said emphatically.

"Get dressed, put books in box, go see doctor," he said again.

"If you want my fucking books, then you fucking pack them, you Saudi cunt. Take them and stuff them sideways up your arse" was my response.

I had intended to ignore him, but the threat posed by the confiscation of my books made me emotional and aggressive. To my surprise, instead of collecting some of my books, he turned on his heel and departed. The door closed behind him with the usual sound of it being locked, and I tried to return to my book. Unfortunately, I was now quite stressed, my pulse elevated, and all possibility of relaxation or sleep was gone. I was unable to concentrate.

What came next I would certainly not have predicted. To me my cell was my final home; freedom of the physical kind was a long-distant memory, something that I would not savour again. I resolved at that moment that if they came in to confiscate my books, this time I would try to do some permanent damage to one of the guards rather than passively resist. Just as these thoughts coalesced in my mind, the familiar double-click sounded again, and I heard the footsteps of more than one person heading toward the door. I sat up and braced myself, looking to my left and right to ensure that I had one or two of the heavier hardback volumes to hand for use as projectiles.

When the door opened Huey walked in as expected. The person following him was Sandy Mitchell, dressed in a white shell suit and trainers. To say that I was astonished or even shocked would be an understatement. I had not seen Sandy since the day I had watched him being assaulted. My only knowledge of his presence from then until now had been the sight of his signature on the court record and of his medication on the shelf outside his cell. I had no idea of how he had fared, nor any real idea of his physical health or his mental state.

As he approached me, I drank in the sight of him. He was clean-shaven and looked reasonably healthy, much as he had done prior to our arrest. My appearance must have shocked him. My hair was nearly shoulder length, lank, matted, and filthy. My beard was full and in the same dirty state. My body was emaciated, barely recovered from my experiment in nutritional deprivation, encrusted with dirt and my own faeces. The smell of my prison cell and of my person must have been overpowering for him.

I am not sure which one of us spoke first, though as I remember it we spoke to each other at the same time. I greeted him as if meeting him unexpectedly in the pub.

"Hello Dinky, what were you doing here then?" I asked.

At the same time, he said, "Get dressed, we are going home."

Those words slammed into me like a runaway train, their import not registering through the shock of hearing them. This was not what I had steeled myself for, not what I had trained myself to expect. Hearing it stated so baldly made me doubt my ears and my imagination, while my brain tried to make sense of those few simple words. Sandy seated himself on the end of the bed plinth and leaned toward me. He repeated his first statement, and followed it up with the few details of our departure that he knew. We were all about to go home, due to be flown from Riyadh on the first flight the next morning. However, I had to get dressed and see the prison doctor first.

I noticed that as he spoke he had trouble not retching at the odour that emanated from both my cell and my body. I had long since gotten used to my own stench and obviously some of my guards had grown immune to it or learned to control their reactions. His expression told me just how shocking my appearance must have been. He kept asking me if I was all right, and I kept reiterating that there was nothing wrong with me that a single malt and a hot bath could not mend. It was not quite the truth. Emotionally I was stretched taut, and I had a plethora of physical problems. Nevertheless, at that moment I actually felt all right.

I looked over at Huey, the guard sergeant. He was still carrying the cardboard box. Behind him another of the sergeants, the one I called Zapata, holding some of my clothes, neatly presented on coat hangers, was looking as tense as he always did when he was around me. I had managed to sink my teeth into him on one occasion. Both men were observing this reunion warily. At that moment, I understood what the box was for – it was for me to pack up my books to take with me. My imminent departure was the reason for sending in a solo guard. Someone must have thought that such an event would have made me more amenable. As no one had bothered to inform me of that fact until Sandy's arrival, my lack of cooperation up to that point was understandable given my track record. Mind you, I probably would not have believed it had the news been delivered to me by the guards or even by their superiors.

As it now finally sank in that we were about to be released, I stood up and said simply, "Let's go." I was completely naked. My intention was to depart the country in the same state in which I had been driven to live for the past two years.

The guards shook their heads. Sandy was incredulous. He reiterated his request that I get dressed. Still I refused, much to the exasperation of everyone concerned. I finally gave in partly, reaching over and collecting the only items of clothing that had been left in my cell. These were a T-shirt and a pair of boxer shorts, last washed in July 2001 and last worn in September of the same year. I had used them to wipe my feet after my daily walks around the cell and were thus as filthy as I was and just as fetid. I put them on, covering at least my nakedness but making myself only marginally more presentable.

The guards refused to accept this compromise. Even Sandy was showing signs of frustration at my bloody-minded behaviour, and he had experienced it for only a few minutes. At this point Sandy and the guards left me, saying that they would speak to Brigadier Mohammed Said on the phone. Within a couple of minutes they returned, saying that I had to change and shower, and once again I adamantly refused.

We had reached an impasse, and I was just not about to grant a concession of any kind to my captors. If they wanted me packaged neat and presentable for whatever purpose, then they would have to do so by force. Again the three of them left frustrated, Sandy telling me that he would speak to the brigadier for a second time. Their departure left me wondering if I would get left behind. Oddly that thought did not faze me. The fight against the bastards who had imprisoned me had sustained me, given me purpose, and filled my days. In my odd and perverse way, though caged, one part of me was free because I still held to my sense of self-determination. I was willing to risk remaining where I was.

When finally they returned, Sandy said the few words that allowed me to cooperate. "The embassy says you are to have a shower and get dressed."

"Which embassy?" I asked.

"The British Embassy" was his reply.

"That is an order I can accept."

At that time, I would accept such a request from British officials, but not from the Canadians, given their behaviour and crass stupidity. If I knew then what I know now of the British government's actions in our case, I would not have acceded to their request either. Then, however, all I had was the brief information from Sandy that the British Embassy officials had stood up to the

Saudis during their visits with the prisoners, a description that contrasted sharply with the actions of Canadian officials who had told me to my face on more than one occasion that I was guilty. So I cooperated, peeled off what I had just put on, and asked for a towel and some soap.

Zapata, who seemed stunned by my rapid *volte-face*, disappeared and returned with the soap, shampoo, toothbrush, and toothpaste that had sat outside my cell unused. I stepped into a shower cubicle and turned on the water. Tepid though it was, it was refreshing – my first shower in two years. I had looked longingly across my cell at these cubicles for all that time, knowing that it would have been so easy to experience this minor pleasure, but resisted, gaining more from the knowledge of the discomfort and embarrassment that my condition caused all my captors. As the water flowed over me and I massaged in the soap, the filth came off my body in grey brown flakes, forming a thick scum on the floor of the shower. While I cleansed myself, Sandy and I kept up a non-stop conversation over our experiences.

I discovered from Sandy that Zapata, whom I had abused in the past and whose actions toward me were purely professional, not friendly, but never abusive, had in fact been quite good to the other prisoners. Possibly he would have been to me as well, had I behaved myself and not drawn his blood with my teeth. As I learned of his kindnesses, I felt a sense of regret that I had insulted and abused him, for he was not responsible for my arrest or my torture, he was just a prison guard, lumbered with containing and constraining those his masters threw into prison. Some prisoners would be guilty, others would not be, but that was beyond his means to determine. He, like a number of others, did his job as humanely as circumstances permitted. I felt sorry for him. Huey, Moussa, the dispenser, the young corporal who had refused to hold me down, the young private who had given me my sweater, and the others like them who had to deal with me were not the enemy.

Zapata had been standing by the cell door while I had my shower, but now that I had finished, dried myself off, and put on fresh clothes, he had moved back into the cell. I went to him and told him of what Sandy had said, thanking him for being kind to my friends and apologizing for everything that I had said and done to him and to some of the others.

"I hope you can understand, but I had to do what I did. I had my reasons, but I am still sorry for what I have done to you" was how I finished my apology.

Zapata listened in disbelief at the reasoned and conciliatory nature of my words. Only a few moments ago, I was an unpredictable animal to be handled only when forcibly restrained or sedated. Now I was expressing sentiments that could hardly have been expected. I was being unpredictable in a new way. As he listened to me, his expression changed and his whole body relaxed, accepting the sincerity of what I was saying. When I had finished, he said simply, "I am sorry too."

Zapata accompanied Sandy and me to the doctor's office for my final medical, another cursory affair. I noted that my weight was only sixty-two kilograms, more than thirty kilograms less than when I was arrested. I was now dressed in the shirt in which I had been arrested, still with tears that the first period of interrogation had caused, along with a pair of khaki trousers that my father brought in on his first visit. The clothes hung on me and looked as though they belonged to someone else. The trousers needed to be folded over at the waistband. Even then they only just stayed up, yet when I had last worn them they were barely large enough.

Back in the cell, I began to pack up some of the books I had received. A couple of large luggage bags had now been provided for the purpose. I left most of the books behind, packing only those that I had dipped into time and time again: *Fortune's Rocks*, *Great Expectations*, *The Strange Last Voyage of Donald Crowhurst*, a couple of mathematics texts, and the Discworld novels of Terry

Pratchett that acted as my book diaries. These had been my friends and companions, helping me pass the time, directing my imagination into tangents from their plots or engaging my intellect in problem solving. As has been the case since my childhood, I had drawn strongly upon the written word for solace and was oddly sad to be leaving some of them behind, even the turgid spy novels.

With this done, I strolled out into the hallway, waiting for Sandy to attend to his own packing, what there was of it. Standing beside Zapata, I watched him light up a cigarette and asked him if he had one to spare. Not one of my smarter ideas for I was at that time free of addiction to the damn things, but as usual I tempted fate. Generously, he obliged my request, and for the remaining time that I spent in his company, every time he lit up, he offered his pack to me. This might seem an insignificant detail, and given current attitudes to smoking it might not appear to be considerate; however, it was to me, for we were treating each other like humans, something absent in my life for too long.

When Sandy rejoined us, our bags were loaded onto a trolley and wheeled off, and the three of us left the cellblock, stopping at the guards' office at the main hub to complete more paperwork. Our arrival sparked nervous activity among the guards relaxing there, most of whom sprang to their feet. Two of the younger guards proceeded to collect shackles and handcuffs from the weapons locker and began to approach us with some of the others in tow. Both Sandy and I bristled at the prospect of being placed again in restraints, swearing at the two who were carrying the items.

I braced for a fight, before turning to Zapata, telling him that there was no way they were going to put them on us without a fight. Nodding to me, he let forth an angry salvo of Arabic at the two guards, who responded just as angrily. At the end of this exchange, Zapata moved a couple of steps away from me, continuing to glare furiously at the two youngsters. As he moved, the other guards moved back, leaving the ones with the restraints distinctly alone. Whatever their reason for wanting to put us in chains, it evaporated when they realized that their older (and wiser) peers were not about to render assistance, leaving them to face two rather unhappy individuals, one of whom did not have the best of behaviour records. The restraints were returned to storage and we were signed out for the next stage, taken to the reception area where I was fingerprinted and photographed for the last time, and then returned to the cellblock to wait, for now it turned out that our transport was not ready.

Finally, Sandy and I were summoned to leave, retracing our footsteps out of the cellblock to the main hub and then into the loading bay and daylight. It was well past dawn, and the release had effectively taken all night, yet somehow it had not seemed that long a time. It was then that I noticed something strange. My instinct for observation had not been disconnected in the euphoria of impending freedom, and I was still taking mental notes of everything I saw. There in the loading bay were armed guards, not in the uniform of the Ministry of the Interior but in the uniform of the National Guard, equipped with 9mm SMGs, their red checkered shemaghs being what first drew my attention. At the edge of the loading dock were a couple of prisoner transport vans, but beyond the bay I saw two 4×4 vehicles in the livery of the National Guard.

What were they doing here? This was the turf of Prince Naif and the Ministry of the Interior, and with the strict division of power and concomitant demarcations that are a hallmark of the internal politics of the Kingdom, it was significant that we were to be escorted from the prison by Crown Prince Abdullah's soldiers of the National Guard.

Placed in the back of the van, obviously in convoy on our way to the airport, Sandy and I talked about our arrests and treatment, going over details of our different experiences. It was then that I first discovered that I had been formally sentenced to death by *al haad*, a brutal means of execution that involves being affixed to two stakes, being partially beheaded, left to die slowly over a period of hours. It is the ultimate sanction under the application of Sharia law in the Kingdom, reserved for particularly heinous murders or acts of terrorism.

When finally we came to a halt, the rear door of the transport opened, and we stepped onto the concrete of the taxiways just in front of the terminal building of the airport. Forming a cordon at a discreet distance were soldiers of the National Guard, with one or two uniformed personnel of the Ministry of the Interior present. I again noted this discordant fact, for airport security was the responsibility of the ministry, yet again the National Guard seemed to be guaranteeing our safe departure.

There about five metres in front of us was the Smiling Knife, Brigadier Mohammed Said. The temptation to avail myself of one last chance to injure was strong. I stared at him as he began to approach, clenching and unclenching my fists. My body language must have been screaming out my desire; he stopped, turning instead to lead us into the terminal building. As we marched along in file, Said two paces in front of Sandy, Sandy two paces in front of me, I began to whistle softly "Colonel Bogey March," one of the tunes I had whistled for hours walking in my cell. I even recited the words that I had composed to the tune:

"Abdullah has only got one ball
Naif has something similar
Khaled is like Mohammed
Because Mohammed has no balls at all."

Said heard me, as I intended him to. He turned his head toward me. His expression reflected his displeasure. He seemed about to say something to me, but changed his mind as I returned his gaze as malevolently as I could. Not for me the meek acquiescence expected in return for the generosity of granting me my freedom.

That was something that was mine by right, stolen from me by the corrupt and brutal thugs of the Al Saud regime, of which Said was one, and I was not going to touch my forelock or kiss the hem of their robes as they might demand. Apologizing to those who had tried to treat me decently was one thing; being subservient to the brigadier and the others who colluded or took part in the torture was something else again. I was still at war with them and have so remained in my fight for redress.

We had been directed into the area of VIP lounges discreetly out of sight of the main area of the terminal. As we walked along the long corridor, passing a couple of doorways on the way toward our allotted waiting area, I saw the first of the delegation that had been assigned to collect us. Standing against the wall was a tall, well-dressed individual; it turned out he was a consul at the British Embassy. I saw a hint of either a grimace or a smile appear on his face as I got close enough for him to recognize the tune of my discordant whistling. No doubt he would have requested its cessation, but as I drew level I stopped, my need to irritate Said temporarily satisfied.

After a brief introduction, we were shown into a small vestibule on the right, in and around which were now milling various members of the British and Canadian embassies and a couple of people from the law firm of Al Hejailan, most of whom were unknown to me. On both sides of the vestibule were large spacious waiting rooms, and Sandy and I were directed into the one on the left. As I walked through the door, I saw Les Walker standing there. My suspicions concerning his arrest had been correct. I was surprised to see other familiar faces. Seated on the sofas that encircled the walls of the room were Pete Brandon, situated directly behind Les, and to my left I recognized James Cottle. Both of them looked haggard. Both of them were thinner than when we last met. My first words to Cottle indicated how much his appearance had changed.

"Hello, Cottle, you have lost weight. You look like Jack Duckworth [a character from *Coronation Street*]."

His reply was short and obscene, but amused and not annoyed. He was obviously relieved that we were on our way home, as were we all.

Within a couple of minutes two more people I knew arrived in the room. The first was James Lee, also much slimmer than when I last saw him. He was followed by Sharon Ballard, the wife of my friend Glenn, and I wondered why she was there, though I assumed that it might be because of her being a nurse. As I spoke to her, I discovered that her husband had been the last to be arrested. A few minutes later he was delivered into our company. The group was now as complete as it was going to be. Two of our number were missing – Raf Schvyens and Carlos Duran.

As I talked to each of my co-detainees, I began to build up a picture of what had happened since my arrest. The scope of the terrorist campaign and correspondent attempts of the Saudi Arabian government to conceal it by arresting westerners was greater than I had imagined. The bombings of western businesses and shootings of westerners had continued throughout 2001 and 2002. I learned then that nine of us had been arrested, but the number expanded considerably when I later began my investigations into the circumstances around my arrest. Raf Schvyens, myself, and Sandy Mitchell were arrested in December 2000. Les Walker, Carlos Duran, Pete Brandon, James Lee, and James Cottle were arrested in the first half of 2001. Finally, Glenn Ballard was arrested in late 2002. Each of those arrested had been subjected to psychological torture (or coercive interrogation, as it is euphemistically labelled), and six of us had also been subjected to several of the brutal methods of physical torture that our captors so enjoyed inflicting.

I had been peppering my fellow detainees with questions. Did they know what had happened to Carlos or to Raf? They did not know. A member of the British Embassy told me that Raf had been deported the night before and should be in Brussels by now. As for Carlos, this was the first he had heard of our Filipino co-detainee. Some weeks later I learned that he had been released and was safe.

While I was apologizing to Les for my role in his arrest, an official from the British Embassy interrupted me and said, "You are not going to hit any of the Saudis, are you?"

This blunt question was the first indication I had that the officials of the British Embassy in the room were watching me with concern.

"Not if they don't stand too close to me."

I was being sarcastic, but I was serious. I was not going to force a confrontation but I would have certainly faced any of them. I found it interesting that this question was not asked of my fellow prisoners.

The second incident occurred a moment or two later. I was standing in the vestibule, just outside the lounge, when I was approached and cornered by a consul from the Canadian Embassy I had not met before. He wanted my signature on various pieces of paper.

I said, "I will not deal with any representative of the Canadian government; I will only deal with representatives of the British government."

"You are my responsibility, and you will do as I tell you. There are documents that you are required to sign and you will sign them."

I don't know why he assumed he could intimidate me. For two years I had rebelled against the violent bullying of my captors, and I was hardly going to be intimidated by a petty official of the Canadian government with an over-inflated sense of his own power or importance. As for my being his responsibility, he should in effect review his understanding of the powers of arrest and detention associated with his position. While I was in Saudi Arabia, I was the legal responsibility of the Ministry of the Interior, which was empowered under what passes for the law in that country to arrest and detain. Had I been in Canada, I could conceivably have been subject to control by the various legitimate authorities responsible for arrest or detention of suspects or criminals. However, the fool before me was a diplomat and thus not imbued with such authority in Saudi Arabia or in Canada. Still, he felt that he had power over me even though the embassy appeared to use no power to protect me from torture.

I bellowed, "I am a British citizen, and I will deal only with representatives of the British government. If you continue to harass me or force yourself upon me, I promise you that you will find yourself being subjected to a legal action and dragged into court so fast that your fucking head will spin."

I watched the man deflate, and Said and the couple of Ministry of the Interior officials present now moved toward us. The consul of the British Embassy interceded, taking the heat out of the moment. The Canadian consul backed away, handing over to his British counterpart the various pieces of paperwork that he had been waving. I then dealt with them, receiving a surprising amount of cash from the Saudi prison service, some of which was the money confiscated on my arrest and some the prison wages I had not been given during the past two years. The Saudis were certainly being painstakingly honest at this late juncture – pity they were not so honest from the outset.

I noticed out of the corner of my eye that the other members of the Canadian delegation, who were now standing in the hallway, backed away even farther from me. Among them I saw a face I recognized, that of Neil Oliver, the Canadian psychiatrist. He had obviously been brought here because of questions that had been raised concerning my sanity. Would it suit all concerned if I could be certified as mentally unhinged? Had my bad-tempered display just added fuel to that particular fire? I switched as quickly as possible to being cooperative with the British consul. I suppose that the ability to quickly turn one's temper on and off is symptomatic of a psychological disorder. I was damned whatever way I turned.

When I returned to the lounge, I sat down on one of the sofas and was handed a black holdall, sent from my father in anticipation of my release. As I inspected its contents, I was joined on the bench by one of the team of medical staff from a British military unit who had been assigned to assess and accompany us. They were specialists in retrieving casualties, supervising their return to Britain, and in more ways than one we fit into their job description. We had been informed that we would be put through a medical prior to our departure, in order to assess our needs during the long flight. Interestingly, though they were serving members of British armed forces, they were not in uniform, thus discreetly avoiding any demonstration of a foreign military presence on Saudi soil, something the Saudi government would have found undesirable.

The chap who sat next to me was a psychiatric nurse, and I was not surprised to find myself becoming friendly with the "shrink" on the team. When he informed me of his specialty, I asked if he had deliberately sought me out or been assigned to me. Although he said he was not assigned to me, I felt this was not the truth. Sometime later I discovered that I was his priority assignment because of information that had been provided to the British officials by their Canadian counterparts. He engaged me in conversation. I knew that I was being probed, but the manner in which it was being conducted did not bother me. I was amused.

These were the first unrestricted conversations I had enjoyed in nearly three years of solitary confinement. I could not stop talking, pausing only to draw breath, and I could not sit still.

"Do you play chess?" my companion asked at one point.

I said I had played competitively "for a brief time" and then added, "I have been playing chess every day for the last two years."

Until this day, I had had no dealings with any British official. The information on my state of mind would have had to come from either the Saudi Arabian or Canadian governments. The Saudis certainly preferred to classify me as crazy. I now know that the information provided by the Canadian government stated that I was suffering from a psychotic disturbance. Given the circumstances, was such a diagnosis appropriate? Whether this was a considered opinion or political spin put on a more equivocal diagnosis I do not know, but it certainly explained the nervousness of many of the British officials whom I dealt with that day.

If it was a considered medical opinion, it raises questions about the validity of psychiatric diagnoses conducted under intolerable circumstances. I was an innocent man locked up for a crime that I did not commit. I was denied access to anything resembling due process or a fair trial and I was living under threat of death. The brief interviews to assess my mental health were conducted in the presence of my torturers. What perspective can be taken regarding the behaviour of those who are wrongly incarcerated? If my actions were looked at in isolation, many of them would seem insane to most people. Every one of the actions in which I indulged was undertaken to provoke a reaction, and a reaction they received, including the characterization that I had become mentally disturbed and dangerous. I am not trying to convey the impression that I am completely normal or free of any tics or eccentricities, but I dispute the ability of mental health professionals to define what is a normal or acceptable mode of behaviour in the circumstances under which I found myself.

The detainees' behaviour as result of their treatment probably did in part reflect the underlying or nascent characteristics of their personalities from the most passive to the most aggressive. It would be remiss of me not to reiterate that it was natural for me to behave in the manner that I did. I do know that early in my incarceration a newspaper article, published about me in the *Vancouver Sun* and detailing a fight in which I was involved at the age of sixteen, characterized me as dangerously aggressive, but that was a misrepresentation of the facts that played into my captors' hands, and I was not able to put forth my side of the story.

During the time I have been writing this book, I have looked into numerous cases of wrongly convicted prisoners and found some disturbing similarities made in psychiatric assessments conducted during their incarceration and parole hearings. Glaswegian Robert Brown is one such case. Imprisoned for murder in 1977, he proclaimed his innocence until his sentence was overturned by the Appeal Court in 2002. He did have the possibility of release on parole before that date, but would have had to "accept" his guilt, which he did not do. His refusal to acknowledge responsibility for a crime he did not commit unfavourably affected the assessments of the prison's psychiatric counsellors. If the mental health professionals are unable to distinguish between those who are guilty but deluded or deceitful in protestation of their innocence from those who are truly innocent, then one has also to question their abilities to determine what is or is not acceptable behaviour in situations of incarceration where extreme duress is the norm.

I am not about to claim that psychiatric counselling is not helpful or appropriate – far from it. After my release, I actively sought counselling, for the circumstances of my imprisonment did cause me emotional damage, and I knew I would need some help in coming to terms with my experiences. But this is a far cry from being assessed against one's will while incarcerated, and on the basis of flawed assumptions. Yet inaccurate and prejudicial assessments occur with too much regularity – just ask any innocent man released after a long period of wrongful imprisonment.

My behaviour in the airport did give cause for concern, particularly when viewed from the perspective that I was dangerously disturbed. For one thing, my appearance would have been unsettling given my lank hair, beard, emaciated appearance, and bulging eyes. Generously, I have described myself as looking like an aging cast member of *Jesus Christ Superstar*. In truth I bore more than a passing resemblance to Charles Manson, and, as I said, I could not stop talking. I was well aware then that my extreme talkativeness was problematic for everyone, myself included. I tried to make myself shut up, but found it impossible, nor could I make myself sit still. I wandered around while my gums flapped. At one point I wandered out into the hallway and walked toward the main part of the terminal for the simple reasons that I could and that I might find a toilet. This apparently set everyone on edge, expecting that I would try to run away.

There was another worry raised by my wanderings. Ibrahim and Khaled were present at the airport for one last demonstration of their power and their miserable egos. Fortunately, the diplomats insisted that they sit behind closed doors in another of the lounges. Because I had attacked them and threatened to kill them, there was a fear about what I might just try to do. There was at least some benefit from everyone considering me to be dangerous. To be frank, if I had seen them, the intensity of the hatred they still inspired in me might have driven me to attempt to harm them. Understandable, but not acceptable, and it would have resulted in a diplomatic hiatus. Fortunately, no one told me of their presence until after we arrived at Heathrow. I marvelled at their temerity.

I had begun drinking fruit juice from the moment of my arrival at the airport lounge, consuming vast quantities of liquid. The amounts that I drank seemed to amaze some of my fellow travellers, but I had survived on black tea and tap water for so long that I could not get enough of the taste, nor could my body seem to get enough of the nutrients. The result was predictable, so not long after my short walk I was guided by the psychiatric nurse to the nearest toilet. There, while washing my hands, I had a proper look at myself in the mirror, commenting more to myself than to my watchdog, "I don't look as bad as I expected."

Having had in my cell only the stainless steel plates that distorted the image reflected, I was unable to see the fine details of my appearance. Now I was able to examine myself in more detail, noting my pallor, my sunken cheeks, and the haunted look in my eyes. I showed the strain of my incarceration, but I had expected it to be worse. This hint of self-awareness was of interest to the psychiatric nurse, who had by this time begun to see me as less difficult than he had been led to expect.

One of my strongest memories of that time pertains to something extremely mundane. I had arrived at the airport wearing sandals, taken from among the items in my cell. The holdall that I was given revealed among other things that my father had packed socks and my old pair of cowboy boots, much to my delight. I slipped off the sandals and immediately began to put on a pair of socks. They were for some reason cool; this and their softness created an unexpected sensual delight as they slid over the coarse, calloused skin of my feet. The expression on my face did not go unnoticed.

My nurse, now my constant companion, said, "I wish I had my camera."

Then I slid on my boots, which were surprisingly comfortable considering that my feet had not been encased in such footwear for a long time. These were such simple things, but so redolent with pleasure and meaning for me. They formed another step toward my becoming civilized again, toward what I saw as my reclamation.

A medical examination was conducted on each one of us in turn, all of us being passed fit for travel. I was offered a sedative for the flight, but refused, saying that what I wanted was a single malt. I informed my examiners that there were only four things I sought, all of which were technically forbidden in Saudi Arabia: a whisky, a bacon sandwich, to place a bet, and to make love. While the first three were easily obtainable, my condition and appearance, alongside the fact that there was no lover awaiting my release, meant that one desire would have to wait. I was informed that there was to be a two-drink limit imposed on us during the flight, which I thought immensely sensible given our enforced abstinence; anyway, all I wanted was one – it was more symbolic than anything else.

Eventually, there was a panic and flap as various of our personal possessions, confiscated at the time our arrests, arrived and had to be checked, and then organized for putting on the aircraft. Because I had no list of what had been taken in the first place, this was an academic exercise, though what was returned was much less than what had been taken. None of my personal papers were there nor any of the books taken from my house, just the smashed remains of my computer and a few computer discs along with the books I had packed in the prison. Amid these exchanges, my passports were finally returned, and a boarding card presented to me. We were rushed through the terminal and straight onto the plane, past the astonished gazes of expatriates and Saudis waiting to board the same flight.

We were whisked into the business class cabin, which had been assigned to our party alone. We were quite a large group, seven former detainees, the medical team, and officials from the Canadian and British embassies. The only one who had to remain behind was Sharon Ballard, much to the distress of her husband, Glenn. She was not allowed to leave for another two weeks, and I often wondered if the delay in releasing her from her obligations at the Specialist Hospital was not just another part of their game.

I found that the watchdog was seated next to me. I was glad of his company, for my non-stop chatter did not faze him as it might the others in the party. Do not take the label I attached to him as derogatory; it is used solely to describe the role he played. He was a likeable individual, and I developed a rapport with him that has been maintained since my release.

The flight was remarkable only in that I did not sleep, even after having my one drink, which was rather disappointingly a Jack Daniel's. I had not slept since the night before yet I did not feel drowsy; I was pumped full of adrenaline, all the stress beginning to bleed out of me as I talked through everything from my treatment in prison, to my survival tactics, to my plans. The nurse beside me listened attentively, giving advice as and when he could get a word in. I did not fail to notice his wanderings to the seats in the rear of our section, where he negotiated on my behalf with the Canadian officials who sat there. My conversations with him had ranged over my refusal to deal with them. He eventually persuaded me to be more pragmatic in my approach and take whatever was on offer. By the time we landed, he had secured for me, and I had accepted, an offer of temporary accommodation in a hotel for the coming weekend and medical treatment for the injuries and ailments accruing from my imprisonment (a promise only partly fulfilled) from the officials of the Department of Foreign Affairs who were travelling with us.

The fact that the promise of medical treatment has been only partly fulfilled can be taken as confirmation that the offers were made for their propaganda value, not out of concern for my condition, nor of any acceptance of the criminal brutality to which I was subjected. When the scope of the physical damage that I had suffered became more apparent and the bills for the cost of my treatments began to mount, the supposed generosity was terminated on the very night before I was to undergo another angioplasty for the damage done to my cardiovascular system. My protests and the threat of legal action (and its subsequent embarrassment) meant that at least the operation was paid for; most other procedures, including necessary orthopaedic surgery, were cancelled. These medical bills should be paid for by the Saudi Arabian government, and if the Canadian government and its representatives in the Department of Foreign Affairs had any moral courage, they would present such a demand to the government that so damaged someone they claim as their citizen. That has not happened, nor is it likely to, for it would appear that appeasement of the Al Sauds is one of the highest political priorities in Canada, as well as in Britain and Belgium.

I have often wondered how the cabin crew coped with our party. I know now that they had been prepared to transport a potentially dangerous passenger suffering from a psychotic disturbance. I cannot but imagine that made them nervous, and the manner of my physical appearance cannot have done anything to ameliorate their concerns. Yet what I remember is being wrapped in a metaphorical blanket of service and warmth, of the captain coming back to greet and congratulate us, of being served champagne, compliments of the captain and crew, just prior to arrival in London. It was an almost overwhelming show of indulgence and sympathy, making this flight to freedom all the more memorable.

Regardless of the fact that I had been handed over to consular officials, had boarded a plane, and was heading to London, I still retained a sense of uncertainty, as if it was all too good to be true, that it was all a dream from which I would wake up, back in my cell. One part of me felt that until I arrived somewhere safe, my flight to freedom could still end short of its destination, resulting in my being taken back to prison. I knew these were paranoid thoughts brought about by the state of mindful distrust in which I had had to live, but I was not able to dispel them.

When finally we touched down in London, I was able to banish these thoughts for good. We were ushered off the flight first, and as I stood momentarily in the doorway of the plane, I felt my last doubts melt away as the dank humidity of the air and the smell of jet fuel assailed my senses. London was in the grip of a heat wave, with temperatures more common to the place I had left behind, but there was no mistaking the airport scene that spread out before my eyes. There before me was my freedom – I was not going back.

We were ushered into a waiting bus that took us to the VIP centre, usually reserved for visiting dignitaries and located well away from the terminal buildings. There we were swept up in the welcome of our families, and the inherent welter of emotion. I stood apart observing my fellow detainees, taking pleasure from their emotional displays. Oddly, it had not crossed my mind that anyone would be there to meet me, as I had never given any thought to the practicalities of being released, not having expected it. The only thought that I had, having been formulated only the night before, was just to take what cash I had and fade away.

While I looked on, I was approached by an official of the Canadian Embassy in London, who informed me that James and Nelia, my father and step-mother, were waiting for me in a separate room. How they managed to get there on short notice is a saga all on its own. They had learned of my release less than twenty-four hours earlier from the other families involved, not from the Canadian government, which would have had much more advance notice. They departed from Vancouver hastily, barely making the flight that brought them into London only a couple of hours before I arrived.

The officials were unsure how I would respond to my father. While in prison I had said that I disowned my father, doing so because of his repeated visits to the Kingdom against my wishes. Although my captors believed me and had stopped trying to use our relationship against me, now the problem everyone faced was whether I had been sincere, for it seemed that I had convinced everyone but my father. The officials hardly needed a scene being created during this most poignant of times for the other detainees, so it was arranged that my family reunion would occur separately from the rest of the group.

As I entered the room in which James and Nelia had been secreted, I was aware of the restrained emotion and worry in my father's eyes. As always, we greeted each other formally – overt emotional displays have never been part of our relationship and never will be. My first statements to my father were effectively to define exactly what his role was now that I had returned and what I planned to do. I did not intend to return directly to the bosom of my family; instead I wanted to spend a couple of days collecting myself before experiencing the emotional intensity that reunion would bring. Some might find such a way of conducting things to be odd, but then they do not know either of us.

I have always tended initially to look inwards to sort out any personal difficulties or problems before I look outward and seek help or sustenance, and I was doing so again. Selfish though it might sound under the circumstances, given the suffering that my family would have endured, my suffering had been the greater and the more damaging. Selfless attention to the needs of others simply had to wait, for now I had to do what was necessary for me. Fortunately, those who are close to me understand this and patiently accept the independence of my character. As for my father, defining his role in the process was necessary, for had I not done so, he would have tended to engage in frantic activity to solve all the problems as he saw them within five minutes, overwhelming me in the process. His intentions would have been for the best, for he is a kind and generous man, but the pace of his actions and their direction might not have been appropriate. This did not stop him sticking his oar in, but at least it slowed him down a bit. With my somewhat strict greeting to my father finished, I turned to Nelia, wrapping her in my arms. Tears welled up in her eyes, and she buried her head in my shoulder, as I said simply, "Don't worry, it's over now."

It felt strange, but it seemed for a brief moment that I was the one doing the comforting, rather than being comforted. Right then, I was not in need of such care, for I was caught up in the euphoria of being released. The need for being comforted would come later as I began to deal with the emotions that the intensity of my captivity caused; at that moment I was just happy and felt amazingly calm. After a few moments, I led James and Nelia over to join the other families and to introduce them to my co-detainees. What followed was a whirl of introductions and conversations that spun around me in a fog of emotion.

After we had joined the other families, my father tried to engage me in deciding what to do with my belongings that were stored in his garage. That was hardly a matter of importance to me at that exact moment, but at his insistence for an answer, I told him that if my possessions were in the way, throw them out, for I had other things to deal with. From this response he finally took the hint and left me to make my own arrangements. To this day most of my possessions are still stuck in his garage, much to his now understandable but amused annoyance.

Gradually, the officials who had accompanied us began to melt away, their duties done; the detainees and their families began exchanging contact details, and almost as soon as it had begun our welcoming party began to disperse.

During the flight home, the detainees, collectively and without coercion, had decided not to hold a press conference or speak to the media, preferring instead to have an official of the Foreign and Commonwealth Office deliver a press release expressing our gratitude for the support that we received while in prison and requesting our desire for privacy and time with our families. It was a sincere request. However, another consideration that played its part was the fact that Sharon Ballard still remained in the Kingdom. We felt that any statements to the media should be done only when she was safely out of Saudi Arabia. Still, the press managed to report that our lack of availability had been forced upon us, something that annoyed me severely at the time.

I took my leave of James and Nelia, joining a group of officials from the Canadian Embassy who had arranged for me to stay at the Heathrow Hilton, little more than a mile from my present location. As we now prepared to leave, a final farewell along with contact details was delivered by an officer of the anti-terrorist branch of the Metropolitan Police. This is when we discovered I had been booked into the hotel under my own name. Everyone but me momentarily panicked about the possibility of press harassment. This might have worried them but it did not me, as I reminded them that after what I had been through, the press would hardly be a problem for me, more likely that I would be a problem for them. As I think back on it, these officials probably were more worried about what I might do to the press than the other way around. Interestingly, it was reported in the media that we had all gone into hiding, even though most of us stayed with family whose addresses were well known. As for me, I had hardly gone underground, residing under my own name for three nights in a hotel from which it was possible to view the runway upon which I had landed.

That night in my hotel room, I was once again able to make choices of my own free will. Some were easy, some were difficult. The first thing I did was to turn on the BBC news channel and hungrily absorb the news and information. I revelled in the freedom to access whatever I wanted. To this day, the sound of the signature of the BBC news can induce a pleasant frisson of excitement, representing as it does to me the sound of freedom. Soaking for hours in the bath was also one of the easy ones, changing the water four times, as I scrubbed and scratched off the accumulated dirt and grime that my last shower had not been able to dislodge. By the time I was finished, the white enamel of the tub was a disgusting grey in colour, despite my modest attempts to rinse it down. At least by then I had begun to feel clean and somewhat refreshed.

Phoning friends and family was the next priority, and I spent hours on the phone over the next couple of nights talking with many whom I had not been in touch with for years but who had come to my support. More difficult was deciding what to eat. I spent more than an hour reading and re-reading the room service menu, before finally choosing a meal of vegetable curry and salad. The most difficult task of all was leaving the hotel room. I had become in part cage-bound due to my isolation. I knew instinctively that I had to seek help with this, to give myself a reason to break from what could become self-imposed isolation. To this end, I phoned Neil Oliver, whom I knew to be staying in the same hotel for the weekend. I had initially avoided his company, as I had done with all the Canadian delegation, but after speaking with family members, I was made to reconsider my opinions on him at least. So with that new information in mind, I made a deal with him: I would act as his tour guide through London, a city I knew well, having lived there as a student, if he would keep an eye on me and report to me his observations and recommendations.

My final act of that evening was to watch one of the in-house movies, selecting it by the simple expedient that any movie with Al Pacino in its cast would be worth watching. Thus I came to view the film *The Recruit*, not knowing of its plot or its subject matter. It turned out to be a reasonably constructed spy story centred on the induction and training of recruits in the CIA. The film contained scenes of interrogation and torture, and watching them did not disturb me. Some might find that surprising, but then I have always had a very dispassionate way of viewing events that happen to me, and so do not always find as disturbing as others would images that bring to mind the brutality I endured.

That is not to say that the film did not affect me. I told friends it was a film that, having watched once, I did not think I would be capable of watching again. A month later I found myself confronted with it again. I had flown to New York for an interview, and on my return the in-flight movie was none other than *The Recruit*. I guess I could have turned off the seat-back screen in front of me and read a book, but I didn't. I had come to feel that watching it again might disturb me, and in effect I had become afraid of it. For whatever reason, I have always confronted my fears head-on. My passion for climbing was derived from my need to overcome my fear of heights, and through spending long hours on cold rock faces I came to terms with it. I never completely conquered it, for when I look over the edge of a precipice or tall building, I still feel a sense of weakness in my limbs, just below the surface, but the fear does not control me either. As I was now confronted with something that symbolically took on the shape of a new fear – in effect, the possible inability to confront or deal with what had happened to me – instinctively I did what I have always done: confront it. I forced myself to watch the film, and perversely I enjoyed it more on the second viewing, despite its content. I had obviously worried too much.

On the Saturday, the day after my arrival in London, I began the process I called reclamation. Neil had accepted my proposal, and so we toured, by foot and by bus, the centre of London. Neil occasionally stopped to look for souvenirs, and I purchased personal items, little things like my favourite cologne and a pair of sunglasses. I deliberately guided us to Harrods, not for the purpose of buying anything, but just to visit its food halls. To one whose senses had been so devoid of stimulation, that place was intensely engaging. The crush of the Saturday shopping crowds, the vast array of items, and most importantly the aromas emanating from the displays, flooded my senses. I stood for moments transfixed, deeply inhaling, savouring each scent and the memories they invoked. Eventually we left, and I continued to show off what can best be described as my London. This was not an excursion that took in the usual tourist destinations, apart from Harrods; it was more an exploration of my old haunts. Each step I took that day invoked memories of my past life, places and events that are that part of me called experience. I knew exactly what I was doing, deliberately recalling the things that shaped my late adolescence and early adult life, the period of my first true independence. The process was the reclamation of a person almost left behind in a prison cell, and Neil good-humouredly tagged along while I regaled him with tales of a pleasantly wasted youth. Slightly foot-sore and hot, we ended our tour in a pub, one in which I had whiled away the odd evening years previously, before returning to the hotel and dinner. It was for me an enjoyable and successful outing, for I no longer felt so cage-bound or vulnerable.

The next day, Sunday, was not so pleasant, but in some respects more informative. I had spent the evening on the phone and had slept for only an hour. I had had too little sleep and too much caffeine before we embarked on the day's outing and found myself to be out of sorts. We headed straight to the British Museum, as Neil had requested, and I looked forward to viewing the exhibits. However, when confronted by the crowds in the museum, and the concomitant heat and closeness, I felt a mounting anxiety that built internally until I had to withdraw. I left Neil to continue his peregrinations through the exhibits, while I found a cooler, quieter spot where I waited for him, slowly getting control of my anxiety. I realized then that I had to take care in my re-introduction into society. When Neil rejoined me, we returned to the hotel and spent the evening watching television as I slowly shook off the effects of my anxiety attack.

On Monday morning it was time for me to join my family. My cousin William came to the hotel to collect me but first joined me at breakfast. He was shocked by both my appearance and behaviour, as I sat hunched over my place setting, eating a bowl of cereal with my fingers. He said nothing then, but thankfully passed comment days later, letting me know that I was lacking in the social graces. The welcome my family gave me was warm and lively, and two aspects stand out in particular. William's younger children, who were well below the age at which my trials and tribulations would mean anything to them, descended on me and expected my attention. Regardless of the fact that when they first met me I was still in my wild and hairy state, I soon became an object for their

amusement and a mobile climbing frame. In their youthful ignorance, they brought me out of myself as I watched their antics, listening to their screams of childish delight and pain as they played
and fought.

The following day, I visited Helga, an elderly relative whom I
held in fond regard. She was recovering in hospital from treatment
for cancer, a disease that sadly claimed her life twelve months later.
Just short of her eightieth birthday, Helga was one of the formida-
ble matriarchs of my family, someone of definite opinions and not
unafraid to express them. She and I had verbally fenced through
the years. She often commented with amusement on my nomadic
and often dissolute lifestyle. I remember one such conversation
provoked by the termination of my engagement to marry.

"Someone needs to get you in harness, boy" was one of her
forthright comments.

I responded, "I am not a dray horse."

"More's the pity," she shot back.

Now though, I walked into the hospital room and stuck my
head around the curtain of her bed. She looked older and frailer
as I expected she would, but she was still as defiant and outspo-
ken as ever. My hair and beard had disappeared the night before,
so I looked a little more civilized than I did in the press photos of
a few days earlier, which would have been all that Helga would
have seen of me. When she saw my grinning countenance at the
end of her bed, her first words were "Thank God you got that
bloody hair cut."

Expressed in her inimical way, it signalled to me more than any
other statement that I was back and things were as they should be.
I had endured 963 days of imprisonment and solitary confinement
for a crime that I did not commit. I was tortured, raped, brutalized
into having a heart attack, and left with a myriad of orthopaedic
and dental problems. In the days just after my release, I had been

given a lesson in my emotional limitations, realizing that the years of my isolation would take more than a day to overcome. Still, I was back and it was time rebuild and civilize myself. I knew I had the strength to do it, just as I had found the strength to endure, but I would need to use the patience I had also developed. In one brief statement, Helga had voiced these expectations and beliefs. I would not have had it any other way.

six

RECLAMATION

﷽ ﷽ ﷽ ﷽

I waited nervously in the arrivals area at Heathrow airport. It would be the first time in years that I had seen Siobhan. I knew time had changed me, and I worried that these changes would appear severe. My body was still gaunt, weighing barely sixty-six kilograms, but what was more noticeable was my face. The skin still appeared stretched and taut, plastered to my skull. My eyes remained hollow and distant; the thousand-yard stare had not yet left me.

The tension of anticipation was almost unbearable. Would she recognize me? Would I recognize her? Should I kiss her? What if she was not ready or interested in even that? Stupid adolescent questions added to the tension. For more than an hour, I waited. Her flight had arrived, but still she did not appear. I phoned her home, I phoned her mobile. Had she left home only to miss the plane? Surely she would have called. I checked at the information desk only to be told that her flight had arrived but that congestion at the gate had delayed the unloading of passengers and baggage. I wandered back to my lonely vigil and then I saw her. I am not sure who was first to recognize the other, for it seemed to happen jointly. One second I was peering into a sea of anonymous faces. The next, our eyes met, recognition being instant and profoundly emotional. She raced toward me as quickly as she could drag her suitcase.

Small and slender, her hair different – no longer straight but lightly curled, wearing a simple white blouse and black trousers, she was a spirit made flesh. Her large eyes and her refined features, angelic and impish both at the same time, filled my vision. Everything dissolved around me, drifting out of focus. I could see only her, as beautiful as ever I remembered, as beautiful as ever I dreamed.

As we fell into each other's embrace, her arms gripped me tightly, fingers pressing into my back as if to confirm the reality of my presence. I too clung to her, enfolding her in my arms, holding on as if to a life raft. I pulled her tighter, sliding my hand along her neck to hold her head as she buried her face into my shoulder and her tears poured forth. Tears of joy and tears of relief flowed down her face, soaking through my shirt to my skin. It was refreshing, it was invigorating, it was soothing, like rain falling on parched earth. I mumbled inept platitudes, things that needed no utterance. At a loss for words, something all too rare for me, I lost myself in the moment, a moment to last an eternity.

When finally we relaxed our embrace, I asked if I could kiss her. Nervously, she said not yet. Her reply added to both my longing and to my fear. Looking back, I know that she was as nervous and frightened as I was. We both needed privacy to overcome the inhibitions that time and circumstance had imposed. There was time. We had a week together to rediscover each other.

Slowly we walked from the airport to the London Underground station and boarded a tube train. We talked only a little. Mainly, we sat in silence absorbing the presence of the other. We held hands as the train began to travel into London toward the flat where I was staying. The journey was long, but it only added to the sense of contentment I had begun to feel. I sat basking in the presence of one who had brought light into my darkness. Our eyes met frequently. As I looked into the softness of her eyes and lost myself in the warmth of her gaze, my tensions and fears were gently allayed. I was ready now to accept whatever happened between us. I could let things proceed at another's pace.

At King's Cross station, I led Siobhan through the crowds and onto the grimy streets that surround the station. No matter what efforts at urban regeneration had occurred in this area, it remained as I first found it years previously: dilapidated, seedy, and rife with the flotsam of London life, a modern Dickensian hole. In the midst of this decay was the flat where I was staying, its balcony overlooking the Regent's Canal, a place populated with narrow boats and barges converted into trendy homes. It was an oasis of peace amid the urban chaos.

Siobhan and I dropped her luggage in her bedroom. With a sense of stilted, almost absurd, courtesy, I showed her around the flat, ending the tour in the living room with its large semi-circular bay window overlooking the canal and converted warehouses opposite. Again we embraced, holding each other tightly. For me each sensation was a revelation. It had been so long since I had experienced such sensual pleasure. The warmth and softness of the woman that I held in my arms was overpowering.

Nervously, I asked again if we could kiss, willing to accept denial without a sense of rejection, such was the strength I drew from her presence. Her head lifted toward mine, her lips parted, and without another word we kissed, gently and delicately. The kisses increased in their fervour, awaking a hunger and desire that we both felt, but were hesitant to express. Then within moments, we found ourselves standing in a state of disarray, exploding with passion. What the office workers opposite thought of this I do not know, but I hope it brightened their day. Breathlessly I pulled back, then whispered into her ear. A silent movement of her head in approval prompted me to take her hand and lead her to the bedroom.

I was now both expectant and frightened. This I wanted, but the thought of physical intimacy also stirred up feelings of trepidation. I was worried that my experiences had rendered me incapable. This was my first such moment of sensuality and consummation of physical desire in years. It would be the first time I had been so physically close to another since my rape. I need not have worried. The tenderness of the moment, the beauty of Siobhan's soul, and the love that I still felt for her overcame all my fears. My inhibitions and pain melted away in the passion and desire into which Siobhan and I led each other. This moment is impossible for me to describe. As she had with a few words delivered to me in prison through my father and the Canadian Embassy, so now she fortified and delivered me. What barriers, emotional and physical, that might have impeded us had gone.

Dinner that night was in a little Italian restaurant near Russell Square. I had first discovered that place twenty-five years ago while, as a student, I had lived nearby. It was owned by a family of Italian immigrants and was now passing into the hands of the third generation of family members to manage. The Cosmoba has always been a place in which I dined, when funds were available, each time I returned or passed through London. It is a pleasant trattoria, slightly off the beaten track, with warm friendly service, good food, and a welcoming atmosphere. During this prolonged stay in London, I dined there more frequently than my limited purse should have permitted, but this time the meals had a far greater significance. I allowed myself this indulgence as it formed part of my personal rediscovery, an essential part of the healing process. So there Siobhan and I dined, as we mapped out our week together and thought of things we wished to do. Plans, as always, never quite worked out as envisaged. Our time together and our walks around London affirmed my freedom and could fill another volume.

Oddly enough, we had not planned to go to London Zoo, though we had decided to explore the Regent's Canal. The balcony of the flat overlooked an old quay that had once been a commercial hub of Regent's Canal. Siobhan had asked me about it and the extent of the canal. My explanations had piqued her curiosity so we planned a walk. The London Zoo was bordered by the canal and became a topic of conversation as we prepared two days later for another walk.

On that day, we stepped from the flat out into the London weather. Up until Siobhan's arrival, London had sweltered in a heat wave that lasted well beyond the usual limits of an English summer. London, with its congestion, tight streets, and old buildings, is a city best suited to cooler temperatures. No matter where I have travelled, I find London to be the city least suited to hot weather. That may in part be due to expectation and prejudice concerning the nature of English weather, but my desire is always for rain when the city has basked too long in high temperatures. I was pleased then when the weather had changed just prior to Siobhan's arrival. It was still sunny, but a strong breeze blew, clouds threatened, and the temperatures had dropped to their autumnal norm. It was perfect walking weather in an old northern European city.

We found our way onto the canal towpath and proceeded westward toward Regent's Park. The path winds its way at the side of the waterway that runs from the east end of London, skirting the northern edge of the park, before heading out to the west and the old canal network that was the mainstay of commercial traffic in the early industrial revolution. These days it is no longer of commercial importance, the barge trade having finally died with the advent of road works and motorways. The towpath now fills a new role as a place for joggers and walkers to find a right of way unhindered by the nuisance of modern traffic.

We meandered along, revelling in the quiet and peace, interrupted only by the sounds of waterfowl claiming the canal and by the rhythmic diesel thump of the odd narrow boat taking its inhabitants on a canal tour. Holding hands, occasionally stopping to embrace and to kiss, we were serenely happy in each other's company. The emotions and passions of the preceding days had given us a heightened sense of the sublimity of these ordinary moments. After couple of hours' walking, stopping only for Thai curry, strawberries, and Belgian chocolate at Camden Lock, we arrived at the north end of the park where the canal widens and the mesh of the zoo's aviary can be seen. Reluctantly, I led Siobhan from the canal, caught as I was in the gentle mood of our walk.

As a child, I had always loved zoos for they sated my interest in what for me were the exotic and the unusual. As I grew older, though, my enthusiasm was tempered by the realization of the essential cruelty that is inherent in maintaining captive exhibits for the entertainment of the public. Having spent so long living like such an exhibit, I was aware of these considerations as we passed through the turnstiles.

As we walked around the exhibits, my attention was more on the customers than the residents. Particularly, I watched the reactions of the children and the wonder that their youth provides them. I must have looked a bit of a fool, wandering arm in arm with another, grin on my face, as I nosily listened in on the expressions of childish fascination. I was so relaxed in Siobhan's presence; I began to enjoy playing the tourist.

At the hippo enclosure, I noticed the deep tan of the animal's hide and said to Siobhan that parts of me had been a similar colour when I had covered myself with my own faeces. Her eyes widened and she began to ask me questions as she finally understood what exactly was meant by my dirty protest. Her look of astonishment turned to one of amusement as I explained the reasons for my actions. She said that with skin as soft mine was now, there clearly had been a tangible benefit to my bathing in my own waste – the idea made both of us laugh.

When we arrived at the primate enclosures, we entered by the chimpanzee exhibit. There standing before us was a large silver-backed male who appeared to be indifferent to the people looking at him. His large dark eyes seemed both sad and bored, and I found seeing him confined quite painful. He, unaware of my anthropomorphic thoughts, began to groom himself with one hand while supporting himself on the knuckles of the other. He slowly scratched the region of his buttocks with great thoroughness. Having completed this he inspected his fingers, sniffing earnestly at them before licking them clean.

Most observers groaned in disgust, prompting me to make a comment on his intelligence or lack of it. A woman standing to my left put me in my place by voicing an altogether more appropriate thought. Who was the more stupid, the chimp for his actions or us for watching in near morbid fascination? Just so, I thought, who am I to judge his actions given my own recent behaviour? I turned to Siobhan and said, as if to reassure her, that his actions were similar to mine not that long ago, but I did not do quite what our enclosed friend had done. She looked at me with amusement, giving me the distinct impression that she would not have been surprised had I acted in just this way to disgust those who watched me in my cage. Somehow, she seemed to understand what for so many was my inexplicable behaviour.

We wandered away, leaving the old chimp to his amusements, and joined another group who with rapt attention were watching a family of gorillas. I assumed they were a family, though I admit that my knowledge of gorilla social organization is hardly comprehensive. As we stood, watching the younger and smaller of these creatures, a large male raced toward us, slamming his palms against the reinforced glass partition of the enclosure. Everyone watching gasped and stepped back. Almost immediately, the shock turned to amusement at the futility of his gesture. As he sauntered away to the outdoor section of his prison, I felt a wave of incredible sadness pass over me. Siobhan leaned into me and amusedly commented that this display was also similar to my antics. Yes, it unfortunately was. Maybe my imprisonment had made me too sensitive, but I could not help empathizing with the frustrations of this curious and human-like creature. A sense of shame and disgust pervaded me at that moment. I suggested that his behaviour was both similar to mine and appropriate given the restricted environment in which he is forced to live, being gawped at all day long.

It is a sad commentary on how humankind treats the creatures with which it shares this planet. Our rapaciousness means that probably the only chance for survival that the gorilla and his kind have is to be caged in an environment far removed from what is natural to them. As I expressed these thoughts, I turned to Siobhan, the pain obviously showing in my face. Seeing this, she gently took my hand in hers, silently trying to assuage my feelings. I felt myself relax as the warmth of her touch calmed me. In a strange way, it was a moment that drew us even closer, and it taught me even more the value of what I had discovered in prison.

I had been planning a trip to Edinburgh ever since my release. Rounds of medical appointments had me stuck in London, as doctors probed and prodded, determining the extent of the damage I had sustained. When Siobhan had finally decided to visit, I postponed this journey in order to share it with someone for whom I cared. Making this decision marked another noticeable change. I was no longer assuming the solitary actions that had been a hallmark of my earlier behaviour. It was a miracle that we had found each other again after so long without contact; even more surprising were the feelings we had awakened in each other. So now, three days after her arrival in London, we were preparing to depart for Scotland, the one place that throughout my life I have regarded as home.

As a child, I had lived in the north of that country in a town called Nairn. The most detailed of my childhood memories are of the time in this small town and the country of the Moray coast. A special fondness and sense of place lodged in my heart and has always remained with me. As an adult, I had the good fortune to study and work in Edinburgh and Glasgow for over eight years. There was not a part of the country that I had not explored through climbing and winter mountaineering. It was on its rivers that I discovered a love for white-water kayaking. It was there that the best of my friendships were forged. In the long hours of my confinement, it was the beauty of its mountains that I travelled.

More than once I fondly remembered sitting on the summit of Arthur's Seat in Holyrood Park, hipflask in one hand, book in the other while peacefully surveying Edinburgh spread out around me. Thus, for me, this was to be my true homecoming, more than my arrival in London or anywhere else. It was something I had craved since I stepped onto a plane in Riyadh two months earlier.

On the day of our departure from London, we travelled to Edinburgh in a small crowded commuter jet, wedged into our places. I had not managed to get a window seat so I sat in the middle of the row and tried not to lean over my fellow passenger who occupied that seat. Siobhan, to my right, must have sensed my nervousness, for she was even more attentive and affectionate, if such a thing was possible. I had been edgy and impatient during the trip to the airport and on our boarding of the aircraft; now that it was in the air, the inevitability of our arrival did not calm me. My anxiety intensified as we drew closer to Edinburgh.

Then through the window, the city appeared below as the plane circled over the Firth of Forth. I could feel the pent-up emotions inside me fighting for release. I gripped Siobhan's hand tightly as tears began to slide from my eyes. There was nothing I could do to stop them, nor would I have. By the time the plane had landed, my face was awash with moisture. This was my time for tears, not of pain, but of joy and release. What my fellow passenger sitting by the window thought of my emotional display I do not know, but her quizzical looks indicated some concern about her neighbour. I did not care then, but now when I look back, I blush at the memory of my sentimentality. Yet I am pleased I have retained and developed the capacity for such feeling. Stepping down the exit stairs, I felt that finally I had come home, though there was still one last thing to do.

The next afternoon, having spent the morning again showing Siobhan another city packed with so many of my personal memories, we went for a walk in Holyrood Park. The centre of this park, like the city around it, is dominated by the spur of Arthur's Seat, which had beckoned me since my release. Stopping in a small tourist shop on the Royal Mile, I bought a pair of small crystal glasses of a size appropriate to accompany the small bottle of Macallan already tucked into my rucksack. Walking down the Royal Mile, we entered the park by Holyrood Palace, passing the construction site that is now the new Scottish parliament. There before us rose Salisbury Crags and behind that the Seat. The walk ahead was neither long nor difficult, but sections were steep and potentially strenuous for me. Thus, I was feeling a bit worried. I had been suffering with angina again and was due for another operation to deal with the problem. In the past couple of weeks, the condition had grown worse, restricting my exercise. I wondered if now it would trouble me, knowing as the question crossed my mind that it would.

We walked across the road, passing by the ruins of St. Anthony's chapel into the bowl of Hunter's Bog. The slightly marshy ground lay immediately below the Seat, ramping gently to the top of Salisbury Crags on the right and Whinny Hill on the left. An intermittent fine drizzle passed over while we meandered our way up to the col between the crags and the Seat. At this point, we decided to head up a steeper path through the rocks of Gutted Haddie. On the lower gentle ground, I had been fine, but as we now ascended, I felt my legs fatigue. Though I had walked some considerable distances in my cell, it was obviously on level ground. I found that my legs would protest on lengthy uphill stretches, as muscles hitherto unemployed for some time were pressed into action and complained. As I continued to walk, I felt some mild discomfort in my chest and had to pause. I knew it would pass and thus decided not to mention it to Siobhan, as it might have worried her and spoiled our pleasure. Silly as it seems, I was determined to achieve the summit. I felt a fleeting sense of absurdity and embarrassment, for this was a path that I had run up in the past. Now, I sweated and puffed as if on a Himalayan trek. Was this discomfort worth it? For me there was only one answer, so I continued slowly, ever vigilant about my discomfort and its potential to worsen.

With Siobhan leading, finally we reached the summit platform and proceeded to the cairn. I sat on the grey damp stone, my angina fading, feeling the coolness of the misty rain as it passed over us. Below me once again was the panorama of Edinburgh with its solid stone buildings looking much as I remembered, much as it did when I first saw this view. Surreptitiously, I squirted my glyceryl trinitrate spray under my tongue, chasing away the last of my discomfort. It would subside and I would be fine, so there was no need to cause concern.

With a restrained sense of ceremony, I opened my rucksack, withdrawing the whisky and the glasses. I poured us each a dram, handing a glass to Siobhan. In a silent toast to each other, we raised the glasses and sipped the fragrant liquid. While we sipped, we looked longingly and intensely at each other. At that moment, I felt love as I never had before. I was thankful for her presence and glad that I had shared this journey with her.

As I sat back on the smooth rocks, I began to reflect, without a trace of pain or difficulty, on all the events that had led to this juncture. The days and weeks of brutalization, the mind-numbing ennui of solitary confinement, the violation of rape, each measured against my responses and my own brutalization of my captors. I had endured, but I had not endured alone. The beauty that I had experienced in life and the love that I had been shown were with me throughout my trials. The process had damaged me, both emotionally and physically. What lay before me now would be difficult, as I would try to put my life together again. There is physical damage that will always be there to remind me, but emotionally, I knew that I would heal. In the midst of all the inhumanity I had suffered, I found my own humanity. In my soul, I felt a better person now than when it all began. Standing beside me was Siobhan, memories of whom had given me so much in the past, and who was now giving me so much again. As I looked at her, I knew, more deeply than ever I had experienced, that I could love and be loved. I was blessed. I was reclaimed.

ACKNOWLEDGEMENTS

Having reached the point that I now have, and reflecting back on both the events I described and the process of writing about them, there are many whose contribution I would like to mention and to whom I owe a debt of gratitude.

Firstly, I would like to thank my family members, particularly my father, James, my step-mother, Nelia, William, Martin, and Cecily for all their efforts, especially during the darkest days of my imprisonment; also Mary Lou and Sarah for their help getting me back on my feet during my first year of freedom, and Helga for keeping my feet on the ground and my head unstuck.

Numerous friends stood by me while I was in prison and since my release, providing everything from moral support to a gas cooker. I would not have rejoined civilization so well had it not been for their kind attention. Most of all I would like to express my gratitude and affection to Siobhan.

Thanks also to the following:

My fellow detainees, particularly Les Walker, Raf Schyvens, and James Lee, who have continued the fight that was started without their choosing, for providing me with information and assistance.

Journalists Francine Dube and Annemie Bulte, the former of whom got me thinking about writing this book, for hearing the worst of my tales and providing encouragement.

Geoffrey Bindman, Tamsin Allen, Mark Emery of Bindman and Partners, Edward Fitzgerald and Richard Hermer of Doughty Street Chambers, for taking on the case and helping me pursue redress. I know that it cannot have been easy dealing with my impatience.

The medical support team, particularly the psychiatric nurse, that brought me home and began the process of bringing me out of the mentality in which I existed in prison.

Dr. Peter Mills, Dr. William Mitchell, Dr. Stuart Morgenstein, and the other members of the medical professions, who helped put me back together. Dr. Kirstine Amris and Dr. Søren Torp-Pedersen of the Parker Institute in Denmark, would it be that their work was not necessary, but I am grateful for their dedication to helping the survivors of torture.

Rosanna Mesquita, Kevin Laue, and Carla of REDRESS, Houshang Bouzari of InCAT, Win Wahrer and Reuben Carter of AIDWYC, for helping not just me but all victims of wrongful imprisonment and abuse.

Of the politicians who involved themselves in my case, I would like to make note of the contributions made by Stéphane Bergeron, MP for Verchères-Les Patriotes, whose support to my family was greatly appreciated, and John Maples, MP for Stratford-on-Avon, whose assistance in bringing my ongoing pursuit before parliament has been most welcome and needed.

Among those I have come to know at my new home, I would like to thank John at the Eden Foyer for computer time and assistance, Sandra and Bob of the Lowther for the relaxing and convivial environment in which much of this book was written, and the regulars of that establishment for the necessary distraction.

Thanks also to my agent, Robert Mackwood, whose hair must by now be a little thinner or a little greyer, as he nursed me through the process of writing this book; to Stacey McNutt, my editor, whose patience went beyond stoicism; and to Doug Pepper, Bruce Walsh, Marilyn Biderman, and the rest of the publishing team at McClelland & Stewart.

ACKNOWLEDGEMENTS

Finally, I would like to acknowledge the contribution made by Prince Naif, Brigadier (formerly Colonel) Mohammed Said, Lieutenant Colonel (formerly Captain) Ibrahim Al Dali, and Captain (formerly Lieutenant) Khaled Al Saleh. Through your lack of humanity, you helped me find my own.